CURRENT TRENDS
IN
PROGRAMMING METHODOLOGY

VOLUME III

Software Modeling

CURRENT TRENDS
IN
PROGRAMMING METHODOLOGY

VOLUME III

Software Modeling

K. MANI CHANDY and **RAYMOND T. YEH,** *Editors*

Department of Computer Sciences
The University of Texas at Austin

PRENTICE-HALL, INC., Englewood Cliffs, New Jersey 07632

Library of Congress Cataloging in Publication Data

Main entry under title:

Current trends in programming methodology.

    Includes bibliographies.
    Includes indexes.
    CONTENTS: v. 1. Software specifications and design.
—v. 3. Software modeling.
    1. Programming (Electronic computers) 1. Yeh,
Raymond Tzuu-Yau (date)
QA76.6.C87   001.6'42   76–46467
ISBN 0–13–195727–9 (v. 3)

Printed in the United States of America

10 9 8 7 6 5 4 3 2 1

PRENTICE-HALL INTERNATIONAL INC., *London*
PRENTICE-HALL OF AUSTRALIA PTY. LIMITED, *Sydney*
PRENTICE-HALL OF CANADA, LTD., *Toronto*
PRENTICE-HALL OF INDIA PRIVATE LIMITED, *New Delhi*
PRENTICE-HALL OF JAPAN, INC., *Tokyo*
PRENTICE-HALL OF SOUTHEAST ASIA PTE. LTD., *Singapore*
WHITEHALL BOOKS LIMITED, *Wellington, New Zealand*

CONTENTS

v

3

SYSTEM DESIGN AND PERFORMANCE ANALYSIS USING ANALYTIC MODELS

HISASHI KOBAYASHI

4

QUEUEING NETWORK MODELS: METHODS OF SOLUTION AND THEIR PROGRAM IMPLEMENTATION

M. REISER
C. H. SAUER

5

GRAPH MODELS IN PROGRAMMING SYSTEMS

J. L. BAER

6

COMBINATORIAL PROBLEMS AND APPROXIMATION SOLUTION   232

C. L. Liu
Donald K. Friesen

7

SYSTEM DEADLOCKS   256

A. N. Habermann

8

OPTIMAL MULTIPROGRAMMED MEMORY MANAGEMENT   298

Peter J. Denning

9

AN INTRODUCTION TO MATHEMATICAL PROGRAMMING APPLIED TO COMPUTER SYSTEMS DESIGN   323

K. Mani Chandy

PREFACE

Performance is an important aspect of programs. Programs serve specific functions, such as computing payrolls or guiding space ships, and these functions have no value if the service is either too slow or too unreliable. We recognize that, in general, it is important to study the performance of the total system (such as spaceships) in which programs play only a part in mission accomplishment. However, in this book our emphasis is on studying the performance of computing systems, and the interface with the larger system is represented by a description of the load offered to the computing system.

Designers of computing systems must have techniques which help them predict system performance because it is too expensive to build a system and later decide that its performance is unsatisfactory. Values have to be selected for a very large number of parameters in any computing system design and system designers need techniques to help them search the large parameter space. This book is concerned with *models* to help designers search large parameter spaces rapidly and also to predict system performance.

Many computer scientists are now aware that performance modeling can have significant practical value in their work. However, a significant portion of computer scientists have only a vague notion of modeling techniques and often presume (incorrectly) that these techniques are very complex and extremely hard to understand. This book reinforces the idea that performance modeling has practical utility and dispels the notion that the modeling area is complex. Professional computer scientists, as well as professors and students will find this book helpful in getting a clear introduction to the use of models in computing system performance analysis. A wide range of models is covered and the relevance of the models is emphasized. Models are discussed in sufficient depth that the reader can immediately grasp key issues and apply the models to his work.

Models such as those discussed in this book have been used for some time in diverse disciplines, though their utility in computing systems design has not been apparent until recently. The general area of modeling has been called Operations Research. Recently, a significant number of operations researchers have become interested in applications of their discipline to computer system design and tuning. There also seems to be increasing agreement among operations researchers that for models to have significant value it is at least as important to gain expertise in the systems being modeled as it is to have expertise in the theory of modeling. This book will prove valuable to operations researchers, management scientists, statisticians, systems engineers, and applied mathematicians who are interested in applying their techniques to analyze computer systems performance. This book shows how different types of models can be usefully applied to computing systems analysis.

Chapter 1 introduces the reader to statistical analysis of performance data at a very basic level. Statistical analysis is the key to performance modeling because without experimental data there cannot be good models and analysis is required to understand large volumes of raw data. This chapter contains clear descriptions of recent advances in the statistical analysis of performance data. Many breakthroughs in this area were discovered by the authors of this chapter.

Discrete-event simulation methods have been used to model systems for a very long time. The question that is most often asked relating to simulation is: How does one know whether a simulation has been run long enough to have a high degree of confidence in simulation results? Even though discrete-event simulation is the most widely used performance modeling tool, very few computer scientists know how probability theory can be used in answering the crucial question regarding confidence in simulation results. Chapter 2 uses the theory of regenerative processes to address this and other related questions. The author of this chapter is a pioneer in this field.

Simulations suffer from the fact that they may require an enormous amount of computation time to obtain meaningful results. Analytic methods based on queueing theory generally require much less computation. It is sometimes helpful for a designer to use an interactive analysis package which rapidly provides estimates of performance metrics. Simulations are generally unsatisfactory in such an interactive environment. Chapter 3 discusses recent results in congestion models of computing systems. Models based on networks of queues have been particularly useful in computing systems analysis. The author of Chapter 3 is a leading figure in the area of queueing network models.

It has been recognized for some time that a key problem in utilizing modeling theory is the paucity of computer scientists with experience in modeling (and operations researchers with experience in computer sciences). Another key problem is that there is generally relatively little time to develop and analyze models; people who demand performance estimates usually should have requested the estimates several months earlier. It is therefore crucial that performance modelers use as many standard, "canned" analysis programming packages as possible. It is also extremely important that modelers have formal languages to describe models to each other and to analysis packages. Chapter 4 discusses a versatile system, called RESQ, which addresses both these problems. There is enough detail in this chapter to help the user build his own versatile analysis package. RESQ is the best analysis package in existence today. The authors are leaders in language development for modeling as well as in queueing models and simulation.

Graph models are widely used in computing systems analysis. Graphs are used in the analysis of programs, recognition of parallelism, scheduling resources, and a variety of other areas. Chapter 5 starts with basic concepts and then discusses recent advances in this area. The reader will obtain a clear understanding of graph models, a thorough knowledge of the application of these models in certain areas of computer sciences, and an appreciation of the value of graph models in all areas of computer sciences. Expository papers by the author of this chapter are among the most widely quoted in this area.

Graph theory is a part of the discipline of combinatories. Chapter 6 discusses applications of combinatories which are not emphasized in the previous chapter. Combinatoric models are used in the analysis of algorithms, resource scheduling, systems design, and in designing communication network topology. Recent developments in complexity theory, particularly the notion of NP-completeness, are of great importance to the professional computer scientist as well as to theoreticians. Computer professionals often refer to some problems as being *tractable* and to others as being *intractable* or *hard*. They develop *optimal* or *exact* algorithms to solve certain problems and *heuristics* to solve others; the former type of algorithm is preferred but the latter type may be used for hard problems. It is vitally important for computer professionals to be aware of the precise definitions of these terms; it is also important that they understand the complexity of the problems that they are dealing with so that they select problem-solving methods most likely to yield satisfactory solutions. Chapter 6 introduces the reader to these important concepts. The authors have made substantial contributions in this area and also have a remarkable capacity for clear exposition.

The problem of scheduling resources is considered in Chapters 5 and 6. However, there is an important aspect of resource scheduling, *deadlocks*, which deserves an entire chapter to itself. Deadlocks arise in concurrent systems when no process can proceed any further because they cannot obtain the resources they require for further processing. The key issues are those of recognizing states which may lead to deadlock and managing resources to avoid (or reduce the possibility of) deadlock. Though resource management has been studied in several branches of engineering and business, the problem of deadlocks has received the most attention in computer sciences. Chapter 7, written by the leader in this field, introduces the reader to the problem of deadlocks with the aid of clear examples and illustrations. This chapter will prove useful to computer scientists and to people concerned with resource management in general.

The performance of computing systems depends in large part upon the effective management of memory. It is crucial that program behavior be understood and that memory be allocated to those programs which are most likely to contribute to effective system performance. Chapter 8 is a comprehensive, lucid discussion of the problem of optimally managing memory. It is written by a pioneer in operating systems theory, who also identified the *working set* principle, which is the key concept in understanding program behavior with reference to memory.

Chapter 9 is an introduction to mathematical programming. No prior acquaintance with mathematical programming is required to understand this chapter though a basic knowledge of linear algebra is assumed. The goal of this chapter is to provide the reader who is unfamiliar with this area with a clear, thorough understanding of the key concepts of optimization theory. This chapter is designed to help the reader (a) to identify situations in which mathematical programming techniques will help in computer systems design problems, (b) formulate systems design problems as mathematical programs, and (c) communicate with operations researchers. This chapter emphasizes intuitive understanding at the expense of rigor. The chapter relies on illustrations and examples in elucidating key concepts.

This book could be used as a text in a beginning graduate course in computer systems modeling. A familiarity with introductory probability theory and simulation is assumed. The text should be supplemented with descriptions of case studies and measurement techniques found in the proceedings of recent workshops such as those sponsored by IFIP working group 7.3. on computer systems performance modeling, measurement and evaluation and ACM SIGMETRICS. Case studies should be selected depending upon the specific interests of students; for instance, case studies can be drawn from computer networks, data-base systems, or multiprogrammed operating systems. The modeling issues descussed in this text apply to a variety of cases. This book, supplemented with case study material, is planned to be used in first-year graduate courses in the Computer Sciences Department, University of Texas at Austin.

K. MANI CHANDY
RAYMOND T. YEH

Austin, Texas

CURRENT TRENDS IN PROGRAMMING METHODOLOGY

VOLUME III

Software Modeling

CHAPTER 1

STATISTICAL METHODS

IN COMPUTER

PERFORMANCE ANALYSIS

Y. BARD

M. SCHATZOFF
IBM Cambridge Scientific Center
Cambridge, Massachusetts

1.1. INTRODUCTION

Application of statistical methodology to the study of computer system performance seems quite natural in light of our ability to generate very large volumes of data on many variables, whether by hardware or software instrumentation, and our need to understand what such data have to say about the system from which they are derived. Statistics provides tools for summarizing the salient features of data, searching for meaningful patterns, detecting instances of anomalous behavior, understanding complex relationships among many variables, and designing efficient experiments for determining the effects of factors that can be controlled.

The types of data generally collected for computer systems usually include utilizations of various system resources such as the central processing unit, I/O devices, and channels; counts of events such as various classes of program interrupts; and tracing of program paths initiated by specified events. The level of detail of data collection depends on the purposes for which the data are to be used. At one level, the purpose might be to provide overall descriptions of system, subsystem, or program behavior. At another level, the objective might be to answer specific questions pertaining to certain aspects of these behavioral phenomena. Or, we might wish to predict, control, or improve system performance under stipulated conditions.

Statistics provides a useful methodology for approaching problems at all of these levels of inquiry. Because of the stochastic nature of events occurring in the operation of a computer system, it is natural to think of describing the resulting data in terms of probability distributions. Such descriptions entail questions of fitting distributions to data, testing goodness of fit, estimating relevant parameters of fitted distributions, and statistical testing of hypotheses concerning such parameters.

In Section 1.2, we shall outline some of the basic notions of probability and statistical inference to be used in subsequent sections. Techniques such as regression and correlation analysis, which apply to the study of the joint distributions of two or more variables, are treated in Section 1.3. Concepts of design and analysis of experiments, pertaining to situations in which one or more factors can be controlled by the investigator, are dealt with in Section 1.4. Finally, in Section 1.5, we shall examine the applicability of design of experiments to the problem of optimizing or tuning computer systems.

As a prelude to the ensuing sections, we shall introduce the idea of a data matrix, in which each row contains observations on a number of variables, taken at a given time. Successive rows then represent observations taken at successive points in time. Determination of the appropriate lengths of sampling intervals is itself a question of some importance, for which there is no definitive answer. The choice depends on factors such as impact of the measurements on system performance, activity level of the system, degree of time dependence in the data, and desired accuracy of results. Exploratory data analysis can usually provide reasonable guidelines as to an appropriate choice of sampling interval.

1.2. STATISTICAL PRELIMINARIES

1.2.1. Random Variables and Probability Distributions

The data for a single variable, as recorded in a particular column of a data matrix, may be viewed as a sample drawn from a hypothetical population consisting of all possible values that the variable might assume. If the data generating mechanism were allowed to run indefinitely, we could observe the frequencies with which observations fall in various intervals. Thus, the characteristics of the hypothetical population could be described in terms of a probability distribution, from which one could calculate the proportion of all possible observations lying within any specified interval. Usually, we are unable to observe the entire population and must confine our inferences about the population to observations taken on a sample drawn from it. Procedures for selecting samples are the subject of sampling theory, whereas methods for making statements about the nature of the underlying population derive from principles of statistical inference.

Let us denote a random variable by X and a possible value of the variable by x. The distribution function $F(x)$ for the random variable X is defined by the following relation: $F(x) = \text{prob}\,(X \leq x) = \int_{-\infty}^{x} dF(y)$. With this definition in hand we can readily express the probability that X lies within a prescribed interval (a, b) by $\text{prob}\,(a < X \leq b) = F(b) - F(a) = \int_{a}^{b} dF(x)$. If $F(x)$ is a continuous function, then

$dF(x) = f(x)\,dx$, and $f(x)$ is said to be the density function of x. In the case of a discrete-valued random variable, the foregoing Stieltjes integral reduces to a summation. For example, if X is defined only on the nonnegative integers, then $F(x) = \sum_{y=0}^{x} f(y)$, where $f(x)$, the probability that $X = x$, is called the frequency function of x.

The mathematical expectation or mean of a random variable is defined by $\mu = E(X) = \int_{-\infty}^{\infty} x\,dF(x)$. This is the center of gravity of the distribution, since $E(X - E(X)) = 0$. The variance or second central moment of a random variable is defined by $V(X) = E(X - \mu)^2 = EX^2 - \mu^2$. It provides a measure of the dispersion, or spread of the distribution. In general, the kth central moment of a distribution is defined by $\mu_k = E(X - \mu)^k$. It is straightforward to verify that the kth moment of CX, where C is a constant, is equal to $C^k \mu_k$ and that $E(X - \theta)^2$ is minimized when $\theta = \mu$.

Let prob (A) be the probability of the event A. Two random variables X and Y are said to be statistically independent if $\text{prob}\,[(X \in I)\text{ and }(Y \in J)] = \text{prob}\,(X \in I) \times \text{prob}\,(Y \in J)$ for all intervals I and J. Let A be the event $X \in I$ and B the event $Y \in J$. Then the conditional probability of the event B occurring, given that A has occurred, is defined as prob $(B \mid A) = [\text{prob}\,(A\text{ and }B)] \div \text{prob}\,(A)$. Thus, if X and Y are statistically independent, prob $(B \mid A) = \text{prob}\,(B)$.

Two events A and B are said to be mutually exclusive if prob $(A\text{ or }B) = \text{prob}\,(A) + \text{prob}\,(B)$. In general, prob $(A\text{ or }B) = \text{prob}\,(A) + \text{prob}\,(B) - \text{prob}\,(A\text{ and }B)$. When A and B are mutually exclusive, prob $(A\text{ and }B) = 0$.

Example 1

Suppose the interarrival times of messages arriving at the CPU of a data processing system are exponentially distributed with density function $f(t) = \lambda e^{-\lambda t}$, $t > 0$. Then the mean and variance of t are given, respectively, by

$$\mu = \int_0^{\infty} t\lambda e^{-\lambda t}\,dt = 1/\lambda \quad \text{and} \quad \sigma^2 = \int_0^{\infty} t^2 \lambda e^{-\lambda t}\,dt - (1/\lambda)^2 = 1/\lambda^2.$$

Example 2

When interarrival times are exponentially distributed, it can be shown that the number of arrivals x in any interval of length t has a Poisson distribution, defined by the probability mass function

$$f(x) = \frac{e^{-\lambda t}(\lambda t)^x}{x!}, \qquad x = 0, 1, \ldots$$

The mean and variance of the Poisson distribution are both equal to λt.

The two preceding distributions, which are very important in the study of queueing problems, are derived from the following two postulates:

1. The distribution of the number of occurrences depends only on the length of the interval and not on its position in time.

2. The number of occurrences in different intervals are statistically independent.

For any two random variables X and Y, $E(X + Y) = E(X) + E(Y)$. The covariance of X and Y is defined by

$$\text{cov}\ (X, Y) = E(X - \mu_X)(Y - \mu_Y)$$

where μ_X and μ_Y are the expectations of X and Y, respectively. If X and Y are statistically independent, then

$$\text{cov}\ (X, Y) = E(X - \mu_X) \cdot E(Y - \mu_Y) = 0$$

and

$$V(X + Y) = V(X) + V(Y)$$

These properties extend to any number of mutually independent random variables $X_1, \ldots, X_n$, so that

$$E\left(\sum_{i=1}^{n} a_i X_i\right) = \sum_{i=1}^{n} a_i E(X_i)$$

and

$$V\left(\sum_{i=1}^{n} a_i X_i\right) = \sum_{i=1}^{n} a_i^2 V(X_i)$$

When the X_i are not mutually independent, we have

$$\text{cov}\left[\left(\sum_{i=1}^{n} a_i X_i\right), \left(\sum_{j=1}^{n} b_j X_j\right)\right] = \sum_{i=1}^{n} \sum_{j=1}^{n} a_i b_j\ \text{cov}\ (X_i, X_j)$$

The correlation coefficient for two random variables X and Y is defined by

$$\rho_{XY} = \frac{\text{cov}\ (X, Y)}{[V(X) \cdot V(Y)]^{1/2}}$$

Given a set of p random variables $X_1, \ldots, X_p$, the covariance matrix is defined as a $p \times p$ matrix whose (i, j) element is given by $\text{cov}\ (X_i, X_j)$. The correlation matrix is defined in an analogous manner.

1.2.2. Sampling Theory

Suppose that we draw a random sample of n observations, $x_1, \ldots, x_n$ from an infinite population having mean μ and variance σ^2. The x_i are observations on mutually independent random variables. Any function $g(x_1, \ldots, x_n)$ of the observations is also a random variable. In particular, we shall be interested in functions such as the sample mean and variance. Let $\bar{x} = (\sum_{i=1}^{n} x_i)/n$ denote the sample mean. From the results of the previous section we have

$$E(\bar{x}) = \sum_{i=1}^{n} E\left(\frac{x_i}{n}\right) = \frac{n\mu}{n} = \mu$$

and

$$V(\bar{x}) = \sum_{i=1}^{n} V\left(\frac{x_i}{n}\right) = \sum_{i=1}^{n} \frac{\sigma^2}{n^2}$$

$$= \frac{n\sigma^2}{n^2} = \frac{\sigma^2}{n}$$

In many instances, it is a simple matter to derive not only the expectations and variances of means of independently distributed random variables but also their entire sampling distributions. The interpretation of a sampling distribution is as follows. Suppose that random samples of size n are drawn over and over again. Each such sample would result in a particular value of $\bar{x}$, so that these sample means may themselves be viewed as random variables having a common probability distribution. Two important theorems relating to the sampling distribution of $\bar{x}$ follow.

Theorem 1   The Law of Large Numbers

Let $X_1, \ldots, X_n$ be a sequence of mutually independent random variables with a common distribution having expectation μ. As $n \rightarrow \infty$, the probability that $\bar{X}$ differs from μ by less than any arbitrarily prescribed value ϵ tends toward 1. In other words, the sample mean tends toward the mean of the parent population with probability 1.

Theorem 2   The Central Limit Theorem

If the random variables in the above sequence have variance σ^2, then as $n \rightarrow \infty$, $Z = n^{1/2} \cdot (\bar{X} - \mu)/\sigma$ tends toward the normal distribution with mean 0 and variance 1, with the density function given by

$$f(z) = (2\pi)^{-1/2} \exp\left(\frac{-z^2}{2}\right)$$

This distribution will be denoted by the notation $N(0, 1)$, and $Z \sim N(0, 1)$ means that Z is distributed as a $N(0, 1)$ random variable. The $N(0, 1)$ distribution is a special case of the normal distribution with mean μ and variance σ^2, denoted $N(\mu, \sigma^2)$. The density function for the $N(\mu, \sigma^2)$ distribution is given by

$$f(x) = (2\pi)^{-1/2} \exp\left\{\frac{-[(x - \mu)/\sigma]^2}{2}\right\}$$

The normal distribution is completely described by its mean and variance. Linear transformations of normally distributed random variables are also normally distributed. In particular, if $X \sim N(\mu, \sigma^2)$, then $Z = (X - \mu)/\sigma \sim N(0, 1)$. The normal distribution is symmetric about μ; the intervals $\mu \pm 1.96\sigma$ and $\mu \pm 2.576\sigma$ contain 95% and 99% of the distribution, respectively.

Although the central limit theorem is an asymptotic result, it can be shown that for a wide class of random variables it provides a good approximation for fairly small values of n, say on the order of 10 or 20. This result is extremely important and provides the basis for development of normal sampling theory. In many real-life applications, observed values of random variables may actually be sums of small random perturbations; furthermore, even when the observations themselves have an arbitrary distribution the sample means are approximately normally distributed.

Since the normal distribution plays such an important role in statistics, we shall list here some of its important properties. Derivations may be found in Fraser (1958) or Kendall and Stuart (1963).

1. If $X \sim N(0, 1)$, then $Y = X^2 \sim \chi_1^2$, where χ_1^2 denotes the chi-square distribution on one degree of freedom. Degrees of freedom refer to the number of independent components into which a random variable may be decomposed.

2. If $Y_1, \ldots, Y_k$ are independently distributed as $N(0, 1)$, then $\sum_{i=1}^{k} Y_i^2 \sim \chi_k^2$, where χ_k^2 denotes the chi-square distribution on k degrees of freedom.

3. If X and Y are independently distributed as $N(0, 1)$ and χ_k^2 random variables, respectively, then $t = k^{1/2} X / Y^{1/2}$ is distributed according to the Student t distribution on k degrees of freedom, denoted t_k.

4. If Y_1 and Y_2 are independently distributed as $\chi_{k_1}^2$ and $\chi_{k_2}^2$, respectively, then $\mathfrak{F} = (Y_1 \div k_1)/(Y_2 \div k_2)$ has the F distribution on k_1 and k_2 degrees of freedom, denoted F_{k_1, k_2}.

The above results provide the basis for distribution theory related to sampling from a normal distribution. Suppose that $x_1, \ldots, x_n$ are a random sample drawn from the $N(\mu, \sigma^2)$ distribution. Then

1. $\bar{x} = (1/n) \sum_{i=1}^{n} x_i \sim N(\mu, \sigma^2/n)$.

2. $(n - 1)s^2 = \sum_{i=1}^{n} (x_i - \bar{x})^2 \sim \sigma^2 \chi_{n-1}^2$.

3. $\bar{x}$ and s^2 are independently distributed.

4. $(n^{1/2})(\bar{x} - \mu)/s^2 \sim t_{n-1}$.

5. $n(\bar{x} - \mu)^2/s^2 \sim F_{1, n-1}$.

Tables of the normal, t, χ^2, and F distribution functions may be found in Pearson and Hartley (1962) as well as in a number of statistics texts.

1.2.3. Statistical Inference

The foregoing results provide the distribution theory essentials for discussing aspects of statistical inference related to the normal distribution. By statistical inference, we refer to the processes by which we make inferences concerning the characteristics of a population based on samples drawn from that population. The subject of statistical inference is a controversial one from a philosophical viewpoint, giving rise to several schools of thought that differ from one another principally in their interpretation of probability. In this section, we shall deal only with the concepts of significance tests and confidence intervals, leaving philosophical discussions of statistical inference to others. More complete discussions of statistical inference are contained in Fraser (1958), Kendall and Stuart (1963), and Lehmann (1959).

Suppose that we draw a sample from some population for the purpose of learning about its characteristics, or possibly making a decision, based on what we have observed. The population may be viewed as having a probability distribution with one or more parameters whose values are unknown. We may be interested in estimating the values of these parameters or in testing hypotheses concerning their values. These notions are perhaps easiest to describe by means of simple examples.

Let us suppose that we have drawn a random sample of n observations $x_1, \ldots, x_n$ from a normal distribution with known variance σ^2 and unknown mean μ. A natural estimator for μ, the mean of the population, is $\bar{x}$, the mean of the sample. It turns out that $\bar{x}$ is the maximum likelihood estimator (see Section 1.3) as well as the least-squares estimator for μ.

Suppose now that we want to test the hypothesis that $\mu \leq \mu_0$, a specified constant. If $\bar{x}$ is very large compared to μ_0, we might tend to believe that our sample had been drawn from a population whose mean was greater than μ_0. As a means of assessing our degree of belief concerning the hypothesis that $\mu \leq \mu_0$, we could calculate the probability that a sample mean based on n observations would be equal to or greater than the observed value, $\bar{x}$, given that $\mu = \mu_0$. Suppose that this probability, say α, was very small. We would then conclude either that $\mu > \mu_0$ or that an event of very small probability α had occurred. The smaller the value of α, the more likely it would be for us to believe that $\mu > \mu_0$, contrary to our hypothesis.

For the case at hand, we know that $z = \sqrt{n}\,(\bar{x} - \mu_0)/\sigma \sim N(0, 1)$ when $\mu = \mu_0$. The probability that a sample mean based on n observations would be equal to or greater than the observed value $\bar{x}$, given that $x_1, \ldots, x_n$ were independently distributed according to the $N(\mu_0, \sigma^2)$ distribution, is given by

$$\alpha = \int_z^\infty \varphi(x)\,dx = 1 - \Phi(z)$$

where $\varphi(x)$ is the standardized $N(0, 1)$ density function and $\Phi(z) = \int_{-\infty}^z \varphi(x)\,dx$ is the corresponding distribution function. Values of $\Phi(z)$ are tabulated in most statistical texts. We could then say that the observed significance level is equal to α.

Generally, one would not know the true value of σ^2 but might still want to carry out a significance test on μ. This case would be handled by the t distribution, using the fact that

$$t = \frac{\sqrt{n}\,(\bar{x} - \mu_0)}{s} \sim t_{n-1}$$

The tests discussed thus far are called one-sided tests, since we are interested only in whether $\mu \leq \mu_0$. Suppose instead that we wanted to test whether the hypothesis $\mu = \mu_0$ were plausible and were willing to consider a sufficiently large value of $|\bar{x} - \mu_0|$ as ample evidence that $\mu \neq \mu_0$. We would now be in a situation calling for a two-sided test. For an observed value of $z = |\sqrt{n}\,(\bar{x} - \mu_0)/\sigma|$, we would calculate

$$\alpha = 1 - \int_{-z}^z \varphi(x)\,dx$$

for the case where σ^2 is known and would reject the hypothesis that $\mu = \mu_0$ for sufficiently small values of α. A similar calculation using the t distribution would be required for the case where σ^2 is unknown.

Although we may be satisfied that $\bar{x}$ provides a reasonable way of estimating μ, we are usually interested in the quality or accuracy of the estimation procedure. How closely $\bar{x}$ is likely to approximate μ depends on its variance, σ^2/n. Thus, it will provide a very good estimate if σ^2 is sufficiently small or if n is sufficiently large. It is generally of interest to speak about confidence intervals for an unknown parameter θ. Suppose that for every possible outcome $\mathbf{x} = [x_1, \ldots, x_n]$ of a sample of n observations we define an interval $I(\mathbf{x})$. If $I(\mathbf{x})$ has the property that it includes the true parameter θ with a preassigned probability $1 - \alpha$, no matter what θ is equal to, then $I(\mathbf{x})$ is called a confidence interval for θ with confidence coefficient $1 - \alpha$.

It should be noted carefully that θ is fixed, though unknown in value, while the interval $I(\mathbf{x})$ is random, being dependent on the particular outcome $\mathbf{x}$. Prior to drawing the sample, we could say that the probability that the interval $I(\mathbf{x})$ will include the unknown parameter θ is equal to $1 - \alpha$. If the experiment were to be repeated over and over again, $100(1 - \alpha)\%$ of the time the random interval $I(\mathbf{x})$ would include θ. Once the sample has been drawn, however, the resulting interval does or does not contain θ. We no longer talk about the probability that θ is contained in $I(\mathbf{x})$, since that probability is equal to 0 or 1. Instead, we use the term *confidence interval* to describe our degree of belief that θ is included in $I(\mathbf{x})$.

We shall illustrate the notion of confidence intervals by means of the example of drawing a sample form the $N(\mu, \sigma^2)$ distribution with σ^2 known. Based on our knowledge that $\bar{x} \sim N(\mu, \sigma^2/n)$, we can construct the random interval $I(\mathbf{x}) = (\bar{x} - 1.96\sigma/\sqrt{n}, \bar{x} + 1.96\sigma/\sqrt{n})$. This interval will contain μ only if the random variable $\sqrt{n}\,(\bar{x} - \mu)/\sigma$ is contained in the interval $(-1.96, 1.96)$, an event of probability .95. Thus, we say that the interval $I(\mathbf{x})$ is a .95 two-sided confidence interval for μ.

Similar reasoning can be used to determine the sample size required to estimate μ within a given precision at a stipulated confidence level. Suppose that σ^2 is known and that we wish to draw a sample of sufficient size to estimate μ with a specified precision (k) at the .95 level. Now, $\mathrm{pr}\,(|\bar{x} - \mu| < k) = \mathrm{pr}\,(\sqrt{n}\,|\bar{x} - \mu|/\sigma < \sqrt{n}\,k/\sigma)$. Therefore, n must satisfy the equation $\sqrt{n}\,k/\sigma = 1.96$ for μ to be estimated with precision k at the .95 level. The required sample size is $n = [(1.96\sigma/k)^2]$, where $[x]$ denotes the smallest integer that is not less than x. The interpretation is that if samples of size n were drawn repeatedly, 95% of the samples would have means lying within k units of the true mean μ.

1.3. MODELING AND REGRESSION

1.3.1. Introduction

In the preceding section we were concerned with purely *stochastic models*, i.e., models in which the properties of a variable are fully described through its probability distribution. We shall now treat models which involve functional relationships among the variables. Such relationships, called *model equations*, may be defined as any procedures which may be used to calculate, at least approximately, the values of certain physically meaningful *dependent variables*, $\mathbf{y} = [y_1, y_2, \ldots, y_m]$, given values of *independent variables* $\mathbf{x} = [x_1, x_2, \ldots, x_k]$, and parameters $\boldsymbol{\theta} = [\theta_1, \theta_2, \ldots, \theta_l]$.

The difference between independent variables and parameters is that the former may be measured directly, whereas the latter must be estimated. For example, in the model of an auxiliary storage device, the response time to an I/O request may be the dependent variable, record length and access rate the independent variables, and device rotation time and average seek time the parameters.

A model may in general be expressed in the form

$$\mathbf{y} = \mathbf{f}(\mathbf{x}, \boldsymbol{\theta}) \tag{1}$$

where $\mathbf{f} = [f_1, f_2, \ldots, f_m]$ is a vector of functions. These functions may have simple analytic forms, e.g., $y = \theta_1 x + \theta_2$, or they may be so complicated that an elaborate simulation is required for their evaluation. In either case, *model building* requires determining the form of the functions $\mathbf{f}$ and estimating the values of the parameters $\boldsymbol{\theta}$.

There are two basic approaches toward determining the form of the model equations. If the nature of the situation being modeled is well understood, the model equations may be derived directly from physical considerations. We then have a *mechanistic* model, which is either *analytic* in nature if the equations can be written down explicitly or *simulative* if evaluation is possible only by direct imitation of the original process. In a mechanistic model, the parameters usually have a direct physical meaning, e.g., the rotation time of a disk or the average time between page faults. The values of such parameters can often be determined by direct measurement, but at other times they must be estimated from other data.

When the relationships among the variables are not well understood, one must resort to *empirical* models. These are models, usually fairly simple in nature, which are derived directly from the data. Here the modeler selects a broad class of models, e.g., linear relationships or polynomials, and then employs statistical techniques to select the most appropriate model from this class, to estimate the parameters, and to verify whether an adequate fit has been obtained. Even in the construction of empirical models, some physical understanding of the phenomena being modeled is helpful in selecting the class of models and the list of variables to which the statistical techniques are applied.

Construction of a model is usually not an end in itself. What one really wants is to predict the behavior of the system being modeled under conditions which have not yet been observed. Statistical techniques are then required if one wishes to know how reliable the prediction is, i.e., how likely it is to be within a certain interval around the true outcome.

To summarize, statistics play the following roles in the process of model construction:

1. Suggest the form of the model, or choose among alternative models.
2. Estimate the values of unknown parameters.
3. Provide confidence limits for the estimated values.
4. Evaluate the adequacy of the model.
5. Provide confidence limits for predictions based on the model.

We shall treat these topics in the succeeding sections. The treatment is necessarily limited to a few highlights which have proven useful in the analysis of system performance.

1.3.2. Estimating Model Parameters

For the time being, assume that a model (1) has been proposed and that for any given $\mathbf{x}$ and $\boldsymbol{\theta}$ we can evaluate $\mathbf{y}$. Further, assume that the values of $\mathbf{x}$ and $\mathbf{y}$, say $\mathbf{x}_\mu, \mathbf{y}_\mu$, have been observed for $\mu = 1, 2, \ldots, n$. The problem is to find a vector of parameters $\boldsymbol{\theta}$ such that the equations

$$\mathbf{y}_\mu = \mathbf{f}(\mathbf{x}_\mu, \boldsymbol{\theta}) \qquad (\mu = 1, 2, \ldots, n) \tag{2}$$

are satisfied as closely as possible. Methods of estimation may be classified according to the criterion of *closeness* being used. A secondary classification relates to the type of equation being fitted. We shall concentrate primarily on the least-squares criterion and its specialization to linear models—so-called *linear regression*. Subsequently we shall indicate some extensions to other criteria and model types.

1.3.2.1. Linear Regression. Suppose there is a single dependent variable y which is supposed to be related linearly to a set of independent variables $\mathbf{x}$:

$$y = \theta_1 x_1 + \theta_2 x_2 + \ldots + \theta_k x_k \tag{3}$$

(Usually there is a constant term θ_0 in the equation. This is best treated by including an extra variable x_0, which is assigned the value 1 for all observations. Then $y = \theta_0 x_0 + \theta_1 x_1 + \ldots + \theta_k x_k$. We shall take the vector $\mathbf{x}$ to include $x_0 = 1$ whenever a constant term appears in the model.) Let $y_\mu, x_{\mu 1}, x_{\mu 2}, \ldots, x_{\mu k}$ be the measured values of $y, x_1, x_2, \ldots, x_k$ at the μth observation. We define the *residual* $r_\mu(\boldsymbol{\theta})$ as the difference between the μth observed and predicted values of y, i.e.,

$$r_\mu(\boldsymbol{\theta}) = y_\mu - \theta_1 x_{\mu 1} - \theta_2 x_{\mu 2} - \ldots - \theta_k x_{\mu k} \tag{4}$$

The function

$$S(\boldsymbol{\theta}) = \sum_{\mu=1}^{n} r_\mu^2(\boldsymbol{\theta}) \tag{5}$$

is the sum of squares of the residuals. The value of $\boldsymbol{\theta}$, say $\hat{\boldsymbol{\theta}}$, for which $S(\boldsymbol{\theta})$ is minimum is called the *least-squares* estimate of $\boldsymbol{\theta}$. The process of determining the least-squares estimate for a linear model of the form (3) is called *multiple* (if $k > 1$) *linear regression*. The independent variables $x_1, x_2, \ldots, x_k$ are said to be *included* in the regression.

Let

$$\mathbf{y} = [y_1, y_2, \ldots, y_n]^T$$
$$\mathbf{r}(\boldsymbol{\theta}) = [r_1(\boldsymbol{\theta}), r_2(\boldsymbol{\theta}), \ldots, r_n(\boldsymbol{\theta})]^T$$

and

$$\mathbf{X} = \begin{bmatrix} x_{11} & x_{12} & \cdots & x_{1k} \\ x_{21} & x_{22} & \cdots & x_{2k} \\ \cdot & & & \\ \cdot & & & \\ \cdot & & & \\ x_{n1} & x_{n2} & \cdots & x_{nk} \end{bmatrix}$$

Then we may write

$$\mathbf{r}(\boldsymbol{\theta}) = \mathbf{y} - \mathbf{X}\boldsymbol{\theta}$$
$$S(\boldsymbol{\theta}) = (\mathbf{y} - \mathbf{X}\boldsymbol{\theta})^T(\mathbf{y} - \mathbf{X}\boldsymbol{\theta})$$

It is easy to show that the least-squares estimate $\hat{\boldsymbol{\theta}}$ is given by the solution to the set of linear equations

$$\mathbf{X}^T\mathbf{X}\hat{\boldsymbol{\theta}} = \mathbf{X}^T\mathbf{y} \tag{6}$$

Hence, provided $\mathbf{X}^T\mathbf{X}$ is nonsingular,

$$\hat{\boldsymbol{\theta}} = (\mathbf{X}^T\mathbf{X})^{-1}\mathbf{X}^T\mathbf{y} \tag{7}$$

The minimum sum of squares, $S(\hat{\boldsymbol{\theta}})$, comes out to be

$$S(\hat{\boldsymbol{\theta}}) = \mathbf{y}^T\mathbf{y} - \mathbf{y}^T\mathbf{X}(\mathbf{X}^T\mathbf{X})^{-1}\mathbf{X}^T\mathbf{y} \tag{8}$$

The term $\mathbf{y}^T\mathbf{y} = \sum_\mu y_\mu^2$ is the sum of squares of the original observations; the term $\mathbf{y}^T\mathbf{X}(\mathbf{X}^T\mathbf{X})^{-1}\mathbf{X}^T\mathbf{y}$ represents the reduction in sum of squares due to the variables included in the regression. It is evident that the more variables included in the regression (i.e., the more independent variables there are), the greater is the reduction in sum of squares. Not every variable included in the regression is, however, likely to be useful. Inclusion of a variable may fail to reduce the sum of squares significantly for one of the following reasons:

1. The variable is irrelevant; i.e., it really has little effect on the dependent variable. The estimated coefficient for such a variable will usually be small, but even so its inclusion in a regression will increase the variance of predictions based on the model (see Section 1.3.5). Hence, an effort should be made to exclude such variables from the regression.

2. The variable is redundant; i.e., it is strongly related to other variables already included in the regression, so that its inclusion adds no further information. For instance, if $x_3 = 2x_1 + 5x_2$ in all observations, then inclusion of any two of the variables x_1, x_2, x_3 is sufficient. Inclusion of a redundant variable in the regression can be catastrophic. For instance, suppose $y = 2x_1$ correctly models a physical situation, and suppose $x_2 = x_1$ at all observations. Then $y = x_1 + x_2$ and even $y = 100x_1 - 98x_2$ are all equally good representations of the data. By including the redundant variable x_2 one loses all ability to estimate either θ_1 or θ_2. It is, therefore, essential to identify any linear dependencies among the independent variables, e.g., by means of principal component analysis (Section 1.3.3).

Various *variable selection* techniques have been devised to choose a useful set of variables for inclusion in a regression. For example, the *forward selection* method works as follows:

1. Start out with no variables included in the regression.

2. Find the nonincluded variable whose inclusion would cause the greatest decrease in the sum of squares. If this decrease is below a predefined threshold (say less than 1% of the original sum of squares—F tests are often used to define this threshold), terminate the procedure. Otherwise, include the variable. Repeat until no includable variables are left.

For computational details, the reader is referred to standard texts on regression, e.g., Draper and Smith (1966). The procedure is likely to eliminate irrelevant variables. It also guarantees that no redundant variables are included. However, there is no telling in advance which one, among a set of linearly dependent variables, will be excluded. If the same procedure is applied to different sets of observations, a different set of variables may be selected each time, even though the underlying structure is the same for all data sets. For this reason, it may be advantageous to identify, a priori, linear dependencies among the independent variables using principal component analysis. This analysis, combined with an understanding of the system being modeled, may then result in a better model from which the proper redundant variables are excluded, as illustrated in the example of Section 1.3.3.

We shall now present two examples of the use of regression in computer performance analysis.

Example 3 Overhead Regression

An operating system provides various services for programs running under it. It is useful to determine the cost of such services, e.g., the amount of CPU time consumed in servicing a single request of any given kind. We shall refer to this amount of CPU time as a *unit overhead coefficient*. One method of estimating the unit overhead coefficients is the following: Suppose the operating system is instrumented to maintain (a) a count of the total number of requests of each type received and (b) the total amount of CPU time used up by the operating system. Suppose that these counters are sampled at regular intervals (say, 1 or 5 minutes). By taking the differences between successive counter readings, one obtains the following values:

$x_{\mu i}$ = number of requests of type i made during the μth observation period $(i = 1, 2, \ldots, k)$

y_μ = CPU time used by the operating system during the μth period

Now, if θ_i is the unit overhead coefficient for the ith request type, then the following relation should hold approximately for each observed period:

$$y_\mu = \theta_0 + \theta_1 x_{\mu 1} + \theta_2 x_{\mu 2} + \ldots + \theta_k x_{\mu k} \qquad (9)$$

where θ_0 is the average CPU time used by the operating system in performing unaccounted for functions. It is now a simple application of linear regression methods to estimate the θ_i. This method has been applied by Bard (1971) to estimate the amount of CPU time required by CP-67[1] to service page exceptions and virtual I/O requests of various types. Some of the results are shown in Table 1.3.1, illustrating the improvement in version 3 of the system over version 2. For instance, the CPU overhead of a paging operation has been reduced from 6.1 to 2.0 milliseconds.

[1]CP-67 is a time-sharing system for the IBM System/360 Model 67 computer [Meyer and Seawright (1970)].

Table 1.3.1. CP-67 Overhead Regression

Request Type	Estimated Overhead Coefficient (msec CPU time per request)	
	CP-67 Release 2	CP-67 Release 3.0
Virtual selector I/O	9.7	7.9
Page read	6.1	2.0
Spool I/O	6.0	4.6

The above may be considered an example of a mechanistic model, since the model equation had a direct physical meaning. The following example is more empirical in nature:

Example 4 Response Time Regression

Leroudier (1973) has measured many variables associated with each transaction executed on an interactive computer system (once more CP-67). Among these were $y =$ response time, $x_1 =$ CPU time, $x_2 =$ number of disk I/O's, $x_3 =$ number of console I/O's, and $x_4 =$ number of users logged on at the time the transaction was completed. Other variables were also measured; however, they turned out to be uncorrelated with response time. Regression analysis produced the following equation for predicting a transaction's response time in seconds:

$$y = 7.62 + 0.11x_2 + 5.75x_3 - 4.77x_1 + 0.21x_1x_4 \tag{10}$$

Although this equation was constructed in a purely empirical manner, Leroudier finds an ex-post-facto mechanistic interpretation for it. The reader is referred to the cited paper for details.

1.3.2.2. Statistical Aspects of Regression. The estimated parameters are computed from the data. Hence, if the data are subject to random errors, so are the estimated parameters. We must investigate the statistical properties of the estimates to answer questions such as "What is the probability that the error of the estimate is no larger than a specified value?" To start with, these depend on the statistical properties of the data and of the model.

Typically, the model (3) does not hold exactly. Instead, one has

$$y_\mu = \theta_1 x_{\mu 1} + \theta_2 x_{\mu 2} + \ldots + \theta_k x_{\mu k} + \epsilon_\mu \tag{11}$$

where ϵ_μ is a random error term. There are generally two sources of error:

1. Errors in the measurements of $\mathbf{x}_\mu$ and y_μ.

2. Errors in the model itself, typically as the result of omitting important terms, e.g., ones for which no data are available.

Let us assume now that the errors $\boldsymbol{\epsilon} = [\epsilon_1, \epsilon_2, \ldots, \epsilon_n]$ are identically and independently distributed random variables with zero means and standard deviations σ. These assumptions are typically justified when the primary source of error is in the measurement of y_μ. It is then easy to show that the least-squares estimate $\hat{\theta}$ is a random variable having the following properties:

$$E(\hat{\theta}) = \theta^*, \tag{12}$$

where θ^* is the true value of θ;

$$E[S(\hat{\theta})] = (n - k)\sigma^2 \qquad (n \geq k) \tag{13}$$

$$V(\hat{\theta}) = \sigma^2(X^TX)^{-1} \tag{14}$$

where $V(\hat{\theta})$ is the covariance matrix of the estimates. Property (12) is equivalent to the statement that $\hat{\theta}$ is an *unbiased* estimate of θ. Property (13) leads to the estimate

$$\hat{\sigma} = \left[\frac{S(\hat{\theta})}{n - k}\right]^{1/2} \qquad (n > k) \tag{15}$$

for the error standard deviation σ. Property (14) provides estimates of the variability of the estimated parameters $\hat{\theta}$. What properties (12) and (14) state is, essentially, the following: Let a set of n observations with the same x_μ ($\mu = 1, 2, \ldots, n$) be taken over and over again. Each set of observations will have a different y because of the random error term ϵ. Let the estimate $\hat{\theta}$ be computed for each set of observations. Then the population of estimates $\hat{\theta}$ has a distribution with mean θ^* and covariance matrix $\sigma^2(X^TX)^{-1}$. In particular, the variance of $\hat{\theta}_i$ is $\sigma^2 Q_{ii}$, and the covariance between θ_i and θ_j is $\sigma^2 Q_{ij}$, where $Q = (X^TX)^{-1}$.

When almost redundant variables are included in the regression, the matrix X^TX is nearly singular. Hence $V = \sigma^2(X^TX)^{-1}$ includes very large elements, indicating that some of the parameter estimates are highly variable.

An estimate θ is *linear* if it has the form $\theta = Ay$, where A is a matrix that does not depend on y. Clearly, $\hat{\theta}$ is linear, with $A = (X^TX)^{-1}X^T$. The Gauss-Markov theorem asserts that of all unbiased linear estimates $\hat{\theta}$ has the least variance, provided that the above assumptions on the errors ϵ hold.

If, in addition, the errors ϵ are *normally* distributed, then so are the estimates $\hat{\theta}$. It can then be shown [Scheffe (1959)] that the quantity

$$\frac{(\theta^* - \hat{\theta})^T X^T X (\theta^* - \hat{\theta})}{k\hat{\sigma}^2}$$

has the $F_{k,n-k}$ distribution. From this it is easy to develop tests for the hypothesis that the true values θ^* are within a specified region around the estimates $\hat{\theta}$. On the other hand, a test for whether a specific parameter θ_i is significantly different from zero is based on the fact that $\hat{\theta}_i/\hat{\sigma}Q_{ii}^{1/2}$ would, if $\theta_i^* = 0$, be distributed as t_{n-k}. Such tests applied to two or more parameters are not independent unless the corresponding variables are mutually orthogonal (i.e., the corresponding $Q_{ij} = 0$).

In the CP-67 overhead regression (Example 3), many of the assumptions on which the above analysis is based are violated. All the variables in equation (9) are measured exactly, and the reason that the equation does not fit the observations exactly is that the θ_i are not in fact constants. The time required to service a given request is quite variable, depending partly on the complexity of the request (e.g., the length of a channel program accompanying a virtual Start I/O) and partly on the state of the system (e.g., whether or not enqueueing of the request is necessary). In addition, θ_0 represents the time spent servicing miscellaneous unaccounted requests, and these are obviously quite variable in number. It is not surprising, therefore, that even though the model fits the data well (values of R^2—see Section 1.3.4—in excess of 0.8), the estimates are considerably more variable than predicted by the above analysis. For instance, while the expected variations in θ_1 from one sample of 600 observations to the next should have had a standard deviation of 0.15 msec according to equation (15), the actual standard deviation computed from six replications of 600 observations each was 0.56 msec [Bard and Suryanarayana (1972)].

1.3.2.3. Some Extensions to Linear Regression

(1) *Ridge regression.* While linear regression provides the best *unbiased* linear estimate, the linear estimate with smallest expected squared error is given by

$$\hat{\theta}(k) = (\mathbf{X}^T\mathbf{X} + k\mathbf{I})^{-1}\mathbf{X}^T\mathbf{y} \tag{16}$$

where k is the solution to the equation

$$k\theta^{*T}(\sigma^2\mathbf{X}^T\mathbf{X} + k^2\theta^*\theta^{*T})^{-1}\theta^* = \text{Tr}(\mathbf{X}^T\mathbf{X} + k\mathbf{I}) \tag{17}$$

(Tr $\mathbf{A}$ is the trace of the matrix $\mathbf{A}$). Since the true value θ^* is not known, the value of k cannot be determined. In the method of ridge regression [Hoerl (1962) and Hoerl and Kennard (1970)], the components of $\theta(k)$ are plotted as functions of k for $k \geq 0$, and a value of k is chosen where they cease to vary rapidly. Hemmerle (1975) provides a method for solving equation (17) explicitly when $\hat{\theta}(k)$ is substituted for θ^*. Other methods for estimating k are given by Dempster et al. (1977).

The method of ridge regression avoids the large errors in the estimate $\hat{\theta}$ which result from the presence of nearly redundant variables.

(2) *Robust regression.* The parameter estimates are sensitive not only to the inclusion of redundant variables but also to the presence of unusually large errors in some observations as well as to other violations of the model assumptions. It is the aim of *robust regression* to guard against such effects. The simplest such technique involves *rejection of outliers*: The parameters are estimated as usual; the residuals $r_\mu(\hat{\theta})$ ($\mu = 1, 2, \ldots, n$) and their standard deviation σ are computed. All observations for which $|r_\mu(\hat{\theta})| > K\sigma$ are rejected, where K is some positive constant. The regression is then rerun on the remaining observations. Another technique is to minimize $\sum_\mu |r_\mu(\theta)|$, i.e., the sum of absolute values of residuals. This estimate is much less sensitive to large errors than is the least-squares estimate.

Both of these methods are special cases of *robust regression* procedures. The general formulation requires the minimization of a function of the form

$$\sum_{\mu=1}^{n} \Phi\left[\frac{r_\mu(\theta)}{\sigma(\theta)}\right]$$

where $\sigma(\theta)$ is some estimate of the *spread* of the errors and $\Phi(z)$ is a function whose form can be adjusted so as to give large residuals relatively small weights. In ordinary least squares, $\Phi(z) = z^2$. Some "robust" functions which have been proposed are

$$\Phi(z) = \begin{cases} -z + K^2 - K, & z < -K \\ z^2, & -K \le z \le K \\ z + K^2 - K, & K < z \end{cases} \tag{18}$$

and

$$\Phi(z) = \begin{cases} 1 + \cos \dfrac{z}{c}, & |z| \le c\pi \\ 0, & |z| > c\pi \end{cases} \tag{19}$$

For details, see Andrews (1974).

(3) *Regression with bounded parameters.* Physical con iderations frequently dictate that the values of certain parameters may not exceed or fall below certain bounds. Most often, parameters are required to be positive: Average CPU overhead per service request, device rotation time, and average time between page faults are all cases in point. A parameter estimate which violates a known bound is of no use, since it is known a priori to be incorrect. The least-squares criterion should therefore be modified as follows:

> Find $\hat{\theta}$ such that $S(\hat{\theta})$ is minimum and such that $a_i \le \theta_i \le b_i$ for all bounded θ_i.

For a linear model, this formulation has the form of a *quadratic programming* problem and may be solved by means of quadratic programming algorithms. Efficient algorithms for the case of bounded parameters are given by Bard (1974) and Lawson and Hanson (1974). The frequently adopted expedient of computing the ordinary regression estimate $\hat{\theta}$ and replacing out-of-bound parameter values with the nearest bound (e.g., zero for negative estimates in case of nonnegativity constraints) does not necessarily produce an optimal solution.

In computing the coefficients in the CP-67 overhead regression (Example 3), nonnegativity constraints were, in fact, imposed on all parameters, since the CPU time required for executing a given function cannot be negative.

(4) *Nonlinear regression.* When the model equation is not a linear function of the parameters, the least-squares estimate cannot be obtained by solving a set of linear equations. Sometimes, the equations may be linearized through a transformation of variables. Mostly, however, iterative techniques must be used to compute the estimates. The best known of these is the Gauss-Newton method:

1. Select an initial guess θ_0.

2. Form a first-order Taylor series approximation to the model equation around θ_0, i.e.,

$$y = f(\mathbf{x}, \theta_0) + \left.\frac{\partial f}{\partial \theta}\right|_{\theta = \theta_0} \delta\theta \tag{20}$$

where $\delta\theta = \theta - \theta_0$. We now have a model which is linear in $\delta\theta$, so that $\delta\theta$ can be estimated using linear regression methods.

3. $\boldsymbol{\theta}_0$ is now replaced by $\boldsymbol{\theta}_0 + \delta\boldsymbol{\theta}$, and step (2) is repeated until convergence occurs ($\delta\boldsymbol{\theta} \approx 0$).

Computational details, and many modifications to improve convergence, are given by Bard (1974). The statistical properties which we have derived for linear models still hold, but only approximately. The role of the matrix $\mathbf{X}$ is played here by $\partial\mathbf{f}/\partial\boldsymbol{\theta}$. Bounded parameters, outliers, etc., can be handled just as in the linear case. On the other hand, since the concept of inclusion or exclusion of a variable does not apply directly, variable selection and principal component techniques are not particularly useful with nonlinear models. Significance tests on parameter values may still be carried out, even though they are at best approximate in nature.

Example 5

A paging drum is receiving page read or write requests at a rate of P per second. If a request arrives while the drum is free, a Start I/O operation is initiated immediately. On the other hand, if several requests arrive while the drum is busy, they are chained together and serviced with a single Start I/O operation which is deferred until the drum becomes free. Let S be the rate of Start I/O's issued per second, and let t be the average length of a busy period. The fraction of time when the drum is free is $1 - St$; hence the rate of immediate Start I/O's is $P(1 - St)$. A deferred Start I/O occurs if at least one request arrives during the busy period. If the arrival process is Poisson, this occurs with a probability of approximately $1 - \exp(-Pt)$ for each busy period. Hence, the total rate of Start I/O's is approximately

$$S = P(1 - St) + S[1 - \exp(-Pt)]$$

or

$$S = \frac{P}{Pt + \exp(-Pt)} \tag{21}$$

The average busy period should be an increasing function of the average number of requests filled per Start I/O, i.e., of P/S. Let us assume $t = \theta_1 + \theta_2 P/S$. Then

$$S = \frac{P}{P(\theta_1 + \theta_2 P/S) + \exp[-P(\theta_1 + \theta_2 P/S)]} \tag{22}$$

This model is nonlinear in the parameters θ_1 and θ_2.

The values of P and S were measured over 178 1-minute intervals on CP-67 with an IBM 2301 paging drum, which has a 17.2-msec rotation time. The Gauss-Newton method was used to fit equation (22) with the results:

$$\theta_1 = 4.8 \text{ msec}; \qquad \theta_2 = 8.0 \text{ msec}$$

The standard deviations of the estimates were 0.9 and 0.5 msec, respectively, showing that the parameters were well determined. The standard deviation of the residuals was 0.08, compared to an average S value of about 40 Start I/O's per second, indicating that the model fit the data well. Further confirmation for the validity of the estimates was obtained as follows: When each page request leads to one Start I/O ($P/S = 1$), the average drum busy time should consist of a $\frac{1}{2}$ revolution of latency time, plus $\frac{2}{9}$ of a revolution for data transfer time (there is room for $4\frac{1}{2}$ pages per revolution). Thus, the total average busy time should be $\frac{13}{18}$ revolution, or $17.2 \times \frac{13}{18} = 12.4$ msec, compared to $4.8 + 8.0 \times 1 = 12.8$ msec as predicted by the model. The discrepancy is well within the tolerance expected from the estimated standard deviations.

(5) *Maximum likelihood.*   Maximum likelihood provides a very general method for estimating parameters which appear in model equations and in probability distributions. For instance, in the linear model (11) one obtains estimates both for the θ_i and for the parameters of the distribution of the errors ϵ_μ.

Formally, the method proceeds as follows: Form the density function of the joint probability distribution of all the random variables occurring in all the observations that were taken. Substitute, where possible, the *observed* values of the random variables. These may be directly measured quantities (Example 6 below), or they may be computed from the measured variables by means of the model equations (Example 7 below). The resulting expression is called the *likelihood function*. The parameter values which maximize the likelihood function are the *maximum likelihood estimates* (MLE's).

Example 6

Suppose the number of messages arriving in a communications computer during independent time periods of lengths t_μ ($\mu = 1, 2, \ldots, m$) were observed to be n_μ. It is hypothesized that the arrival process is Poisson with mean interarrival time $1/\lambda$. The probability of n_μ arrivals in time t_μ is then

$$p_\mu = \frac{(\lambda t_\mu)^{n_\mu}}{n_\mu!} \exp(-\lambda t_\mu) \tag{23}$$

The joint pdf is

$$p = \prod_{\mu=1}^{m} \frac{(\lambda t_\mu)^{n_\mu}}{n_\mu!} \exp\left(-\lambda \sum_{\mu=1}^{m} t_\mu\right) \tag{24}$$

In this case, no model equation exists; hence no substitution is necessary, and the likelihood function is simply $L(\lambda) = p$. Taking logarithms, we find

$$\log L(\lambda) = -\lambda \sum_{\mu=1}^{m} t_\mu + \sum_{\mu=1}^{m} n_\mu \log \lambda + \ldots \tag{25}$$

where the omitted terms do not depend on λ. Now the same value of λ which maximizes $L(\lambda)$ also maximizes $\log L(\lambda)$; hence we can find the MLE for λ by equating the derivative of equation (25) to zero:

$$-\sum_{\mu=1}^{m} t_\mu + \frac{1}{\lambda} \sum_{\mu=1}^{m} n_\mu = 0$$

i.e.,

$$\hat{\lambda} = \frac{\sum n_\mu}{\sum t_\mu} \tag{26}$$

Example 7

Consider the model

$$y_\mu = f(\mathbf{x}_\mu, \mathbf{\theta}) + \epsilon_\mu \qquad (\mu = 1, 2, \ldots, n) \tag{27}$$

where the ϵ_μ are distributed independently and normally with zero mean and standard deviation σ. The joint pdf is

$$p(\epsilon_1, \epsilon_2, \ldots, \epsilon_n) = (2\pi)^{-n/2}\sigma^{-n} \exp\left(-\sum_{\mu=1}^{n} \frac{\epsilon_\mu^2}{2\sigma^2}\right) \tag{28}$$

Making the substitution $\epsilon_\mu = y_\mu - f(\mathbf{x}_\mu, \mathbf{\theta})$, we obtain the likelihood function:

$$L(\mathbf{\theta}, \sigma) = (2\pi)^{-n/2}\sigma^{-n} \exp\left\{-\sum_{\mu=1}^{n} \frac{[y_\mu - f(\mathbf{x}_\mu, \mathbf{\theta})]^2}{2\sigma^2}\right\} \tag{29}$$

It is quite evident that L is maximum when $\sum [y_\mu - f(\mathbf{x}_\mu, \mathbf{\theta})]^2$ is minimum. In this case, then, the least-squares and maximum likelihood estimates coincide. An exercise in elementary calculus shows the MLE for σ to be

$$\hat{\sigma} = \left\{\sum_\mu \frac{[y_\mu - f(\mathbf{x}_\mu, \hat{\mathbf{\theta}})]^2}{n}\right\}^{1/2} \tag{30}$$

This is close to the estimate (15) when n is much larger than k.

The statistical properties of the MLE may be summarized as follows: The covariance matrix of the estimates is approximately $[\partial^2 L/\partial\mathbf{\theta}\,\partial\mathbf{\theta}]_{\mathbf{\theta}=\hat{\mathbf{\theta}}}^{-1}$. The estimate is consistent (approaches the true value as $n \longrightarrow \infty$) and asympotically efficient (has minimum possible variance as $n \longrightarrow \infty$). These properties may not hold when the parameters are subject to constraints or if the pdf is discontinuous.

The maximum likelihood method greatly expands the range of situations for which estimates may be routinely derived. One can handle problems where the independent variables are subject to errors [Bard (1974)] and even where the parameters themselves are random variables with specified distributions. In the latter case, one estimates the parameters—e.g., mean and variance—of that distribution.

1.3.3. Suggesting the Form of the Model

The most obvious way to select the form of a model is to fit various forms to the data and then select the one which gives the best fit. Statistical techniques can, however, to a limited extent point out what relationships exist among the variables and hence point the way to a model. The techniques are essentially limited to *linear* models, i.e., models having the form

$$y = \theta_0 + \theta_1 x_1 + \theta_2 x_2 + \ldots + \theta_k x_k \tag{31}$$

and therefore most purely empirical models are restricted to this class. Nevertheless, such models are often useful, either because they are in fact physically justifiable (e.g., the CP-67 overhead model described above) or because they express the approximate effects that small perturbations in the independent variables have on the dependent variable (e.g., in the analysis of designed experiments; see Section 1.4).

In many analyses of computer performance data one does not even know in advance which variables are related to each other. Nor can one, a priori, distinguish between dependent and independent variables. We shall refer to the entire set of measured variables as $\mathbf{w} = [w_1, w_2, \ldots, w_r]$ and to the data from the μth observation $(\mu = 1, 2, \ldots, n)$ as $\mathbf{w}_\mu = [w_{\mu 1}, w_{\mu 2}, \ldots, w_{\mu r}]$. The starting point of the analysis here is the correlation matrix $\mathbf{R}$ of the data. Simple inspection of the elements of $\mathbf{R}$ immediately reveals which variables are simply related to each other. Thus, if R_{ij} is close to 1 (-1), then large values of w_i generally occur in observations where w_j is large (small). A small absolute value of R_{ij} indicates the lack of a monotone relationship between these variables. Suppose w_i and w_j are two independent normally distributed random variables, and suppose $w_{\mu i}$ and $w_{\mu j}$ $(\mu = 1, 2, \ldots, n)$ are samples drawn at random from w_i and w_j. Let R_{ij} be the sample correlation. Then [Anderson (1958)] the quantity $R_{ij}[(n - 2)/(1 - R_{ij})^2]^{1/2}$ has Student's t distribution with $n - 2$ degrees of freedom. Given the value of R_{ij}, it is then easy to test the hypothesis that w_i and w_j are indeed uncorrelated. Note, however, that when such tests are applied to different elements of $\mathbf{R}$, the results are generally not independent.

While inspection of the correlation matrix may reveal the presence or absence of relationships among different variables taken two at a time, a more incisive analysis is required to uncover richer relationships. This purpose is served by *principal component* analysis [Bard (1974) and Webster et al. (1974)].

Let us transform the original variables into normalized form:

$$z_i = \frac{w_i - \bar{w}_i}{\sigma_i} \qquad (i = 1, 2, \ldots, r) \tag{32}$$

where $\bar{w}_i$ and σ_i are the mean and standard deviation of w_i, respectively. Clearly, the z_i have zero means and unit variances. Also, the covariance matrix of the $\mathbf{z}_\mu$ is precisely the correlation matrix $\mathbf{R}$ of the $\mathbf{w}_\mu$. The purpose of this transformation is to reduce all the variables to scales in which they have equal variances. The sum of all these variances is r, and this may be regarded as the total variablity present in all the observations. We would like to find a small number of *statistically independent* linear combinations of the variables which account for as much of the variation in the observations as possible and for other combinations which have as little variation as possible. Both of these aims are satisfied by the *principal components*, which are defined below.

Let λ_i $(i = 1, 2, \ldots, r)$ be the ith eigenvalue of $\mathbf{R}$, and let $\mathbf{v}_i = [v_{i1}, v_{i2}, \ldots, v_{ir}]$ be the corresponding normalized eigenvector. We have, then, $\mathbf{R}\mathbf{v}_i = \lambda_i \mathbf{v}_i$ and $\mathbf{v}_i^T \mathbf{v}_i = 1$. Furthermore, since $\mathbf{R}$ is nonnegative definite, $\lambda_i \geq 0$, and since $\mathbf{R}$ is symmetric, $\mathbf{v}_i^T \mathbf{v}_j = 0$ for $i \neq j$ (see any text on linear algebra for details). Let us assume for the moment that $\mathbf{R}$ is the true population correlation matrix. Then the $\mathbf{v}_i$ and λ_i are not random. Hence, the random variable $u_i = \mathbf{v}_i^T \mathbf{z} = v_{i1} z_1 + v_{i2} z_2 + \ldots + v_{ir} z_r$ has the following properties:

$$E(u_i) = E(\mathbf{v}_i^T \mathbf{z}) = \mathbf{v}_i^T E(\mathbf{z}) = 0 \tag{33}$$

and

$$E(u_i u_j) = E(\mathbf{v}_i^T \mathbf{z} \mathbf{z}^T \mathbf{v}_j) = \mathbf{v}_i^T E(\mathbf{z}\mathbf{z}^T) \mathbf{v}_j$$
$$= \mathbf{v}_i^T \mathbf{R} \mathbf{v}_j = \mathbf{v}_i^T \lambda_j \mathbf{v}_j = \lambda_j \mathbf{v}_i^T \mathbf{v}_j = \begin{cases} \lambda_i & i = j \\ 0, & i \neq j \end{cases} \tag{34}$$

The u_i are called *principal components* and form a set of k uncorrelated linear combinations of the random variables **w**, whose variances are the eigenvalues of the correlation matrix **R**.

Of greatest practical interest are the *largest* and *smallest* components, i.e., those with the largest and smallest eigenvalues. These components are the solutions to the following problem: Find the normalized (i.e., sum of squares of coefficients equal to 1) linear combination of the z_i having largest/smallest variance. The second largest/smallest components are the normalized linear combinations orthogonal to the largest/smallest component having largest/smallest variance, and so on.

We shall now explain the usefulness of first the small and then the large components. If λ_i is very small, the corresponding u_i has small variance. This is the same as saying that the value of u_i does not vary much from one observation to the next. Hence, the relation

$$v_{i1}z_1 + v_{i2}z_2 + \ldots + v_{ir}z_r = 0 \qquad (35)$$

holds approximately for most observations. It follows that we now have an equation relating the variables of the problem. There are two possibilities: Maybe this relationship is accidental, perhaps the result of a poorly designed experiment. At any rate, one of the variables entering the expression is redundant in the present data set and should be dropped from further analysis. On the other hand, the equation we have discovered may express a genuine relationship among the variables, in which case it should be included in the model, as illustrated in the example below. The determination of which of these two possibilities holds requires an understanding of the system being modeled and of the data acquisition method. Experimental design techniques (see Section 1.4) should be used to guard against introduction of spurious relationships among independent variables.

Inspection of the coefficients in equation (35) usually reveals some which are nearly zero, showing that the corresponding variables should probably not be included in the equation. Precisely which variables should be included is perhaps better determined by variable selection regression methods (Section 1.3.2). The identification of a *dependent variable* requires understanding of the system, as illustrated by the example below.

A few details need to be ironed out before we can come up with a usable equation. Recall that the normalized variables z_i are related to the original variables w_i by means of equation (32). One easily verifies then that equation (35) is equivalent to

$$a_1w_1 + a_2w_2 + \ldots + a_rw_r = b \qquad (36)$$

where

$$a_j = v_{ij}/\sigma_j \quad \text{and} \quad b = \sum_j v_{ij}\bar{w}_j/\sigma_j$$

These ideas will be illustrated in the following example [Bard and Suryanarayana (1972)]. In the CP-67 overhead regression, the estimated coefficients were subject to large fluctuations, partly due to the high degree of correlation among the independent variables. To reveal dependencies that may exist among the latter, a principal component analysis was carried out on the covariance matrix. The results are displayed in Table 1.3.2; also see Table 1.3.3. It appears that there are four small eigenvalues. The

Table 1.3.2. Principal Component Analysis, CP-67
Release 3.1 Data

Variable (see Table 1.3.3 for definitions)	Eigenvalue of Correlation Matrix			
	0.00109	0.0155	0.178	0.302
	Coefficient in Normalized Eigenvector [1]			
x_1 VSIO	—	—	0.510	0.354
x_2 VMIO	—	—	0.401	0.128
x_3 DIAGIO	—	—	—	—
x_4 SPOOL	—	—	0.137	—
x_5 PAGES	−0.757	0.299	—	—
x_6 UNSIO	—	—	—	—
x_7 TIO	—	—	—	—
x_8 PGMINT	—	—	—	0.492
x_9 IOINT	—	—	−0.663	—
x_{10} DISP	—	—	0.194	−0.765
x_{11} PAGEIO	0.113	−0.815	—	—
x_{12} PAGEIN	0.643	0.496	—	—
x_{13} HIO	—	—	—	—
x_{14} TCH	—	—	−0.258	—

[1] Only coefficients in excess of 0.1 are displayed. The largest coefficient in each eigenvector is underlined.

Table 1.3.3. Definition of CP-67 Variables

Variable	Definition
VSIO	Virtual selector I/O
VMIO	Virtual multiplexer I/O
DIAGIO	Special virtual I/O
SPOOL	Spool I/O
PAGES	Page read or write
UNSIO	Unsuccessful Start I/O
TIO	Test I/O
PGMINT	Program interrupt
IOINT	I/O interrupt
DISP	Dispatch
PAGEIO	I/O to paging device
PAGEIN	Page read
HIO	Halt I/O
TCH	Test channel

two smallest ones have eigenvectors whose only sizable coefficients are associated with paging variables. They merely reflect the fact that since the three paging variables are very highly correlated, there are two linear relationships among them and only one truly independent variable. The next smallest eigenvalue has a particularly large coefficient associated with the I/O interrupt rate. This component seems to reflect the fact that I/O interrupts result from I/O operations; hence the number of interrupts is a function principally of the number of virtual selector and multiplexor Start I/O operations. The next component seems to reflect the dependency of the dispatching rate on the various functions performed by the control program. Thus, the relationships uncovered by the analysis could have been hypothesized a priori from a close study of the system.

The relationships thus uncovered may be combined with the CP-67 overhead regression in a two-stage process:

1. Perform regressions[2] relating the number of I/O interrupts and dispatches to their explanatory variables. On the data summarized in Table 1.3.2, this yields the relations

$$x_9 = 0.853x_1 + 0.485x_2 \tag{37}$$

$$x_{10} = 77.6 + 5.76x_1 + 3.57x_3 + 2.37x_5 + 1.66x_8 \tag{38}$$

2. Define two new variables, r_9 and r_{10}, as the residuals from the above equations.

3. Use r_9 and r_{10} in addition to the remaining variables as independent variables in the overhead regression, which now yields the relation

$$y = 15.8 + 5.03x_1 + 1.5x_2 + 2.06x_3 + 1.74x_4 + 1.63x_5$$
$$+ 0.38x_6 + 0.47x_7 + 0.37x_8$$
$$+ 0.24r_9 + 1.08r_{10} \tag{39}$$

The advantage of this procedure over straightforward regression of y on x_1 through x_{10} is that whereas x_9 and x_{10} are nearly redundant with the other variables, r_9 and r_{10} are uncorrelated with them. Hence, the estimated coefficients of equation (39) exhibit smaller variance than those obtained in a straightforward regression. The interpretation of a typical coefficient in equation (39) is the following: θ_1, say, is the contribution of one virtual selector Start I/O, including the 0.853 I/O interrupts and 5.76 dispatches that such a request engenders, on the average. On the other hand, $\theta_9 = 0.24$ expresses the average contribution of an I/O interrupt, without regard to its origin.

If small eigenvalues of **R** identify combinations of variables which have small variability, the converse is true of the large eigenvalues. Suppose we compute the values of two principal components, say, u_i and u_j, for each observation. We now draw a point whose coordinates are u_i and u_j on a plot with suitably labeled axes. By the time we are finished with all n observations, we have a swarm of n points. If λ_i and λ_j are the two *smallest* eigenvalues, then the points will exhibit the least possible

---

[2] A forward selection regression program was used. Only the selected variables are shown in equations (37)–(39). Some variables not suggested by Table 1.3.2 were selected in equation (38).

scatter: Most of them will be clustered around the origin. Conversely, if λ_i and λ_j are the two *largest* eigenvalues, the points will have the largest possible scatter. Inspection of such a plot is most likely to show if the observations may be naturally classified into distinct *clusters*. The presence of well-defined clusters may indicate that radically different conditions prevailed during various subsets of the observations. For instance, Figure 1.3.1 clearly reveals the presence of at least two distinct clusters. Later investigation revealed that the points in the lower left-hand cluster all belonged to night-shift operation, when the system work load was quite different from that of the day shift. Similar analysis has enabled Anderson et al. (1973) to classify the work load of a time-sharing system into different types of transactions.

Classifying the observations into clusters may reveal that the relationships between variables vary from one cluster to another. Therefore, it may be profitable to cluster the observations first and then to apply the principal component analysis again to the observations within each cluster.

In summary, principal component analysis has two important applications:

1. A scatter plot of the first two components (those with the largest eigenvalues) is a useful clustering tool.

2. The components with the smallest eigenvalues yield candidates for model equations.

A third useful application of principal component analysis is the following: Instead of regressing the dependent variable on the original independent variables, one transforms into principal components and uses the latter as the independent variables in the regression procedure. The advantage is that one thus has a set of uncorrelated variables, and one obtains regression coefficient estimates which are uncorrelated. This procedure is referred to as *regression on principal components*.

1.3.4.   Evaluating the Adequacy of the Model

Two points of view may be taken in evaluating the adequacy of a model. The one is statistical: Is the model consistent with the data? The other one is utilitarian: Does the model serve its purpose? The answers to these questions may not be the same. For instance, if the data are poor (large measurement errors), then even a poorly fitting model will be statistically adequate, although its predictions may have no practical value. On the other hand, a model (such as the CP-67 overhead regression) may be statistically inadequate (because some of the model assumptions are violated), yet produce a very good fit to the data and perform well in predicting future observations.

Decision theory [Raiffa and Schlaifer (1961)] presents a formal basis for resolving utilitarian questions, but we shall discuss only a frequently used intuitive goodness of fit measure. Let $\bar{y}$ be the average of the y_μ, and let $S = \sum_\mu (y_\mu - \bar{y})^2$. The quantity S is a measure of the total variability in the observed y_μ. On the other hand, $S(\hat{\theta})$ is a measure of the variability left after the model equation was fitted to the data.

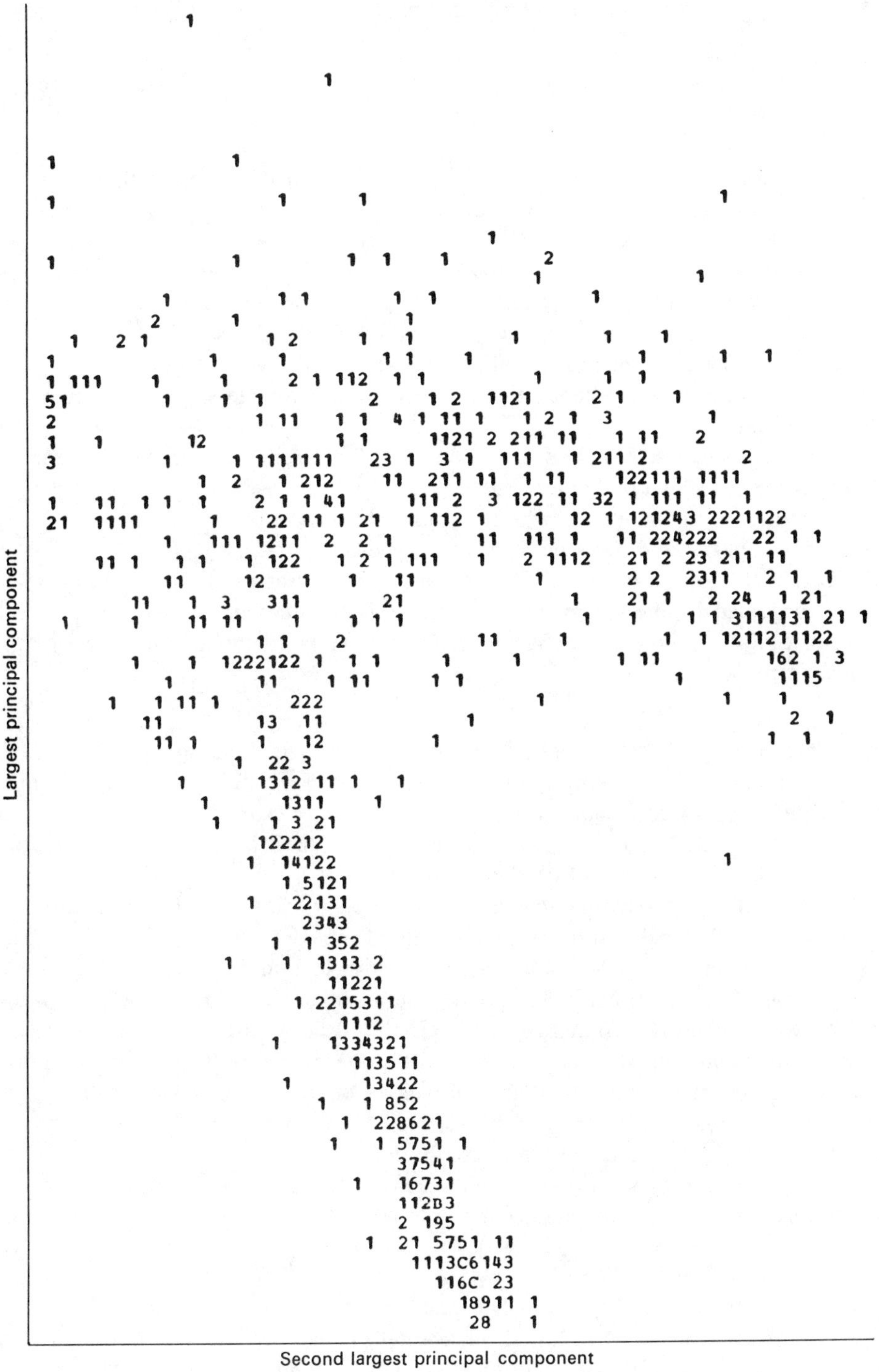

Largest principal component

Second largest principal component

Figure 1.3.1. Scatter plot of largest principal components, computer performance data. Digits indicate number of observations falling in each square.

Thus,

$$R^2 = \frac{S - S(\hat{\theta})}{S} \tag{40}$$

is the fraction of the total variability which is "explained" by the model equation. When $R^2 = 0$, i.e., $S = S(\hat{\theta})$, the model has contributed nothing toward explaining the variations in y, whereas when $R^2 = 1$, i.e., $S(\hat{\theta}) = 0$, the model explains the observations perfectly. The R^2 criterion is particularly useful when the measurement errors are small and lack of fit is mostly due to missing terms or other approximations made when deriving the model. In such cases, one would take an R^2 exceeding 0.5 as promising, exceeding 0.8 as good, and exceeding 0.9 as excellent. Even models with very small R^2 values may provide excellent estimates for certain parameters, as illustrated by the following example.

One wishes to discover the average amount of "free" main storage space required per logged-on user in a computer system (such storage is used for control blocks and status information). Available were 1115 observations on the variables P = number of pageable pages and U = number of logged-on users. Now $P = M - N - F$, where M is the total number of main storage page frames, N is the number of page frames occupied by the system nucleus, and F is the number of used "free" pages. Since M and N are constants, changes in P are directly attributable to changes in F. Hence, in the model

$$P = \theta_1 - \theta_2 U \tag{41}$$

the parameter θ_2 is the required free storage per user. Equation (41) was fitted to the observed data, with a rather poor $R^2 = 0.37$. However, the estimate $\theta_2 = 0.595 \pm 0.023$ corresponded well with preliminary estimates and was very well determined indeed. The poor R^2 is due to the fact that there is much random variation in F even when the number of users remains constant.

Statistical tests for model adequacy—or *goodness of fit*—are generally based on the residuals $r_\mu(\theta)$. Each residual is an estimate of the corresponding error ϵ_μ, and the distribution of the residuals should resemble (with certain reservations) that of the errors. Thus, if the errors are independently and normally distributed with zero means and known standard deviation σ, then $\sum_\mu \epsilon_\mu^2/\sigma^2$ has the χ^2 distribution with n degrees of freedom. Similarly, the normalized sum of squares of residuals $S(\theta^*)/\sigma^2$ should have a χ^2 distribution, but the number of degrees of freedom is reduced to $n - k$ by the k estimated parameters. This provides a test for the hypothesis that the residuals are explainable by the assumed error distribution.

The χ^2 test determines only whether the *magnitude* of the residuals is acceptable. It does not test their randomness. For the latter purpose, various residual plots are useful. Among these are

1. Normal probability plot. The residuals are sorted in ascending order of algebraic value and plotted on normal probability paper. The plot will be nearly linear if the distribution is normal. Outliners will be clearly noticeable as deviations from linearity at either end of the plot.

2. Trend plot. The residuals are plotted against the magnitude of variables which may or may not appear in the model equations (time of observation may be an example of the latter).

Other useful trend plots are residuals vs. the fitted values of the dependent variable and the squared or absolute values of the residuals vs. any other variable of interest. Any obvious deviations from randomness in these plots may point to effects that were neglected in the model.

An interesting deviation from randomness appears in the residuals of the CP-67 overhead regression. The average of all residuals is, of course, zero (why?). However, the average of all large residuals (say, all those exceeding 2.5σ in absolute value) is strongly positive. The obvious explanation is that during some observation periods the system was heavily engaged in some unaccounted for activities, which increased the overhead way beyond the value predicted for the accounted activities.

1.3.5. Model-Based Predictions

Suppose the model $y = f(\mathbf{x}, \boldsymbol{\theta}) + \epsilon$ is to be used to predict the value of y for a specified value of $\mathbf{x}$. Parameter estimates $\hat{\boldsymbol{\theta}}$, with an associated covariance matrix $\mathbf{V}$, have been obtained from past observations. An estimate of the error variance σ^2 has also been obtained, either from equation (15) or from knowledge of the measurement process. It may also be the case that the values of $\mathbf{x}$ are not known precisely in advance but may be subject to errors $\delta\mathbf{x}$ with covariance matrix $\mathbf{U}$. If f is continuous and differentiable, then to a first-order approximation,

$$y + \delta y = f(\mathbf{x}, \hat{\boldsymbol{\theta}}) + \frac{\partial f}{\partial \mathbf{x}} \delta\mathbf{x} + \frac{\partial f}{\partial \boldsymbol{\theta}} \delta\boldsymbol{\theta} + \epsilon$$

Assuming that the errors $\delta\mathbf{x}$, $\delta\boldsymbol{\theta}$, and ϵ are uncorrelated, then the expected squared error of the prediction is approximately

$$s^2 = E(\delta y^2) \approx \left(\frac{\partial f}{\partial \mathbf{x}}\right)^T \mathbf{U} \frac{\partial f}{\partial \mathbf{x}} + \left(\frac{\partial f}{\partial \boldsymbol{\theta}}\right)^T \mathbf{V} \frac{\partial f}{\partial \boldsymbol{\theta}} + \sigma^2$$

In particular, in the linear model $y = \boldsymbol{\theta}^T \mathbf{x}$ we have

$$s^2 = \hat{\boldsymbol{\theta}}^T \mathbf{U} \hat{\boldsymbol{\theta}} + \mathbf{x}^T \mathbf{V} \mathbf{x} + \sigma^2$$

1.4. DESIGN OF EXPERIMENTS

1.4.1. Introduction

Design of experiments deals with situations in which there are variables, or factors, that can be controlled by the experimenter, as in a laboratory environment. The aim of carrying out designed experiments is usually to identify those factors that have significant effects on the dependent variables or responses, to estimate the magnitude of these effects, and to determine the nature of possible interactions among the factors. In this spirit, a computer system may be viewed as a laboratory in which we can carry out scientific experiments to learn how to control and improve its performance. Factors under our control might be related to the hardware, the operating system, or the workload. For example, factors which may be varied in a controlled manner to determine their effects upon system performance are disabling of system components such as main memory banks, drums, and channels; setting operating system parameters to prescribed values; or changing the job mix in the work load.

Experiments in which the work loads are controlled are usually referred to as benchmark tests. Although such experiments can be controlled very effectively, inferences drawn from analysis of the results are necessarily conditioned on the work load, and it is difficult, if not impossible, to extrapolate the results to other work loads. Experiments can also be carried out on systems while they are processing actual work loads, and valid inferences are possible provided that the experiments are designed in such a way as to control the effects of variations in the work loads upon the responses of interest. Ideally, one would like to understand the salient characteristics of work loads sufficiently to be able to parameterize them effectively and include the resulting parameters as factors in the experiment. In this way, it would be theoretically possible to study the joint effects of hardware, operating system, and workload characteristics on relevant aspects of system performance and to draw valid inferences as to the probable effects of these factors in other environments.

The model employed to study designed experiments is identical to that used to study linear regression, with the controlled factors taking the place of the independent variables. The goal of the theory of design of experiments is to provide methods for obtaining the greatest amount of information concerning the phenomena to be studied, at a given cost. Some general principles of importance in this regard include the following:

1. When the effects of two or more factors are to be studied, the factors should be varied simultaneously in a single (factorial) experiment rather than one at a time in separate experiments. The benefits accruing from factorial experiments are twofold:

    a. Equivalent levels of information pertaining to the effects of the individual factors, hereafter referred to as main effects, can be achieved in a factorial experiment with a smaller number of trials than required for separate single-factor experiments.

    b. Interaction effects resulting from the joint variation of two or more factors can be estimated in a factorial experiment, since it allows for joint variation of factors.

2. The factors in a factorial experiment should where possible, be varied in such a way as to ensure that they are mutually orthogonal (or uncorrelated). Then the main effects and interactions can be estimated independently of one another, thereby eliminating problems arising from dependencies among the independent variables. Furthermore, in orthogonal experiments, regression-type computations reduce to very simple forms not requiring matrix inversions.

3. The experimental trials should be conducted in random order to avoid the possible inadvertent introduction of systematic bias into the experiment. This principle is commonly referred to as randomization.

4. If there are uncontrollable sources of variation that may affect the measured responses, it may be possible to arrange the experimental trials in such a way as to substantially reduce their effects. This can be accomplished by arranging the trials in blocks (or groups) of equal size such that the effects of the uncontrollable sources of variation are believed to be small within blocks. The experiment should then be designed in such a manner as to ensure that the effects of variations between blocks and variations due to the controllable factors are mutually orthogonal. It is then possible to estimate the factorial effects independently of the blocking effects. This device is called blocking, and experiments which employ randomization within blocks are referred to as randomized block experiments.

5. It is frequently possible to estimate main effects and low-order interactions (i.e., two- or three-factor interactions) without carrying out complete factorial experiments. For example, a complete factorial experiment involving six factors, each at two levels (e.g., high and low or on and off), would require 64 trials, or runs. However, if one could safely ignore the higher-order interactions, it would be possible to design a $\frac{1}{2}$ replicate fractional factorial experiment in just 32 runs and estimate all main effects and two-factor interactions.

In the following sections we shall illustrate these principles with examples of designed experiments carried out on computer systems.

1.4.2. Single-Factor Experiments with Real Work Loads

Margolin et al. (1971) carried out an experiment with actual work loads to evaluate the relative merits of two different free storage management algorithms on CP-67. A naive way of conducting such an experiment might have been to run the system with algorithm A for several days and then run it for an equal number of days with algorithm B. One could then compare system variables of interest, such as interactive response time, proportion problem state time, or overhead for the two algorithms. If the experiment had been run in this way, it would have been difficult to ascertain whether observed differences were due to the effects of the different algorithms or to differences in the work loads that were encountered from day to day. In most computer installations, daily variations in work loads are usually very substantial, so that the issue in question is quite real.

A simple means of achieving some degree of control over this situation might have been to conduct a completely randomized experiment in which the algorithms were assigned randomly to the different days during which the experiment was to be run. For example, suppose it was decided that the experiment should be run during the normal workweek, Monday through Friday, for two weeks. Each day, the experimenter could flip a coin and run algorithm A or B depending on whether the result was a head or a tail. With this procedure, each algorithm would have an equal chance of being used on each day, but one might end up being used more often than the other. To achieve balance, the coin tossing would be abandoned once one of the algorithms had been run five times, and the other algorithm would be run for the balance of the time. With this procedure, each algorithm would be used exactly five times, while the randomization would tend to prevent any systematic bias in the work loads associated with a particular week or day of the week. However, it might be that algorithm A was used four times in the first week and only once in the second. If the work load had changed significantly from one week to the next, we would be in trouble. Or perhaps algorithm A happened to have been selected on the Tuesdays and Fridays of both weeks. If certain jobs tend to be run on particular days of the week, we would again encounter difficulties in separating the effects of the algorithms from those of the work loads.

The design finally used in this experiment is shown in Table 1.4.1. The randomi-

Table 1.4.1. Experimental Design for Free Storage
Experiment

	Monday	Tuesday	Wednesday	Thursday
Week 1	A	B	B	A
Week 2	B	A	A	B

zation consisted only of choosing at random which algorithm would be run on the first day. This design has the following properties:

1. Each algorithm is run twice each week.

2. Each algorithm is run once each day.

3. Comparisons of the two algorithms cannot be affected by any possible linear or quadratic time trends in the work loads.

Thus, the effects of week, day of the week, linear trend component, and quadratic trend component are orthogonal to difference in algorithms. These properties are illustrated by Table 1.4.2 in which the design factors are coded as indicator variables to denote the presence ($+1$) or absence (0) of a particular level of a given factor. The effects due to varying the levels of a factor are expressed in the linear model as deviations about the overall mean and hence must sum to zero. To express this restriction, the last level of each factor is represented, by convention, as the negation (-1) of all of the other levels of that factor. For example, observations 4 and 8 in Table 1.4.2, corresponding to the last level of the factor "day," are coded as the negation of the effects of Monday, Tuesday, and Wednesday. The final two columns of the matrix contain the first- and second-degree orthogonal polynomials for eight equally spaced observations. They provide a means of independently estimating linear and quadratic effects in the data by regressing the observations on these two variables. Cochran and

Table 1.4.2. Design Matrix for Free Storage Experiment

Observation	Week	Mon.	Tues.	Wed.	Alg. A	Orthogonal Polynomials Linear	Quadratic
1	1	1	0	0	1	−7	7
2	1	0	1	0	−1	−5	1
3	1	0	0	1	−1	−3	−3
4	1	−1	−1	−1	1	−1	−5
5	−1	1	0	0	−1	1	−5
6	−1	0	1	0	1	3	−3
7	−1	0	0	1	1	5	1
8	−1	−1	−1	−1	−1	7	7

Cox (1957) describe applications of this type. It is a simple matter to compute the inner products of the column corresponding to algorithm with those of the different work-load factors and check that they are equal to zero. Thus, the treatment and work-load factors are mutually orthogonal, so that comparisons of the two algorithms are free of any contamination from work-load variations that are due to week, day, and linear and quadratic trend components. The indicator variables play the roles of the independent variables in the linear regression model.

The results of the experiment are reproduced in Table 1.4.3, which gives the average CPU time per call to the FREE and FRET modules,[3] where these denote demands

Table 1.4.3. Results of Free Storage Experiment, CPU Time Per Call (microsec)

	Monday	Tuesday	Wednesday	Thursday
Week 1				
FREE	325	50	45	426
FRET	221	38	34	287
Week 2				
FREE	37	346	313	45
FRET	27	236	217	33

for blocks of free storage and return of such blocks to the free storage pool, respectively. The results are so striking as to obviate the need for formal statistical analysis. However, for purposes of illustration, we shall present in Table 1.4.5 the analysis of variance of the results for calls to FREE.

Briefly, the analysis of variance subdivides the total sum of squares of the observations about their mean into additive components attributable to the various factors.

[3]Such algorithms are commonly referred to by the terminology DEACTIVATE and ACTIVATE, respectively.

In terms of the linear regression model described in the previous section, we can compute the reduction in the sum of squares due to all of the main effects and interactions. In an orthogonal design, these sums of squares are mutually independent and may be calculated in any sequence. Furthermore, it is possible to derive simple computational formulas not involving matrix inversions. Details may be found in Scheffe (1959).

Suppose, in our example, that we wanted to compute sums of squares corresponding to day, week, and algorithm. The computational formulas can be deduced from the example of a two-factor experiment, as given in Table 1.4.4. Let Y_{ij} be the observed response when factor A is at level i and factor B is at level j, and let $Y_{i.}$, $Y_{.j}$, and $Y_{..}$ be the averages of responses with factor A at level i, the responses with factor B at level j, and all responses, respectively [e.g., $Y_{i.} = (\sum_j Y_{ij}) \div J$]. Furthermore, let $C = IJY_{..}^2$, where $I =$ the number of levels of factor A and $J =$ the number of levels of factor B. Table 1.4.4 gives formulas for SS_A (the sum of squares due to the factor A main effect), SS_B, etc. An alternative formula for SS_A is $J \sum_i (Y_{i.} - Y_{..})^2$, so that it is readily seen that a main effect sum of squares measures the variability of the average responses at each level of the given factor about the general mean.

If the responses are linear functions of the factors and their interactions plus independent normally distributed errors with mean zero and constant variance, then it can be shown, under the null hypothesis that all effects equal zero, that the sums of squares are independently distributed as chi-square random variables. In a completely replicated experiment, that is, one in which there are two or more observations at each design point, the error sum of squares would be estimated from the replicated measurements. For instance, suppose that in our two-factor example each design point were replicated K times. Let Y_{ijk} denote the response at the kth replication of factor A at level i and factor B at level j. Then SS_A would be given by $JK \sum_i (Y_{i..} - Y_{...})^2$, and the sum of squares for error (SS_e) would be given by $\sum_i \sum_j \sum_k (Y_{ijk} - Y_{ij.})^2$ and would have $IJ(K - 1)$ degrees of freedom. In the absence of replications or any other independent source of estimate of the error variance, the highest-order interaction sums of squares are generally used to estimate the error variance, on the assumption that such interactions are nonexistent or negligible. In either case, the statistical significance of an individual effect may be tested by dividing its mean square by the error mean square and subjecting the ratio to an F test. Because the various sums of squares are independently distributed as chi-square random variables under the null

Table 1.4.4. Analysis of Variance for a Two-Factor Experiment

Source	Sums of Square	Degrees of Freedom	Mean Squares
A main effects	$SS_A = J \sum_i Y_{i.}^2 - C$	$I - 1$	$SS_A/(I - 1)$
B main effects	$SS_B = I \sum_j Y_{.j}^2 - C$	$J - 1$	$SS_B/(J - 1)$
AB interaction	$SS_{AB} = \sum_i \sum_j (Y_{ij} - Y_{i.} - Y_{.j} + Y_{..})^2$	$(I - 1)(J - 1)$	$SS_{AB}/(I - 1)(J - 1)$
Total	$SS_{tot} = \sum \sum Y_{ij}^2 - C$		

hypothesis of zero effects, the resulting F tests are mutually independent. This important property holds only for orthogonal designs.

The analysis of variance given in Table 1.4.5(a) reveals that variations in work load from day to day and week to week were not significant. Differences in algorithms were so huge that the precautions taken in designing the experiment were really not necessary. However, one never knows beforehand whether such considerations are important, and it usually costs little or nothing extra to design and run an experiment in such a way as to provide protection against uncontrollable factors that might completely invalidate the experiment.

Table 1.4.5. Analysis of Variance of FREE Calls

Source	Sums of Squares	Degrees of Freedom	Mean Squares
(a) Day	4,111.375	3	1,370.458
Week	1,378.125	1	1,378.125
Algorithm	190,036.125	1	190,036.125
Error	2,358.250	2	1,179.125
Total	197,883.875	7	
(b) Linear component	102.149	1	102.149
Quadratic component	1,703.720	1	1,703.720
Algorithm	190,036.125	1	190,036.125
Error	6,041.881	4	1,510.470
Total	197,883.875	7	

Although we have already seen that work-load variations had no effect on the results of this experiment, we shall present, for pedagogical purposes, an alternative analysis that treats the linear and quadratic trend components explicitly. The analysis of variance is given in Table 1.4.5(b). Since we have used only two degrees of freedom to model the temporal variations, we now have two additional degrees of freedom for error.

Frequently, one needs to be able to detect much more subtle effects in the presence of actual work-load variability. A case in point is discussed by Bard (1973), who carried out an on-line experiment to measure the effect of two different page replacement algorithms on the performance of CP-67. This experiment was carried out as a block experiment in which the system automatically switched from one algorithm to the other every 5 minutes. Thus, each 10-minute interval could be regarded as a block, providing a comparison between the two algorithms. Because the treatments were orthogonal to the blocks, the design effectively removed the effects of work-load variations (between successive 10-minute intervals) from the comparison of the algorithms. In the experiment data were recorded at 1-minute intervals, while in the analysis the first observation in each 5-minute interval was discarded in order to eliminate the transient effects due to the switching. An analysis of variance of the results is given in Table 1.4.6. It is interesting to note that about two thirds of the variability in the experiment was due to work-load fluctuations, as measured by the

Table 1.4.6. Analysis of Variance for Paging
Experiment

	Percent Problem State Time			
Source	SS	d.f.	MS	*F*
Blocks, day 1	5.02	26	0.19	17.04
Blocks, day 2	5.28	26	0.20	17.91
Blocks, day 3	6.40	26	0.25	21.71
Blocks, day 4	6.59	26	0.25	22.35
Days	0.81	3	0.27	23.73
Algorithms	0.29	1	0.29	25.97
Replications	7.34	648	0.0113	
Lack of fit	4.14	107	0.0387	3.41
Total	35.87	863		

sum of squares of blocks within days, and that due to day-to-day variations. The estimate of SS given by the replicated observations is probably an underestimate because observations at 1-minute intervals are highly correlated and therefore not independent. The sum of squares attributed to lack of fit, computed by subtraction of all the other sums of squares from the total sum of squares, probably provides a more appropriate measure of error. It represents the interaction of blocks and days with algorithm, and there is certainly no reason to expect this to be of any significance. Recalculation of *F* ratios based on this estimate of error sum of squares would still produce highly significant results.

The results of the experiment in terms of average response time, average problem state time, and average page reads per second by day are given in Table 1.4.7. They show that algorithm A is always superior to algorithm B. However, the day-to-day variation was so large that on day 4, algorithm A exhibited worse response times and paging rates than did algorithm B on days 1–3. Similarly, algorithm A had a lower level of problem state time on day 3 than was achieved by algorithm B on days 1–2. These results provide dramatic demonstrations of the highly beneficial effects of blocking in the experiment.

Table 1.4.7. Results of Paging Experiment

	Response Time		*Problem State Time*		*Page Read Rate*	
Day	A	B	A	B	A	B
1	7.0	8.4	45.6	42.6	29.0	29.7
2	7.6	8.5	49.7	43.6	30.0	32.6
3	7.7	10.4	39.5	37.5	26.9	32.1
4	12.1	16.6	42.8	39.3	33.1	36.1
Average	8.6	11.0	44.4	40.7	29.7	32.6

1.4.3. A Multifactor Factorial Experiment

Tsao et al. (1972) report the results of an experiment to study the effects of four factors, memory size (M), problem program (P), load sequence of system program subroutine decks (D), and page replacement algorithm (A) on the paging characteristics of a demand paging system, CP-40 (a forerunner of CP-67). Each factor was varied at three levels, low, medium, and high, producing a total of $3^4 = 81$ trials, each of which was carried out in a single program environment. Three response variables, page swaps (PS), activity count (AC), and inactivity count (IC) were measured. Activity count is the average number of resident pages referenced at least once between successive page swaps, relative to the number of pages in main memory. Inactivity count is the average number of page swaps occurring between the time a page is swapped out and the time it is swapped in again, relative to the size of main memory. The authors carried out statistical analyses on all three dependent variables, including analyses of residuals from the fitted linear models, to determine the adequacy of the models. In the case of page swaps, a logarithmic transformation was used because of the high variability of these measurements. It was concluded that activity count was the best measure to use for comparison of page replacement algorithms because it could be demonstrated from the data that this measure was least affected by differences in problem program. The analysis of variance for AC is reproduced in Table 1.4.8. It shows that the largest effects are the A, D, and M main effects and the $D \times M$ interaction. Sums of squares for all other effects are an order of magnitude

Table 1.4.8. Analysis of Variance for AC

Source of Variation	d.f.	SS	MS
Total	80	1472.0	
Main effects	8	910.5	112.6
A	2	350.2	
D	2	338.5	
P	2	6.0	
M	2	215.8	
First-order interaction	24	440.3	18.3
AD	4	46.7	
AP	4	21.4	
AM	4	38.2	
DP	4	39.5	
DM	4	262.0	
PM	4	32.5	
Second-order interaction	32	105.2	3.3
ADP	8	9.4	
ADM	8	45.2	
APM	8	12.4	
DPM	8	38.2	
Third-order interaction ($ADPM$)	16	16.0	1

smaller than these. The model and parameter estimates, fitting only these four effects, are given in Table 1.4.9. The precise definitions of the factor levels are as follows:

(A) Replacement algorithm
        level 1. LRUV—least recently used
        level 2. FIFO—first in, first out
        level 3. RAND—random

(D) Deck sequence of CMS
        level 1. GROUP—operating version of CMS. It grouped together subroutines that called each other frequently.
        level 2. FREQY—grouping of subroutines causing most page swaps on a previous experiment.
        level 3. ALPHA—alphabetical arrangement by subroutine name.

(M) Main memory size—available pages
        level 1. 24
        level 2. 20
        level 3. 16

(P) Problem program size
        level 1. Small
        level 2. Medium
        level 3. Large

Table 1.4.9. Fitted Model for AC

---

1. *Notation:* Let
    Z_{ijkl} = AC for the ith algorithm, jth deck arrangement, kth problem program, and lth memory size, where $i, j, k, l = 1, 2, 3$
    $\hat{Z}_{ijkl}$ = fitted value for corresponding AC, Z_{ijkl}.
2. *Fitted model:*
    $\hat{Z}_{ijl} = \mu + A_i + D_j + M_l + DM_{jl}$
3. *Estimated parameters:*
    $\mu = 36.7$

$A_1 = 2.8$	$A_2 = -2.1$	$A_3 = -0.7$
$D_1 = 2.4$	$D_2 = 0.1$	$D_3 = -2.5$
$M_1 = 1.5$	$M_2 = 0.7$	$M_3 = -2.2$
$DM_{11} = -2.7$	$DM_{12} = 1.4$	$DM_{13} = 1.3$
$DM_{21} = -0.6$	$DM_{22} = 0.8$	$DM_{23} = -0.2$
$DM_{31} = 3.3$	$DM_{32} = -2.2$	$DM_{33} = -1.1$

    [e.g., $\hat{Z}_{1231} = 36.7 + (2.8) + (0.1) + (1.5) + (-0.6)$
                   $= 40.5$]

1.4.4. Fractional Factorial Experiments

In the previous section, we saw that a full factorial experiment with four factors, each at three different levels, required a large number of trials, namely 81. Since all of the factors could be ordered from high to low in terms of the expected effects on the paging characteristics, one might well question whether it would have sufficed to use only the highest and lowest level of each factor, reducing the size of the experiment from 81 to 16 runs, as shown in Table 1.4.10. The analysis that would have resulted is shown in Table 1.4.11(a). The same conclusions could have been drawn from this experiment, namely that the largest effects were A, D, M, and DM. Alternatively, a $\frac{1}{3}$ fractional factorial could have been carried out in 27 runs. In this situation, all main effects are estimable, but there is some confusion among the two-factor interactions. The procedure for designing this type of experiment is described by Cochran and Cox (1957).

The rationale for fractional factorial experiments in which all factors are at two levels is relatively simple to explain. Suppose we have three factors, each at two levels. The eight treatment combinations can be represented by the vertices of a cube, as in Figure 1.4.1. A half-replicate could be represented by the circled vertices. In this design, there are two observations on each face of the cube, and the differences between the means of the observations on each pair of parallel faces provide estimates of the main effects of factors corresponding to the particular directions. Furthermore, the points are chosen in such a way as to maintain orthogonality. In experiments involving larger numbers of factors, low-order interactions can also be estimated. Within the mathematical restrictions imposed by the particular design (i.e., number of factors and size of fraction), one can specify which particular interactions will be estimable and which ones will be confounded with others. The methodology is explained in Cochran and Cox (1957).

Table 1.4.10. Activity Counts

A	P	D	M	AC
1	1	1	1	29.4*
1	1	1	−1	41.2*
1	1	−1	1	35.6*
1	1	−1	−1	39.2*
1	−1	1	1	29.4
1	−1	1	−1	37.5
1	−1	−1	1	35.6
1	−1	−1	−1	34.6
−1	1	1	1	32.5
−1	1	1	−1	42.5
−1	1	−1	1	41.2
−1	1	−1	−1	44.2
−1	−1	1	1	33.1
−1	−1	1	−1	40.4
−1	−1	−1	1	42.5
−1	−1	−1	−1	40.0

Notes: 1. Observations forming half-replicate are underlined.

2. Observations marked by * provide data for separating AP and DM interaction in the half-replicate.

Table 1.4.11. Analysis of Variance of Activity Counts (2^4 subset of original experiment)

Source	SS	d.f.
(a) Full 2^4		
A	71.82	1
P	10.08	1
D	45.23	1
M	101.50	1
AP	0.95	1
AD	8.85	1
AM	1.38	1
PD	0.33	1
PM	17.01	1
DM	72.68	1
Error	1.11	5
Total	330.95	15
(b) $\frac{1}{2}$ replicate of 2^4		
A	28.50	1
P	4.65	1
D	22.78	1
M	49.51	1
AP(DM)	28.50	1
AD(PM)	0.66	1
AM(PD)	1.53	1
Total	136.13	7

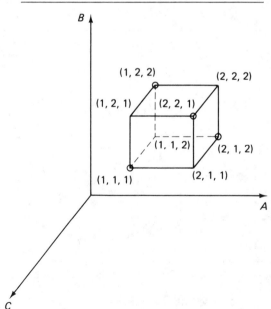

Figure 1.4.1. One-half replicate of a 2^3 fractional factorial design.

As an illustration, we shall consider a one-half fraction of the full 2^4 formed by taking the high and low levels of each factor in the Tsao et al. experiment. The data corresponding to the half-replicate are shown in Table 1.4.10 as the underlined observations. The analysis of variance is shown in Table 1.4.11(b). It again verifies that factors A, D, and M produce the large main effects. However, now the two-factor interactions are confounded with one another, as indicated in the table. For example, the computations required for the AP sum of squares are exactly the same as those needed for the DM sum of squares. All we can say is that at least one of these interactions is large. A supplementary 2×2 experiment with either pair of factors would have enabled us to separate the results. This would only have required two additional trials, as indicated in Table 1.4.10, where we have arbitrarily selected those observations corresponding to $A = P = 1$. We could have selected any other subset of four observations for which the levels of A and P did not change and carried out a similar analysis. The resulting two-way layout shown in Table 1.4.12 indicates that the DM interaction is indeed large, being almost four times the size of the D main effect. Verification that the AP interaction is negligible could have been obtained by a similar analysis using observations 1, 5, 9, and 13, requiring two additional trials. The foregoing analyses indicate that the main conclusions reached in the Tsao et al. experiment could have been reached with far fewer observations. Since they used 60 hours of CPU time on a System 360/40, the savings would have been substantial.

Table 1.4.12. Two-way Layout for Experiment to Estimate DM interaction

		D		
		-1	1	
M	-1	39.2	41.2	80.4
	1	35.6	29.4	65.0
		74.8	70.6	

Source	Effects	SS
D	$\frac{1}{2}(29.4 - 35.6 + 41.2 - 39.2) = -2.1$	4.21
M	$\frac{1}{2}(29.4 - 41.2 + 35.6 - 39.2) = -7.7$	59.29
DM	$\frac{1}{2}(29.4 - 35.6 - 41.2 + 39.2) = -4.1$	16.81

Further examples of the use of fractional factorial experiments in computer studies are provided by Schatzoff and Tillman (1975), who carried out identical half-replicates of a 2^5 experiment both on CP-67 and on a simulator of CP-67. The factors represented parameters of the dispatching algorithm. By comparing the main effects and two-factor interactions from each experiment, the authors were able to verify that the simulator provided an accurate representation of the real system.

1.5. AN EXPERIMENTAL APPROACH TO SYSTEM TUNING

1.5.1. Introduction

System tuning may be defined as finding operating conditions which optimize the system's performance. Much of system tuning lore has been concerned with placement of data sets on storage devices, selection of resident operating system modules, and other decisions which are discrete in nature. Operating systems, however, also contain numeric parameters whose values may influence performance, e.g., buffer sizes, maximum multiprogramming level, or time slice length. In this section we shall be concerned with the selection of optimal values for a moderate number of such parameters.

We shall not concern ourselves here with the question of how to choose the performance criterion to be optimized. We shall assume that such a criterion has been defined and that its value for a given running period can be computed from collectable data. We shall refer to the value of the criterion for a given computer run as the run's *response*.

While we shall be concerned primarily with tuning the system for a repeatable benchmark work-load stream, similar methods may be applied in uncontrolled real work-load environments. This point is discussed further in Section 1.5.9.

1.5.2. Problem Statement

Let $\boldsymbol{\theta} = [\theta_1, \theta_2, \ldots, \theta_k]$ be a vector of parameters defined within the system and suppose that each parameter θ_i may be assigned values between a lower bound a_i and an upper bound b_i. Let a benchmark work-load stream be given, and suppose that for any run through the work load we can characterize the system's performance by computing some response function R. If repeated runs are made at fixed parameter values $\boldsymbol{\theta}$, the responses R will vary randomly around some mean value which is a function f of $\boldsymbol{\theta}$. Thus,

$$R = f(\boldsymbol{\theta}) + \epsilon \qquad (42)$$

where ϵ is a random variable with zero expectation. We refer to the function $f(\boldsymbol{\theta})$ as the *response surface*.

The problem may now be stated as follows: Find $\boldsymbol{\theta}$ satisfying $\mathbf{a} \leq \boldsymbol{\theta} \leq \mathbf{b}$ such that $f(\boldsymbol{\theta})$ is maximum. Remember that the function $f(\boldsymbol{\theta})$ is not known; all one can do is observe R for specified values of $\boldsymbol{\theta}$.

Equation (42) implies that even in repeated runs with identical work-load and parameter settings, the results vary in a random fashion. This has been observed to be the case on real systems (see Section 1.5.8).

Generally, the system parameters may assume only certain discrete values. This may be inherent in the nature of the parameter (e.g., the maximum allowed multiprogramming level must be an integer). In other cases this results from the limited precision with which the parameter is represented in the system (e.g., the maximum allowed paging rate is represented as an integral number of page reads per second). In principle, then, we have a stochastic integer programming problem. Observe that not only must the optimal θ vector be integral, but every trial value must also be such, since we can observe the system's performance only for permitted values of θ. In the sequel, however, we shall treat the θ_i as continuous variables, and we shall assume that observing the system at $\langle \theta \rangle$ is indistinguishable from observing it at θ, where $\langle \theta_i \rangle$ is taken to be the rounded-off value of θ_i. This assumption is reasonable in view of the presence of the relatively large noise component ϵ.

From a practical point of view, any value of θ that gives near-optimal operating conditions suffices. Perhaps more important than optimality is robustness. For instance, $f(\theta)$ may have a maximum at $\theta = \theta_1$, but perturbing θ_1 slightly causes a sharp decline in performance; on the other hand, $f(\theta_2)$ may be slightly less than $f(\theta_1)$, but even sizable departures from θ_2 affect performance only slightly. Clearly θ_2 is a better operating point than θ_1. For that reason, we want to maximize not $f(\theta)$ but its average value within some region surrounding θ. This modified objective function will be defined in Section 1.5.5.

1.5.3. Optimization Procedure

The problem of determining experimentally the optimum operating point of a process whose behavior can only be measured approximately has been addressed by the method of *evolutionary operation* [Box and Draper (1969)]. A certain number of observations are taken in a region of parameter space, a smooth surface is fitted to the observed responses, and one then attempts hill climbing to a better point on the surface. We shall describe below a specially adapted variant of this method.

We assume that at any point in time a certain number n of runs has been made with parameter settings $\theta_1, \theta_2, \ldots, \theta_n$, yielding observed responses $R_1, R_2, \ldots, R_n$. The question of initialization will be dealt with subsequently. We shall define a function $F_n(\theta)$ which has the following properties:

1. It has a closed analytic form which can be evaluated easily for any feasible value of θ.

2. It is continuous and has continuous first and second derivatives (this is required for ease of optimization).

3. It approximates the observed data. That is, if, say, $\theta_1 \approx \theta_2 \approx \ldots \approx \theta_m$ (i.e., m runs were made at similar values of θ), then $F_n(\theta_i) \approx (R_1 + R_2 + \ldots + R_m)/m$ for $i = 1, 2, \ldots, m$. In particular, if $m = 1$ (single run in a given parameter region), then $F_n(\theta_1) \approx R_1$.

Once $F_n(\theta)$ has been constructed, it is possible by purely numerical methods to find the value of θ, say θ_n^*, which maximizes $F_n(\theta)$. This is the value to which we wish to set the parameters for the next run. The optimization procedure may be summarized as follows:

1. Preselect a set of m parameter settings $\boldsymbol{\theta}_1, \boldsymbol{\theta}_2, \ldots, \boldsymbol{\theta}_m$. Run the system at those settings, obtaining responses $R_1, R_2, \ldots, R_m$.

2. Set $n = m$.

3. Construct the function $F_n(\boldsymbol{\theta})$.

4. Using a nonlinear programming routine, find a parameter vector $\boldsymbol{\theta}_n^*$ which maximizes $F_n(\boldsymbol{\theta})$ within a suitable feasible region.

5. Set $\boldsymbol{\theta}_{n+1} = \langle \boldsymbol{\theta}_n^* \rangle$ and run the system at that parameter setting, obtaining the response R_{n+1}.

6. Increase n by 1, and return to step 3.

Steps 3–6 are repeated until one has run out of time, completed a prespecified number of experiments, or convinced oneself that no significant further improvement can be expected.

We refer to the first m experiments (step 1 above) as the *initial design* and to the remaining experiments as *hill climbing*. It remains to define the procedure for selecting the initial design and the construction of the hill-climbing objective function $F_n(\boldsymbol{\theta})$.

1.5.4. The Initial Design

The initial set of runs should provide a good view of the overall behavior of the response surface. A well-known experimental design which satisfies this requirement is the composite rotatable balanced design [Cochran and Cox (1957)], which permits (1) fitting of a full quadratic surface to the data, with all coefficients determined to the same degree of accuracy, and (2) direct assessment of the "experimental error," i.e., of the properties (e.g., standard deviation), of the random variable ϵ. We have adopted this type of design, although we shall make no explicit use of either one of these properties.

The design (illustrated for the two-dimensional case in Figure 1.5.1) consists of three types of experiments:

1. A number of replicate runs at some centrally located parameter vector $\boldsymbol{\theta}_0$.

2. A complete or fractional 2^k factorial design centered at $\boldsymbol{\theta}_0$ (points $\boldsymbol{\theta}_1$–$\boldsymbol{\theta}_4$ in Figure 1.5.1).

3. Two points on each coordinate axis outside the area covered by the factorial (points $\boldsymbol{\theta}_5$–$\boldsymbol{\theta}_8$ in Figure 1.5.1).

The number of replications of $\boldsymbol{\theta}_0$, the required fraction of the complete 2^k factorial, and the relative distances of type 3 and 2 points from $\boldsymbol{\theta}_0$ can be computed for a given value of k (number of parameters) if the design is to be optimal for fitting a quadratic equation to the response surface. Since this is of no great concern to us, we may choose some convenient values, e.g., those shown in Table 1.5.1. The order in which

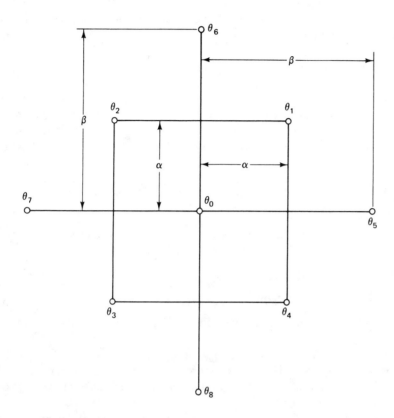

θ_0: Central points
$\theta_1 - \theta_4$: Factorial points (dropping θ_2 and θ_4 would leave a half replicate fractional factorial)
$\theta_5 - \theta_8$: Extreme points

Figure 1.5.1 Composite rotatable design for initial experiments.

Table 1.5.1. Initial Designs

No. of Parameters k	No. of Replications at Center	No. of Points in Fractional Factorial	No. of Extreme Points	β-α (see Figure 1.5.1)	Total No. of Points
3(1)	6	8(2)	6	1.682	20
4	5	8(3)	8	1.7	21
5(1)	6	16(3)	10	2	32
6	6	16(4)	12	2.5	34

Notes: 1. This design is optimal.
2. Full 2^k factorial.
3. Half-replicate of 2^k factorial.
4. Quarter-replicate of 2^k factorial.

the initial experiments are carried out should be randomized to compensate for any unknown time-dependent effects.

1.5.5. The Objective Function

As before, let $R_1, R_2, \ldots, R_n$ be the observed system responses at parameter settings $\theta_1, \theta_2, \ldots \theta_n$. We assign to each observation an *influence function* $G_i(\theta)$ which defines the effect of a unit observed response at θ_i on the value of the objective function at an arbitrary parameter setting θ. We require that $G_i(\theta)$ satisfy the following conditions:

1. $G_i(\theta)$ is continuous and has first and second continuous derivatives.

2. $G_i(\theta) \geq 0$ for all feasible θ.

3. $G_i(\theta)$ is fairly constant in a small region around θ_i but then decreases sharply as a function of the distance of θ from θ_i.

The following is a suitable influence function:

$$G_i(\theta) = \exp\left[-\lambda r_i^2(\theta)\right] \tag{43}$$

where λ is an arbitrary positive parameter, and $r_i(\theta) = \|\theta - \theta_i\|$ is the Euclidean distance between θ and θ_i.

It is tempting to define $F_n(\theta) = C_n \sum_{i=1}^{n} R_i G_i(\theta)$, where $C_n^{-1} = \sum_{i=1}^{n} G_i(\theta)$. Indeed, if λ is taken sufficiently large, $F_n(\theta)$ approximates R_i in the neighborhood of θ_i. This definition, however, has one fault: If m observations are taken at identical or nearly identical parameter settings, they will contribute m terms to $F_n(\theta)$, and hence the influence of this region will be increased m-fold *for every* value of θ. To counteract this effect, we must define quantities d_i which approximate the *density* of observations in the region around θ_i. The following is a suitable definition:

$$d_i = \sum_{j=1}^{n} \exp\left[-\lambda r_i(\theta_j)\right] \tag{44}$$

The d_i have the following properties:

1. If θ_i is an isolated point, i.e., $\|\theta_j - \theta_i\|$ is large for all $j \neq i$, then $d_i \approx 1$.

2. If m observations are taken at θ_i, or very near to it, and if all other observations are far removed, then $d_i \approx m$. Thus, d_i may be viewed as a count of the number of observations at or near θ_i.

The objective function may now be defined as follows:

$$F_n(\theta) = C_n \sum_{i=1}^{n} \frac{R_i G_i(\theta)}{d_i} \tag{45}$$

where

$$C_n^{-1} = \sum_{i=1}^{n} \frac{G_i(\theta)}{d_i}$$

Introduction of the d_i factors essentially means that the effects of several observations at neighboring points are averaged rather than summed. The objective function $F_n(\boldsymbol{\theta})$ may, in fact, be regarded as accomplishing two things: (1) smoothing the observed responses and (2) interpolating between the smoothed values. It achieves both of these objectives while retaining all the important features of the response surface and not being bound to any specific global form, such as a quadratic. In this sense, the objective function is similar to a spline approximation. Indeed, a spline approximation would be used were it not for the difficulty of finding one to fit irregularly placed data points in a higher-dimensional parameter space.

The degree of smoothing provided by $F_n(\boldsymbol{\theta})$ is controlled by the value of λ. As λ approaches zero, $F_n(\boldsymbol{\theta})$ approaches a constant value—the average of all observations. As λ approaches infinity, all smoothing disappears, and $F_n(\boldsymbol{\theta}_i)$ approaches R_i (or the average R_i if multiple observations were taken at $\boldsymbol{\theta}_i$). It can be seen from equation (43) that the *radius of influence* of an observation at $\boldsymbol{\theta}$ is proportional to $\lambda^{-1/2}$.

Note that a new objective function is defined before each hill-climbing experiment. It will generally be the case that $F_q(\boldsymbol{\theta}) \neq F_p(\boldsymbol{\theta})$ for $q \neq p$.

1.5.6. Finding the Maximum

In practice, to avoid instabilities, the search for the maximum of $F_n(\boldsymbol{\theta})$ is confined to a subset of the entire feasible region surrounding the observation with the best current value of $F_n(\boldsymbol{\theta})$. Furthermore, all parameters are scaled to lie in the region 0 to 1; otherwise, the Euclidean distance required for computing $r_i(\boldsymbol{\theta})$ would be meaningless. With this scaling, the value $\lambda = 200$ has been found to give an effective though not excessive degree of smoothing. The algorithm proceeds as follows:

1. Compute $Q_i = F_n(\boldsymbol{\theta}_i)$ for $i = 1, 2, \ldots, n$.

2. Select $\boldsymbol{\theta}_j$ so that $Q_j = \max_i Q_i$.

3. Let $\mathbf{a}' = \max\,[\boldsymbol{\theta}_j - \mathbf{c}, (\boldsymbol{\theta}_j + \mathbf{a})/2]$, and let $\mathbf{b}' = \min\,[\boldsymbol{\theta}_j + \mathbf{c}, (\boldsymbol{\theta}_j + \mathbf{b})/2]$, where $\mathbf{a}$ and $\mathbf{b}$ are the lower and upper bounds on $\boldsymbol{\theta}$, and $\mathbf{c} = (\mathbf{b} - \mathbf{a})/10$. Thus, $\mathbf{a}'$ and $\mathbf{b}'$ are temporary bounds which allow $\boldsymbol{\theta}$ to depart from $\boldsymbol{\theta}_j$ by no more than one-tenth the feasible span of $\boldsymbol{\theta}$ values and by no more than half the distance to the boundary of the feasible region. (Note that after scaling all elements of $\mathbf{b}$ became 1's.)

4. Find the maximum of $F_n(\boldsymbol{\theta})$ subject to the constraints $\mathbf{a}' \leq \boldsymbol{\theta} \leq \mathbf{b}'$. In practice, a modified Newton method with gradient projection [Bard (1974)] is used to find the maximum.

5. Once the maximum is found, it is unscaled and rounded to the nearest integer vector to obtain the next trial point $\boldsymbol{\theta}_{n+1}$.

Qualitatively, the behavior of the algorithm may be described as follows: When a parameter setting with favorable response is first encountered, further experiments are carried out in its neighborhood. If the results of these experiments are unfavorable, the value of $F_n(\boldsymbol{\theta})$ in that neighborhood becomes depressed (due to the averaging effect), and the algorithm moves over to another region. If, on the other hand, the new experiments confirm the favorable results, then the algorithm continues to explore this region. If a setting better than the original one is found, this becomes the new center of exploration, and the temporary bounds are moved accordingly. Thus, the region of exploration can move systematically to areas of increasingly favorable smoothed response.

1.5.7. Experimental Procedure

To conduct a series of tuning experiments, a suitable benchmark job stream should be defined. A data set, which we call TUNE, is maintained. It contains the parameter settings and responses for all experiments conducted to date. Each experiment conducted on the system requires that one perform the following steps:

1. Initialize the system.
2. Determine the parameter settings for the forthcoming experiment and save them in the TUNE data set. See Figure 1.5.2 for a flowchart of this step.
3. Store the parameter values into their proper locations in the operating system.
4. Initiate the benchmark work load and the performance monitor.
5. When the run has completed, obtain the required monitor data and compute the response value R.
6. Save the response value in the TUNE data set alongside the parameter values.

An automatic procedure for cycling through steps 1–6 indefinitely (or until a specified number of experiments have been run) without operator intervention is highly desirable. The procedure should be interruptable at any point and resumable at a later time, with only the already completed portion of the interrupted experiment needing to be repeated.

1.5.8. An Example

The aim of the experiments reported here was to tune the parameters in an experimental version of the VM/370[4] system scheduler [Bard (1975)]. This so-called Ψ-scheduler uses feed-forward and feed-back control strategies to determine the allowed multiprogramming level at any moment. The four parameters whose values were to be optimized are listed in Table 1.5.2. All parameters were restricted to integer values within the specified ranges. According to Table 1.5.1, the preliminary design consisted of 21 experiments. The parameters of this design are also listed in Table 1.5.2. In each experiment, 40 users were logged on automatically at 1-second intervals and were allowed to run prepared scripts for 8 minutes to establish *steady-state* conditions. Measurements were then initiated and continued for 10 minutes. The average percent

---

[4]VM/370 is a time-sharing system for IBM System/370 virtual memory computers [IBM (1972)].

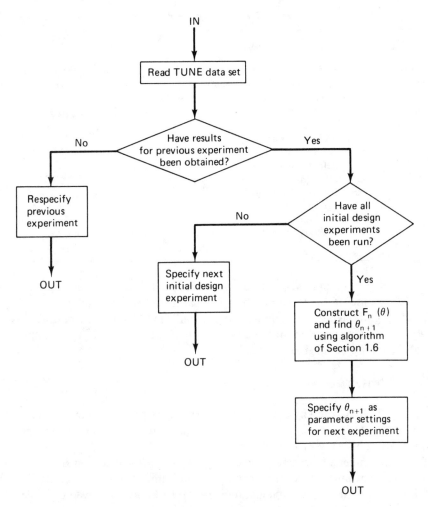

Figure 1.5.2. Selecting parameter settings for next experiment.

CPU time in the problem state during those 10 minutes was taken as the response R. Two complete series of tuning experiments on an IBM System/370 Model 155–II were made, one with main storage size of 768K bytes and the other with 1024K. Deliberately poor choices of parameter values were used to center the initial design. Runs were terminated when no further improvement was expected.

Tables 1.5.3 and 1.5.4 show the results of the two series. In both cases, parameter settings as good as any known to the experimenters were found within a dozen experiments beyond the initial design. Also apparent in Tables 1.5.3 and 1.5.4 is the variability of the results of replicate runs (type 1). The results at and around the best parameter settings, however, appear quite stable.

Table 1.5.2. Ψ-Scheduler Parameters

Para-meter	Explanation	a (mini-mum)	b (maxi-mum)	θ_0 (center of initial design)	α (see Figure 1.5.1)	β-α (see Figure 1.5.1)
Ψ_c	Used for predicting programs' working sets	3	60	30	10	7
Ψ_m	Minimum allowed value of Ψ (no. of CPU bursts before unreferenced page is removed)	3	60	30	10	7
P_M	Maximum allowed paging rate (page reads per sec)	20	100	30	10	7
S_M	Maximum allowed page steals per 1000 page reads	20	1000	100	25	17

The smoothing and averaging properties of $F_n(\boldsymbol{\theta})$ are well illustrated by experiments 29, 33, and 35–38 of Table 1.5.4. The parameter settings for these experiments vary only slightly, while the responses range from 56.6 to 59.3. The smoothed response $F_{38}(\boldsymbol{\theta}) = 58.0$ is assigned to all these experiments, and the parameter settings for any one of these may be taken as optimal.

1.5.9. Extensions

We shall discuss briefly two important extensions to the tuning technique. These deal with how to handle a larger number of parameters and how to perform tuning experiments in a live work-load environment.

As the number of parameters increases beyond the half dozen or so which can be handled conveniently by our technique, some initial screening process must be established. In many cases, some parameters will be known to have negligible effects, while near optimal values may be guessed at for others. If all this fails to reduce the number of parameters to a manageable level, a series of experiments using the random balance design [Satterthwaite (1959)] is suggested. This scheme in its simplest form works as follows: An even number of experiments, say $2n$, is performed. For each one of the k parameters θ_j, select a high value θ_j^H and a low value θ_j^L. For each j ($j = 1, 2, \ldots, k$), assign the parameter value θ_j^H to n experiments selected at random and the parameter value θ_j^L to the remaining n experiments. After the experiments are performed, the "effect" of the jth parameter is estimated as the difference between the average response of the θ_j^H experiments and the average response of the θ_j^L experiments. Only those parameters with large effects are chosen for further tuning—and hopefully there won't be more than half a dozen of these.

The desirability of tuning the system under real live operating conditions is obvious. There are two fundamental difficulties in applying experimental design techniques

Table 1.5.3. Tuning Experiments, System
with 768K Main Storage

Experiment No.	Type Code (see key below)	Parameter Settings				Response (percent problem state, maximum underlined)	$F_{40}(\theta)$ (smoothed response computed after last experiment)
		Ψ_c	Ψ_m	P_M	S_M		
1	1	30	30	30	100	36.5	36.9
2	2	20	20	35	125	42.4	41.7
3	2	40	40	25	75	34.6	35.4
4	3	13	30	30	100	33.9	33.9
5	3	30	47	30	100	36.1	36.1
6	1	30	30	30	100	35.8	36.9
7	2	40	40	35	125	44.8	44.0
8	3	30	30	39	100	47.5	43.9
9	2	20	40	35	75	41.3	40.7
10	3	47	30	30	100	35.2	35.2
11	1	30	30	30	100	34.2	36.9
12	3	30	30	21	100	33.3	34.3
13	2	40	20	35	75	41.4	40.8
14	2	20	20	25	75	34.0	34.7
15	2	20	40	25	125	33.5	34.1
16	1	30	30	30	100	35.8	36.9
17	3	30	13	30	100	34.1	34.1
18	3	30	30	30	58	36.7	36.9
19	3	30	30	30	142	37.0	36.9
20	2	40	20	25	125	33.5	34.1
21	1	30	30	30	100	35.8	36.9
22	4	46	46	43	223	48.7	48.8
23	4	52	49	48	188	51.0	51.0
24	4	56	54	56	104	47.7	47.7
25	4	56	46	56	286	53.0	52.5
26	4	58	42	63	335	51.2	51.4
27	4	58	52	49	384	49.7	49.8
28	4	58	47	56	254	<u>53.6</u>	52.4
29	4	59	47	58	210	<u>50.0</u>	51.5
30	4	57	43	48	297	52.5	52.9
31	4	52	49	60	309	52.7	52.5
32	4	55	47	55	298	51.3	52.4
33	4	58	43	49	274	52.9	52.9
34	4	59	37	44	176	53.1	51.4
35	4	59	31	49	134	51.5	51.5
36	4	59	41	36	116	52.0	52.0
37	4	59	34	36	274	51.9	51.9
38	4	59	38	46	190	49.2	51.1
39	4	58	44	48	288	<u>53.6</u>	53.0
40	4	59	46	40	280	<u>53.6</u>	<u>53.4</u>

Type codes: 1: initial design, central point 2: fractional factorial; 3: extreme point; 4: hill climbing.

Table 1.5.4. Tuning Experiments, System
with 1024K Main Storage

Experiment No.	Type Code (see key below)	Parameter Settings				Response (percent problem state, maximum underlined)	$F_{38}(\theta)$ (smoothed response computed after last experiment)
		Ψ_c	Ψ_m	P_M	S_M		
1	1	30	30	30	100	35.3	36.5
2	2	20	20	35	125	51.8	49.4
3	2	40	40	25	75	20.2	22.7
4	3	13	30	30	100	35.6	35.6
5	3	30	47	30	100	34.5	34.5
6	1	30	30	30	100	36.6	36.5
7	2	40	40	35	125	52.4	50.0
8	3	30	30	39	100	56.7	52.0
9	2	20	40	35	75	50.6	48.2
10	3	47	30	30	100	35.8	35.8
11	1	30	30	30	100	40.6	36.5
12	3	30	30	21	100	17.3	23.5
13	2	40	20	35	75	51.3	48.8
14	2	20	20	25	75	20.6	23.0
15	2	20	40	25	125	18.3	20.7
16	1	30	30	30	100	31.5	36.5
17	3	30	13	30	100	39.4	39.4
18	3	30	30	30	58	38.2	37.1
19	3	30	30	30	142	34.5	35.9
20	2	40	20	25	125	18.8	21.2
21	1	30	30	30	100	38.7	36.5
22	4	30	30	47	94	58.2	57.4
23	4	30	30	55	57	57.4	57.3
24	4	30	30	52	192	57.7	57.9
25	4	30	28	50	118	57.6	57.4
26	4	30	34	50	114	56.5	57.1
27	4	30	26	49	83	55.9	56.9
28	4	30	28	60	290	55.6	55.8
29	4	30	30	48	217	59.1	<u>58.0</u>
30	4	29	35	42	315	56.8	57.0
31	4	36	25	43	285	56.8	56.9
32	4	25	26	45	260	56.7	56.9
33	4	32	31	46	237	<u>59.3</u>	<u>58.0</u>
34	4	38	34	48	248	56.9	57.2
35	4	32	31	45	242	59.0	<u>58.0</u>
36	4	32	31	45	243	56.6	<u>58.0</u>
37	4	31	30	47	235	56.6	<u>58.0</u>
38	4	31	32	47	223	58.0	<u>58.0</u>

Type codes: 1: initial design, central point; 2: fractional factorial: 3: extreme point; 4: hill climbing.

to such an environment. First, only small changes in parameter settings from the best currently known values are permitted, since service to users must not be severely degraded. Second, the measured responses are subject to extensive random variations due to fluctuations in the work load. The original evolutionary operation technique [Box and Draper (1969)] consists of carrying out at any time a relatively simple local experimental design in the neighborhood of current operating conditions; the region of operation may then be shifted in a direction indicated by the results of the experiments. Thus, the first problem may be solved, although one expects to require many more experiments than when one is allowed to range freely over the entire parameter space. The second problem is overcome by switching rapidly (say, every 5 minutes) back and forth between the different parameter settings which comprise the experiments of the local design. The response R_i is then taken to be the average observed response over all the periods when the parameter setting θ_i was in effect. The random variations due to work-load fluctuations are thereby averaged out to a large extent (see Section 1.4.2).

CHAPTER 2

THE REGENERATIVE METHOD

FOR

SIMULATION ANALYSIS[1]

DONALD L. IGLEHART
Stanford University
Stanford, California

2.1. INTRODUCTION

Performance evaluation of computer systems frequently requires the analysis of complex networks of queues. As the complexity of these networks grows, our ability to carry out a complete stochastic analysis is quickly exceeded. At this point stochastic simulation is usually the only feasible way of analyzing the system.

The stochastic simulation of a computer system, for example, should be viewed as a statistical experiment. Just as in classical statistics observations are taken with an eye toward making statistical inferences about some unknown parameters associated with the system being simulated. Most simulations are vastly more complicated statistically than the experiments which are analyzed by classical methods of statistics. As computer running times for such simulations tend to be large, it is very important to use statistical methodology which will enable the simulator to achieve his desired statistical precision as quickly as possible. Classical methods of statistics are not well suited for direct application to most stochastic simulations. This is the case because the observations made on the stochastic process being simulated are highly correlated and nonstationary in time. Lack of a suitable methodology has prevented many simulators from presenting a convincing statistical analysis of the output of their simulations.

In the last five years a statistical methodology has been developed for analyzing the output of a certain class of simulations. This method, which we call the regenerative method, has been used with some success in conjunction with simulations of computer

[1]This research was supported by the Office of Naval Research under contract N00014-72-C-0086 (NR-047-106) with Control Analysis Corporation, Palo Alto, California.

systems. Examples of such simulations may be found in Cochi (1973), Lavenberg and Slutz (1975a), Sauer (1975), Smith (1974), and Wilheim (1973). While the regenerative method is certainly not a panacea for analyzing the output of all simulations, it does substantially enhance the state-of-the-art. Our goal in this chapter is to present the highlights of the regenerative method.

The general problem of analyzing the output of simulations and the basic ideas behind the regenerative method are discussed in Section 2.2. In Section 2.3 these ideas are illustrated for the case of semi-Markov processes. The statistical problem and confidence intervals are dealt with in Section 2.4. A discrete time method for reducing computational time is covered in Section 2.5, and quantile estimation is covered in Section 2.6. Selecting among competing systems and tests of hypotheses are the subjects of Section 2.7. A numerical example which illustrates most aspects of the regenerative method covered in this chapter is discussed in Section 2.8. Finally, approximation techniques to be used when the regenerative structure is absent are the subject of Section 2.9. The reference list contains all papers dealing with the regenerative method known to the author at the time this chapter was written.

2.2. THE PROBLEM AND REGENERATIVE METHOD

Suppose $\{X(t): t \geq 0\}$ is the vector-valued output of a discrete-event stochastic simulation. Assume that we know that $X(t)$ "approaches a steady state" as $t \to \infty$; that is, $P\{X(t) \leq x\} \to P\{X \leq x\}$ as $t \to \infty$, where X can be viewed as the *steady state* of the stochastic system. This type of convergence is known as weak convergence and will be written $X(t) \Rightarrow X$. The objective of many simulators is to estimate $E\{f(X)\} \equiv r$, where f is a specified real-valued function. Examples of f functions of interest will be given later. Ideally, we would like to produce both point and interval estimates for r.

The classical method of handling this problem runs something like this. A "good" initial state x_0 is selected and the simulation is allowed to run T_0 time units "until the initial transient wears off." Then the simulation is allowed to run for an additional t units of time. Finally, the point estimate

$$\hat{r}(t, T_0, x_0) = t^{-1} \int_{T_0}^{T_0+t} f[X(s)]\, ds$$

is given for r. No confidence interval is given. This method is unsatisfactory for many reasons. No guidance is given for selecting x_0, T_0, and t, and no confidence interval is obtained for r.

The stochastic processes of concern in this chapter are regenerative processes. A regenerative process $\{X(t): t \geq 0\}$ with state space R^k, k-dimensional Euclidean space, is a stochastic process which starts from scratch at an increasing sequence of regeneration times $\{\beta_i: i \geq 1\}$. That is, between any two consecutive regeneration times β_i and β_{i+1}, say, the portion $\{X(t): \beta_i \leq t < \beta_{i+1}\}$ of the regenerative process is an independent, identically distributed replicate of the portion between any other two consecutive regeneration times. However, the portion of the process between times 0 and β_1, while independent of the rest of the process, is allowed to have a different distribution. For complete details on the construction of these processes, consult Crane and Iglehart (1975a). The typical situation in which our regenerative assumption is satisfied is when β_i represents the time of the ith entrance to a fixed state $\mathbf{r}$, say, and upon hitting this state the simulation proceeds without any knowledge of its past history.

The regenerative property is an extremely powerful tool for obtaining analytical results for the process $\{\mathbf{X}(t): t \geq 0\}$. Before stating these results, we shall first introduce some notation and make a few assumptions. Let α_i denote the time between the ith and $(i + 1)$th regeneration times, that is, $\alpha_i = \beta_{i+1} - \beta_i, i \geq 1$, and assume $E\{\alpha_i\} < \infty$. We speak of the time interval $[\beta_i, \beta_{i+1})$ as the ith cycle. Let F denote the common distribution function of the α_i's. We shall say that F is *arithmetic with span* λ if it assigns probability 1 to a set $\{0, \lambda, 2\lambda, \ldots\}$ for some $\lambda > 0$. For our simulation applications we shall assume that the process $\{\mathbf{X}(t): t \geq 0\}$ is piece-wise constant and right-continuous and makes only a finite number of jumps in each finite time interval. Then if F is not arithmetic, it is known that $\mathbf{X}(t) \Rightarrow \mathbf{X}$ as $t \to \infty$; i.e., there exists a random vector $\mathbf{X}$ such that the $\lim_{t \to \infty} P\{\mathbf{X}(t) \leq \mathbf{x}\} = P\{\mathbf{X} \leq \mathbf{x}\}$ for every $\mathbf{x} \in R^k$ at which $P\{\mathbf{X} \leq \mathbf{x}\}$ is continuous. On the other hand, if F is arithmetic with span λ, then there exists a random vector $\mathbf{X}$ such that $\mathbf{X}(n\lambda) \Rightarrow \mathbf{X}$ as $n \to \infty$.

Now let $f: R^k \to R^1$ be a nice (measurable) function and define

$$Y_i = \int_{\beta_i}^{\beta_{i+1}} f[\mathbf{X}(s)] \, ds, \qquad i \geq 1.$$

For discrete time processes the integral should be replaced by a sum. The goal of our simulation is to estimate $E\{f(\mathbf{X})\}$. A confidence interval for this quantity may be obtained through application of the following two propositions. The first follows from the structure of regenerative processes, and the second is proved in Crane and Iglehart (1975a).

(1) **Proposition**

The sequence $\{(Y_i, \alpha_i): i \geq 1\}$ *consists of independent and identically distributed random vectors.*

(2) **Proposition**

If $E\{|f(\mathbf{X})|\} < \infty$, *then*

$$E\{f(\mathbf{X})\} = \frac{E\{Y_1\}}{E\{\alpha_1\}}.$$

This regenerative structure is present for $GI/G/s$ queues in light traffic [Crane and Iglehart (1974b)], positive recurrent Markov chains [Crane and Iglehart (1974c)], and semi-Markov processes. To illustrate the regenerative structure the special case of semi-Markov processes will be discussed in the next section. We shall show in Section 2.4 how Propositions 1 and 2 may be used to obtain a confidence interval for $E\{f(\mathbf{X})\}$.

2.3. PROBABILISTIC STRUCTURE OF SEMI-MARKOV PROCESSES

Semi-Markov processes occur frequently in modeling networks of queues. In this section we shall spell out the details of the regenerative structure in the context of a Markov renewal process, the basic process from which a semi-Markov process is defined. Excellent elementary accounts of Markov renewal processes can be found in Çinlar (1975a,b). Here we shall only mention those aspects relevant to simulation; proofs may be found in Çinlar (1975a).

Let E be a countable (or finite) set, the state space for a stochastic process $\{X_n: n \geq 0\}$, and let $\{T_n: n \geq 0\}$ be an increasing $(0 = T_0 \leq T_1 \leq T_2 \leq \ldots)$ sequence of random variables.

(3) **Definition**

The process $\{(X_n, T_n): n \geq 0\}$ is a Markov renewal process with state space E if

$$P\{X_{n+1} = j, T_{n+1} - T_n \leq t \,|\, X_0, \ldots, X_n; T_0, \ldots, T_n\}$$
$$= P\{X_{n+1} = j, T_{n+1} - T_n \leq t \,|\, X_n\}$$

for all $n \geq 0, j \in E$, and $t \geq 0$.

The given datum for a Markov renewal process is the semi-Markov kernel Q, defined as follows:

$$Q(i, j, t) = P\{X_{n+1} = j, T_{n+1} - T_n \leq t \,|\, X_n = i\},$$

$i, j \in E$ and $t \geq 0$. It is easily shown that $\{X_n: n \geq 0\}$ is a Markov chain and that the successive T_n's for which $X_n = j$ comprise a renewal process, provided $X_0 = j$. We shall always assume that $\sup_{n \geq 0} T_n = +\infty$ with probability 1, in keeping with most processes being simulated. This rules out the possibility of "explosions" (infinite number of jumps) at a finite time. If E is finite, this is automatic. From a Markov renewal process we construct a semi-Markov process, the process of principal interest for simulation.

(4) **Definition**

The process $\{X(t): t \geq 0\}$ is a semi-Markov process if

$$X(t) = X_n \qquad \text{on } \{T_n \leq t < T_{n+1}\}.$$

Two special cases of semi-Markov processes are worthy of mention. When $T_{n+1} - T_n = 1$ for all $n \geq 0$, $\{X(t): t \geq 0\}$ is essentially a discrete time Markov chain (although it is defined for all t, not just the nonnegative integers). When $T_{n+1} - T_n$ has an exponential distribution whose parameter only depends on the value of X_n, $\{X(t): t \geq 0\}$ is simply a continuous time Markov chain.

Assume that $\{X_n: n \geq 0\}$ is an irreducible, aperiodic, positive recurrent Markov chain with transition matrix $\{p_{ij}: i, j \in E\}$. Then $\{X_n: n \geq 0\}$ will have a stationary (*steady-state*) distribution:

$$\lim_{n \to \infty} P\{X_n = j \,|\, X_0 = i\} = \pi_j \qquad \text{for all } i, j \in E,$$

where $\pi_j > 0$, $\sum_{j \in E} \pi_j = 1$, and $\pi_j = \sum_{i \in E} \pi_i p_{ij}$. Furthermore, the Markov chain $\{X_n : n \geq 0\}$ will visit each state in E infinitely often. Also the recurrence time (in discrete time units) of each state in the state space E has a finite mean.

To describe the stationary (steady-state) distribution of the semi-Markov process, $\{X(t) : t \geq 0\}$, we need to introduce the mean sojourn time m_j of each visit to state j:

$$m_j = E\{T_1 \,|\, X_0 = j\}, \qquad j \in E.$$

We shall always assume that the m_j's are finite, an innocuous assumption for processes being simulated. When $\{X(t) : t \geq 0\}$ is a continuous time Markov chain, m_j is simply the expected value of the exponential holding time in state j. Since we have assumed that $\sup_{n \geq 0} T_n = +\infty$ and $\{X_n : n \geq 0\}$ is a positive recurrent Markov chain, the semi-Markov process $\{X(t) : t \geq 0\}$ will visit each state of E infinitely often. If we select a fixed state i_0 (say) and let β_i be the time of ith entrance of $\{X(t) : t \geq 0\}$ to i_0, then $\{\beta_i : i \geq 1\}$ will constitute a sequence of regeneration times since the process starts from scratch at these points without regard to its past. From the general regenerative theory $X(t) \Rightarrow X$ as $t \longrightarrow \infty$ provided the distribution of $\beta_2 - \beta_1 = \alpha_1$ is nonarithmetic. The distribution of X is indicated next; see Çinlar (1975a, p. 342) for a proof.

(5) **Proposition**

> *If $\{X_n : n \geq 0\}$ is an irreducible, aperiodic, positive recurrent Markov chain with stationary disribution $\{\pi_i : i \in E\}$ and $m_j < \infty$ for all $j \in E$, then for all $i, j \in E$*
>
> $$\lim_{t \to \infty} P\{X(t) = j \,|\, X_0 = i\} = \frac{\pi_j m_j}{\sum_{i \in E} \pi_i m_i} = P\{X = j\},$$
>
> *provided α_1 is nonarithmetic.*

Let f map E into $R_1 = (-\infty, +\infty)$. Simulators are often interested in estimating $E\{f(X)\} = \sum_{j \in E} f(j) P\{X = j\}$. Possible functions f of interest are the following:

(6)   If $f(i) = \begin{cases} 1, & i = j \\ 0, & i \neq j \end{cases}$, $j \in E$, then $E\{f(X)\} = \pi_j$;

(7)   If $f(i) = \begin{cases} 1, & i \geq j \\ 0, & i < j \end{cases}$, $j \in E$, then $E\{f(X)\} = P\{X \geq j\}$;

(8)   If $f(i) = i^p$, $p > 0$, then $E\{f(X)\} = E\{X^p\}$;

(9)   If $f(i) = c_i = \text{cost of being in state } i$, then $E\{f(X)\} = \sum_{i \in E} c_i P\{X = i\}$

     (the stationary expected cost per unit time).

Suppose $E = \{0, 1, \ldots, N\}$, $f(x) = x$, and β_i is the time of the ith entrance to state 0. Then a typical sample path of the semi-Markov process is illustrated in Figure 2.3.1. To estimate $E\{X\}$ the simulator will record the values of the Y_i's and α_i's.

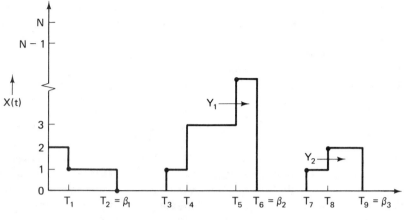

Figure 2.3.1

An alternative goal of the simulator may be to estimate the $\lim_{t \to \infty} t^{-1} C(t; f_1, f_2)$, where $C(t; f_1, f_2)$ is a cost (or reward) function that cumulates costs $f_1(x, y)$ for transitions from state x to state y and $f_2(x, y, s)$ per unit time in state y at s time units after a change of state from x. If we let $Y_i(f_1, f_2)$ be the cost accumulated during the ith cycle, then the pairs $\{Y_i(f_1, f_2), \alpha_i : i \geq 1\}$ are again independent and identically distributed, and $\lim_{t \to \infty} t^{-1} C(t; f_1, f_2) = E\{Y_1(f_1, f_2)\}/E\{\alpha_1\}$ with probability 1, provided $E\{Y_1(|f_1|, |f_2|)\} < \infty$.

A second alternative of interest is to estimate the transient behavior of the process $\{X(t): t \geq 0\}$. Suppose the simulator desires to estimate $E\{f[X(10)]\}$ when $X(0) = i_0$, say. Now think of cycles based on returns to state i_0. Then independent samples of $f[X(10)]$ can be read off 10 time units after the start of a cycle, the samples being based on nonoverlapping portions of the process.

The regenerative structure which has been illustrated here for semi-Markov processes is ideally suited for obtaining point estimates and confidence intervals for $E\{f(X)\}$ or $E\{Y_1(|f_1|, |f_2|)\}/E\{\alpha_1\}$. We shall take up this topic in the next section.

2.4. STATISTICAL ESTIMATION PROBLEM

Suppose we are interested in estimating $r = E\{f(X)\} = E\{Y_1\}/E\{\alpha_1\}$. The ratio $E\{Y_1(f_1, f_2)\}/E\{\alpha_1\}$ discussed in Section 2.3 can be estimated by the same methods presented here. On the other hand, the transient $E\{f[X(10)]\}$ can be estimated by classical methods of statistics.

We are given the following observations: $\{\mathbf{X}_k = (Y_k, \alpha_k): 1 \leq k \leq n\}$, independent and identically distributed (i.i.d.), with $E\{\mathbf{X}_1\} = \boldsymbol{\mu} = (\mu_1, \mu_2)$, $\mu_2 \neq 0$.

Problem

Estimate $E\{Y_1\}/E\{\alpha_1\} \equiv r = \mu_1/\mu_2$.

Let

$$\bar{Y} = \frac{1}{n} \sum_{i=1}^{n} Y_i, \qquad \bar{\alpha} = \frac{1}{n} \sum_{i=1}^{n} \alpha_i,$$

the sample means of the Y_i's and α_i's. Let

$$s_{11} = \frac{1}{n-1} \sum_{i=1}^{n} (Y_i - \bar{Y})^2, \qquad s_{22} = \frac{1}{n-1} \sum_{i=1}^{n} (\alpha_i - \bar{\alpha})^2,$$

and

$$s_{12} = \frac{1}{n-1} \sum_{i=1}^{n} (Y_i - \bar{Y})(\alpha_i - \bar{\alpha}),$$

the sample variances and covariance. Suppose we are interested in a $100(1 - \gamma)\%$ confidence interval for r and let $k = [\Phi^{-1}(1 - \gamma/2)]^2/n$, where Φ is the mean zero variance one normal distribution function. Let $z_{1-\gamma/2} = \Phi^{-1}(1 - \gamma/2)$.

We shall consider next a variety of point and interval estimates for r. The following five point estimates for the ratio r will be considered:

(10) *Fieller estimator*

$$\hat{r}_f(n) = \frac{\bar{Y}\bar{\alpha} - ks_{12}}{\bar{\alpha}^2 - ks_{22}}.$$

(11) *Beale estimator*

$$\hat{r}_b(n) = \frac{\bar{Y}}{\bar{\alpha}} \cdot \frac{1 + s_{12}/n\bar{Y}\bar{\alpha}}{1 + s_{22}/n\bar{\alpha}^2}.$$

(12) *Classical estimator*

$$\hat{r}_c(n) = \frac{\bar{Y}}{\bar{\alpha}}.$$

(13) *Jackknife estimator*

$$\hat{r}_j(n) = \frac{1}{n} \sum_{i=1}^{n} \theta_i,$$

where $\theta_i = n(\bar{Y}/\bar{\alpha}) - (n-1)(\sum_{j \neq i} Y_j / \sum_{j \neq i} \alpha_j)$.

(14) *Tin estimator*

$$\hat{r}_t(n) = \frac{\bar{Y}}{\bar{\alpha}} \left[1 + \left(\frac{s_{12}}{\bar{Y}\bar{\alpha}} - \frac{s_{22}}{\bar{\alpha}^2} \right) n^{-1} \right].$$

The Fieller estimator is the midpoint of the confidence interval proposed by Fieller (1940) and treated by Roy and Potthoff (1958); it should be mentioned that Fieller did not propose that it be used as a point estimator. The Beale estimator was first suggested in Beale (1962), the classical estimator has undoubtedly been around for years, and the Tin estimator was first proposed by Tin (1965). The jackknife estimator is an outgrowth of work by Quenouille (1949, 1956); for a current review of the jackknife method, consult Miller (1974), which also contains a list of references dealing with ratio estimators. We note in passing that all four estimators are strongly consistent (converge to r with probability 1) and generally are biased. The Beale, jackknife, and Tin estimators were all concocted with the aim of reducing the bias of the classical estimator.

The problem of constructing confidence intervals for r can be approached in a number of ways. As a first approach, let $Z_i = Y_i - r\alpha_i$. Note that the Z_i's are i.i.d. since the X_i's were. Also observe that $E\{Z_i\} = 0$ and $\sigma^2\{Z_i\} = \sigma_{11} - 2r\sigma_{12} + r^2\sigma_{22} \equiv \sigma^2$. Assuming (as we do) that $0 < \sigma^2 < \infty$, the central limit theorem (c.l.t.) tells us that

$$(15) \qquad \sum_{i=1}^n \frac{Z_i}{\sigma n^{1/2}} \Rightarrow N(0, 1) \qquad \text{as } n \longrightarrow \infty,$$

where $N(0, 1)$ stands for a mean zero, variance one normal r.v. and $\Rightarrow$ denotes weak convergence. Rewriting (15), we see that

$$(16) \qquad \frac{n^{1/2}[\hat{r}_c(n) - r]}{\sigma/\bar{\alpha}} \Rightarrow N(0, 1) \qquad \text{as } n \longrightarrow \infty.$$

Since $\bar{\alpha} \longrightarrow E\{\alpha_1\}$ with probability 1, we could replace $\bar{\alpha}$ by $E\{\alpha_1\}$ in (16) and not change the result. Similarly, since $n^{1/2}[\hat{r}_c(n) - \hat{r}_b(n)] \longrightarrow 0$ and $n^{1/2}[\hat{r}_c(n) - \hat{r}_t(n)] \longrightarrow 0$ with probability 1, we could also replace $\hat{r}_c(n)$ in (16) by either $\hat{r}_b(n)$ or $\hat{r}_t(n)$ and not change the result. In simulations one can very rarely compute σ. Even in cases where it has been computed it is a difficult task. Thus it is evident that the principal task in deriving confidence intervals for r is to estimate σ. The Fieller method for obtaining confidence intervals which was used in Crane and Iglehart (1974b,c, 1975a) results from estimating σ in (16) by $(s_{11} - 2rs_{12} + r^2s_{22})^{1/2}$ and then solving a quadratic inequality in r to obtain the $100(1 - \gamma)\%$ confidence interval

$$(17) \qquad \hat{I}_f(n) = \left(\hat{r}_f - \frac{D^{1/2}}{\bar{\alpha}^2 - ks_{22}}, \hat{r}_f + \frac{D^{1/2}}{\bar{\alpha}^2 - ks_{22}} \right)$$

where $D = (\bar{Y}\bar{\alpha} - ks_{12})^2 - (\bar{\alpha}^2 - ks_{22})(\bar{Y}^2 - ks_{11})$. The classical method estimates σ by $(s_{11} - 2\hat{r}_c s_{12} + \hat{r}_c^2 s_{22})^{1/2} \equiv \hat{s}_c(n)$. Combining this estimate for σ together with the classical point estimator for r yields a $100(1 - \gamma)\%$ confidence interval

$$(18) \qquad \hat{I}_c(n) = \left(\hat{r}_c - \frac{z_{1-\gamma/2}\hat{s}_c}{\bar{\alpha}n^{1/2}}, \ \hat{r}_c + \frac{z_{1-\gamma/2}\hat{s}_c}{\bar{\alpha}n^{1/2}} \right).$$

The third type of confidence interval considered comes from the jackknife method. In terms of the notation introduced above, let $\hat{s}_j(n) = \{\sum_{i=1}^n [\theta_i - \hat{r}_j(n)]^2/(n - 1)\}^{1/2}$. Then the following limit theorem provides a basis for our confidence interval:

$$\frac{n^{1/2}[\hat{r}_j(n) - r]}{\hat{s}_j} \Rightarrow N(0, 1) \qquad \text{as } n \longrightarrow \infty.$$

Thus the jackknife method yields the $100(1 - \gamma)\%$ confidence interval

$$(19) \qquad \hat{I}_j(n) = \left(\hat{r}_j - \frac{z_{1-\gamma/2}\hat{s}_j}{n^{1/2}}, \ \hat{r}_j + \frac{z_{1-\gamma/2}\hat{s}_j}{n^{1/2}} \right).$$

The variance estimates that enter in the confidence intervals (17)–(19) converge with probability 1 as $n \longrightarrow \infty$ to $\sigma/E\alpha$. Furthermore, it is known at least in the parametric case where (Y_i, α_i) has a bivariate normal distribution that the point estimators

(10)–(14) are asymptotically minimum bound estimators in the sense of the Cramér-Rao inequality; see Tin (1965) for this result. Thus one would expect the five point estimators, (10)–(14), and the three confidence intervals (17)–(19) to yield comparable results for large values of n.

In an attempt to provide some guidance for simulators we have evaluated in Iglehart (1975a) the performance of these estimators on three simple stochastic models: the $M/M/1$ queue with $\rho = 0.5$, the classical repairman model, and an (s, S) inventory model. Our objective was to compare both the small- and large-sample properties of the point and interval estimators described above. Here is a brief summary of our conclusions.

Point Estimators of r

Of the five point estimators studied the Fieller estimate can be immediately discarded. In all three models it showed considerably more bias than the other estimators for short runs. The jackknife estimator appeared to be the best in terms of small bias for short runs. The Beale and Tin estimators were about the same and only slightly more biased than the jackknife estimator. In fourth place comes the classical estimator. For the $M/M/1$ queue and inventory models all five point estimators gave comparable results for long runs. For the repairman model the jackknife and classical estimators gave good results for long runs, while the Beale and Tin estimators overestimated the true value of r, and the Fieller estimator underestimated r.

Point Estimators of $\sigma/E\alpha$

The estimators of $\sigma/E\alpha$ determine the lengths of the confidence intervals for r. Asymptotically for long runs, the Fieller, jackknife, and classical estimators of $\sigma/E\alpha$ performed comparably in the three models. For short runs the jackknife method appeared to be best in terms of small bias and most rapid convergence to the true value of $\sigma/E\alpha$. It was about a toss-up between the Fieller and classical estimators for second place. In all three models the estimate for $\sigma/E\alpha$ stablized after a moderate number of cycles.

Coverage of Various Confidence Intervals

Let A/B denote the confidence interval centered about the point estimate A and using method B to estimate $\sigma/E\{\alpha_1\}$. Asymptotically for long runs, the Fieller/Fieller, jackknife/jackknife, Tin/classical, and classical/classical confidence, intervals gave accurate coverage of the parameter r for all models with one exception. The Tin/classical confidence interval for the repairman model did not give adequate coverage, presumably because the Tin point estimator has a significant upward bias. For short runs all four methods produced short confidence intervals which do not adequately cover r. This is caused primarily by low estimates of $\sigma/E\alpha$. However, for short runs the jackknife/jackknife method did best, followed by the Tin/classical and classical/classical, which are about the same. The Fieller/Fieller method came in last.

Recommendations

The jackknife method for point and interval estimation of r produced slightly better statistical results than the other methods and is recommended. We point out, however, that the length of confidence intervals produced (relative to r) was quite large for those run lengths where the jackknife's superiority was visible. This suggests that the jackknife method is particularly appropriate for any short exploratory runs the simulator might make. Two minor drawbacks of the jackknife method are a larger memory requirement and slightly more complex programming. Additional storage addresses of the order of $2n$ are required, where n is the number of cycles observed.

If the storage requirements for the jackknife method are excessive, we would recommend using the Beale or Tin methods for point estimates and the classical method for interval estimates. The classical/classical method is the easiest to program and pedagogically the simplest to explain. Thus for the long runs it is an attractive candidate. Finally, the Fieller/Fieller method appears to be dominated statistically for short runs by the jackknife method and to be more complex than the classical method, which performs comparably for long runs.

The methods discussed above are all for a fixed sample size of n cycles. Suppose now we are interested in estimating a parameter r with a $100(1 - \gamma)\%$ confidence interval whose half-length is $100\delta\%$ of r. If we knew the values of r, σ^2, and $E\{\alpha_1\}$, then the number of cycles, n, required is given roughly by

$$(20) \qquad n = \left(\frac{z_{1-\gamma/2}}{\delta}\right)^2\left(\frac{\sigma}{rE\{\alpha_1\}}\right)^2.$$

Thus the value of $(\sigma/rE\{\alpha_1\})^2$ gives a good measure of the length of simulation run required for a fixed level of accuracy. For the $M/M/1$ queue, (s, S) inventory model, and repairman model the true values of $(\sigma/rE\{\alpha_1\})^2$ are 14.5, 0.0154, and 0.317, respectively. Thus the $M/M/1$ queue requires runs about 46 times as long as those for the repairman model, which in turn requires runs about 21 times as long as those for the (s, S) inventory model. Note also that σ^2 contains a term $-2r\sigma_{12}$ so that if σ_{12} increases, σ^2 decreases, assuming all other parameters remain fixed. Thus a high value of the correlation coefficient $\rho_0 = \sigma_{12}/(\sigma_{11}\sigma_{22})^{1/2}$ yields a smaller value of σ, which in turn means the simulation will not require as long runs. Our estimates of ρ_0 in the $M/M/1$, inventory, and repairman models were 0.8643, 0.9895, and 0.9720, respectively, which is consistent with the above remark.

Since in practice the values of r, σ^2, and $E\{\alpha_1\}$ are unknown, we cannot calculate the value of n (number of cycles to be simulated) given in (20). This situation will require us to use either a sequential or two-stage sampling plan. We shall sketch these ideas here. For a more detailed discussion of these issues, see Robinson (1976).

A sequential sampling plan would stop simulating after a random number of cycles, N, where N is the least integer m such that

(21)
$$\left(\frac{\hat{s}(m)}{\bar{\alpha}(m)\hat{r}(m)}\right)^2 \left(\frac{z_{1-\gamma/2}}{\delta}\right)^2 \leq m,$$

where $\hat{s}(m)[\hat{r}(m)]$ is either the classical or jackknife estimate of $\sigma[r]$. Sampling plans of this general type have been studied by Chow and Robbins (1965) in the context of classical statistics. They show that such plans give, asymptotically as $\delta \downarrow 0$, the prescribed coverage probability $1 - \gamma$ and are efficient relative to the fixed sample size procedure, (20), when $\sigma/rE\{\alpha_1\}$ is known. Since this sequential procedure is a large-sample one, we recommend tempering the definition of N based on (21) to force N to be larger than some fixed number of cycles. This will enable us to employ the various normal approximations with greater safety.

The other alternative is to use a two-stage sampling plan. In the first stage a fixed number of cycles, n_0, are simulated primarily to obtain a preliminary estimate of $\sigma/rE\{\alpha_1\}$. This estimate is then used to determine the length of the second stage. The second stage would consist of $N_1 - n_0$ cycles. Here N_1, the total number of cycles, is given by

(22)
$$N_1 = \max\left\{n_0, \left[\left(\frac{\hat{s}(n_0)}{\bar{\alpha}(n_0)\hat{r}(n_0)}\right)^2 \left(\frac{z_{1-\gamma/2}}{\delta}\right)^2 + 1\right]\right\},$$

where $[\cdot]$ is the integer-part function and the other quantities are defined as in (21). For a discussion of similar two-stage procedures, see Dudewicz and Dalal (1975).

Because of the close relationship between the expressions in (21) and (22), we would expect the performances statistically of the sequential and two-stage sampling plans to be comparable. Computationally, however, we point out that use of the jackknife estimates of σ and r together with a sequential sampling plan will greatly increase the amount of computer time required, because the so-called pseudovalues, θ_i, will have to be computed after each cycle. Our suggestion is that the classical [jackknife] estimates be used with the sequential [two-stage] sampling plan.

2.5. DISCRETE TIME METHOD FOR SEMI-MARKOV PROCESSES

Suppose we are simulating a semi-Markov process of the type discussed in Section 2.3. Two types of randomization enter into such simulations. First uniform $(0, 1)$ random numbers will be required to generate the successive values (in E) of the Markov chain $\{X_n : n \geq 0\}$. Once two successive values, say $X_n = i$ and $X_{n+1} = j$, of the Markov chain have been determined the length of the sojourn $T_{n+1} - T_n$ must be generated having a distribution $Q(i, j, t) = P\{X_{n+1} = j, T_{n+1} - T_n \leq t \mid X_n = i\}$. In general, of course, this will require the generation of a nonuniform random number which may be expensive in terms of computing time. Here is a simple idea which avoids this time-consuming complication; see Hordijk et al. (1976) for details.

Observe from Proposition 5 that the stationary distribution of the semi-Markov process, $P\{X = j\}$ for $j \in E$, depends on the distribution of the sojourn times, $T_{n+1} - T_n$, only through their means, $\{m_j : j \in E\}$. Hence if we modify our original semi-Markov process, $\{X(t) : t \geq 0\}$, so that the sojourn times in state j are constant with value m_j, then the modified process will have the same stationary distribution and thus the same value of $r = E\{f(X)\}$. But the modified process has the distinct advantage of not requiring the generation of sojourn times. The potential computational savings here can be quite significant. Furthermore, it can be shown that the value of $\sigma/E\{\alpha_1\}$ for the modified process is less than that for the original process. Since this is the parameter that appears in the denominator of the central limit theorem for r, (16), the modified process will lead to shorter confidence intervals for r for a fixed number of cycles. The smaller value of $\sigma/E\{\alpha_1\}$ should be expected since we have removed some of the uncertainty by making the sojourn times constant.

2.6. QUANTILE ESTIMATION

Instead of estimating $E\{f(X)\}$, we might wish to estimate the quantiles of the distribution function of $f(X)$. Here for simplicity we shall assume X is a real-valued random variable and take $f(x) = x$. Then our problem is to estimate the quantiles of the distribution function, F, of X. The pth quantile, $Q(p)$, of F is defined to be

$$Q(p) = \inf\{x: F(x) \geq p\}, \quad 0 < p < 1.$$

Of course in nice cases $Q(p) = F^{-1}(p)$. As in classical statistics, the problem of estimating quantiles is significantly more difficult than estimating moments.

From a practical point of view the problem of estimating quantiles is quite important. Suppose the simulator is designing a computer system and wants to determine the size of a certain memory. He may then want an estimate of the 0.95 quantile of the stationary distribution of the number of storage locations used. Similarly, in designing the waiting room for a complex queueing system the characteristic of interest may be the 0.90 quantile of the stationary waiting time of a customer. For inventory models we may wish to know the 0.95 quantile of the inventory level in order to assign storage capacity.

In this section we shall discuss the sample quantile approach to estimating quantiles; for complete details, see Iglehart (1975b). Since our desire is to produce a confidence interval for quantiles, we naturally begin by proving a c.l.t. Suppose we agree to run the simulation for n cycles. Assume for simplicity that β_1 has the same distribution as α_1. (This will not affect any of our limit theorems and is generally the case in practice.) Then we only simulate to time β_n. Let 1_A be the indicator function of the set A. Then for real x the function

$$F_n(x) = \beta_n^{-1} \int_0^{\beta_n} 1_{(-\infty,\, x]}[X(s)]\, ds$$

can be viewed as the empirical distribution of the regenerative process $\{X(t): t \geq 0\}$. We define the sample quantile, $Q_n(p)$, based on n cycles by the relation

$$Q_n(p) = \inf\{x: F_n(x) \geq p\}, \quad 0 < p < 1.$$

Our next task is to prove a c.l.t. for $Q_n(p)$. Select a particular p, $0 < p < 1$. As in the classical theory, we shall need to make some regularity assumptions on F, the distribution function of X, whose quantiles we are attempting to estimate. We shall assume that

(23)
$$Q(p) = F^{-1}(p);$$

(24)
$$F'[Q(p)] \text{ exists and is positive and finite};$$

and

(25) $F''(x)$ exists, and $|F''(x)| \leq M < \infty$ for x in some neighborhood of $Q(p)$.

The force of (23)–(25) is to permit a Taylor series expansion with remainder of $F(x)$ in the neighborhood of $Q(p)$. If the state space of $\{X(t): t \geq 0\}$ is discrete, these assumptions obviously do not hold. The stationary distribution F will be purely discrete in this case, jumping only at the states of the process. In this case the conditions (23)–(25) are blatantly violated. Here is a way around this difficulty.

Suppose for sake of discussion that $E = \{0, 1, \ldots, N\}$. Define a new distribution function $\tilde{F}$ from F by linear interpolation between the jumps of F. For $-1 \leq x \leq N$,
$$\tilde{F}(x) = F([x]) + (x - [x])\{F([x] + 1) - F([x])\}.$$
The new distribution function $\tilde{F}$ is illustrated in Figure 2.6.1 for the case $N = 5$. The conditions (23)–(25) are satisfied for the distribution $\tilde{F}$ except in those rare instances when $\tilde{Q}(p)$ is one of the integers of I, where $\tilde{Q}(p) = \tilde{F}^{-1}(p)$. In the latter case left- and right-hand derivatives of $\tilde{F}$ exist at the point $\tilde{Q}(p)$. We shall define $\tilde{F}_n$ and $\tilde{Q}_n(p)$ in a similar way based on F_n. Clearly, $Q(p) - 1 < \tilde{Q}(p) \leq Q(p)$, and $\tilde{Q}_n(p) - 1 < \tilde{Q}_n(p) \leq Q_n(p)$. Assume from here on that the transition from F to $\tilde{F}$ has been made when necessary. The basic c.l.t. on which our confidence intervals will be based is contained in

(26)   **Proposition**

If conditions (23)–(25) hold and $E\{\alpha_1^{2+\epsilon}\} < \infty$ for some $\epsilon > 0$, then as $n \to \infty$
$$\frac{n^{1/2}[Q_n(p) - Q(p)]}{\sigma[Q(p)]/E\{\alpha_1\}F'[Q(p)]} \Rightarrow N(0, 1),$$
where $\sigma^2(x)$ is the variance of a certain random variable.

The problem of estimating the constant $\sigma[Q(p)]/E\{\alpha_1\}F'[Q(p)]$ is considerably more complicated than was the corresponding problem in Section 2.4 and hence will be omitted here. The c.l.t. above plus this estimate yields a confidence interval for $Q(p)$ in the usual way.

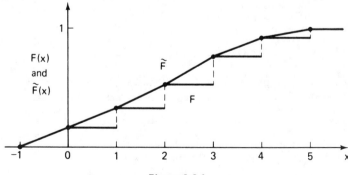

Figure 2.6.1

2.7. TESTS OF HYPOTHESES AND SELECTING THE BEST SYSTEM

Our concern in this section is a methodology which can be used in conjunction with the regenerative method to compare the performance of k (≥ 2) systems which are being simulated; for details of the material in this section, see Iglehart (1976b). A convenient situation to keep in mind is k alternative system designs which are being considered. For the sake of discussion, suppose these k designs each give rise to a regenerative process $\{X^i(t): t \geq 0\}$, $i = 1, 2, \ldots, k$, which we shall simulate. Suppose our measure of system performance for the ith system is $r_i = E\{f(X^i)\}$, the expected value of some given function f of the steady-state random variable X^i. For example, if the system being simulated is a queue, we might wish to base system performance on the expected number of customers waiting. Our goal is to select from the k systems the one with the largest (or smallest) value of r_i. As we do not know the values of the r_i's, we shall have to simulate the k systems and estimate the r_i's.

Consider first the special case of $k = 2$. In this case the simulator desires to compare r_1 and r_2. If system 1 is presently in operation and system 2 is a proposed improvement, he may wish to test whether $r_1 = r_2$ or $r_1 < r_2$ ($r_1 > r_2, r_1 \neq r_2$). Let the regeneration times for the ith system be $\{\beta_n^i: n \geq 0\}$, $i = 1, 2$, and for $n \geq 1$ set

$$\alpha_n^i = \beta_n^i - \beta_{n-1}^i$$

and

$$Y_n^i = \int_{\beta_{n-1}^i}^{\beta_n^i} f[X^i(s)]\, ds,$$

where in the case of discrete parameter processes the integral should be replaced by the corresponding sum over the nth cycle. Next set $Z_n^i = Y_n^i - r_i \alpha_n^i$ and observe that the sequence $\{Z_n^i: n \geq 1\}$ is i.i.d. and that $E\{Z_n^i\} = 0$. Let $\sigma_i^2 \equiv \sigma^2(Z_1^i) = \sigma^2(Y_1^i) - 2r_i \,\text{cov}\,(Y_1^i, \alpha_1^i) + r_i^2 \sigma^2(\alpha_1^i)$, $\bar{Y}^i(n) = (1/n) \sum_{k=1}^n Y_k^i$, and $\bar{\alpha}^i(n) = (1/n) \sum_{k=1}^n \alpha_k^i$.

The test of the null hypothesis, $H_0: r_1 = r_2$, again either $r_1 \neq r_2$, $r_1 > r_2$, or $r_1 < r_2$, is based in the usual way on the following easily proved c.l.t.

(27) **Proposition**

If $r_1 = r_2$, $0 < \sigma_1^2$, $\sigma_2^2 < \infty$, and $n_2 = [an_1]$ for some constant $a > 0$, then as $n_1 \longrightarrow \infty$

(28)
$$\frac{\{[\bar{Y}^1(n_1)/\bar{\alpha}^1(n_1)] - [\bar{Y}^2(n_2)/\bar{\alpha}^2(n_2)]\}}{\{(\sigma_1^2/E^2\{\alpha_1^1\}n_1) + (\sigma_2^2/E^2\{\alpha_1^2\}n_2)\}^{1/2}} \Rightarrow N(0, 1).$$

The values of σ_1, σ_2, $E\{\alpha_1^1\}$, and $E\{\alpha_1^2\}$ are of course unknown and will have to be estimated. To that end, let s_{11}^i and s_{22}^i be the unbiased sample variances of Y_1^i and α_1^i, and let s_{12}^i be the unbiased sample covariance between Y_1^i and α_1^i. A strongly consistent estimate for σ_i^2 is given by

(29)
$$\hat{s}_c^i(n_i) = s_{11}^i - 2\left[\frac{\bar{Y}^i(n_i)}{\bar{\alpha}^i(n_i)}\right]s_{12}^i + \left[\frac{\bar{Y}^i(n_i)}{\bar{\alpha}^i(n_i)}\right]^2 s_{22}^i$$

and for $E\{\alpha_1^i\}$ is given by $\bar{\alpha}^i(n_i)$. The classical estimate $[\hat{s}_c^i(n_i)/\bar{\alpha}^i]$ is one of the estimates we might use for $\sigma_i/E\{\alpha_1^i\}$. Another possibility is the jackknife estimate for $\sigma_i^2/E^2\{\alpha_1^i\}$, given by

$$\hat{s}_j^i(n_i) = \sum_{k=1}^{n_i} \frac{[\theta_k^i - \hat{r}_j^i]^2}{n_i - 1},$$

where

$$\theta_k^i = n_i \frac{\bar{Y}^i}{\bar{\alpha}^i} - (n_i - 1)\frac{\sum_{j \neq k} Y_j^i}{\sum_{j \neq k} \alpha_j^i}$$

and

$$\hat{r}_j^i = \frac{1}{n_i} \sum_{k=1}^{n_i} \theta_k^i.$$

Denote the left-hand side of (28) by $T(n_1, n_2)$ after $E\{\alpha_1^i\}[\sigma_i^2]$ is replaced by $\bar{\alpha}^i[\hat{s}_c^i]$. For a level γ test of $H_0: r_1 = r_2$ versus $H_1: r_1 \neq r_2$

(30)   *reject H_0 if and only if* $|T(n_1, n_2)| > z_{1-\gamma/2}$,

where $z_{1-\gamma/2} = \Phi^{-1}(1 - \gamma/2)$ and Φ is the standard normal distribution function. For a level γ test of $H_0: r_1 = r_2$ versus $H_2: r_1 > r_2$

(31)   *reject H_0 if and only if* $T(n_1, n_2) > z_{1-\gamma}$.

Finally, for a level γ test of $H_0: r_1 = r_2$ versus $H_3: r_1 < r_2$

(32)   *reject H_0 if and only if* $T(n_1, n_2) < -z_{1-\gamma}$.

Of course, we could carry out these tests using the jackknife estimates $\hat{s}_j^i$ instead of $\hat{s}_c^i/\bar{\alpha}^i$.

For the general case of $k \geq 2$, suppose we are interested in selecting the system with the largest r_i. We begin by specifying two numbers P^* and δ^*. Our goal will be to select with probability P^* the system with the largest r_i whenever that value of r_i is separated by at least δ^* from the other r_i's. Because certain variances are unknown and have to be estimated, there is no fixed sample size procedure that will guarantee the above goal. Two procedures are given in Iglehart (1976b). The first procedure is sequential and the second two-stage. The sequential procedure has a stopping rule based on estimates of certain variances. The two-stage procedure uses the first stage to estimate these variances. The length of the second stage is then determined by these variance estimates. Details of these procedures will not be given due to space limitations.

Tests of hypotheses ($k = 2$) and the two selection procedures ($k = 3$) were carried out for the classical repairman model. The numerical results for the tests of hypotheses were in good agreement with the theory. Both the sequential and two-stage methods attained the required goals for the probability of correct selection, P^*. Again the estimates used in the two methods must be chosen properly in order to both attain the desired statistical results and minimize the computational time required to carry out the simulations.

2.8.   A NUMERICAL EXAMPLE

The example we shall discuss here is a simple network of queues. In Figure 2.8.1 the flow of jobs in the network is depicted. This network first arose in the context of the classical repairman problem. Jobs in service at the n servers in stage 2 are viewed

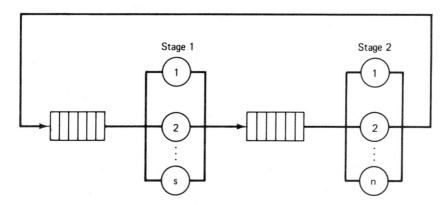

Figure 2.8.1

as machines whose failure times are exponentially distributed. Upon failure a machine is sent to the repair facility (stage 1) for service. At the repair facility there are s repairmen with exponentially distributed repair times. Once a machine is repaired it goes back into operation if less than n machines are currently operating. There are other interpretations in terms of computer systems.

Let $X(t)$ be the number of units waiting for or undergoing service at stage 1 at time t. Assume the service times at stage 1 [stage 2] are exponentially distributed with parameter μ [λ] and that there are $m + n$ jobs in the system. Then $\{X(t): t \geq 0\}$ is a birth-death process with state space $E = \{0, 1, \ldots, m + n\}$, birth parameters $\lambda_i = (n - [i - m]^+)\lambda$, and death parameters $\mu_i = (i \wedge s)\mu$, where $a \wedge b = \min(a, b)$ and $[x]^+ = \max(x, 0)$. Since E is finite and irreducible, $P\{X(t) = j\} \rightarrow P\{X = j\} = \pi_j$ as $t \rightarrow \infty$, for all $j \in E$.

In Table 2.1 some simulation results are given for a variety of parameters of the form $E\{f(X)\}$. The point estimates are Fieller estimates, (10), and the confidence intervals are Fieller intervals, (17). The random number generator used was one written by G. E. Forsythe following the discussion in Knuth (1969, pp. 155–156) for use on the IBM 360/67. First a sequence of random integers $\{X_n: n \geq 0\}$ uniformly distributed on $[0, 2^{31})$ is generated as follows: $X_{n+1} = [(314159269)X_n + 453806245] \bmod (2^{31})$, $n \geq 0$, where X_0 is a given seed. Then a sequence of uniformly distributed numbers, $\{Y_n: n \geq 1\}$, is obtained by setting $Y_n = X_n/2^{31}$.

Next we shall discuss some simulation results which are intended to illustrate the various point estimators and confidence intervals mentioned in Section 2.4. The function $f(x) = x$ was used, and hence we estimated $E\{X\} = 3.471$. We set $X(0) = 0$ and used 0 as the return state for the regenerative method. The model was run for either 40 or 100 cycles, and observations were taken at periodic intervals. Then the runs of 40 [100] cycles were replicated 200 [100] times. Table 2.2 gives the mean (over the various replications) of the five point estimates (10)–(14) as a function of the number of cycles. Confidence intervals for these means are also indicated. All confidence intervals are taken to have a 90 % degree of confidence. Table 2.3 gives the mean (over the replications) and confidence intervals of estimates of $\sigma/E\{\alpha_1\}$

Table 2.1. Simulation Results ($\lambda = 1$, $\mu = 4$, $s = 3$, $n = 10$, $m = 4$; run length 300 cycles) Level of Confidence = 90%

Parameter	Theoretical Value	Point Estimate	Confidence Interval
$E\{X\}$ = expected no. jobs at stage 1	3.471	3.406	[3.205, 3.607]
$E\{X^2\}$	17.278	16.844	[15.094, 18.594]
$P\{X > m\}$ = prob. less than n jobs at stage 2	.306	.294	[.260, .328]
$P\{X > s\}$ = prob. of a queue at stage 1	.438	.429	[.393, .465]
$E\{[s - X]^+\}$ = expected no. of idle servers at stage 1	.678	.705	[.637, .773]
$P\{X > 0\}$ = prob. at least one job at stage 1	.939	.930	[.919, .942]
$P\{X = 0\}$ = prob. no jobs at stage 1	.061	.070	[.058, .081]

Table 2.2. Mean and Confidence Intervals of Point Estimators for $E\{X\}$ = 3.471 in a Repairman Model with $n = 10$, $m = 4$, $s = 3$, $\lambda = 1$, $\mu = 4$

No. of Cycles	Point Estimator of $E\{X\}$				
	Fieller	Jackknife	Beale	Tin	Classical
4	6.8681	3.4589	3.0391	3.0489	2.9747
	±3.7471	±0.1673	±0.1229	±0.1235	±0.1206
8	−3.9251	3.5496	3.3737	3.3939	3.2692
	*	±0.0979	±0.0824	±0.0836	±0.0794
12	3.0112	3.5870	3.5226	3.5481	3.4006
	±0.5291	±0.0724	±0.0665	±0.0679	±0.0632
20	3.1368	3.5175	3.5501	3.5748	3.4239
	±0.0524	±0.0525	±0.0526	±0.0536	±0.0502
40	3.2977	3.4687	3.5603	3.5860	3.4238
	±0.0340	±0.0357	±0.0371	±0.0379	±0.0350
60	3.3475	3.4570	3.5648	3.5905	3.4278
	±0.0376	±0.0390	±0.0411	±0.0424	±0.0385
70	3.3576	3.4508	3.5636	3.5894	3.4258
	±0.0348	±0.0365	±0.0391	±0.0404	±0.0360
80	3.3747	3.4570	3.5747	3.6013	3.4349
	±0.0315	±0.0323	±0.0344	±0.0355	±0.0320
90	3.3782	3.4516	3.5729	3.5999	3.4318
	±0.0311	±0.0318	±0.0339	±0.0349	±0.0315
100	3.3933	3.4598	3.5851	3.6122	3.4419
	±0.0309	±0.0312	±0.0326	±0.0334	±0.0311

*Overflowed the machine.

Table 2.3. Mean and Confidence Interval of Point Estimators $\sigma/E\{\alpha_1\} = 1.9553$ in a Repairman Model with $n = 10$, $m = 4$, $s = 3$, $\lambda = 1$, $\mu = 4$

No. of Cycles	Point Estimator of $\sigma/E\{\alpha_1\}$		
	Fieller	*Jackknife*	*Classical*
4	-4.4548	1.8404	0.9368
	± 4.5332	± 0.1607	± 0.0544
8	13.4331	2.1105	1.3815
	± 18.3457	± 0.1533	± 0.0674
12	2.0163	2.1323	1.5795
	± 1.157	± 0.1361	± 0.0691
20	2.1151	1.9769	1.6771
	± 0.1036	± 0.0917	± 0.0611
40	1.9921	1.9652	1.8056
	± 0.0635	± 0.0655	± 0.0542
60	1.9414	1.9336	1.8224
	± 0.0818	± 0.0867	± 0.0729
70	1.9229	1.9165	1.8218
	± 0.0720	± 0.0759	± 0.0656
80	1.9212	1.9174	1.8317
	± 0.0667	± 0.0704	± 0.0613
90	1.9238	1.9213	1.8438
	± 0.0654	± 0.0687	± 0.0605
100	1.9513	1.9508	1.8791
	± 0.0615	± 0.0645	± 0.0576

generated by the Fieller, jackknife, and classical methods, namely, $(nD)^{1/2}/(\bar{\alpha}^2 - ks_{22})z_{0.95}$, $\hat{s}_j$, and $\hat{s}_c/\bar{\alpha}$. Finally, Table 2.4 gives the fraction of replications for which the confidence intervals given by (17)–(19) and a combination of the Tin point estimator with the classical variance estimator cover the true parameter being estimated. Again confidence intervals for these coverage variables are indicated. For this simulation 4 [100] cycles produced confidence intervals whose half-length was 46% [9%] of the true value of $E\{X\} = 3.471$. For 100 cycles the means over 100 replications of $\bar{\alpha}$, $\bar{Y}$, $\bar{s}_{11}$, $\bar{s}_{12}$, and $\bar{s}_{12}/(\bar{s}_{11}\bar{s}_{22})^{1/2}$ were

$$\bar{\alpha} = 1.6618\ (0.2106), \qquad \bar{\bar{Y}} = 5.7437\ (0.9471), \qquad \bar{s}_{11} = 103.4559\ (35.6320),$$

$$\bar{s}_{12} = 22.2238\ (7.1927), \qquad \bar{s}_{22} = 5.0540\ (1.5350),$$

$$\overline{s_{12}/(s_{11}s_{12})^{1/2}} = 0.9720\ (0.0103),$$

where the figures in parentheses are the sample standard deviations of the 100 numbers averaged.

The quantiles of X were also estimated. Here are some typical results for the same parameter values used above. Because of the discrete state space, the transition from F to $\tilde{F}$ has been made. The estimates in Table 2.5 are the sample means of 100 replica-

Table 2.4. Mean and Confidence Intervals of
Coverage of Various 90% Confidence
Intervals for $E\{X\}$ in a Repairman
Model with $n = 10$, $m = 4$, $s = 3$,
$\lambda = 1$, $\mu = 4$

No. of Cycles	$\dfrac{\text{Fieller}}{\text{Fieller}}$	$\dfrac{\text{Jackknife}}{\text{Jackknife}}$	$\dfrac{\text{Tin}}{\text{Classical}}$	$\dfrac{\text{Classical}}{\text{Classical}}$
	Confidence Interval [1] *for* $E\{X\}$			
4	0.3300	0.7050	0.5250	0.5100
	±0.0548	±0.0532	±0.0582	±0.0583
8	0.6350	0.8050	0.7050	0.6900
	±0.0561	±0.0462	±0.0532	±0.0539
12	0.7600	0.8500	0.7600	0.7750
	±0.0498	±0.0416	±0.0498	±0.0487
20	0.8350	0.8550	0.7900	0.8550
	±0.0433	±0.0411	±0.0475	±0.0411
40	0.8450	0.8600	0.8250	0.8400
	±0.0422	±0.0405	±0.0443	±0.0428
60	0.8900	0.9000	0.8800	0.8900
	±0.0517	±0.0496	±0.0537	±0.0517
70	0.8300	0.8700	0.8300	0.8800
	±0.0621	±0.0556	±0.0621	±0.0537
80	0.8600	0.9100	0.8100	0.8900
	±0.0574	±0.0473	±0.0649	±0.0517
90	0.9000	0.9000	0.7700	0.9000
	±0.0496	±0.0496	±0.0696	±0.0496
100	0.8800	0.8900	0.7900	0.9000
	±0.0537	±0.0517	±0.0673	±0.0496

[1]Confidence interval A/B is centered about the point estimator A
and uses method B to estimate $\sigma/E\alpha$.

Table 2.5. Quantile Estimation

p	*True Value of* $Q(p)$	*Estimate of* $Q(p)$	*True Value of* $\sigma/E\{\alpha_1\}F'$	*Estimate of* $\sigma/E\{\alpha_1\}F'$
.50	2.608	2.575	2.151	2.125
.75	4.507	4.439	2.887	2.897
.90	6.238	6.165	3.686	3.451

tions each of length 200 cycles. These estimates yielded confidence intervals consistent
with the theory.

The discrete time method proposed in Section 2.5 was used for this repairman
problem with $f(x) = x$. For the continuous time simulation the theoretical value of
the constant $\sigma/E\{\alpha_1\}$ is 1.9553, whereas the theoretical value for the discrete method

is 1.9022. Thus only a 2.6% statistical saving is realized. However, the continuous time simulation required 1.79 minutes to replicate 100 cycles 100 times and the discrete time simulation only 0.99 minute, a computational saving of about 44.7%. In all examples run thus far the statistical saving is minor but the computational saving significant.

Because of the additional complications of the selection procedures discussed in Section 2.7, numerical results will not be described here. Numerical examples can be found in Iglehart (1976b).

2.9. APPROXIMATION TECHNIQUES

A discrete-event simulation may not possess the nice regenerative property exploited above. Furthermore, even if it does possess the regenerative property, the return states may be hard to identify or may not occur frequently enough to use the regenerative method. Nevertheless, it may still be the case that $\mathbf{X}(t) \Rightarrow \mathbf{X}$, and estimating $E\{f(\mathbf{X})\}$ may be of interest. Here are two approximation techniques which may be employed in this situation; for more details, see Crane and Iglehart (1975b).

In the first method, select a fixed state $\mathbf{x}$, and construct a small region A surrounding $\mathbf{x}$. Define β_i, α_i, Y_i in terms of returns to A rather than $\mathbf{x}$. Compute confidence intervals by the old method. Here the pairs (Y_i, α_i) will not be independent or identically distributed. But if A is "small," the distributions should be close, and dependence should fall off rapidly. This method has been used by Rivera-Garza (1974) with some success for a simulation of a job shop.

The second method forms a modified process by setting the original process equal to $\mathbf{x}$ each time it enters A. This modified process is then a regenerative process to which the regenerative method can be applied. However, in this case the confidence intervals produced are with respect to the modified process, not the original one.

CHAPTER 3

SYSTEM DESIGN
AND PERFORMANCE ANALYSIS
USING ANALYTIC MODELS

HISASHI KOBAYASHI
IBM Thomas J. Watson Research Center
Yorktown Heights, New York

Abstract

In the past several years noteworthy progress has been achieved in development of various analytic techniques pertinent to computer system modeling and performance evaluation. In this chapter we review these analytic models and their application methods for system design and analysis of complex systems.

In Section 3.1 we briefly discuss historical developments of computer system methodologies and review several cases in which analytic models played important roles.

In Sections 3.2 through 3.4 we present self-contained and cohesive discussions of a class of Markovian queueing models. Section 3.2 is a preliminary section in which *single* resource models (including $M/M/1$, $M/G/\infty$, and $M/G/1$ with processor sharing) will be reviewed and related mathematical theory will be duly discussed. Open and closed queueing networks of Sections 3.3 and 3.4 provide a basic framework of *multiple* resource models which capture dynamics and interactions among various hardware and software resources in a complex computing system. Our discussion starts with the classical exponential server model and ends with the most general queueing network model for which a closed form solution has been found. Computational algorithms for numerical evaluation of various performance measures are also discussed in Section 3.4.

In Section 3.5 we review two important areas of approximation techniques currently pursued in an attempt to solve non-Markovian models. They are the iterative technique and the diffusion approximation models.

In Section 3.6 we discuss applications of the solution techniques discussed in the earlier sections. A modular approach with hierarchical structure is discussed as a practical solution to complex system modeling, and various examples are discussed: (1) memory interference and software lockout problems in a multiprocessor system, (2) a multiprogrammed virtual storage system model, and (3) an interactive time-shared system model.

3.1. INTRODUCTION

A contemporary computer system can be viewed as an organized collection of resources (both software and hardware), which are demanded and competed for by multiple tasks or processes concurrently in the system. A major role of an operating system is to effectively schedule conflicting requests and appropriately handle queues waiting for resource allocation and scheduling. Thus, queueing theory provides a basic framework and the mathematical tools for modeling and analysis of computer system hardware and software.

The purpose of this chapter is to review thoroughly the state-of-the-art of queueing theory and its applications pertinent to computer system modeling. It is the author's hope that this chapter provides the reader with a clear picture concerning which problems one can solve analytically and which problems one must solve by simulation.

In view of the enormous costs and time involved in simulation efforts of any scale, it is vital for system analysts to make sensible decisions as to when they should adopt approximate analyses and when they should resort to detailed simulation. Even when a decision is made for simulation, an analytic solution, however crude it may be, should be sought. It often saves a considerable amount of time and effort if one detects major errors made in the design and implementation phases of a simulator. Analytically obtained solutions also serve as guidelines in narrowing down the range of system configuration and parameters which a simulator must model.

Theoretical research into the properties of queues began in connection with problems of telephone operation. The earliest systematic mathematical work on queueing problems is that of Erlang at the beginning of this century. In the design of automatic telephone exchanges, one had to predict the effect of random fluctuations of service demands (both in terms of incoming calls and holding times of the individual calls) on the utilization of the telephone exchange equipment as well as delay or loss of the calls. Only recently has it been realized that the mathematical theory begun specifically for telephone problems has applications in a variety of operations research problems [see, for example, Hiller and Lieberman (1967)]. Certainly applications of queueing theory to computer system modeling and analysis is one of the newest developments.

With the advent of time-shared systems in the mid-1960's, a new class of queueing system problems were formulated and investigated by a number of people. Figure 3.1.1 depicts the type of model investigated in these studies. A time-shared computer system is represented as a single entity, which constitutes a single server system. In many cases it is assumed that the job arrival mechanism is characterized by a Poisson process (which is equivalent to assuming an infinite population source) but that the

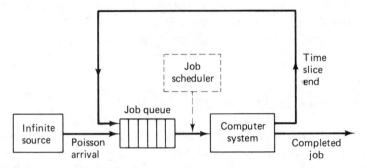

Figure 3.1.1. An infinite source model.

service time distribution is of general form. In such models, various job scheduling algorithms were investigated and compared, notably the round-robin scheduling algorithm and feed-back (or, as it is often called, forground-background) scheduling algorithm. Coffman and Denning (1973) and Kleinrock (1976) discuss these models in full detail. The reader is also referred to a survey paper by McKinney (1969).

In parallel with these developments, the finite source model of Figure 3.1.2 (or as it is often called in queueing literature, a machine-repairman model) was introduced

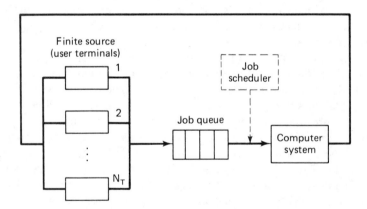

Figure 3.1.2. A finite source model.

to represent interactions between the time-shared system and a finite number of user terminals. In this model we assume that there are always a constant number, N_T, of active terminals and that *terminal blocking* is explicitly modeled: A terminal is in blocked mode while its transaction (or job) is serviced or waiting in the job queue. Thus the job arrival rate is not constant (unlike in an infinite source model) but is proportional to $N_T - n$, where n is the number of outstanding transactions (or equivalently the number of blocked terminals at the present moment). In this type of model, both service times and user terminal times were assumed to be exponentially distributed. Scherr (1967) used this model successfully in the performance analysis of the Compatible Time-Sharing System (CTSS) at M.I.T. Subsequently the same model was applied by Lassettre and Scherr (1972) in system design and performance prediction of IBM's Time Sharing Option (TSO) with a single partition with swapping mechanisms. In both studies the mean service time at CPU was estimated as the sum of the mean program execution time and swapping time. The user terminal time consists of *think* time, terminal inputting time, and outputting time. Then the mean response time per transaction was predicted as a function of N_T, the number of active terminal users, and compared with the measured performance in the actual systems and simulators. They report that surprisingly good agreements were observed despite a number of simplifications and assumptions introduced in their analytic models. In view of the exponential assumptions of compute time and user time (which are usually known to be poor fits insofar as the distributions themselves are concerned), some readers may feel rather skeptical about their claims. A recent result in queueing network analysis, however, substantiates their empirical findings that the performance measures such as the average delay or throughput are rather insensitive to the distribution of both user terminal time and CPU service time. This point will be further discussed later in Section 3.6.

Another class of analytic model extensively studied from late 1960's and early 1970's is a two-stage cyclic queueing model as depicted in Figure 3.1.3, in which the overlap of CPU and I/O executions is represented by use of two independent servers.

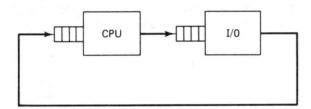

Figure 3.1.3. A cyclic queueing model.

The work by Gaver (1967) is the earliest work that explicitly formulated a multiprogrammed system model in which the central processing unit and I/O processing unit (or data channel) operate simultaneously and asynchronously. Shedler and Lewis (1972) and Adiri (1972) pursued further analysis by incorporating the effect of system overhead incurred by task switching and I/O transfers. Among other related works on the cyclic queue model is a recent work by Reiser and Kobayashi (1974b) which analyzes the effect of distributional form of service times on queue size distributions (as well as on the throughput and utilization).

It was not until around 1970–1971 when the computer modeling community came to realize that a queueing network representation provides a more realistic framework for some of the system and subsystem models, in which parallel executions of CPU, data channels, and various I/O devices and multiplexing of a CPU (or CPU's) are appropriately represented. Moore (1971) at the University of Michigan applied Jackson's result (1963) on a network of queues to the Michigan Terminal System

(MTS), which runs on a dual processor version of the IBM 360/67. In Moore's analysis the model parameters (i.e., the mean service times at various resources and the job transition probabilities from a resource to others) were estimated from measurement data of the system in operation. He observed that the exponential distributions for service times were found to be rather poor fits, yet the predictions from the analytic model and measurement results came fairly close to each other in most test cases: The performance measures such as the mean response time and utilizations were predicted typically within 10% of the observed values. In retrospect, the satisfactory agreements are not entirely surprising for the same reasons discussed above regarding the work by Scherr (1967) and Lassetre and Scherr (1971).

It was at the ACM-SIGOPS workshop in 1971 that Arora and Gallo (1971) and Buzen (1971a) presented their work on applications of Gordon and Newell's result (on closed queueing networks) to analyses of multiprogramming systems. Around the same period Brown (1971) of IBM, independently of the above authors, applied Gordon and Newell's model to performance prediction of a multiprocessor system. Figure 3.1.4 shows a special class of closed queueing network models, which Buzen (1971a) named central server models, which allow simultaneous operation of CPU and secondary storage, and in which peripheral I/O devices and the CPU are explicitly represented as independent servers, so that their interactions can be analyzed. Following the work by these authors, queueing network models have been drawing considerable attention from the computer system modeling community, and we are observing an increasingly large number of applications to system design and performance analysis. Some of these applications will be discussed in Section 3.6.

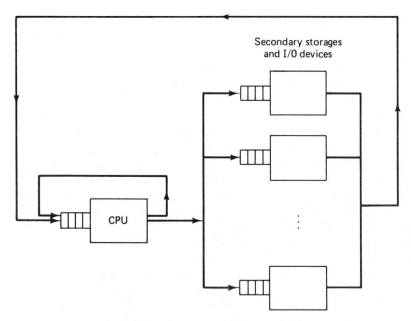

Figure 3.1.4. A central server model.

In the past several years a number of extensions and generalizations have been made on a queueing network model of Jackson's type by Chandy (1972), Baskett and Muntz (1972), Baskett et al. (1975), Kobayashi and Reiser (1975), and others. Sections 3.2 through 3.4 of this chapter are devoted to a cohesive and self-contained treatment of these important results. Our presentation does not necessarily follow the actual sequence of generalizations contributed by these authors but is organized in a unified and inductive manner so that the typical reader with modest knowledge can comprehend the state-of-the-art of this subject. In addition to the references cited in the text, the reader is referred to survey articles by Baskett and Muntz (1973) and Muntz (1975) which contain an extensive list of references and historical reviews.

3.2. REVIEW OF SINGLE RESOURCE MODELS

Although the material of the present and subsequent sections is more or less self-contained, the presentation may be too concise or terse for some of the readers. They are urged to consult introductory chapters of many books on the subjects, for example, Coffman and Denning (1973), Conway et al. (1967), Cox and Smith (1968), Cooper (1972), and Kleinrock (1975).

3.2.1. $M/M/1$ with Work-Conserving Queue Discipline

Consider a system $M/M/1$,[1] i.e., a single server queueing system in which the job arrival process is a Poisson process with rate $\lambda(n)$ [jobs/sec], service demands[2] of individual jobs are exponentially distributed with mean $\bar{w}$ [work units/job], and the processing rate of the server is $C(n)$ [work units/sec], where n is the number of jobs in system and represents the *state* of the system $M/M/1$. As for the queue discipline, we allow any *work-conserving* queue disciplines [see Kleinrock (1976) and Wolff (1970)]. A queue discipline is said to be work-conserving if (1) the service time of each job is not affected by the queue discipline, (2) the discipline cannot take advantage of knowledge about ssrvice times and/or arrival times of the individual jobs, and (3) the server should not be idle if there are some jobs waiting for service.

Let $P(n; t)$ be the probability that the system is in state n at time t. To calculate $P(n; t + \Delta t)$ we note that the system can be in state n at time $t + \Delta$ only if one of the following conditions is satisfied: (1) At time t, the system is in state n, and no change occurs during $(t, t + \Delta)$; (2) at time t the system is in state $n - 1$, and a transition to n occurs; (3) at time t the system is in $n + 1$, and a transition to n occurs; (4) during

[1]Quite often the system $M/M/1$ is defined as one in which $\lambda(n)$ and $\mu(n)$, defined here, are constant. Our general model discussed in this section is often called a *birth-and-death-process* model.

[2]The unit of measure to describe *service* or *work* depends on the nature of server and jobs. If the server is CPU and jobs are programs, an appropriate unit should be [instructions]. If the server is a transmission line and jobs are messages or data, the unit should be [bits] or [bytes].

$(t, t + \Delta)$ two or more transitions occur. By our assumption, the probability of the last event is $o(\Delta)$, where the notation $o(\Delta)$ denotes any function that goes to zero as Δ approaches zero but faster than Δ itself. Since the first three contingencies are mutually exclusive, we can write

$$P(n; t + \Delta) = P(n; t)\{1 - \lambda(n)\Delta - \mu(n) \cdot \Delta\}$$
$$+ P(n - 1; t)\lambda(n - 1)\Delta$$
$$+ P(n + 1; t)\mu(n + 1)\Delta + o(\Delta) \qquad (3.2.1)$$

where $\mu(n)$ is the job completion rate when the system is in state n:

$$\mu(n) = \frac{C(n)}{\bar{w}} \qquad (3.2.2)$$

Subtracting $P(n; t)$ from both sides of (3.2.1) and dividing the equation by Δ and then letting $\Delta \longrightarrow 0$, we obtain the following differential-difference equations:

$$\frac{dP(n; t)}{dt} = -\{\lambda(n) + \mu(n)\}P(n; t) + \lambda(n - 1)P(n - 1; t)$$
$$+ \mu(n + 1)P(n + 1; t), \qquad \text{for } n \geq 1 \qquad (3.2.3)$$

and

$$\frac{dP(0; t)}{dt} = -\lambda(0)P(0; t) + \mu(1)P(1; t) \qquad (3.2.4)$$

If we are interested only in the statistical equilibrium properties of the system, we first take limits as $t \longrightarrow \infty$ throughout equations (3.2.3) and (3.2.4) and then $\lim_{t \to \infty} (d/dt)P(n; t) = 0$, thus obtaining the following linear difference equations:

$$\lambda(n)P(n) - \mu(n + 1)P(n + 1) = \lambda(n - 1)P(n - 1) - \mu(n)P(n), \qquad n = 1, 2, 3, \ldots$$
$$(3.2.5)$$

and

$$\lambda(0)P(0) - \mu(1)P(1) = 0 \qquad (3.2.6)$$

From the above two equations we immediately have the *balance equation*

$$\mu(n)P(n) = \lambda(n - 1)P(n - 1), \qquad n = 1, 2, 3, \ldots \qquad (3.2.7)$$

The left-hand side of (3.2.7) represents the rate of transition from state $n - 1$ to state n, and this quantity is balanced by the transition rate from state n to state $n - 1$, which is given by the right-hand side of (3.2.7). The equilibrium state probabilities are calculated by recurrence:

$$P(n) = \frac{\lambda(n - 1)}{\mu(n)} P(n - 1) = P(0)\Lambda(n)\beta(n)\bar{w}^n \qquad (3.2.8)$$

where

$$\Lambda(n) = \prod_{i=1}^{n} \lambda(i - 1) \qquad (3.2.9)$$

and

$$\beta(n) = \prod_{i=1}^{n} \frac{1}{C(i)} \qquad (3.2.10)$$

Based on the steady-state distribution of (3.2.8), we can show that the departure process is also a Poisson process [see, for example, Burke (1972), Kleinrock (1975), and Muntz (1973)]. To establish this property, it suffices to show that

$$\lim_{\Delta \to 0} \frac{P[\text{departure in } (t - \Delta, t) \mid n(t) = n]}{\Delta} = \lambda(n) \qquad (3.2.11)$$

where $\lambda(n)$ is the arrival rate and $n(t)$ is the state of the system, i.e., the number of jobs in the system, at time t. This, together with the observation that the rate of multiple departures is zero, shows that the departure process with time *reversed* is dependent on the *current* state of the system through the parameter $\lambda(n)$. Note this dependency is equivalent to that of the arrival rate on the system state. Thus, if the arrival process is a state-independent Poisson process, i.e., $\lambda(n) = \lambda$ for all n, so is the departure process.

3.2.2. $M/G/\infty$: A Queueing System with Ample Servers

Consider a service station in which the number of parallel servers is sufficient such that no waiting line exists. If the source has an infinite population, the number of servers must be, theoretically speaking, also infinite to meet such a requirement. If the source is of the finite type, it suffices to have as many servers as the total population size. We call such a station an infinite server (IS) station, and denote it by $M/G/\infty$, when the arrival process is a Poisson process and service demands of individual jobs have a general service distribution, which we denote as $F(w)$.

Mirasol (1963) showed that for a stationary Poisson arrival process with λ, the number of jobs in a system is Poisson distributed with mean $\lambda \bar{w}/C_0$, where, as before, $\bar{w}$ is the average work per job and C_0 is the servicing rate of the individual server. We shall now derive a more general result by using the *method of stage* representation of general service time distributions.

Let $\Phi(s)$ be the Laplace-Stieltjes transform of the distribution $F(w)$,

$$\Phi(s) = \int_0^\infty e^{-sw} \, dF(w) \qquad (3.2.12)$$

and assume that $\Phi(s)$ is a rational function of s,

$$\Phi(s) = \frac{N(s)}{D(s)} \qquad (3.2.13)$$

where $D(s)$ is a polynomial of degree d and thus $N(s)$ is a polynomial of degree at most d. If the zeros of the denominators are at $-w_j^{-1}$ $(j = 1, 2, \ldots, d)$, we can expand $\Phi(x)$ in partial fractions in many ways. The particular expansion we adopt here is of the form

$$\Phi(s) = b_0 + \sum_{j=1}^{d} a_0 a_1 \ldots a_{j-1} b_j \prod_{i=1}^{j} \frac{1}{1 + sw_j} \qquad (3.2.14)$$

where a_i and b_i are expansion constants and satisfy the conditions $a_i + b_i = 1$, for $0 \leq i \leq d - 1$, and $b_d = 1$. The partial fraction of the form (3.2.14) is due to Cox

(1955) and is schematically shown in Figure 3.2.1 as a series of d exponential distributions of parameter w_i^{-1}, $1 \le i \le d$. We recognize this expansion as a generalization of Erlang's representation.

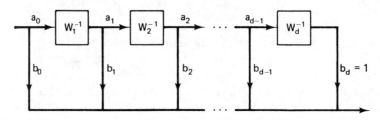

Figure 3.2.1. Cox's representation of a general service distribution.

We define the state of the system $M/G/\infty$ by $\mathbf{n} = \{n_j, 1 \le j \le d\}$, where n_j is the number of jobs which are in the jth stage of service in the above representation. By following an argument similar to the one that has led to (3.2.5), we can write the following linear difference equations for the steady-state distribution $P[\mathbf{n}] = \lim_{t \to \infty} P[\mathbf{n}; t]$:

$$\lambda(n)P[\mathbf{n}] - \sum_{j=1}^{d} (n_j + 1)b_j\mu_j(n+1)P[\mathbf{n}(j^+)] = \lambda(n-1)P[\mathbf{n}(1^-)] - n_1\mu_1(n)P[\mathbf{n}]$$

$$+ \sum_{k=2}^{d} \{(n_{k-1} + 1)a_{k-1}\mu_{k-1}(n)P[\mathbf{n}(k-1^+, k^-)] - n_k\mu_k(n)P[\mathbf{n}]\} \quad (3.2.15)$$

and

$$\lambda(0)P[\mathbf{0}] - \sum_{j=1}^{d} (n_j + 1)b_j\mu_j(1)P[\mathbf{0}(j^+)] = 0 \quad (3.2.16)$$

where the various states in the above equations are defined by

$$\mathbf{n}(k^-) = \{n_1, n_2, \ldots, n_{k-1}, n_k - 1, n_{k+1}, \ldots, n_d\} \quad (3.2.17)$$

$$\mathbf{n}(j^+) = \{n_1, n_2, \ldots, n_{j-1}, n_j + 1, n_{j+1}, \ldots, n_d\} \quad (3.2.18)$$

$$\mathbf{n}(k-1^+, k^-) = \{n_1, n_2, \ldots, n_{k-2}, n_{k-1} + 1, n_k - 1, n_{k+1}, \ldots, n_d\} \quad (3.2.19)$$

and $\mu_i(n)$ is the rate of completion at the ith exponential stage, given by

$$\mu_i(n) = \frac{C(n)}{n\bar{w}_i}, \quad 1 \le i \le d \quad (3.2.20)$$

where $C(n)$ is the entire processing rate of the IS when there are n jobs in the station. The processing rate of the individual server is, therefore, $C_0(n) = C(n)/n$. Let us multiply the following identity by the first terms $\lambda(n)$ and $\lambda(0)$ of (3.2.15) and (3.2.16), respectively:

$$1 = a_1 + b_1 = a_1 + b_1(a_2 + b_2) = \ldots = \sum_{j=1}^{d} e_j b_j \quad (3.2.21)$$

where e_j is the probability that a job comes through up to the jth state:

$$e_j = \prod_{k=1}^{j-1} a_k, \quad j \ge 1 \quad (3.2.22)$$

Then a *sufficient* condition for (3.2.15) to hold is given by the recurrence relation

$$n_k \mu_k(n) P[\mathbf{n}] = e_k \lambda(n-1) P[\mathbf{n}(k^-)], \qquad \text{for } 1 \le k \le d \qquad (3.2.23)$$

which is a generalization of (3.2.7). Equation (3.2.23) is what Chandy (1972) named the *local balance* equation, or the *individual balance* equation [Whittle (1965)], as opposed to the *global balance* equation (3.2.15). By applying this recurrence relation repeatedly, we obtain the following expression, analogous to (3.2.8):

$$P[\mathbf{n}] = P(0)\Lambda(n)\beta(n)n! \prod_{k=1}^{d} \frac{1}{n_k!} (e_k \bar{w}_k)^{n_k} \qquad (3.2.24)$$

where $\Lambda(n)$ and $\beta(n)$ were defined earlier by (3.2.9) and (3.2.10), respectively. The probability distribution of n, the number of jobs in the IS station, is obtainable by summing $P[\mathbf{n}]$ over $\mathbf{n}$ such that $n_1 + n_2 + \ldots + n_d = n$:

$$P(n) = P(0)\Lambda(n)\beta(n)\bar{w}^n \qquad (3.2.25)$$

where

$$\bar{w} = \sum_{k=1}^{d} e_k \bar{w}_k = \int_{0}^{\infty} \{1 - F(w)\} \, dw \qquad (3.2.26)$$

is the average work demanded by a job. Note that the solution form (3.2.25) is the same as (3.2.8). If the processing rate of the individual server is constant C_0, i.e., $C(n) = nC_0$, then (3.2.25) is reduced to

$$P(n) = P(0)\Lambda(n)\frac{1}{n!}\left(\frac{\bar{w}}{C}\right)^n \qquad (3.2.27)$$

Furthermore, if the arrival rate is independent of n, i.e., $\lambda(n) = \lambda$, then (3.2.27) becomes the following Poisson distribution:

$$P(n) = \frac{\rho^n}{n!} e^{-\rho} \qquad (3.2.28)$$

where

$$\rho = \frac{\lambda \bar{w}}{C_0} \qquad (3.2.29)$$

The departure process from the $M/G/\infty$ system possesses exactly the same property as that from the system $M/M/1$ discussed earlier: If the arrival process is a stationary Poisson process with rate λ, so is the departure process.

Different Classes of Jobs in $M/G/\infty$. Now consider the system $M/G/\infty$ in which the input traffic consists of R different classes of jobs. The total arrival process is assumed to be a Poisson process with rate $\lambda(n)$, where n is the total number of jobs currently is the station. If successive arrivals come from one of the R classes with fractional probabilities f_r, $(\sum_{r=1}^{R} f_r = 1)$, then we obtain R independent Poisson substreams with rates $\lambda_r(n) = f_r \lambda(n)$, $r = 1, 2, \ldots, R$. We assume that the service distribution function for class r jobs is given by a general distribution $F_r(w)$. We then define the system state by the vector

$$\mathbf{n} = [\mathbf{n}_1, \mathbf{n}_2, \ldots, \mathbf{n}_r \ldots \mathbf{n}_R] \qquad (3.2.30)$$

where $\mathbf{n}_r$ is a vector of dimension d_r, which is the degree of the denominator in (3.2.13) for the class r job work distribution, $1 \leq r \leq R$. We can obtain the steady-state distribution of the vector (3.2.30) by generalizing our previous arguments. Then the $\{n_r\}$'s, the number of class r jobs in the system, are found to have the following joint distribution:

$$P[\{n_r\}] = P(0)\Lambda(n)\,\beta(n)n! \sum_{r=1}^{R} \frac{1}{n_r!} (f_r \bar{w}_r)^{n_r} \qquad (3.2.31)$$

where n is the total number of jobs, i.e., $n = \sum_{r=1}^{R} n_r$, and $\bar{w}_r$ [work units] is the average work of a class r job:

$$\bar{w}_r = \int_0^\infty \{1 - F_r(w)\} \, dw \qquad (3.2.32)$$

Then it readily follows that the marginal distribution of the variable n is

$$P(n) = P(0)\Lambda(n)\beta(n)\bar{w}^n \qquad (3.2.33)$$

where $\bar{w}$ is the expected work load brought in by a job:

$$\bar{w} = \sum_{r=1}^{R} f_r \bar{w}_r \qquad (3.2.34)$$

If both the arrival rate and the processing rate of the individual server are independent of n, i.e., $\Lambda(n) = \lambda^n$ and $\beta(n) = C_0^{-n}/n!$, then we find from (3.2.31) that

$$P[\{n_r\}] = \prod_{r=1}^{R} P_r(n_r) \qquad (3.2.35)$$

where

$$P_r(n) = \frac{\rho_r^n}{n!} e^{-\rho_r} \qquad (3.2.36)$$

which is a Poisson distribution. Here ρ_r is the traffic intensity of class r jobs:

$$\rho_r = \frac{\lambda f_r \bar{w}_r}{C_0} \qquad (3.2.37)$$

The marginal distribution of n is given by the Poisson distribution of (3.2.28):

$$P(n) = \frac{\rho^n}{n!} e^{-\rho} \qquad (3.2.38)$$

where

$$\rho = \sum_{r=1}^{R} \rho_r = \frac{\lambda \bar{w}}{C_0} \qquad (3.2.39)$$

As to the departure process, our previous result is generalized in a straightforward manner. That is,

$$\lim_{\Delta \to 0} \frac{P[\text{a class } r \text{ job departs in } (t, t + \Delta t) \,|\, \mathbf{n}(t) = \mathbf{n}]}{\Delta} = \lambda(n)f_r \qquad (3.2.40)$$

Thus the departure process of each class r job, with time reversed, is a state-dependent Poisson process with rate $\lambda(n)f_r$.

3.2.3. M/G/1 with Processor-Sharing Queue Discipline

Let us now consider an $M/G/1$ system; i.e., the arrival is Poisson as before, the work load brought by each arrival has a general distribution, and the number of servers is one. However, we restrict the queue discipline to be of a particular type: the so-called processor-sharing (PS) discipline. Under this discipline, when there are n jobs in the service station, each job receives service at the rate of $C(n)/n$ [work units/sec], where $C(n)$ is the processing rate of the server, as defined earlier. The PS discipline can be also viewed as a limiting case of round-robin (RR) scheduling in which the time quatum approaches zero.

When a job arrives at the system, the job immediately starts receiving its share of service; thus there are no waiting lines. This situation is exactly what we observed in the system $M/G/\infty$. It is not difficult to see, therefore, that the system balance equation for the PS case is the same as that obtained for the IS system. Thus, the distribution of n is given by

$$P(n) = P(0)\Lambda(n)\beta(n)\bar{w}^n \qquad (3.2.41)$$

which is, of course, the same as (3.2.8) and (3.2.25).

The properties of the departure process is also the same as in the $M/G/\infty$ and $M/M/1$ systems. Therefore, we can conclude that the PS discipline effectively transforms a general work-load distribution $F(w)$ with mean $\bar{w}$ into the exponential distribution with the same mean, insofar as the steady-state queue distribution and departure process are concerned.

Another important property known for PS scheduling is that when the processing rate is constant, i.e., $C(n) = C$ for all $n \geq 1$, the expected waiting time given w, the work load of a job, is a linear function of w:

$$E[\text{waiting time} \mid \text{service demand} = w] = \frac{\rho w}{(1 - \rho)C} \qquad (3.2.42)$$

where

$$\rho = \frac{\lambda E[w]}{C} \qquad (3.2.43)$$

Similarly, the expected response time is a linear function of w:

$$E[\text{response time} \mid \text{service demand} = w] = \frac{w}{(1 - \rho)C} \qquad (3.2.44)$$

Thus, PS is a scheduling scheme which favors smaller jobs while penalizing larger ones. For detailed discussions of the results (3.2.42) and (3.2.44), see Coffman and Denning (1973) and Kleinrock (1976).

The probability distribution functions of waiting time and response time have not yet been solved analytically for the system $M/G/1$ with PS except for the case of exponential service time, discussed by Coffman et al. (1970).

Chandy (1972) has also shown that the last-come, first-served scheduling with preemptive-resume (LCFS-PR) prossesses properties similar to the PS algorithm.

In LCFS-PR the most recently arrived job uses the server entirely until it is either preempted by a newly arriving job or until it receives its total required service. The properties of PS scheduling, such as (3.2.41), (3.2.42), and (3.2.44), hold also under LCFS-PR. The main shortcoming of the latter scheduling algorithm, however, is that the variances of the waiting and response times are much larger than those for PS.

3.3. QUEUEING NETWORKS FOR MULTIPLE RESOURCE MODELS

Now we are ready to generalize the results of the preceding section to a network of queues. We shall start with a brief review of the classical result due to Jackson (1963).

3.3.1. A Queueing Netowrk with Exponential Servers

Let us assume that we have M separate service stations, labeled as $0, 1, \ldots, M-1$,[3] each of which has it own queue. If the service demand at each service station has exponential distribution (of mean $\bar{w}_i$, $i = 0, 1, \ldots, M-1$) and the scheduling discipline at each station is a work-conserving queue discipline, then the state of the system is given by the vector

$$\mathbf{N} = [n_0, n_1, \ldots, n_i, \ldots, n_{M-1}] \tag{3.3.1}$$

where n_i represents the number of jobs waiting or in service at station i. The processing rate of station i can be dependent on the local queue size n_i, and we denote it by $C_i(n_i)$, $0 \le i \le M-1$. Then the job completion rate at station i is also dependent on the local queue size and is given by

$$\mu_i(n_i) = \frac{C_i(n_i)}{\bar{w}_i} \tag{3.3.2}$$

A job arrives from a source according to a Poisson process with rate $\lambda(N)$, where N is the total number of jobs present in the entire network:

$$N = \sum_{i=0}^{M-1} n_i \tag{3.3.3}$$

A new job originating from the source s will first go to station i with probability p_{si}, $i = 0, 1, 2, \ldots, M-1$. The routing path of a job within the system is governed by a first-order homogeneous Markov chain $\{q_{ij}\}$, $0 \le i, j \le M-1$. The job, after its completion at station i, departs from the system with probability q_{id}.[4]

Let $P[\mathbf{N}; t]$ be the probability that the system is in state $\mathbf{N}$ at time t. By following exactly the same sequence of steps as we developed in Section 3.2, we find that the

---

[3]We use $0, 1, \ldots, M-1$ instead of $1, 2, \ldots, M$ for the notational convenience of our later discussions in Section 3.4.

[4]Here d in subscripts stands for *departure*, and it should be distinguished from the d defined in (3.2.14).

steady-state distribution $P[\mathbf{N}] = \lim_{t\to\infty} P[\mathbf{N}; t]$, if it exists, must satisfy the following equations:

$$\lambda(N)P[\mathbf{N}] - \sum_{j=0}^{M-1} q_{jd}\mu_j(n_j + 1)P[\mathbf{N}(j^+)] - \left\{ \lambda(N-1)\sum_{i=0}^{M-1} q_{si}P[\mathbf{N}(i^-)] \right.$$

$$\left. - \sum_{i=0}^{M-1} \mu_i(n_i)P[\mathbf{N}] \right\} - \sum_{i=0}^{M-1} q_{ji} \left\{ \sum_{j=0}^{M-1} \mu_j(n_j + 1)P[\mathbf{N}(j^+, i^-)] \right\} = 0 \qquad (3.3.4)$$

and

$$\lambda(0)P[\mathbf{0}] - \sum_{j=0}^{M-1} q_{jd}\mu_j(1)P[\mathbf{0}(j^+)] = 0 \qquad (3.3.5)$$

which are quite similar to equation (3.2.15) and (3.2.16). Recall that in Section 3.2.2 we introduced the quantities $\{e_j\}$ to break up the global balance equation (3.2.15) into the set of *local balance* equations (3.2.23), in which $e_j\lambda(n)$ was the rate of job arrival to stage j. If we now define $e_j\lambda(N)$ as the job arrival rate to station j of the network under consideration, the vector $\mathbf{e} = [e_0, e_1, \ldots, e_j, \ldots, e_{M-1}]$ should be given as the solution of the following linear equation:

$$e_j = q_{sj} + \sum_{i=0}^{M-1} e_i q_{ij} \qquad (3.3.6)$$

Then the identity equation which corresponds to (3.2.21) is

$$1 = \sum_{j=0}^{M-1} q_{sj} = \sum_{j=0}^{M-1} \left\{ e_j - \sum_{i=0}^{M-1} e_i q_{ij} \right\} \qquad (3.3.7)$$

Then our procedure for searching for local balance equations is essentially the same as that of Section 3.2, and we find that the recurrence equation

$$e_j\lambda(N-1)P[\mathbf{N}(j^-)] - \mu_j(n_j)P[\mathbf{N}] = 0 \qquad \text{for all vectors } \mathbf{N} \text{ and } j = 0, 1, \ldots, M-1$$

$$(3.3.8)$$

is a sufficient condition for the global balance equation (3.3.4) to hold. This immediately leads to

$$P[\mathbf{N}] = P(\mathbf{0})\Lambda(N) \prod_{i=0}^{M-1} \beta_i(n_i)W_i^{n_i} \qquad (3.3.9)$$

where

$$W_i = e_i \bar{w}_i \qquad (3.3.10)$$

represents the *expected total work load that a job places on the server during its entire life.*

If, in particular, the external arrival rate function $\lambda(N)$ and service rates $C_i(n_i)$ are all constant, the solution is simplified to

$$P[\mathbf{N}] = \prod_{i=0}^{M-1} (1 - \rho_i)\rho_i^{n_i} \qquad (3.3.11)$$

where

$$\rho_i = \frac{\lambda W_i}{C} \qquad (3.3.12)$$

The result (3.3.11) is often called *Jackson's decomposition theorem* since the joint distribution of **N** is decomposable into a product of the marginal distributions; that is, in the equilibrium state the variables $n_0, n_1, \ldots, n_{M-1}$ are statistically independent.

3.3.2. A Generalized Network of Queues

Now we are ready to discuss significant extensions of Jackson's model of the last section. These results are originally due to Chandy (1972), Chandy et al. (1972), Baskett and Muntz (1972), and Baskett et al. (1975). Our presentation will be stated in slightly more general terms than the above author's results.

The readers may have already noticed the strong resemblance of the results of Section 3.3.1 to those of Sections 3.2.2 and 3.2.3. This resemblance, in fact, is not a mere coincidence. Recall that in both the $M/G/\infty$ and $M/G/1$ cases we decomposed a given general distribution into cascaded exponential service stages as given in Figure 3.2.1. Thus, the exponential stage representation of Figure 3.2.1 can be viewed as a special type of queueing network. An important distinction to be made, however, is that if the service discipline is FCFS, for instance, the number of jobs within the entire stages must not exceed 1 at any time. Namely, a job moves through the fictitious stages in sequence, and until the job leaves the system, the next job cannot enter the first stages. This is equivalent to assuming that the entrance stage is *blocked* whenever a job already exists in some stage. Only without blocking, however, does the steady-state distribution take a simple form. Once blocking is introduced, the solution becomes quite complicated even for a simple queueing system. This is why we had to assume that the service distribution is exponential (i.e., d, the number of stages in the representation of Figure 3.2.1, is unity) if that service station is under FCFS or any other work-conserving queue discipline.

In the cases of PS or IS, however, the problem of blocking disappears. In an infinite-server queue, there are always at least as many servers available as the number of jobs; thus no waiting line develops, and hence blocking is nonexistent. A single server under PS, as discussed before, can be viewed as a set of infinitely many parallel servers, with their service rates being inversely proportional to n. Thus, blocking is not an issue in a PS station either.

A similar interpretation can be given to service station under LCFS-PR discipline: Each time a new job arrives at this station, it immediately enters the first stage of the representation of Figure 3.2.1. A job which has been in service up to now is then *frozen* on the spot and will resume receiving service when it becomes the youngest among those remaining in the system. Since any newly arriving job can immediately enter the service station without being blocked, the queue size distribution takes the product form solution (3.2.38). One can substantiate the last statement more formally by writing down a system balance equation similar to (3.2.15).

Then by extending this observation one step further, we can now consider a network of queues in which some or all of the service stations are any of the special types discussed in Sections 3.2.1 through 3.2.3, i.e., (1) exponential service distribution with a work-conserving queue discipline, (2) an IS station in which service distribution is of general form, (3) a PS station with general service distribution, and (4) a LCFS preemptive-resume station with general service distribution. Furthermore, in types (2), (3), and (4), we can have different classes of jobs with service distributions $F_{ir}(w)$, $i = 0, 1, \ldots, M-1$ and $r = 1, 2, \ldots, R$. The job routing is now characterized by a Markov chain $\{q_{ir,jr'}\}$ over an extended state space, where $q_{ir,jr'}$ is the probability that a class r job completing at station i goes next to station j as a class r' job. The state of the system is then defined by the vector

$$\mathbf{N} = [\mathbf{N}_0, \mathbf{N}_1, \ldots, \mathbf{N}_i, \ldots, \mathbf{N}_{M-1}] \tag{3.3.13}$$

where $\mathbf{N}_i$ is the state vector of station i and is decomposable into

$$\mathbf{N}_i = [\mathbf{n}_{i1}, \mathbf{n}_{i2}, \ldots, \mathbf{n}_{ir}, \ldots, \mathbf{n}_{iR}], \qquad 0 \leq i \leq M-1 \tag{3.3.14}$$

in which $\mathbf{n}_{ir}$ itself is a vector and represents the state of class r jobs at station i:

$$\mathbf{n}_{ir} = [n_{ir1}, n_{ir2}, \ldots, n_{irk}, \ldots, n_{ird_{ir}}] \tag{3.3.15}$$

Here n_{irk} is the number of class r jobs in the kth stage at service center i, $1 \leq k \leq d_{ir}$, where d_{ir} is the number of stages in the Cox representation of service distribution $F_{ir}(w)$. The total dimension of the state vector $\mathbf{N}$ is $\sum_{i=0}^{M-1} \sum_{r=1}^{R} d_{ir}$, and it can be a very large number. This is not a problem, however, since the steady-state distribution of $\mathbf{N}$ is again given in terms of product form:

$$P[\mathbf{N}] = P(0)\Lambda(N) \prod_{i=0}^{M-1} \beta_i(n_i) n_i! \sum_{r=1}^{R} \prod_{k=1}^{d_{ir}} \frac{1}{n_{irk}!} (e_{irk} w_{irk})^{n_{irk}} \tag{3.3.16}$$

Here e_{irk} is the expected number of visits that a job makes to the kth stage of $F_{ir}(d)$ and is given by

$$e_{irk} = \left(\prod_{l=1}^{k-1} a_{irl} \right) e_{ir} \tag{3.3.17}$$

which is a generalization of (3.2.22). The parameters $\{a_{irl}\}$ and $\{\bar{w}_{irk}\}$ are those given by the Cox representation of $F_{ir}(w)$. The $\{e_{ir}\}$'s of (3.3.17) are the solutions to the simultaneous equations

$$e_{jr'} = q_{s,jr'} + \sum_{i=0}^{M-1} \sum_{r=1}^{R} e_{ir} q_{ir,jr'} \tag{3.3.18}$$

Thus, on the average a job visits station i e_{ir} times as a class r job during the job's entire stay in the system.

The joint distribution of $n_{ir} = \sum_{k=1}^{d_{ir}} n_{irk}$ is obtained as a marginal distribution of (3.3.16). Using the *reproducing property*[5] of multiple Poisson distribution, we obtain

$$P[\{n_{ir}\}] = P(0)\Lambda(N) \prod_{i=0}^{M-1} \beta_i(n_i) n_i! \prod_{r=1}^{R} \frac{1}{n_{ir}!} (e_{ir} \bar{w}_{ir})^{n_{ir}} \tag{3.3.19}$$

---

[5]Given k independent random variables $X_1 X_2 \ldots X_k$ with Poisson distributions of parameters $\lambda_1, \lambda_2, \ldots, \lambda_k$, respectively, the sum of the variables $Y = X_1 + X_2 + \cdots + X_k$ *reproduces* a Poisson distribution of parameter $\lambda = \lambda_1 + \lambda_2 + \cdots + \lambda_k$.

Proceeding one step further, the joint distribution of $n_i = \sum_{r=1}^{R} n_{ir}$ is immediately derivable from (3.3.19):

$$P[\{n_i\}] = P(0)\Lambda(N) \prod_{i=0}^{M-1} \beta_i(n_i) W_i^{n_i} \qquad (3.3.20)$$

where

$$W_i = \sum_{r=1}^{R} e_{ir} \bar{w}_{ir} \qquad (3.3.21)$$

is a generalization of (3.3.10).

3.3.3. Generalization of Job Routing Characteristics

Thus far we have assumed that job routing behavior in a network is governed by a *homogeneous* and *first-order* Markov chain. We are going to eliminate these restrictions entirely, and yet we shall show that the simple product form solution still holds. Due to space limitations, our treatment here is rather brief; those who are interested in further details are referred to Kobayashi and Reiser (1975).

Let us assume, as before, that there are M service centers $0, 1, 2, \ldots, M-1$ in a given queueing network. The job routing transitions are assumed to be characterized by an hth-order Markov chain; i.e., the probability that a job at station i moves next to station j depends not only on i but also on its previous $h-1$ transitions. Let us denote by $i_1, i_2, k_3, \ldots, i_h$ the sequence of the past h stations that the job has visited, where i_h is the station that a job is currently in, i.e., $i_h = i$. We define that the *state of a job* by an h-tuple,

$$s = (i_1, i_2, \ldots, i_h) \qquad (3.3.22)$$

The values that s can take on range from $(0, 0, \ldots, 0), (0, 0, \ldots, 1)$ to $(M-1, M-1, \ldots, M-1)$, which we represent, for notational conciseness, by integers $s = 0, 1, \ldots, M^h - 1$. Then the job transition behavior governed by an hth-order Markov chain is characterized by $q_{ss'}$, the probability that a job in state s moves next to state s'. We can further generalize this model by assuming a *nonstationary* transition mechanism; i.e., $q_{ss'}$, can be explicitly dependent on t, the current transition step counting from the entrance stage of the job into the network.[6]

This characterization will be best illustrated by the *trellis* diagram of Figure 3.3.1, which depicts the case of $m = 2$ and $h = 2$. Each node of the diagram corresponds to an ordered pair of job state s and transition step t. For example, a job is in state $(01) = 1$ at *time* t if it was at service station 0 at the $(t-1)$th step and is currently at station 1. Similarly, a job is in state $(10) = 2$ at t if it just moved from station 1 to station 0. Without loss of generality, we can assume that every entering job starts at either state $(00) = 0$ or $(01) = 1$. The probability $q_{ss'}(t)$ is the conditional probability of a transition from a given state s at time $t-1$ to state s' at time t.

---

[6]Note the transition step parameter t has no direct relation to *real time*. $t = 0$ corresponds the initial step of a job which arrives in the network.

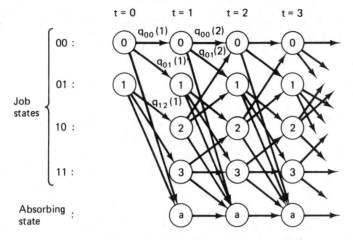

Figure 3.3.1. Trellis diagram representation of job routing.

Included also in Figure 3.3.1 is an absorbing state $s = a$. A transition to this absorbing state means that a job leaves the network forever. With all these generalizations, we now define the system state by the following vector of infinite dimension:

$$\mathbf{N} = \{n_{stk}\} \tag{3.3.23}$$

where $s = 0, 1, \ldots, M^h - 1$, $t = 0, 1, 2, \ldots$, and $k = 1, 2, \ldots, d_{st}$. Here n_{stk} is the number of jobs which are at job state s in their tth transition and currently in the kth stage of service at server i. d_{st} is the number of exponential stages in the Cox representation of the service time distribution $F_{st}(w)$. Note that in our integer representation of state s the current server i is determined by the relation[7]

$$i = s \quad (\text{modulo } M) \tag{3.3.24}$$

Then by generalizing (3.3.16), we obtain the steady-state distribution of $\mathbf{N}$ as

$$P[\mathbf{N}] = P(0)\Lambda(N) \prod_{i=0}^{M-1} \beta_i(n_i)n_i! \prod_{\substack{s=i \\ (\bmod M)}}^{\infty} \prod_{t=0}^{\infty} \prod_{k=1}^{d_{st}} \frac{1}{n_{stk}!} (e_{stk}\bar{w}_{stk})^{n_{stk}} \tag{3.3.25}$$

Here the definition and derivation of $\bar{w}_{stk}$ will both be self-evident. e_{stk} is defined similar to (3.3.17),

$$e_{stk} = \left(\prod_{l=1}^{k-1} a_{stl} \right) e_{st} \tag{3.3.26}$$

where e_{st} is the *probability* that a job is at state s at its tth transition step and is uniquely determined by $\{q_{ss'}(t)\}$. By use of the reproducing property of multiple Poisson distributions, marginal distributions are also all given in product form. For example, the joint distribution of n_i

$$n_i = \sum_{\substack{s=i \\ (\bmod M)}}^{\infty} \sum_{t=0}^{\infty} \sum_{k=0}^{d_{st}} n_{stk} \tag{3.3.27}$$

[7]Equation (3.3.24) reads "i and s are congruent modulo M." Here i is a unique integer between 0 and $M - 1$ such that $s - i$ is an integral multiple of M.

is again reduced to the simple form of (3.3.20). The parameters W_i in that solution are given, instead of by (3.3.21), by

$$W_i = \sum_{\substack{s=i \\ (\text{mod } M)}} \sum_{t=0}^{\infty} \sum_{k=0}^{d_{st}} e_{stk}\bar{w}_{stk}$$

$$= \sum_{\substack{s=i \\ (\text{mod } M)}} \sum_{t=0}^{\infty} e_{st}\bar{w}_{st} \qquad (3.3.28)$$

The last expression looks rather complicated but has the same physical meaning as before: the total amount of work that a job places on server i during its entire life.

The notion of the job state defined by (3.3.22) can be further extended to the case with different classes of jobs:

$$s = [(i_1 r_1), (i_2 r_2) \dots (i_h r_h)] \qquad (3.3.29)$$

The interpretation of this vector will be self-evident. Now there are $(MR)^h$ distinct states. It will be clear that our previous discussions can be extended to the present case in an obvious way. The joint distribution of variables $\{n_{ir}; 0 \leq i \leq M - 1, 1 \leq r \leq R\}$, for example, will be given exactly in the same form as (3.3.19).

3.4. CLOSED QUEUEING NETWORKS AND COMPUTATIONAL ALGORITHMS

3.4.1. A Closed Network of Queues

In our discussions thus far we always assumed that there exists a source of infinite population which generates a sequence of Poisson arrivals with rate λ or $\lambda(N)$. In many problems of practical interest, however, this infinite population model is inadequate or unrealistic. Then we must deal with a finite population model. The central server model discussed in Section 3.1 and the so-called machine-repairman (or machine-interference) model are typical examples of a closed queueing network.

When the number of jobs is finite, one can formulate, theoretically speaking, almost any model in terms of a Markov chain of finite dimension. This does not mean, however, that any closed queueing system is practically solvable. On the contrary, even for a system model of moderate size the dimension of the underlying Markov chain often becomes prohibitively large, and algebraic manipulations (e.g., inversion) of a large matrix become exceedingly tedious and costly.

If we restrict our attention to the class of models defined below, however, a closed form analytic solution can be derived based on the results of Section 3.3. Let us assume that a given closed network contains M stations which we now label as stations $1, 2, \dots, M.$ [8]

The types of service stations, queue discipline, service demand distributions, and job behavior may all be as general as those we defined in Section 3.3. The only differ-

---

[8]Of course we could still use $0, 1, \dots, M - 1$ as in Section 3.3, but most of the expressions would become rather awkward.

ence is that we allow no arrivals or departures. Thus there are constant number, N, of jobs moving around in the network. We could start with the system balance equation of the type discussed in Sections 3.2 and 3.3. Jackson (1963) showed, however, that one can derive a solution more quickly by utilizing results on open networks.

Let us control the job arrival rate function $\lambda(n)$ as follows:

$$\lambda(n) = \begin{cases} 0, & n \geq N \\ \lambda^*, & n \leq N-1 \end{cases} \tag{3.4.1}$$

Let λ^* then increase without bound. As soon as a job leaves the system and n becomes less than N, a new job will be instantaneously triggered into the system; thus the number of jobs is maintained at constant N. Then equation (3.3.20), for example, can be interpreted for a closed network as follows: From (3.2.9) and (3.4.1) we have

$$\Lambda(N) = \lambda^* \Lambda(N-1) \tag{3.4.2}$$

and

$$\Lambda(n) = 0, \quad n > N \tag{3.4.3}$$

Then as $\lambda^* \to \infty$, it follows that $P(0) \to 0$, but $P(0)\Lambda(N)$ approaches constant; thus we obtain the following limit form of (3.3.20):

$$P[\{n_i\}] = \begin{cases} g^{-1}(N, M) \prod_{i=1}^{M} \beta_i(n_i) W_i^{n_i} & \text{if } \{n_i\} \in \mathcal{F}(N) \\ 0, & \text{otherwise} \end{cases} \tag{3.4.4}$$

where $g(N, M)$ is the normalization constant to be duly discussed below and $\mathcal{F}(N)$ is a set of feasible values of $\{n_i\}$; i.e.,

$$\mathcal{F}(N) = \left\{ \{n_i\} \mid n_i \geq 0 \text{ for all } i \text{ and } \sum_{i=1}^{M} n_i = N \right\} \tag{3.4.5}$$

The parameters $\{W_i\}$ of (3.3.10) [and similarly those of (3.3.21) and (3.3.28)] require a new interpretation: The values of $\{e_i\}$ (and similarly $\{e_{ir}\}$ and $\{e_{si}\}$) in the expression are unique only to within a multiplicative constant. Note that the vector $\mathbf{e} = [e_1, e_2, \ldots, e_M]$ is now the eigenvector of the $M \times M$ Markov transition matrix $\mathbf{Q} = [q_{ij}]$ associated with an eigenvalue of unity:

$$\mathbf{eQ} = \mathbf{e} \tag{3.4.6}$$

If we introduce the additional constraint

$$\sum_{i=1}^{M} e_i = 1 \tag{3.4.7}$$

then $\mathbf{e}$ represents the stationary distribution of the Markov chain, and it is given by the following simple form:

$$\mathbf{e} = \mathbf{1} \cdot [\mathbf{Q} + \mathbf{E} - \mathbf{I}]^{-1} \tag{3.4.8}$$

where $\mathbf{1}$ is a row vector size M whose elements are all unity; E is $\mathbf{1} \cdot \mathbf{1}^T$, i.e., an $M \times M$ matrix whose entries are all unity; and I is the identity matrix of size $M \times M$.

If we choose, instead of (3.4.7), a constraint such that $e_1 = 1$, then e_i represents the expected number of visits that a job makes to server i during two successive trips server 1. Then W_i is the expected total amount of work that a job brings into server i during such a cycle.

The normalization constant $g(N, M)$, in either case, should be chosen in such a way that values of $P[\{n_i\}]$ over $\mathfrak{F}(N)$ add up to 1:

$$g(N, M) = \sum_{\{n_i\} \in \mathfrak{F}(N)} \prod_{i=1}^{M} \beta_i(n_i) W_i^{n_i} \tag{3.4.9}$$

The number of the feasible states, i.e., the cardinality of the set $\mathfrak{F}(N)$, is $\binom{N + M - 1}{M - 1}$, and it becomes an astronomically large number even for moderate sizes of N and M. The computational algorithms are therefore of practical importance in the numerical evaluation of $g(N, M)$ of (3.4.9) and various performance measures of a given queueing network.

3.4.2. Computational Algorithm

The recursive algorithms to be discussed below were reported independently by Buzen (1973), Reiser and Kobayashi (1973), and Muntz and Wong (1974). Moore (1972) discussed the same subject, but his model and solution are much more restrictive. As to the results for a closed network model, Buzen's earlier work in his Ph.D. thesis (1971b) apparently predates the others. The generating function method adopted by Reiser and Kobayashi (1975c) has led to substantial generalizations of the algorithm: (1) open and mixed networks as well as closed networks, (2) different classes of jobs, and (3) the case in which job routing is characterized by multiple closed chains. The last model is important when a common machine supports multiple subsystems for different applications. Because of space limitations, we shall present only the case of a closed network with a homogeneous job population.

Let us define a transformed (or generating) function

$$B_i(z) = \sum_{n=0}^{\infty} \beta_i(n) z^n \tag{3.4.10}$$

Then it is not difficult to see that $g(n, m)$ defined above is the coefficient of the term z^n in

$$G_m(z) = \prod_{i=1}^{m} B_i(W_i z) \tag{3.4.11}$$

or equivalently

$$g(n, m) = \frac{1}{n!} \left[\frac{\partial^n}{\partial z^n} \prod_{i=1}^{m} B_i(W_i z) \right]_{z=0} \tag{3.4.12}$$

By rewriting $G_m(z)$ as

$$G_m(z) = G_{m-1}(z) B_m(W_m z) \tag{3.4.13}$$

we obtain the following iterative formula:

$$g(n, m) = \frac{1}{n!} \left[\frac{\partial^n}{\partial z^n} G_{m-1}(z) B_m(W_m z) \right]_{z=0}$$

$$= \sum_{k=0}^{n} g(n - k, m - 1) \beta_m(k) W_m^k, \qquad 1 \leq m \leq M, 0 \leq n \leq N \tag{3.4.14}$$

with the boundary condition

$$g(n, 0) = \delta_{n,0} \tag{3.4.15}$$

where $\delta_{n,0}$ is Kronecker's delta: $\delta_{n,0} = 0$ for $n \neq 0$ and $\delta_{0,0} = 1$. Formula (3.4.14) is obtained based on the well-known fact that the product of two generating functions corresponds to the convolutional sum of the two sequences.

The computation of $\{g(i, m); 0 \leq i \leq n\}$ given the values of $\{g(i, m-1); 0 \leq i \leq m\}$ requires $[n(n+1)]/2$ multiplications and additions. Thus, the evaluation of $g(N, M)$ requires, in total, $[(M-1)N(N+1)]/2$ multiplications and additions, which is a substantial saving compared with $\binom{N+M-1}{M-1}$.

The iterative formula (3.4.14) can be further simplified if the processing rate of server m is independent of the local queue size, i.e., if $C_m(n) = C_m$ for all $n = 1, 2, 3, \ldots$. Then $\beta_m(n) = C_m^{-n}$ from the definition (3.2.10). This leads us to a simpler expression of $B_m(z)$:

$$B_m(z) = \sum_{n=0}^{\infty} (C_m^{-1}z)^n = \frac{1}{1 - C_m^{-1}z} \tag{3.4.16}$$

Substitution of (3.4.16) into (3.4.13) results in

$$G_m(z) = G_{m-1}(z) + W_m C_m^{-1} G_m(z) \tag{3.4.17}$$

which yields a formula simpler than (3.4.14):

$$g(n, m) = g(n, m-1) + W_m C_m^{-1} g(n-1, m) \tag{3.4.18}$$

If all the M stations have constant processing rates, then evaluation of $g(N, M)$ requires, in total, $(M-1)N$ multiplications and additions.

Kobayashi (1976) discusses a computational algorithm based on the Polya theory of enumeration, an application of group theory to combinatorial problems. The amount of computations required in this algorithm is the order of N^2, thus the algorithm is preferable to (3.4.18) when $M > N$.

3.4.3. Computation of Various Performance Measures

We define the M-dimensional probability generating function (p.g.f.) of the probability distribution (3.4.4) by

$$
\begin{aligned}
Q(z) &= E[z_1^{n_1} z_2^{n_2} \cdots z_M^{n_M}] \\
&= g^{-1}(N, M) \sum_{n \in \mathcal{I}(N)} \prod_{i=1}^{M} \beta_i(n_i)(W_i z_i)^{n_i} \\
&= g^{-1}(N, M) \frac{1}{N!} \left[\frac{\partial^N}{\partial \theta^N} \prod_{i=1}^{M} B_i(W_i z_i \theta) \right]_{\theta=0}
\end{aligned}
\tag{3.4.19}
$$

The marginal distribution of server M, for example, is obtained by setting $z_1 = z_2 = \cdots = z_{M-1} = 1$ and $z_M = z$ in (3.4.19):

$$
\begin{aligned}
Q_M(z) &= E[z^{n_M}] = g^{-1}(N, M) \frac{1}{N!} \left[\frac{\partial^N}{\partial \theta^N} G_{M-1}(\theta) B_M(W_M \theta z) \right]_{\theta=0} \\
&= g^{-1}(N, M) \sum_{k=0}^{N} g(N-k, M-1) \beta_M(k)(W_M z)^k
\end{aligned}
\tag{3.4.20}
$$

Hence inverting the p.g.f. (3.4.20), we obtain the marginal distribution of n_M as

$$P_M(n) = g^{-1}(N, M)g(N - n, M - 1)\beta_M(n)W_M^n, \quad 0 \le n \le N \qquad (3.4.21)$$

Thus the throughput, $\lambda_M(N)$, of server M in the network of job population N is given by

$$\lambda_M(N) = \sum_{n=0}^{N} P_M(n)\mu_M(n) \qquad (3.4.22)$$

Substituting (3.2.2) and (3.2.10) into (3.4.22), we obtain

$$\lambda_M(N) = g^{-1}(N, M) \sum_{n=0}^{N} g(N - n, M - 1)\beta_M(n - 1)\frac{W_M^n}{\bar{w}_M}$$

$$= \frac{g(N - 1, M)e_M}{g(N, M)} \qquad (3.4.23)$$

where we used the relation $W_M = e_M\bar{w}_M$.

Utilization, U_M, of server M is readily obtainable from (3.4.21):

$$U_M = 1 - P_M(0) = 1 - g^{-1}(N, M)g(N, M - 1) \qquad (3.4.24)$$

Since $U_M \ge 0$, we establish the following relation for the g function:

$$g(N, M) \ge g(N, M - 1) \qquad (3.4.25)$$

The jth moment of the queue length at server M is defined as

$$E[n_M^j] = \sum_{n=0}^{\infty} n^j P_M(n) \qquad (3.4.26)$$

Substitution of (3.4.21) yields

$$E[n_M^j] = \frac{g_M^{(j)}(N, M)}{g(N, M)} \qquad (3.4.27)$$

where $g_M^{(j)}(N, M)$ is defined by

$$g_M^{(j)}(N, M) = \sum_{k=0}^{\infty} g(N - k, M - 1)k^j\beta_M(k)W_M^k \qquad (3.4.28)$$

From (3.4.14) and (3.4.28) it is apparent that $g_M^{(j)}(N, M)$ is what $g(N, M)$ would be should we substitute $n^j\beta_M(n)$ for $\beta_M(n)$. In particular,

$$g_M^{(0)}(N, M) = g(N, M) \qquad (3.4.29)$$

Of particular importance among the various moments is the first moment or the average queue length:

$$\bar{n}_M = E[n_M] = \frac{g_M^{(1)}(N, M)}{g(N, M)} \qquad (3.4.30)$$

The response time at station M, i.e., the expected amount of time that a job must spend each time it visits station M, is given by

$$T_M = \frac{\bar{n}_M}{\lambda_M(N)} = \frac{g_M^{(1)}(N, M)}{g(N - 1, M)e_M} \qquad (3.4.31)$$

Throughout the discussions of the present section we have restricted our attention to station M. It will be clear that the marginal probability and other related quantities for any chosen station are given by the same formulas: All we need to do is renumber the labels of stations, so that the station of interest is denoted by M.

3.5. APPROXIMATE MODELS

3.5.1. The Approximate Method of Chandy, Herzog, and Woo

Consider the type of model discussed in the previous section, i.e., a network which has M service stations with N jobs and satisfies the local balance equations, Let us single out one service station, say station M, as illustrated in Figure 3.5.1 and break up the entire network into the station M and its complement or remainder. The solution form (3.4.21) for the marginal distribution of the queue size n_M at service station M will suggest the question "Is it possible to represent the remainder part of

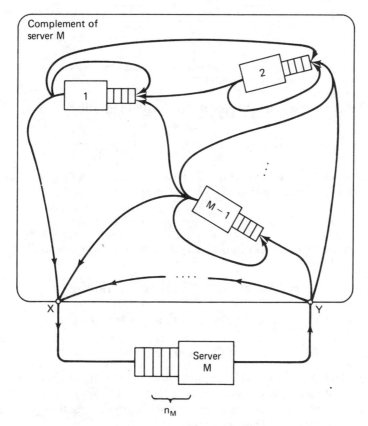

Figure 3.5.1. Decomposition of a queueing network.

the network in terms of an *equivalent* single exponential server as shown in Figure 3.5.2?" If we can represent the job arrivals to the station M by a Poisson process with rate $\lambda^*(N - n)$ when the queue size at the station M is n, it is equivalent to having an exponential server whose job eompletion rate is $\lambda^*(n')$, where $n' = N - n$ is its local queue size. From the simple balance equation of the type discussed in Section 3.2, we

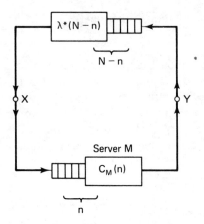

Figure 3.5.2. A conjectured equivalent model of the network of Fig. 3.5.1.

readily find that the queue length probability distribution at the server M should take the form

$$P_M(n) = G^{-1} \left\{ \prod_{i=1}^{n} \lambda^*(N - i + 1) \right\} \beta_M(n) \bar{w}_M^n \qquad (3.5.1)$$

where G is the normalization constant. By a careful inspection of (3.4.21) and (3.5.1), we shall naturally conjecture that $\lambda^*(i)$ be given by

$$\lambda^*(i) = \frac{g(i - 1, M - 1)e_M}{g(i, M - 1)} \qquad (3.5.2)$$

In fact, substitution of (3.5.2) into (3.5.1) results in a form essentially identical to (3.4.21):

$$P_M(n) = G^{-1} \frac{g(N - n, M - 1)}{g(N, M - 1)} \beta_M(n) W_M^n \qquad (3.5.3)$$

from which we can determine the normalization constant G to be

$$G = \frac{g(N, M)}{g(N, M - 1)} \qquad (3.5.4)$$

Chandy, Herzog, and Woo (1975a) have found that $\lambda^*(i)$ of (3.5.2) possesses the following interesting and important property. Let us set $\bar{w}_M = 0$ (hence $W_M = 0$) in the original system of Figure 3.5.1 and in the recurrence relation in (3.4.18) [and (3.4.14) for a general case]. Then we have

$$[g(n, M)]_{W_M=0} = g(n, M - 1) \qquad \text{for all } n \qquad (3.5.5)$$

By comparing (3.5.2) and (3.4.23) we shall find that $\lambda^*(i)$ can be interpreted as the throughput observed from points X and Y in Figure 3.5.1, i.e., the job flow rate from point X to point Y, when the total population is i, that is,

$$\lambda^*(i) = \lambda_M(i)\Big|_{W_M=0} \tag{3.5.6}$$

where $\lambda_M(i)$ is the throughput at server M as defined by (3.4.23). Because of its resemblance to Norton's theorem in linear circuit theory, Chandy et al. (1975a) designate equation (3.5.6) as "Norton's theorem in queueing networks."

Thus the complement of server M seen from X-Y can be represented precisely by the exponential server as conjectured in Figure 3.5.2. If we then replace server M by a general server (i.e., the service time distribution of general form), an equivalent system can be represented by an $M/G/1$ system with queue-dependent Poisson arrival rate. An exact solution of such a model is given by Courtois and Georges (1970) and Chow (1975). Their solution techniques are based on an embedded Markov chain approach.

Chandy et al. (1975b) considered the case in which not only server M but also all the other servers have general distributions (but not dependent on queue size). Clearly in this case there is no equivalent model of the type given in Figure 3.5.2. To obtain an *approximate* solution, however, they propose an algorithm by which a queueing network with general service distribution is replaced by a *nearly equivalent* queueing network with exponential servers. The criteria for *near equivalence* are

1.   The sum of the average queue sizes in the network is as close to N as possible.

2.   The throughputs of server i should be proportional to e_i [the parameter defined by (3.4.6)].

Recall that $\{e_i\}$'s are based purely on *conservation of flows* and are independent of service distributions and queue disciplines. In their algorithm the *equivalent* exponential network is obtained in an iterative fashion by adjusting the mean service times in the network simultaneously. For the description of the algorithm and the degree of accuracy, the reader is referred to the original report in which a number of case examples are reported. An approximate and quick analysis technique to handle priority queueing in a central server model is discussed by Sauer and Chandy (1975), and its accuracy is assessed in a few examples.

3.5.2.   Diffusion Approximation Models

Another avenue to the development of approximate models to deal with non-exponential service distribution is a technique based on the diffusion approximation of a queueing process. In this method a discrete-state jump process such as a queue size process is approximated by a continuous-path Markov process which is usually referred to as a *diffusion process*. The reason that we deal with a diffusion process is simply because we are able to obtain a system equation in the form of partial differential equations, as will be presented below, and this equation is quite often more amenable to mathematical analysis than that of the jump process.

Consider a single server queueing system, and let $Q(t)$ be the queue size (the number of jobs in service or waiting) at time t. Let the interarrival times and service times both be i.i.d. (independent and identically distributed) random variables with

$$\frac{1}{\mu_a} = \text{mean interarrival time} \tag{3.5.7a}$$

$$\sigma_a^2 = \text{variance of interarrival time} \tag{3.5.7b}$$

$$\frac{1}{\mu_s} = \text{mean service time} \tag{3.5.7c}$$

$$\sigma_s^2 = \text{variance of service time} \tag{3.5.7d}$$

Then on the basis of a *central-limit-theorem* argument [see, e.g., Cox and Miller (1965)], we can show that if Δ is sufficientlly large, many events (i.e., arrivals and departures) take place between times t and $t + \Delta$. If $Q(t)$ does not become zero (i.e., the server is kept busy in this interval), then the change in queue size $\Delta Q(t) = Q(t + \Delta) - Q(t)$ should be approximately normally distributed with mean

$$E[\Delta Q(t)] = (\mu_a - \mu_s)\Delta = \beta \cdot \Delta, \qquad \beta < 0 \tag{3.5.8}$$

and variance

$$\text{var}\,[\Delta Q(t)] = (\mu_a^2 \mu_a^3 + \sigma_s^2 \mu_s^3)\Delta = \alpha \cdot \Delta \tag{3.5.9}$$

This observation leads us to approximate a jump process $Q(t)$ by a continuous path process $X(t)$, whose incremental change $dX(t) = X(t + dt) - X(t)$ is normally distributed with mean $\beta \cdot dt$ and variance $\alpha \cdot dt$. Typical behavior of $Q(t)$ and $X(t)$ is illustrated in Figure 3.5.3. Let $p(x_0, x; t)$ be the probability density function of $X(t)$ given that its initial value $X(t) = x_0$. It can be shown that $p(x_0, x; t)$ satisfies the equation

$$\frac{\partial}{\partial t} p(x_0, x; t) = \frac{\alpha}{2} \frac{\partial^2}{\partial x^2} p(x_0, x; t) - \beta \frac{\partial}{\partial x} p(x_0, x; t) \tag{3.5.10}$$

which is called Kolmogorov's diffusion equation or the Fokker-Planck equation [see Cox and Miller (1965) and Newell (1971)]. The solution must satisfy the boundary condition

$$p(x_0, x; t) = 0 \qquad \text{for } x < 0 \tag{3.5.11}$$

since the queue size cannot be negative. A natural way to handle this condition will be to treat $x = 0$ as a reflecting (or elastic) barrier. However, for general distributions with coefficients of variation $c_a = \mu_a \sigma_a$ and/or $c_s = \mu_s \sigma_s$ appreciably different from unity, the simple reflecting barrier model tends to introduce considerable error in the solution of queue size distribution. Various ways of modifying the boundary condition are discussed by Gaver and Shedler (1973), Kobayashi (1974a), Reiser and Kobayashi (1974a), and Gelenbe (1975).

Applications of the diffusion approximation method to a cyclic queueing model (of the type of Figure 3.1.3) for the analysis of a multiprogramming system are discussed in Gaver and Shedler (1973) and Kobayashi (1974a). These models can capture

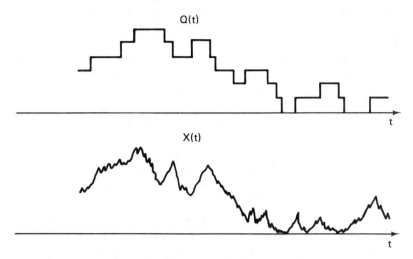

Figure 3.5.3. Typical behavior of the queue-size process $Q(t)$ and the diffusion process $X(t)$.

major effects of nonexponential distributions on such performance measures as server utilization, throughput, queue size distribution, etc., because the first two moments can generally extract a significant portion of information concerning the distribution form, and the diffusion approximation model is one in which the first two moments are explicitly incorporated. A more crude approximation technique is one in which only the mean values are used; such an approximation method is called *fluid approximation*. A monograph by Newell (1971) serves as an excellent introduction to the fluid and diffusion approximations. In Section 3.6 we shall present an application of the fluid approximation model.

Various studies have shown that the diffusion approximation model generally yields more accurate results than a straightforward exponential server model which totally ignores information on the second moments.[9] Kobayashi (1974a) investigated the use of the diffusion approximation to a queueing network of the type discussed in Sections 3.3 and 3.4 but with general service distributions. The approach he takes is essentially to represent the M-dimensional queue size process $\mathbf{Q}(t) = [Q_1(t), Q_2(t), \ldots, Q_M(t)]$ by an M-dimensional diffusion process $\mathbf{X}(t)$, whose probability density function $p(\mathbf{x}_0, \mathbf{x}; t)$ satisfies the multidimensional diffusion equation

$$\frac{\partial}{\partial t} p(\mathbf{x}_0, \mathbf{x}; t) = \frac{1}{2} \sum_{m=1}^{M} \sum_{n=1}^{M} \alpha_{mn} \frac{\partial^2}{\partial x_m \, \partial x_n} p(\mathbf{x}_0, \mathbf{x}; t)$$
$$- \sum_{m=1}^{M} \beta_m \frac{\partial}{\partial X_m} p(\mathbf{x}_0, \mathbf{x}; t) \qquad (3.5.12)$$

[9]The approximation method of Chandy et al. (1975b) discussed in Section 3.5.1 can be interpreted as a model in which the effects of second and higher moments of service distributions are to be reflected in adjustment of values of the first moment.

where the $\{\beta_m\}$'s depend on the mean service and interarrival times and job routing transition probabilities, whereas the $\{\alpha_{mn}\}$'s depend on the variances of service and interarrival times as well.

Another possible advantage of the diffusion approximation method is that quite often we are able to obtain not only the equilibrium state solution, $p(x) = \lim_{t\to\infty} p(x_0, x; t)$ but also the nonequilibrium solution $p(x_0, x; t)$ of the system. The non-equilibrium solution contains transient terms which decay as time elapses; it shows how long the initial value $x_0 = x(0)$ of the system state (i.e., the initial queue size) influences the future $t > 0$. Such information is quite valuable in measurement of operational systems and simulation experiments, because an approximate estimate of transient time will allow us to determine the proper sampling interval to obtain nearly independent sampled (in time) data and hence to estimate the minimum required duration of the simulation or experiment to meet a given confidence level with a specified confidence interval. In simulation an estimate of transient time may be also useful in determining the duration of the initial portion of the simulation run which should be discarded in order to avoid a possible bias introduced in the simulation estimate due to atypical values of the starting condition. Kobayashi (1974b) obtained the transient solution for a cyclic queueing model by solving the diffusion equation of (3.5.10) based on separation of variables and eigenfunction expansion.

3.6.   APPLICATIONS

3.6.1.   Model Formulation

So far we have primarily discussed what classes of queueing models can be solved, exactly or approximately. To analyze a queueing model is one thing; it is quite another to formulate a real system or system under design as an abstract mathematical model. In fact the model formulation task is often more difficult and more crucial than model solving. The main difficulty lies in the fact that tasks or processes in computer systems often utilize more than one resource at a time. For example, a task executing a CPU holds not only the prime resource, i.e., CPU, but also main memory as the secondary resource. Another source of difficulty is that the same object can be viewed as a customer or as a server depending on the problem addressed. As an example, consider a multiple CPU system. From the process scheduling point of view CPU's are certainly servers, and tasks or processes are customers. However, when we deal with the software lockout problem, CPU's are customers and system data bases with locks are servers. Clearly these two problems cannot be formulated in terms of a single queueing model.

A practical approach to overcome the type of difficulties cited above is to structure a system model in a hierarchical manner, as proposed and formulated by Sekino (1972), Courtois (1975a), Browne et al. (1975), and others. Figure 3.6.1 depicts in an abstract way what we call a hierarchical model structure. In this representation model A is at the lowest level and analysis results of model A should be summarized in a

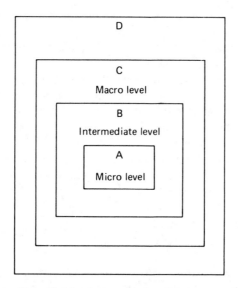

Figure 3.6.1. A hierarchical model structure.

form (such as a constant scaling factor, random variable with known distribution, etc.) usable in the next level, model *B*. Abstracted results of model *B* should then be incorporated in the higher-level model *C*, and so on.

Of course a complete decomposition of a total system model into submodels in such a clear manner as depicted in Figure 3.6.1 is rarely feasible. In practice these submodels are *near-completely* decomposable in the sense of Courtois (1975a), and the analysis of model *A* can be done *almost* independently of its complementary part in model *B*, etc. As observed by Courtois (1975a), the basic requirement for *near-complete decomposition* is that subsystem *A* has transient time constants which are much shorter than the mean time between interactions between subsystem *A* and subsystem model *B*. In other words, a large number of state changes (or events) occur in *A* between state changes in *B*. To be more concrete, let us cite an example taken from an article by Baskett and Muntz (1973): When the time between events being modeled in subsystem *A* is on the order of nanoseconds or microseconds, we shall say that *A* is a microlevel model. An example of a system at this level will be one with multiple CPU's, each of which has a cache and occasionally makes read/write requests to a large main memory or to a multiple module memory. Such issues as memory interference of a multiprocessor, the effect of interleaving, cache mapping algorithm, etc., should be analyzed at this level of model. Some examples will be given in the next section.

When the time between events in system *B* is on the order of milliseconds we shall say that *B* is an intermediate-level model. The most common example at this level is a multiprogramming system model where the customers are tasks concurrently in the multiprogramming mix. The tasks are either engaging in data transfer on I/O devices, executing instructions with a CPU, or are waiting for one of these servers.

Such operating system components as processor scheduling, I/O scheduling memory management, etc., should be studied using a model of this level. The central server model of Figure 3.1.4 is typically used for a model at the intermediate level. See Section 3.6.3 for further discussions.

When the time between events is expressed in seconds, we shall say that we have a macrolevel model. One example at this level is a time-sharing system model such as Figure 3.1.2 in which the servers are the computer and a set of user terminals. Studies on job scheduling algorithms, analysis of terminal response time, etc., are typical issues addressed in a model of this level. In Section 3.6.4 we shall elaborate on the model of Figure 3.1.2 using the results obtained in Sections 3.3 and 3.4. Although not covered in this chapter, the design of a computer communications network should be on top of this macrolevel model.

3.6.2. Memory Interference and Software Lockout in a Multiprocessor System

(a) Memory Interference. One of the well-recognized performance problems in multiprocessor systems is the so-called memory interference or memory contention problem. In general multiple CPU's have independent paths to memory and share a common main memory which usually consists of multiple memory modules. The ability of any processor to address the entire memory space and consequently to execute shareable routines and data provides the flexibility of the operating system. But this apparent advantage is not obtainable without sacrifice. When more than one CPU attempts to access the same module, only one of them can be granted access, while the other CPU's must be queued up. Such situations will be often found when these CPU's wish to use a common operating system program or when they are executing the same problem task. This memory contention has the effect of "stretching" the average memory access time, or equivalently the processing rate of CPU's will slow down by some factor.

Performance analysis of memory interference was studied by Skinner and Asher (1969), Bhandarkar (1975), Chow (1974), and others. Let us consider a multiprocessor configuration as shown in Figure 3.6.2(a) in which N_p processors are all connected to M memory modules. Suppose N CPU's are active at a given time ($N_p - N$ CPU's are idle either because there are not enough tasks or because other tasks are in wait state, waiting for completion of I/O execution). Then we construct the closed queueing model of Figure 3.6.2(b) in which customers or jobs are reference requests issued by these N CPU's. We could also consider the CPU's as customers, since there is always one-to-one correspondence between a reference request and the CPU that issues it. Note also that there is always only one outstanding reference request per CPU. A CPU is in execution state as long as it is executing instructions found in its local memory or cache. If the reference location is not in the local memory, the request is then routed to main memory (one of M modules). If we assume no contention in local store, this stage is representable in terms of an *infinite-server* station, discussed in Section 3.2.2. We label this station as station $M + 1$, as depicted in Figure 3.6.3. The M

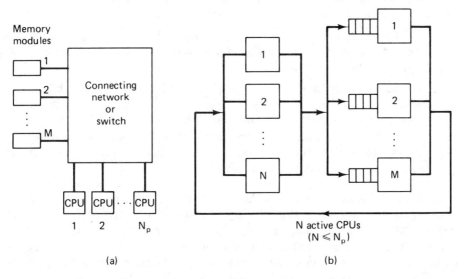

Figure 3.6.2. (a) A physical structure of multiple CPUs and multiple memory modules; (b) a queueing network representation of system (a).

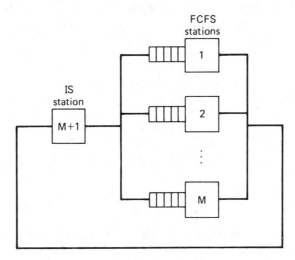

Figure 3.6.3 An equivalent queueing diagram of Fig. 3.6.2.

memory modules are separate independent servers with FCFS discipline, and we denote them by stations $1, 2, \ldots, M$. The closed queueing model of Figure 3.6.3 can be solved by the techniques developed in Section 3.4 if we make the following assumptions:

1. The interval that a CPU is in execution at local store is a random variable with general distribution of mean value $1/\lambda$.

2. Each time a reference to the jth module is generated, it requires τ seconds in the absence of memory contention, and we assume that τ is exponentially distributed with mean $1/\mu$.

3. In the long run a processor references module j with probability e_j, $j = 1, 2, \ldots, M$ and $\sum_{j=1}^{M} e_j = 1$. Note that the memory access pattern need not be assumed to be a first-order Markov chain. In fact the memory module that a processor references will be heavily dependent on those modules it has referenced in the recent past. If M-way interleaving is used, then the reference pattern is highly sequential.

Let C [instructions/sec] represent the total *nominal* processing rate of the central processing station which consists of N_p parallel CPU's. Then each CPU has nominal capacity of C/N_p, where the nominal capacity means the full productivity of a CPU observed when there is no conflict with other processors and there is no idle period incurred due to I/O wait. Let p be the cache *hit ratio*, i.e., the probability that an instruction is found in cache. Then

$$W_{M+1} = \frac{1}{1-p} \text{ [instructions]} \qquad (3.6.1)$$

is the average number of instructions to be executed between two consecutive references to main memory. Thus we have

$$\beta_{M+1}(n) = \frac{(C/N_p)^n}{n!} \qquad (3.6.2)$$

As for stations $1, 2, \ldots, M$, we define their work load directly in terms of service times $1/\mu$. Therefore we set

$$C_j(n_j) = 1 \qquad \text{for all } n_j \geq 1 \text{ and } j = 1, 2, \ldots, M \qquad (3.6.3)$$

which in turn determines

$$\beta_j(n_j) = 1 \qquad \text{for all } n_j \geq 0 \text{ and } j = 1, 2, \ldots, M \qquad (3.6.4)$$

and

$$W_j = \frac{e_j}{\mu}, \qquad j = 1, 2, \ldots, M \qquad (3.6.5)$$

On substituting these model parameters into formula (3.4.4), we obtain the steady-state distribution of $\mathbf{n} = [n_1, n_2, \ldots, n_{M+1}]$:

$$P[\mathbf{n}] = \begin{cases} g^{-1}(N, M+1)\dfrac{(1/\lambda)^{n_{M+1}}}{n_{M+1}!} \displaystyle\sum_{j=1}^{M}\left(\dfrac{e_j}{\mu}\right)^{n_j} & \text{if } \mathbf{n} \in \mathcal{F}(N) \\ 0 & \text{if } \mathbf{n} \notin \mathcal{F}(N) \end{cases} \qquad (3.6.6)$$

where

$$\frac{1}{\lambda} = \frac{W_{M+1}}{(C/N_p)} = \frac{N_p}{(1-p)C} \qquad (3.6.7)$$

is the mean CPU execution time between memory references, and $\mathcal{F}(N)$ is a set of **n** such that

$$n_1 + n_2 + \ldots + n_{M+1} = N \tag{3.6.8}$$

The normalization constant $g(N, M + 1)$ can be computed following the recursive steps discussed in Sections 3.4.2 and 3.4.3, namely

$$g(N, M + 1) = \sum_{k=0}^{N} g(N - k, M)\frac{(1/\lambda)^k}{k!} \tag{3.6.9}$$

and

$$g(n, m) = g(n, m - 1) + \frac{e_m}{\mu} g(n - 1, m), \qquad 0 \le n \le N, 1 \le m \le M \tag{3.6.10}$$

with the boundary conditions

$$g(n, 1) = \left(\frac{e_1}{\mu}\right)^n, \qquad n = 0, 1, \ldots \tag{3.6.11}$$

$$g(n, m) = 0, \qquad n < 0 \tag{3.6.12}$$

If in particular $1/e_j = 1/M$ for $j = 1, 2, \ldots, M$, i.e., all the modules are accessed with equal frequencies in *the long run* (we should emphasize again that this assumption is much less restrictive than assuming branching probabilities $p_{M+1,j} = 1/M, j = 1, 2, \ldots, M$), then the marginal distribution of n_{M+1} (i.e., the number of CPU's executing in local store) is reduced to the following simple form:

$$P_{M+1}(n) = K \cdot \frac{(1/\lambda)^n}{n!} \left(\frac{1}{M\mu}\right)^{N-n}\binom{N - n + M - 1}{M - 1}$$

$$= K^*\binom{N - n + M - 1}{M - 1}\frac{1}{n!}\left(\frac{\mu M}{\lambda}\right)^n \tag{3.6.13}$$

where K^* is the normalization constant

$$K^{*-1} = \sum_{n=0}^{N}\binom{N + M - n - 1}{M - 1}\frac{1}{n!}\left(\frac{\mu M}{\lambda}\right)^n \tag{3.6.14}$$

An appropriate performance index will be the throughput measured in memory references per unit time. This quantity is $\lambda_{M+1}(N)$, defined by (3.4.22):

$$\lambda_{M+1}(N) = \sum_{n=1}^{N} n\lambda P_{M+1}(n) = \lambda E[n_{M+1}] \tag{3.6.15}$$

An alternative expression is from (3.4.23).

$$\lambda_{M+1}(N) = \frac{g(N - 1, M + 1)}{g(N, M + 1)} \tag{3.6.16}$$

Then the effective processing rate of the CPU station is given by

$$C_{\text{CPU}}(N) = \begin{cases} W_{M+1}\lambda_{M+1}(N), & N \le N_p \\ W_{M+1}\lambda_{M+1}(N_p), & N > N_p \end{cases} \tag{3.6.17}$$

where N is now defined as the number of tasks attended by one of the CPU's or waiting in the CPU dispatching queue.

(b) *Software Processor Lockout.* In the operation of the multiple processor system with logically decentralized processor scheduling (as opposed to master/slave scheduling) it is necessary to establish good coordination and communication among processors. When a task becomes blocked due to an operation such as waiting for an I/O completion, the processor may be assigned to some other tasks in ready state. This is called a *suspend* lock since the task is suspended for a while. Consider now a situation where a task enters suspend state, and after saving the status of this task, the processor tries to access the ready list (process scheduling list) and finds that it is locked because the ready list is being used by another processor. In this case the processor must keep "spinning its wheels" until the lock is released. Such a lock is called a spin lock, and we say that the second processor is locked out. The lockout problem is a direct result of multiple processors' attempts to process common data bases asynchronously. This situation resembles the memory interference discussed above except that the resources were hardware (i.e., memory modules), whereas a lockout is due to contention for software resources. There are many such shared data bases besides the ready list, e.g., the memory allocation table, the page allocation table, the I/O list, etc.

The effect of software lockout upon system performance can be analyzed using the same type of model we used for memory interference analysis. The queueing diagram is given in Figure 3.6.4 in which customers are active N CPU's, the N servers

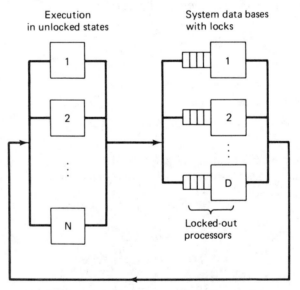

Figure 3.6.4. A software processor lockout model.

on the left side represent users' programs or system's reentrant programs, and the D servers on the right side are D different data bases with separate spin locks.

To analyze the model of Figure 3.6.4 we make the following assumptions:

1. The processing rate of the CPU is given by $C_{CPU}(N)$, obtained above [equation (3.6.17)], where N is the number of active CPU's. Thus the effective rate of a processor is $C_{CPU}(N)/N$.

2. A processor in data base d ($1 \leq d \leq D$) runs in the locked state, executing the number of instructions determined by exponential distribution (geometric distribution, to be precise) of mean W_d [instructions].

3. The number of instructions during which a task is being executed in unlocked state is a random variable with arbitrary distribution of mean W_{D+1} [instructions].

4. The access frequencies to different data bases with locks are given the long-run distribution $\{e_d\}$, where $\sum_{d=1}^{D} e_d = 1$.

Based on these parameters specifications in the closed network with $D + 1$ stations, the effect of lockouts can be analyzed just as we did for the analysis of memory interference.

3.6.3. A Multiprogrammed Virtual Storage System Model

Many contemporary computer systems provide each programmer with a virtual address space, which is much greater than the main memory space actually available to him. This is done by means of a dynamic address translation mechanism called *paging*. Figure 3.6.5 depicts a queueing model of such a virtual storage system operating under multiprogramming. The number, $N(t)$, of tasks multiprogrammed at given time t is a variable controlled by the job scheduler. But the rate of change in $N(t)$ is usually much slower compared with activities such as paging I/O's and file I/O's; thus we can apply the steady-state analysis with $N(t) = N$ being fixed, as discussed in Section 3.6.1. Thus the system with level of multiprogramming N can be represented as a closed network with N customers. The queueing network consists of $M = p + f + 1$ independent service stations out of which p stations are paging stores (usually drums), f stations are file stores (usually disks), and the Mth station is the central processor station, which consists of N_p multiple CPU's.

The total nominal productivity of the CPU station of this model is specified by the curve $C_{CPU}(n)$ of Figure 3.6.6, which reflects the number of processors N_p, the degradation factors due to memory interference, and software lockout. Thus the curve $C_{CPU}(n)$, $n \leq N_p$, is essentially the one we derived in the previous section when the active number of processors is n.

When a process either issues a file I/O request or creates a page fault, it will release its processor to another ready process and wait for completion of I/O transactions. The page fault rate is *not* a quantity entirely intrinsic to that program. It also depends on memory management policies, such as

1.   How many pages of memory are allocated to the program.

2.   What policy is adopted to determine which of the program's pages reside in main memory.

The number of instructions $\{L_i\}$ that a task executes between the ith page fault and the $(i + 1)$st page fault is a random sequence which depends on memory

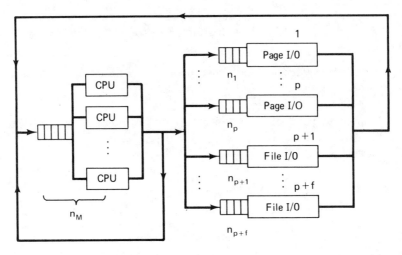

$$N = n_1 + \ldots + n_p + n_{p+1} + \ldots + n_{p+f} + n_M$$

Figure 3.6.5.   A multiprogrammed virtual storage system model.

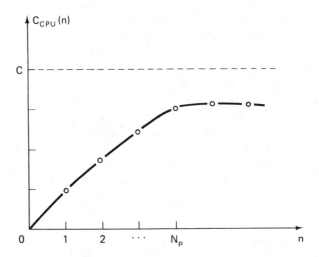

Figure 3.6.6.   The processing rate of CPU (the Mth station) in Fig. 3.6.5.

space $\{S_i\}$ [pages] allocated at that moment and the specific page replacement algorithm employed. The statistical characterization of $\{L_i\}$ is a key issue in the understanding of the dynamic behavior of memory management policy.

As a first-order approximation model we shall characterize the program behavior and memory management in terms of the average, $\bar{L}$, as a function of $\bar{S}$, the average memory space allocated to the program. A typical curve of $\bar{L}$ vs. $\bar{S}$ is shown in Figure 3.6.7. When we scale $\bar{L}$ by processing rate, the curve $\bar{L}$ [in seconds] vs. $\bar{S}$ is sometimes called the lifetime function, and its inverse, i.e., $\bar{L}^{-1}$ vs. $\bar{S}$, is called the parachor curve. For detailed discussions of these curves, see, e.g., Madnick and Donovan (1974) and Denning and Graham (1975).

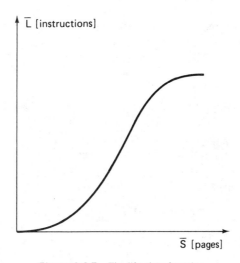

Figure 3.6.7.   The life-time function.

When one attempts to apply formula (3.4.4) to the model of Figure 3.6.5 one must be careful in specifying the model parameters. Let W_{CPU} be the average number of instructions in a page. Then the total number of page faults experienced in running the program will be, on the average, $W_{\text{CPU}}/\bar{L}$. Let f_i be the proportion of page requests that go to device i, $1 \leq i \leq p$. Then the average number of page faults that a program generates to paging device i during the program's entire life in the system is

$$W_i = f_i \frac{W_{\text{CPU}}}{\bar{L}} \qquad 1 \leq i \leq p \qquad (3.6.18)$$

The number of total file I/O requests is, on the other hand, independent of operating system components and thus can be viewed as an intrinsic component of the program's work load. Thus let

$W_j = $ total number of file I/O requests made to I/O station j, $\qquad p+1 \leq j \leq p+f$
$$(3.6.19)$$

Experimental studies by Bard (1975), Anderson et al. (1975), and others have shown that the CPU overhead consumed by the page fault handling routine is a rather significant portion of CPU busy time. Therefore it is important to incorporate this overhead factor explicitly. Let W_{pf} be the number of instructions of the page fault handler; then the total number of instructions that a program creates is

$$W'_{\text{CPU}} = W_{\text{CPU}} + \frac{W_{\text{CPU}}}{L} \cdot W_{pf} = W_{\text{CPU}}\left(1 + \frac{W_{pf}}{L}\right) \tag{3.6.20}$$

With these paremeter specifications, we obtain from (3.4.4) the following expression for the joint queue size $\mathbf{n} = [n_1, n_2, \ldots, n_{p+f}, n_M]$, where n_M is the number of tasks in the CPU station:

$$P[\mathbf{n}] = g^{-1}(N, M)\beta_{\text{CPU}}(n_M)W'^{n_M}_{\text{CPU}}\prod_{i=1}^{p}\left(\frac{W_i\bar{\tau}_p}{L}\right)^{n_i}\prod_{j=1}^{p+f}(W_j\bar{\tau}_f)^{n_j} \tag{3.6.21}$$

where τ_p is the time required to access a required page on the drum and load it into main memory and $\bar{\tau}_p$ is its average. Here we assume that τ_p is exponentially distributed. (A more elaborate model will allow dependency of $\bar{\tau}_p$ on the individual queue length n_i at the paging devices.) Similarly, $\bar{\tau}_f$ is the average time required to handle a file I/O request.

By applying the computational algorithm of Sections 3.4.2 and 3.4.3, we can obtain the throughput of the CPU station according to formulas (3.4.22) and (3.4.23). This quantity, however, is expressed in terms of the number of I/O requests including both types. This is clearly not an appropriate measure of system productivity. We should compute, instead, the following effective productivity of this multiprogrammed system running at the level N:

$$C_{MP}(N) = \sum_{n=1}^{N} C_{\text{CPU}}(n)p_{\text{CPU}}(n) \tag{3.6.22}$$

where $p_{\text{CPU}}(\cdot)$ is equivalent to the marginal distribution $p_M(\cdot)$ of (3.4.21). Figure 3.6.8

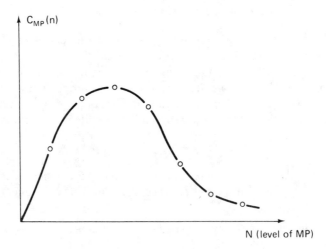

Figure 3.6.8. Effective throughput of a multiprogrammed system as a function of the level of multiprogramming.

illustrates a typical curve of $C_{MP}(N)$ vs. N. As the level of multiprogramming increases, initially the CPU productivity also increases because more and more CPU's are active simultaneously and because overlap between CPU execution and file I/O operations becomes pronounced. However, as N increases further the memory space available to an individual program becomes smaller and smaller; thus the page fault rate tends to rise sharply, as can be predicted from the curve of Figure 3.6.7.

Then it will create a situation in which the CPU's are busy primarily handling paging activities and very little useful work is done. [In equation (3.6.20), W_{CPU} is useful work, whereas $W'_{\text{CPU}} - W_{\text{CPU}}$ is the overhead work.] Such an undesirable phenomenon of excessive paging activities is often called *thrashing* [see Coffman and Denning (1973) and Denning and Graham (1975)]. Once thrashing becomes pronounced due to an increase in N (or poor memory management policy), productivity of the processors deteriorates sharply, as depicted in Figure 3.6.8. Thus it is important that the job scheduler control the system congestion by maintaining appropriate levels of multiprogramming. This problem will be discussed in the next section.

3.6.4. An Interactive Time-Shared System Model

In the Section 3.1 we discussed a time-shared system model which is basically a machine-repairman model with exponential service distributions. In this section, we shall be able to extend the model based on results of Section 3.4 and also discuss how to incorporate the multiprogramming model of the preceding section into this macrolevel model.

A system diagram of an interactive time-shared system is depicted in Figure 3.6.9, in which the multiprogramming system is essentially the part we just analyzed. Let there be N_T logged-on terminals, each of which spends, on the average, T_U seconds

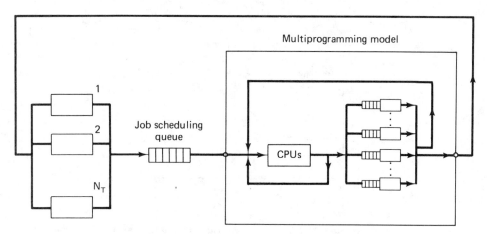

Figure 3.6.9. A multiprogrammed time-sharing system model.

to generate a new transaction. Here T_U is called user terminal time (which consists of think time, input time, and output time). Assume that there are n outstanding transactions in the system (either in the multiprogrammed mix or in the job scheduling queue).

Since each of the n terminals is *blocked* until the outstanding transaction is completed, only $N_T - n$ terminals are able to generate new transactions in the next short interval. Let W_{CPU} be the average total number of instructions in a transaction. Then the inflow rate of work load into the multiprogramming system is given by $[(N_T - n)W_{CPU}]/T_U$ [instructions/sec], whereas the outflow from the system is $C_{MP}(n)$ [instructions/sec], obtained in the previous section. Figure 3.6.10(a) illustrates a crude but simple graphical method for finding an operating point in equilibrium state. In this figure the *uncontrolled* $C_{MP}(n)$ is the one given in Figure 3.6.8, whereas the *controlled* $C_{MP}(n)$ represents the throughput obtained when the job scheduler controls the level of multiprogramming not to exceed the critical value N_c. In the case of the uncontrolled system, there are three possible operating points; A, B, and C. It is not difficult to see that B is an unstable point, whereas A and C represent stable points. Certainly C is an undesirable point, since throughput is virtually zero. Even if the system is initially operating at point A, there is always nonzero probability of moving

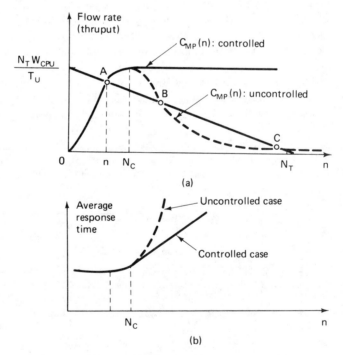

Figure 3.6.10. An approximate analysis of (a) throughput, and (b) average response time of the model of Fig. 3.6.9.

into point C, when some clustered arrivals take place and/or jobs in service at that moment have extraordinarily long execution times. The controlled scheme, on the other hand, guarantees that the system always operates around the desirable stable point A, even when N_T further increases. An approximate estimate of the response time is obtained based on the formula

$$T_R = \frac{n}{C_{MP}(n)} \tag{3.6.23}$$

and is plotted in Figure 3.6.10(b). As can be seen, the optimal point for the fastest response is not the same as that for the highest throughput, although in this region both throughput and response time are not so sensitive to the change in n.

These graphical estimates, however, tend to underestimate the average queue size (n) and the response time (T_R), since the fluctuation or variation of interarrival times and/or service times is completely ignored in this type of crude analysis. The only quantity used in the graph is the mean time and its inverse, i.e., flow rate averaged over a long term. This approximation technique based only on the *first moment* is known as *fluid approximation* in queueing theory [see Newell (1971)], and its application to similar or related problems is discussed by Courtois (1975), Kleinrock and Lam (1975), and Kobayashi et al. (1977). Note that the diffusion approximation discussed in Section 3.5.2 utilizes both the first and second moments of interarrival and service times. Thus a more informative result will generally be obtained. For example, instead of the single point A, its distribution is obtainable.

For more accurate and quantitative analysis of the model of Figure 3.6.9 we use the results of Section 3.4. In a time-sharing system the round-robin scheduling or its variant based on the *time-slicing* technique is commonly used. Its motive is to give preferential treatment to shorter jobs by preventing larger jobs from holding CPU's for an excessive number of periods. It has been analyzed and empirically verified by Baskett (1971) and others that if the time slice is chosen close to the total processing time of trivial jobs, the model of processor sharing discussed in Section 3.3 is a satisfactory approximation for the round-robin algorithm. Each time the slice ends, the memory space that has been allocated to that task should be deallocated. Conversely, when its turn comes up, an appropriate set of pages (often called a *working set*) of the program must be loaded into main memory. These swap-out and swap-in operations consume additional CPU and I/O time. By estimating the average number of swappings per transaction life period, this additional work load should be included in the parameters used in the analysis of (3.6.21).

One of the main properties of processor sharing discussed in Sections 3.3 and 3.4 was that the simple product form solution for the queue size distribution holds for an arbitrary service distribution. The only parameter that appears in the final result is its mean value. Similarly, our earlier result shows that the set of parallel terminals is mathematieally equivalent to a single station with infinitely many servers. Furthermore, the results of Sections 3.3 and 3.4 suggest that the user terminal time T_U can also be arbitrarily distributed. We can even assume that different terminals have different distributions and different service distributions in their transactions. This generalization is possible because of the results discussed in Sections 3.3 and 3.4 concerning different classes of jobs.

Thus the time-shared system model of Figure 3.6.9 is now expressed simply in terms of a closed network with two service stations; one is IS (infinite servers), which represents N_T terminals, and the other is a PS (processor-shared) server, which is a mathematical idealization of the multiprogramming system with time slicing. Note that the service rate of the PS station is equal to $C_{MP}(n)$ obtained earlier, and therefore we define $\beta_{PS}(n)$ by

$$\beta_{PS}(n) = \prod_{i=1}^{n} \frac{i}{C_{MP}(i)} \tag{3.6.24}$$

Then the probability that there are n transactions in the PS station is

$$P(n) = \begin{cases} g^{-1}(N_T, 2)\beta_{PS}(n)W_{CPU}^n \cdot \dfrac{T_U^{N_T-n}}{(N_T - n)!}, & 0 \le n \le N_T \\ 0, & \text{elsewhere} \end{cases} \tag{3.6.25}$$

The normalization constant $g(N_T, 2)$ is simply obtained by setting $N = N_T$ in the formula

$$g(N, 2) = \sum_{k=0}^{N} \frac{T_n^{n-k}}{(N - k)!} \beta_{PS}(k)W_{CPU}^k \tag{3.6.26}$$

and the system throughput (i.e., the number of transactions handled by the time-shared system) is

$$\lambda_{ps}(N_T) = \frac{g(N_T - 1, 2)}{g(N_T, 2)} \tag{3.6.27}$$

The other quantities such as utilization, the average response time, the average queue length, etc., are all immediately derivable from (3.6.25)–(3.6.27).

3.7.   CONCLUDING REMARKS

In this chapter we highlighted recent advances in queueing network models. Generalized model assumptions and the computational algorithms now available to us allow one to model complex systems much more realistically and economically than before. Since most of analytic results discussed in this chapter are very recent accomplishments, examples of applications and model validations are rather scanty at the time of this writing. In view of several successful case studies discussed in Section 3.1, however, it is reasonable to believe that we shall see within the next few years an increasing number of practical applications of these analytic models. It is the author's hope that this chapter will serve as a guide to those who make special endeavors toward such goals.

CHAPTER 4

QUEUEING NETWORK MODELS:
METHODS OF SOLUTION
AND THEIR
PROGRAM IMPLEMENTATION

M. REISER AND C. H. SAUER*

IBM Thomas J. Watson Research Center
Yorktown Heights, New York

Abstract

We present a class of parameterized queueing networks which are rich enough in systems and work-load features to allow meaningful modeling of many computer/ communications systems. Methods of solution for this class of networks are discussed. These methods encompass simulation, approximate analytic solution, and exact solutions for the restricted class of separable networks. The convolution algorithm for separable networks is highlighted. Finally we discuss the design and implementation of queueing network software, which embodies the three methods of solution. It is the goal of such a program package to facilitate tybrid analytic/simulation models and to improve modeling productivity. An actual system, RESQ (research queueing analyzer) is described.

4.1. INTRODUCTION

The ever-increasing complexity of contemporary computing systems requires that more attention be paid to performance. Queueing network models have proven to be one promising approach toward a quantitative theory of performance. There are two problem areas to be distinguished, namely,

- How to map system and work-load features into a queueing network.
- How to solve queueing network problems.

*Current address: Department of Computer Sciences, The University of Texas at Austin.

The first area is called *modeling*; the second one deals with suitable *methods of solution*. The modeling question is least well understood. On the one end, we find extremely simplified analytical models; on the other end, we see the designers resorting to costly, highly imitative simulations. We believe that there is an intermediate level of abstraction in modeling which yields sufficient accuracy for many performance questions. It is our object in this chapter to describe a program package, called RESQ (research queuieng analyzer), which provides the modeler with efficient methods of solution for a spectrum of queueing models of varying complexity, ranging form analytically tractable separable networks to rather general stochastic models. The chapter is organized as follows:

- In Section 4.2, we shall introduce a general class of queueing network models which is rich in systems and work-load features but which still allows a relatively simple parameterized definition.

- In Section 4.3, we shall discuss methods of solution. These methods encompass the algebraic solution of balance equations, the approximate analytic solution, and simulation. Since the last two methods are dealt with elsewhere in this volume, we shall highlight the numerical methods for separable queueing networks.

- In Section 4.4, finally, we shall discuss the design of software which implements the various methods of solution. Some typical examples are also given.

We shall present the material on an introductory level. In particular in Section 4.3, we shall omit the technicalities of proofs which were given elsewhere [Reiser(1976b)]. It is, however, our goal to give enough detail to enable the reader to create his own queueing network software.

The structure of RESQ is given in Figure 4.1.1. RESQ should encourage the modeler to combine the various methods of solution to construct hybrid analytic/ simulation models. We see three ways in which the two methods of solution can support each other, namely,

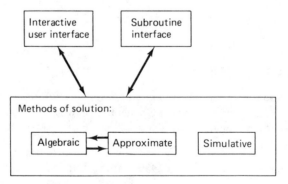

Figure 4.1.1. Functional structure of RESQ (research queueing analyzer).

- A simple analytic model can support a more detailed simulation model of the same system. The analytic model is used to narrow down the range of parameters and to reduce the necessary number of simulation runs.

- A simulation model can support an analytic model in the sense that the sensitivity of the analytic model with respect to unjustified assumptions can be investigated (we call this an internal validation to distinguish it from validating the model against the real system).

- One or more subsystems are modeled and solved separately by an analytic method. Then they are included in a global simulation model by means of substitute queues with queue-dependent rates (see the schematic diagram of Figure 4.1.2). This method is sometimes called hierarchical modeling [some practical examples are found in Browne et al. (1975) and Sauer and Woo (1977)].

- Analytic models may be used on a gross level, while simulation models may resolve more details.

The hierarchical decomposition has also been applied to systems which have no tractable analytic solution but whose components α and $\mathcal{S}$ both have such an analytic

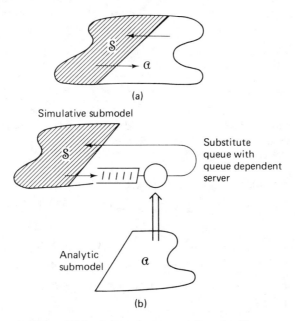

(a)

Simulative submodel

Substitute queue with queue dependent server

Analytic submodel

(b)

Figure 4.1.2. Schematic representation of a hierarchical analytic/simulation model. (a) System consisting of parts $\mathcal{S}$ and α; (b) the analytic model subsystem α is used to determine the rate function of the substitute queue, which represents the subsystem α in the simulation model $\mathcal{S}$.

solution. The iterative approximate analytic solution of Chandy et al. (1975b) (which is also provided in RESQ) is based on such a decomposition. The hierarchical decomposition has been found to be exact for separable networks; see Chandy et al. (1975b). In general, however, it can only be expected to be an approximation. Intuitively, one expects the hierarchical decomposition of Figure 4.1.2 to be most accurate when the time constants of system α are much smaller than those of subsystem $\mathcal{S}$ [some progress toward formalyzing this notion has been made recently by Courtouis (1975b) and Reiser and Konheim (1976)]. Note that it is precisely in this good case where the most can be gained from the hybrid analytic/simulation model.

4.2. A CLASS OF QUEUEING NETWORKS

Stochastic models may be characterized in order of decreasing complexity as follows:

1. General stochastic models driven by dependent processes and controlled by a centralized algorithm which has access to the full system state at all times.

2. Stochastic models structured as a network of locally scheduled queues and driven by renewal processes. The flow of jobs is governed by a sequence of decisions made upon service completion at one of the queues.

3. Network of queues restricted to simplify the mathematical solution (separable queueing networks).

We shall subsequently define a class of stochastic models, Q, say, which is of the second type. It is our goal to define Q such that it allows a simple parameterized definition (see Section 4.4.1) yet provides enough systems and work-load features to allow meaningful application to many computer system and communication network problems.

A queueing network in Q consists of

· Active resources which provide service for which jobs have to queue.

· Passive resources which regulate the population in subnetworks.

· A population of jobs which place a load on the resources.

· A routing rule which governs the flow of jobs through the network. The routing may make use of job attributes and of the system state.

· Sources, fission gates, and split gates which generate jobs.

· Sinks and fusion gates which destroy jobs.

4.2.1. Resources

An *active resource* (we also use the term active queue) is composed of a waiting room, a set of servers, and a queue discipline, which is a rule governing how jobs are to receive service. The waiting room may be divided into a set of individual local waiting rooms each of which holds jobs of a particular class. For brevity, shall term these individual waiting rooms simply classes. The class concept is used in the routing, in the generation of work load, and for scheduling. In particular, we assume the following service mechanism:

1. Jobs arrive and join waiting rooms corresponding to one of the local classes.

2. Upon arrival, the job places a work demand on the queue. The work demand is generated by a stochastic process which we assume to be a renewal process. Each local class may have its own work demand distribution (WDD) from which successive work demands are sampled. We require the mean and the standard deviation of the WDD to be finite.

3. Servers provide work with a given work rate (or service rate). Jobs stay at the queue until all work is done, and then they depart instantly. The way jobs are served is governed by the queue discipline. The queue discipline may make use of the local classes (e.g., as priority classes) and may subdivide the work into various slices (e.g., round-robin queue discipline). It may also imply an ordering on the jobs (e.g., order of arrival). The work rate of the servers may depend on congestion (queue-dependent rate).

4. Noninterruptable overhead periods may occur before service begins. The amount of overhead activity performed is defined in the same manner as the work demand. The overhead mechanism may depend on the queue discipline (e.g., setup overhead, priority switching overhead, polling overhead, etc.).

A schematic diagram of an active resource is given in Figure 4.2.1. We shall use open buckets to denote waiting lines and circles for the servers.

Note that our definition of the class concept differs from the one used by Baskett et al. (1975) and in Chapters 2 and 3. We define a job to be of a certain class only with respect to an active resource. The same job may be of class j at resource m and later of class i at resource n. This class concept is local to resources as compared with the global class concept where a job keeps its class distinction over possibly several

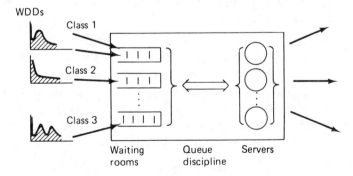

Figure 4.2.1. Schematic representation of an active resource.

resources. The advantage of the local class concept is the minimization of job attributes and a simplification of the routing description. This will become apparent in Section 4.2.3 where we introduce the arrow notation, which is well suited for a concise inter- active network definition (see also Sections 4.4.1 and 4.4.4). It is important, however, to realize that both class concepts are of exactly the same generality.

In most of the queueing literature, job completion rates (rather than work rates) or service times are used to describe the service mechanism. We feel, however, that work rate and work demands simplify the treatment of queue-dependent servers and queue disciplines such as processor sharing. They are also somewhat closer to the language of the systems engineer, who tends to think in terms of MIPS rates or byte transfer rates and path lengths or record sizes. Clearly, if the work rate, μ, say, is a constant, service times and work demands are simply related by

$$\tau = \mu w \tag{4.2.1}$$

where τ denotes the service time and w the work demand.

The main purpose of a *passive resource* is to regulate (and limit) the population in subsystems. The passive resource consists of

- A pool of tokens,
- A set of allocate gates with associated waiting rooms, and
- A set of release gates.

The following mechanism governs passive resources:

1. A job which passes through an allocate gate requests a certain number of tokens from the pool associated with the gate. This number may be a constant or a random variable.

2. If there is a sufficient number of tokens in the pool, the request is satisfied. The job holds the tokens and proceeds according to its routing. The amount of tokens in the pool is decremented by the number requested. The allocation of tokens is an instantaneous process.

3. If there are not enough tokens to satisfy the request, the job waits in the allo- cate gate's waiting room.

4. Jobs which proceed through a release gate return their tokens to the associ- ated pool. Jobs not holding tokens pass through the gate unaffected. In any event, jobs are not delayed by the release gate.

5. If jobs are waiting, one or several of them may be able to satisfy their request and to proceed on their routing. The order in which requests are granted and the manner in which released tokens are distributed among the allocate gates are determined by the passive resource's queue discipline.

A passive resource is shown schematically in Figure 4.2.2. We shall use triangles for allocate and release gates and rectangles for the pool of tokens. Broken lines indicate the flow of tokens.

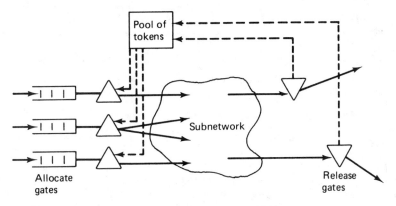

Figure 4.2.2. Passive resource with gates.

Figure 4.2.3 gives an example of the use of a passive resource to limit the population in a certain subsystem.

Besides the allocate and release gates, it is sometimes desirable to have other types of gates associated with the passive resource, such as the create gate and its counterpart, the destroy gate. These gates allow the number of tokens to fluctuate (see Example 2, Section 4.4.1).

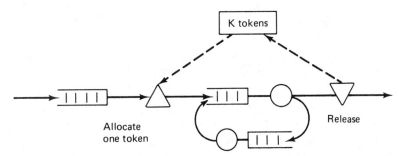

Figure 4.2.3. Use a passive resource to limit the population in the waiting rooms of the two queues to at most *K*. One token is allocated at the gate.

4.2.2. Job Attributes, Job Creation, and Job Deletion

The population in Q may be fixed (closed network) or variable (open networks). A job has the following attributes:

- A job variable (JV) whose value may be set or changed by set gates,
- A set of tokens (may be empty), and
- A tag which identifies whether the fob is a member of a set generated by splitting a job into several copies.

The job variable may be used by the routing rule (possibly also by the service mechanisms of active resources). If the job passes a *set gate*, the following may happen:

- A constant is assigned to the JV.

- A sample value of a random variable is assigned to the JV (the distribution of this random variable is an attribute of the set gate).

- The JV is incremented/decremented by a constant.

- The JV is assigned the name of the waiting room, which the job just left (i.e., the class number).

Set gates are represented by squares in future queueing diagrams.

There are three ways in which jobs can be generated, namely by sources, fission gates, and split gates. In analogy to their creation, jobs may be destroyed by sinks or fusion gates, respectively.

A *source* generates jobs according to a renewal process which is specified by the interarrival time distribution. We assume that a source produces only single jobs (note that batch arrivals may be obtained by means of a split gate; see Figure 4.4.2). Upon creation, the job variable is set to zero. Jobs entering a *sink* leave the network (they may be considered destroyed). Upon leaving, all tokens are returned. A network with the symbols used for sources and sinks is portrayed in Figure 4.2.4.

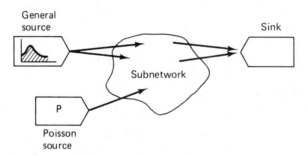

Figure 4.2.4. A network with sources and sinks.

Fission gates, *split gates*, and *fusion gates* are a means to spawn subjobs and to reunite copies thus created. The following rules govern fission gates and fusion gates:

1. The job entering a fission gate is split into a given number of copies. The job which entered the gate is called parent job; the copies are called offsprings.

2. The parent job keeps tokens and JV value; offsprings have no tokens, and their JV value is set to zero.

3. Parent job and offsprings may leave the gate along different paths. The order in which they leave is left undefined.

4. The union gate provides a waiting room. Any job which passed a fission gate (parent and offsprings) waits at the gate until all jobs generated at the same

time have arrived. Then the copies units. The fused job possesses the characteristics of the parent job. Tokens held by offsprings are released to their
respective pools. Jobs not created by a fission gate pass the union gate
unaffected.

The split gate is similar to the fission gate with the exception that jobs leaving the
split gate are not tagged as relatives. The parent job keeps tokens and the job variable;
offsprings hold no tokens, and their job variables are set to zero. Once generated, jobs
originating from a split gate are indistinguishable from regular jobs. In particular, they
pass a fusion gate unaffected. The symbols used for fission, fusion, and split gates are
given in Figure 4.2.5.

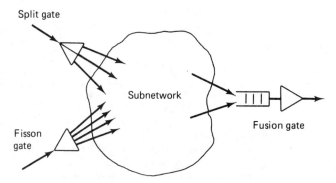

Figure 4.2.5. Split, fission, and fusion gates.

4.2.3. Routing

The routing is a rule describing how jobs proceed through the network. It is convenient to view the routing as a sequence of routing decisions made upon job completion or upon passage through a gate. The structure imposed by the routing on Q may
be visualized by a directed graph. Nodes of this graph may represent sources/sinks,
gates, or local classes. Alternatively, they may serve the sole purpose of being points of
division or points of confluence of routing transitions. Nodes are connected by edges
if a routing transition between these nodes is feasible. The routing may define equivalence classes of nodes such that any two nodes within a class may be connected by a
sequence of routing transitions but no two nodes in different classes can be connected
that way. We call such equivalence classes *routing chains* (or simply chains); Figure
4.2.6 shows a network with two chains. Chain 1 consists of the job classes 1 and 3 and
contains a source (node 7) and a sink (node 8). Chain 2 contains the job classes 2, 4, 5,
and 6. The dashed rectangles indicate how job classes are grouped into active resources
(or queues). The first queue, for example, contains classes 1 and 2. A chain is either
open (i.e., has sources and sinks) or closed (i.e., has a fixed set of jobs circulating
indefinitely). Open and closed chains may coexist in a network. See Figure 4.2.6 for an
example of such a mixed network.

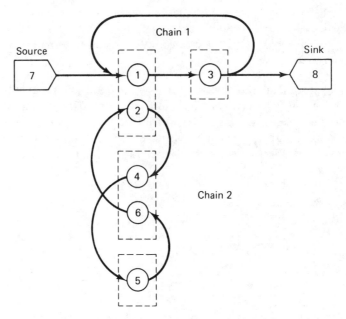

Figure 4.2.6. A network in $\mathbb{Q}$ with two chains. The dashed lines delineate active resources. Note that the two chains are coupled through an active resource (otherwise the network would separate into two in-dedependent networks).

If a node, i, say, has more than one successor node, a job leaving i must make a decision where to go next. This decision is dictated by the routing. It may be based on

•   A random selection (stochastic or probabilistic routing),

•   The value of a predicate on the job characteristic or on network states, or

•   On a combination of both.

To state the routing of a network in $\mathbb{Q}$ consisely, we introduce the following notation:

$$i \rightarrow j_1, j_2, \ldots, j_n; \, \mathcal{P}_1, \mathcal{P}_2, \ldots, \mathcal{P}_m \quad else \quad p_{m+1}, p_{m+2}, \ldots, p_n \qquad (4.2.2)$$

where $\{j_1, j_2, \ldots, j_n\}$ are successor nodes of a given node i, $\{\mathcal{P}_1, \mathcal{P}_2, \ldots, \mathcal{P}_m\}$ are predicates, and $\{p_{m+1}, \ldots, p_n\}$ are real numbers denoting probabilities. In (4.2.2) it is not required that the sets $\{j_1, j_2, \ldots, j_m\}$ and $\{j_{m+1}, j_{m+2}, \ldots, j_n\}$ be mutually exclusive. It suffices that all successor nodes of i appear at least once in $\{j_1, j_2, \ldots, j_n\}$. The routing rule (4.2.2) has the following interpretation:

1.   The predicates $\mathcal{P}_k$ are evaluated in order of increasing indices $k = 1, 2, \ldots, m$. Let $\mathcal{P}_l$ denote the first predicate whose value is "true." Then the job joins node j_l.

2. If all predicates have the value "false," then a random choice is made among nodes $\{j_{m+1}, j_{m+2}, \ldots, j_n\}$ with probabilities $\{p_{m+1}, p_{m+2}, \ldots, p_n\}$.

Any predicate on the state of the network can be admitted. The following are some possibilities:

- Tests on job attributes such as JV = 5, JV ≠ 5, JV > 5, or RJ (related job) which is true if the job has been created by a fission gate (~RJ denotes the negation of RJ).

- Tests on the status of passive resources. Examples of such predicates are TA for "token available" and its negation ~TA. Clearly, the successor node corresponding to a TA predicate must be an allocate gate.

- Tests on queue lengths such as the predicate SQ, which is true if the corresponding queue size is the shortest one among all the successor nodes of the root node i.

It is possible that probabilities are missing in (4.2.2). In this case, we simply write

$$i \longrightarrow j_1, j_2, \ldots, j_n; \; \mathcal{P}_1, \mathcal{P}_2, \ldots, \mathcal{P}_n \qquad (4.2.3)$$

It is required in this case that $\mathcal{P}_1 \vee \mathcal{P}_2 \vee \ldots \vee \mathcal{P}_n \equiv true$. Similarly, predicates may be absent, in which case (4.2.2) specializes to

$$i \longrightarrow j_1, j_2, \ldots, j_n; \; p_1, p_2, \ldots, p_n \qquad (4.2.4)$$

The form (4.2.4) is the familiar stochastic or probabilistic routing rule. If node i has just one successor node so that the transition is taken with certainty, we may omit the probability; i.e., we may write

$$i \longrightarrow j \qquad (4.2.5)$$

instead of the more cumbersome $i \longrightarrow j; 1.0$.

The routing of an entire network is specified by a set of statements of the form (4.2.2) to (4.2.5). Each feasible transition $i \longrightarrow j$ must be described at least once.

A network in Q which possesses a unique steady-state solution is called stable or well defined. Stability imposes a condition on the structure and on the parameters. An obvious requirement for well definition is

$$\sum_{j=1}^{M} p_{ij} = 1 \qquad \text{for all } i = 1, 2, \ldots, M \qquad (4.2.6)$$

where p_{ij} is the probability of a job joining node i after service completion of node i.

More material on well-defined and on ill-defined networks is given in Section 4.2.4. Examples of ill-defined networks are shown in Figures 4.2.7 and 4.2.8.

4.2.4. Ill-Defined Networks

Having defined such a rich class of queueing networks, we must be aware that we have allowed networks which do not attain equilibrium or which have complex transient behavior before reaching equilibrium or have several mutually exclusive equilibrium conditions. We shall not give a formal characterization of well-defined networks but shall discuss only some examples of ill-defined networks. The problems within our examples will be readily apparent. However, similar problems can exist in complex networks without such a transparency.

A simple example of a queueing system which does not attain equilibrium is a single server queue with external arrivals and with work intensity (or traffic intensity) greater than 1. Similarly, a network with such a queue would be unstable. In general, stability can be relatively easily determined in a network consisting of active resources alone. The situation is much more difficult, however, in a network with passive resources resulting in blocking effects. Some interesting stability tests for special systems with blocking are found in Reiser and Konheim (1976) and Lavenberg (1975b), but in general, a full solution is required to establish stability.

In addition to reducing the work capacity of active resources of a network, contention for passive resources can cause deadlocks ("deadly embraces"). Deadlocks have been the subject of much study, and we shall not discuss them in detail here (see chapter 8 of this volume). Figure 4.2.7 shows a system which may become deadlocked. The problem is that two jobs may request the same two resources in different order. If there is only one token in each of the passive resources, then it is possible for each job to hold one of the resources and wait (forever) for the other one.

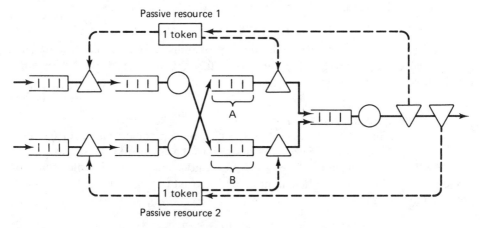

Figure 4.2.7. A queueing network with deadlock. The pools of both passive resources contain only one token. An example of a deadlock state is: one job in waiting line *A* and another one in waiting line *B*. Neither job can move.

Fission and fusion gates also introduce possible contentions leading to deadlock. Figure 4.2.8 illustrates such a possibility. If there is only one unit of the passive resource (i.e., only one token in the pool), then one job may wait at the allocate gate for the resource while another job waits at the fusion gate before releasing the resource. (Note also that if the number of units of a resource may fluctuate due to create and destroy gates, then it is even harder to determine whether deadlocks will occur.)

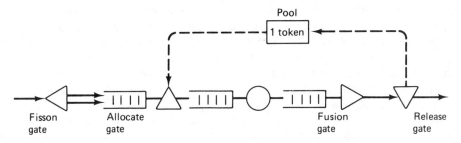

Figure 4.2.8. Potential deadlock with fission/fusion gates. The pool consists of one token.

These examples show certain deadlocks in isolation; there may be several such situations in a given network. The deadlocks may be partial in that other customers can proceed through other parts of the network, unaffected by the deadlocks. Thus several equilibrium conditions may be possible, depending on which one of the partial deadlcks occurs.

4.3. METHODS OF SOLUTION

If we restrict the work demand distributions and interarrival time distributions to those distributions which can be represented by a network of exponential stages [Cox (1955)], then the class of networks, Q, introduced in Section 4.2 is part of the class of *Markovian queueing networks* (also sometimes called memoryless queueing networks). The steady-state joint queue size distribution of Markovian networks is determined by a set of linear equations, called balance equations. It may seem that this problem formulation is well suited for a numerical evaluation by means of computers. Unfortunately, however, the state space is either infinite or grows combinatorially with the size of the problem. For all but the most simple models a numerical solution of the balance equations becomes impractical. Some works on the assemblage of the balance equations (which is in itself a nontrivial problem) and on their solution by iterative methods is found in Wallace (1972), Wallace and Rosenberg (1966), and Herzog et al. (1975). We think that considerable progress can still be made in this area and that one can expect that problems with up to 50,000 states will become tractable. Yet presently, a numerical solution of the balance equations is not a practical method for a solution package designed for general topology networks.

The following alternatives remain:

- To restrict the class of queueing networks to $Q^* \subset Q$, say, such that in Q^* the need for a numerical solution of the balance equations does not arise,

- To try to approximate the original problem by solutions which are in Q^*, possibly aided by a numerical evaluation of certain reduced systems of balance equations [Chandy et al. (1975b)], and

- To solve a network in Q by execution on a simulation processor.

It is our primary purpose in this section to discuss in some detail the first method. Approximation methods such as the diffusion approximation approach "Kobayashi (1974a, 1974b) and Reiser and Kobayashi (1974a)] or the forced decomposition approach [Chandy et al. (1975b)] are still somewhat controversial since general theoretical foundations are not fully established. A discussion of approximation methods is found in Chapter 3 and need not be repeated here. Similarly important recent progress in the simulative method of solution (regeneration point method) is dealt with in great detail in Chapter 2 of this volume. We shall discuss some practical aspects of the regeneration point method in Section 4.3.13.

4.3.1. Separable Queueing Networks

We define a subset Q^* of Q as follows:

- No passive resources,
- Active resources restricted to the cases of Table 4.3.1,
- Poisson sources only, no fission and fusion gates,
- Routing predicates limited to tests on the job variable. If the sample value of a random variable is assigned to the JV, the distribution of this random variable must be a mixture of geometric distributions (i.e., must have a rational z-transform).

Table 4.3.1   Types of Active Resources in Q^*
(note that possible overhead activity must be included in the work demand distribution)

Type Code	No. of Servers	Queue Discipline	Work Demand Distribution
LCFSPR	1	Last come, first served (pre-emptive-resume)	General, class-dependent
PS	n	Progessor sharing	General, class-dependent
IS	∞	Any	General, class-dependent
FCFS	n	Work-conserving	Negative exponential, independent of classes

Q^* is called the class of *separable queueing networks* because the balance equations can be solved by separation of variable techniques (the terms locally balanced networks [Baskett et al (1975)] or networks with product form solutions are also used).

Exponential server queueing networks as described by Jackson (1963) and Gordon and Newell (1967) are part of Q^*. Multiple classes and the active resources of Table 4.3.1 have been added by Baskett et al. (1975). Multiple chains and predicates on the job variable are dealt with in Reiser and Kobayashi (1975c) and Kobayashi and Reiser (1975) (see also Chapter 3).

4.3.2. Open Networks, Jackson's Theorem

We consider a network with M local classes and N active resources (or queues). The state of this network is determined by the population vector

$$\mathcal{K} = (k_1, k_2, \ldots, k_M) \tag{4.3.1}$$

where k_m ($m = 1, 2, \ldots, M$) is the number of jobs in class m. The state of an individual queue is given by

$$\mathbf{k}_n = (k_{s_n(1)}, k_{s_n(2)}, \ldots, k_{s_n(t_n)}), \tag{4.3.2}$$

where t_n is the number of local classes and $s_n(j)$ ($j = 1, 2, \ldots, t_n$) are the class names at queue n ($n = 1, 2, \ldots, N$). An example of a network with the corresponding state vectors is provided in Figure 4.3.1. Since classes are local to queues, the state space of Q^* is the Cartesian product of the state space of individual resources.

The stationary queue size distribution of Q^*, if it exists, is obtained as follows:

1. Determine the throughput θ_m ($m = 1, 2, \ldots, M$) of class m.

2. Determine the steady-state queue size distribution (marginal distribution) of queue n ($n = 1, 2, \ldots, N$) *as if* this queue would be subjected to Poisson arrivals of intensity $\theta_{s_n(j)}$, ($j = 1, 2, \ldots, t_n$) (determined in step 1).

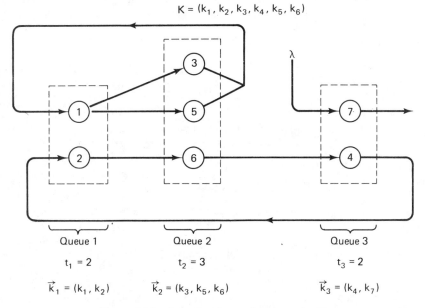

$K = (k_1, k_2, k_3, k_4, k_5, k_6)$

Queue 1	Queue 2	Queue 3
$t_1 = 2$	$t_2 = 3$	$t_3 = 2$
$\vec{k}_1 = (k_1, k_2)$	$\vec{k}_2 = (k_3, k_5, k_6)$	$\vec{k}_3 = (k_4, k_7)$

Figure 4.3.1. Examples of states in a network with $M = 7$ and $N = 3$. The circles represent job classes, the dashed rectangles delineate active resources.

3. Obtain the joint distribution as the product of the distributions of step 2, i.e.,

$$p(\mathcal{K}) = \prod_{n=1}^{N} p_n(\mathbf{k}_n) \qquad (4.3.3)$$

Obtain performance measures by summing over (4.3.3).

This three-step procedure is sometimes called Jackson's theorem (1963). The way in which routing (step 1) is decoupled from step 2 is a most remarkable property. So is the fact that the queues behave as if they were subjected to Poisson arrivals even though the flows in Q^* are not Poisson.

The determination of $\{\theta_m\}$ in step 1 is a problem which involves the routing only. If we restrict the problem to the case of probabilistic routing (i.e., no predicates on the JV), then the $\{\theta_n\}$'s are obtained by solving the system of linear equations

$$\theta_m = \lambda_m + \sum_{j=1}^{M} p_{jm}\theta_j, \qquad m = 1, 2, \ldots, M \qquad (4.3.4)$$

where p_{jm} is the probability of joining class m after service completion at class j and λ_m is the rate of exogenous arrivals at class m. Note that (4.3.4) is a forced flow problem. Note also that if there are multiple chains, (4.3.4) is decomposable in as many subsystems as there are chains. System (4.3.4) has an unique solution if each chain contains at least one node j such that $\lambda_j \neq 0$ and at least one node i (may be the same as j) such that the ith row sum of the routing matrix $[p_{ij}]$ is less than unity. The calculation of $\{\theta_m\}$ with predicates on the job variable is found in Kobayashi and Reiser (1975).

To state the queue size distribution $p_n(\mathbf{k}_n)$ of queue n ($n = 1, 2, \ldots, N$), we introduce

Definition 1

- Capacity coefficient of queue n ($n = 1, 2, \ldots, N$):

$$a_n(i) = \frac{(\mu_n^0)^i}{\prod_{j=1}^{i} \mu_n(j)} \qquad (4.3.5)$$

  where $\mu_n^0 =$ unit work rate of queue n,
  $\mu_n(j) =$ work rate as a function of the queue size j.

- Capacity function:

$$c_n(x) = \sum_{i=0}^{\infty} a_n(i)x^i \qquad (4.3.6)$$

- Work intensity of class m ($m = 1, 2, \ldots, M$):

$$\rho_m = \theta_m \bar{W}_m / \mu_{n(m)}^0 \qquad (4.3.7)$$

  where $n(m) =$ queue which contains class m,
  $\bar{W}_m =$ expectation of the work demand distribution of class m.

Some important capacity functions are given below:

- Single server queue with constant rates $\mu_n(j) = \mu_n^0 = $ const.:

$$C_n(x) = \frac{1}{1 - x} \qquad (4.3.8)$$

- Limited queue-dependent server[1] defined by $\mu_n(j) = $ arbitrary for $1 \leq j < d$, $\mu_n(j) = \mu_n^0 = $ const. if $j \geq d$:

$$C_n(x) = \frac{\gamma_n(x)}{1 - x} \qquad (4.3.9)$$

where $\gamma_n(x)$ is a polynomial of degree $d - 1$, given by

$$\gamma_n(x) = 1 + \sum_{i=1}^{d-1} [a_n(i) - a_n(i - 1)]x^i \qquad (4.3.10)$$

- Infinite servers whose rate function is $\mu(j) = j\mu_n^0$:

$$C_n(x) = \exp(x) \qquad (4.3.11)$$

where μ_n^0 is the rate of an individual server.

Theorem 1

The generating function (g.f.) of an improper distribution $p_n^*(\mathbf{k}_n)$ of queue n $(n = 1, 2, \ldots, N)$ is given by

$$p_n^*(\mathbf{z}_n) = C_n(\mathbf{\rho}_n \cdot \mathbf{z}_n) \qquad (4.3.12)$$

where

$$\mathbf{\rho}_n = (\rho_{s_n(1)}, \rho_{s_n(2)}, \ldots, \rho_{s_n(t_n)})$$

$$\mathbf{z}_n = (z_{s_n(1)}, z_{s_n(2)}, \ldots, z_{s_n(t_n)})$$

and $\mathbf{\rho}_n \cdot \mathbf{z}_n$ denotes the inner product of vectors. The g.f. of the proper distribution, if it exists, follows from (4.3.12) by normalization, i.e.,

$$p_n(\mathbf{z}_n) = \frac{C_n(\mathbf{\rho}_n \cdot \mathbf{z}_n)}{C_n(|\mathbf{\rho}_n|)} \qquad (4.3.13)$$

where $|\cdot|$ is the L_∞-norm (i.e., sum of absolute values of components).

For the proof of the theorem we refer to Reiser and Kobayashi (1975c).

Thus, $p_n^*(\mathbf{z}_n)$ is simply *the capacity function of queue n evaluated at a linear combination of the work intensities*, a very simple result indeed. The advantage of the g.f. method becomes clear if one compares (4.3.12) with its inverse, as given in Baskett et al. (1975).

For example, a single class fixed rate queue has $C = 1/1 - x$, and hence

$$p(z) = (1 - \rho)\frac{1}{1 - \rho z} \longleftrightarrow p(k) = (1 - \rho)\rho^k \qquad (4.3.14)$$

the familiar expression for the $M/M/1$ system. Similarly, for an IS queue

$$p(z) = e^{-\rho}e^{\rho z} \longleftrightarrow p(k) = \frac{e^{-\rho}\rho^k}{k!} \qquad (4.3.15)$$

again, the well-known form of the $M/G/\infty$ queue. The two examples are shown in Figure 4.3.2.

---

[1] A multiserver of mutfiplicity d is equivalent to a limited queue-dependent server with rate function $\mu_n(j) = (j\mu_n^0$ if $j \leq d$, $d\mu_n^0$ otherwise).

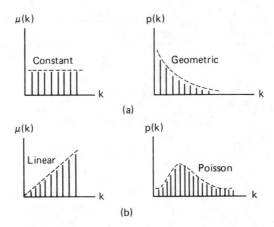

Figure 4.3.2. Rate function $\mu(k)$ and queue size distribution $p(k)$ for a single class constant rate server (a) and a single class IS queue (b).

We have now completed the discussion of the open network. Once $\{\theta_n\}$ is known, the numerical evaluation of (4.3.13) is a rather simple problem. The numerical effort is negligible.

4.3.3. Conditioned Solution and Closed Chains

In practice, one is often interested in conditioned queue size distributions. An important case is to require the population in a chain to have a given, fixed value. A motivating example of such conditioning is the familiar breakdown of measurements according to levels of multiprogramming.

In this section, we are interested in the conditioned distribution

$$p(\mathcal{K}, \mathbf{K}) = \Pr\{\text{state} = \mathcal{K} \mid \text{chain } l \text{ contains } K_l \text{ jobs, } l = 1, 2, \ldots, L\} \quad (4.3.16)$$

where $\mathbf{K} = (K_1, K_2, \ldots, K_L)$ and L is the number of conditioned chains (we assume that the first L chains are the conditioned ones). From the law of conditioned probabilities, we have

$$p(\mathcal{K}, \mathbf{K}) = \begin{cases} \dfrac{p(\mathcal{K})}{g(\mathbf{K})} & \text{if } \mathcal{K} \text{ feasible} \\ 0 & \text{otherwise} \end{cases} \quad (4.3.17)$$

where $g(\mathbf{K})$ is given as

$$g(\mathbf{K}) = \Pr\{\text{chain } l \text{ contains } K_l \text{ jobs, } l = 1, 2, \ldots, L\} \quad (4.3.18)$$

We can interpret the conditioned solution as follows: Assume that we observe and sample the queueing system only during time intervals when the system state is feasible. As soon as the system moves out of the feasible state, we halt our observations until a feasible state is entered the next time. The long-term sample statistics obtained this way are the conditioned statistics introduced above. Note the similarity with stratified sampling techniques, which play an important role in the practical parameter estimation for queueing network models. An example of such a conditioned chain is given in Figure 4.3.3.

A conditioned chain is equivalent to a closed chain up to renaming of jobs. This is easy to understand intuitively and to prove formally by writing down the steady-state equations for both cases. If all chains are conditioned, we call the network closed; otherwise we call it mixed.

Clearly, $g(\mathbf{K})$, which is also called the normalization constant, is given by the sum

$$g(\mathbf{K}) = \sum_{\mathcal{K} \in \mathcal{F}} p(\mathcal{K}) \qquad (4.3.19)$$

with the set of feasible states $\mathcal{F}$. From (4.3.4) it follows that θ_m ($m = 1, 2, \ldots, M$) is a linear functional of the exogenous arrival rates $\lambda_1, \lambda_2, \ldots, \lambda_M$. But the parameters $\{\theta_m\}$ appear as the same powers in the numerators and in the denominator of (4.3.17). Hence, *the conditioned solution is independent of the arrival rates to the underlying open network* for jobs in chain $l, l = 1, \ldots, L$. We shall use this degree of freedom for scaling purposes later on.

Let Ch_l denote the set of nodes in chain l ($l = 1, 2, \ldots, L$); i.e., $\text{Ch}_l = \{m: \text{node } m \text{ belongs to chain } l\}$. For the example of Figure 4.3.1 we have $\text{Ch}_1 = \{1, 3, 5\}$ and Ch_2

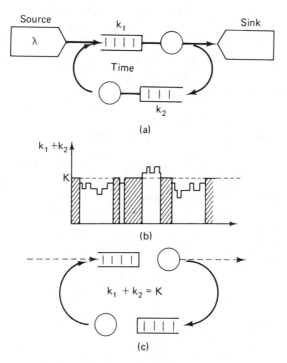

Figure 4.3.3. The concept of a conditioned chain. (a) The underlying open chain; (b) sample system only when $k_1 + k_2 = K$ (shaded time slices); (c) the resulting conditioned chain.

$= \{2, 4, 6\}$. Using this notation, (4.3.18) may be written as follows:

$$g(\mathbf{K}) = \Pr\{ \sum_{m \in \text{Ch}_l} k_m = K_l, \quad l = 1, 2, \ldots, L\} \qquad (4.3.20)$$

But the distribution of the sum of independent random variables is given by the convolution of the individual distributions; hence,

$$g(\mathbf{K}) = (p_1 * p_2 * \ldots * p_N) \qquad (\text{at } \mathbf{K}) \qquad (4.3.21)$$

where p_n ($n = 1, 2, \ldots, N$) are the individual queue distributions given by (4.3.13) and * denotes the convolution operator. *Thus the normalization constant is the convolution of the N individual queue size distributions, taken at the point of chain populations.* Our algorithms for the computation of $g(\mathbf{K})$ are based on this interpretation.

We now revert to the use of generating functions and state (4.3.21) more precisely as follows:

Theorem 2

The g.f. of the improper normalization constant is given by

$$G^*(\mathbf{Z}) = \prod_{n=1}^{N} C_n(r_n^0 + \mathbf{r}_n \cdot \mathbf{z}) \qquad (4.3.22)$$

where $\mathbf{Z} = (Z_1, Z_2, \ldots, Z_L)$ is a vector of transform variables associated with $\mathbf{K}$,

$r_n^0 = \sum \rho_m$ summed over all nodes m which are in queue n and in open chains,

$r_{n,l} = \sum \rho_m$ summed over all nodes m which are in queue n and in conditioned chain l,

$\mathbf{r}_n = (r_{n,1}, r_{n,2}, \ldots, r_{n,L})$.

For the example of Figure 4.3.1, we have $r_1^0 = 0$, $r_2^0 = 0$, $r_3^0 = \rho_7$, $\mathbf{r}_1 = (\rho_1, \rho_2)$, $\mathbf{r}_2 = (\rho_3 + \rho_5, \rho_6)$, and $\mathbf{r}_3 = (\rho_4)$. The proof of Theorem 2 is given in Reiser and Kobayashi (1975c).

From the theorem it follows that multiple classes at queue n within a given chain l add nothing to the complexity of the result. Similarly, all that open chains contribute is a shift in the origin of the capacity function. In (4.3.22) multiplication of transform functions substitute for the convolutions in the usual manner.

Once the normalization constant is known, the problem is solved in principle. However, for practical applications, the joint queue size distribution (4.3.17) is of little value. Performance measures such as throghput, utilization, mean queue size, and response times are required. These statistics can be expressed as sums over $p(\mathcal{K}, \mathbf{K})$. The structure of these sums is similar to the one defining the normalization constant (4.3.19). We shall aim at relating the desired statistics to $G^*(\mathbf{Z})$ since this will save computation. We introduce

Definition 2

$$G^*_{(m^-)}(\mathbf{Z}) = \prod_{\substack{n=1 \\ n \neq m}}^{N} C_n(r_n^0 + \mathbf{r}_n \cdot \mathbf{Z}) \qquad (4.3.23)$$

and

$$G^*_{(m^+)}(\mathbf{Z}) = C_m(r_m^0 + \mathbf{r}_m \cdot \mathbf{Z})G^*(\mathbf{Z}) \qquad (4.3.24)$$

Let $p_n(k, \mathbf{K})$ be the marginal queue size distribution in conditioned network. $p_n(z, \mathbf{Z})$ denotes its g.f., which is given in

Theorem 3

The g.f., of the improper marginal distribution $p_n^*(k, \mathbf{K})$ is

$$p_n^*(z, \mathbf{Z}) = C_n(z[r_n^0 + \mathbf{r}_n \cdot \mathbf{Z}])G_{(n^-)}^*(\mathbf{Z}) \qquad (4.3.25)$$

where z is a transform variable associated with k. The proper distribution is obtained by normalization, i.e., division through $g^*(\mathbf{K})$.

From (4.3.25) follows the mean queue size by standard manipulations on generating functions. We summarize the results for the mean in

Corollary 1

•   The g.f. of the improper mean queue size of queue n is

$$Q_n^*(\mathbf{Z}) = (r_n^0 + \mathbf{r}_n \cdot \mathbf{Z})C_n'(r_n^0 + \mathbf{r}_n \cdot \mathbf{Z})G_{(n^-)}^*(\mathbf{Z}) \qquad (4.3.26)$$

where

$$C_n'(x) = \frac{dC_n(x)}{dx}$$

•   If queue n has a *fixed rate server*,

$$Q_n^*(\mathbf{Z}) = (r_n^0 + \mathbf{r}_n \cdot \mathbf{Z})G_{(n^+)}^*(\mathbf{Z}) \qquad (4.3.27)$$

•   If queue n has an *infinite server*,

$$Q_n^*(\mathbf{Z}) = (r_n^0 + \mathbf{r}_n \cdot \mathbf{Z})G^*(\mathbf{Z}) \qquad (4.3.28)$$

The throughput in a conditioned chain differs from the implied $\{\theta_m\}$ values of (4.3.4) by a proportionality constant, which is given in

Theorem 4

The throughput through a class m in a conditioned chain l ($m \in \text{Ch}_l$) is proportional to θ_m,

$$\theta_m(\mathbf{K}) = \theta_m g^*(\mathbf{K} - \mathbf{e}_l)/g^*(\mathbf{K}) \qquad (4.3.29)$$

where $\mathbf{e}_l$ is the lth unit vector of dimension L.

For proofs of Theorem 3, Corollary 1, and Theorem 4, we refer once more to Reiser and Kobayashi (1975c).

4.3.4. The Convolution Algorithm

In the following discussion, we shall consider r_n^0 and $\mathbf{r}_n$ ($n = 1, 2, \ldots, N$) as given parameters. Their computation via $\{\theta_m\}$ does not pose serious problems. In many cases, the system of equations (4.3.4) can be solved by inspection. In most cases, (4.3.4) is very sparse.

As we have mentioned, open (or unconditioned) networks require only a negligible computational effort. However, the situation is different if there are condtioned (or closed) chains. In this case, the computational effort increases rapidly with L and $\mathbf{K}$. It is our object in this and subsequent sections to discuss efficient numerical algorithms for networks with conditioned chains.

It follows from Theorem 2 that all that nonconditioned chains contribute to the solution is a shift in the argument of the capacity functions. Furthermore, the mathematical form of the shifted capacity function remains unchanged for the cases of infinite servers, fixed rate servers, and limited queue-dependent servers. This leads to the conclusion that in general open chains do not increase the computational complexity (the only exception is the evaluation of marginal queue size distribution).

Since open chains bring nothing new computationally, we shall not include them in the subsequent discussion. This will simplify the notation. We shall also drop the asterisk notation used previously to denote improper distributions.

The basic problem, then, is the computation of $g(\mathbf{K})$, whose g.f. is known by (4.3.22), i.e.,

$$G(\mathbf{Z}) = \prod_{n=1}^{N} C_n(\mathbf{r}_n \cdot \mathbf{Z}) \tag{4.3.30}$$

The number of terms in the defining sum (4.3.19) which grows combinatorially with $\mathbf{K}$ and L clearly excludes a naive term-by-term summation for all but the smallest problems. Practical methods fall into two categories:

1.   Inversion of generating functions, and

2.   Convolution of the N known inversions c_n of the trems $C_n(\mathbf{r}_n \cdot \mathbf{Z})$ of (4.3.30).

The first approach does not lead to well-behaved algorithms. Clearly, the general inversion formula of (4.3.30), which requires integration on a complex hyperdisk, is not well suited for a numerical evaluation. If the problem is restricted to $L = 1$ and fixed rate servers at all queues, then $g(K)$ can be obtained by a partial fraction expansion of $G(Z)$, a rational function in Z. Moore (1972) has given the solution under the additional constraint that all r_i be distinct (i.e., $r_i \neq r_j, i = 1, 2, \ldots, N, j = 1, 2, \ldots,$ N, and $i \neq j$). The latter constraint was later removed by Lam (1975). Computational schemes based on partial fraction expansions are only *conditionally stable numerically* since they involve alternating sign sums. They are clearly inferior to the convolution methods, especially since they are of the same efficiency [i.e., O(NK) operations] and considerably less versatile.

Convolution methods for simple closed networks were introduced by Buzen (1973) and independently by Reiser (1976b) and Reiser and Kobayashi (1973). The last authors also showed the connection with Horner's rule for the evaluation of polynomials [Reiser and Kobayashi (1975a)] and later generalized the convolution method to systems with multiple chains (i.e., $L > 1$) [Reiser and Kobayashi (1975b 1975c)]. The convolution method is discussed in detail subsequently. An error analysis is also provided. Great emphasis is placed on efficiency, both with respect to operations and storage. Of special practical interest is Section 4.3.9, in which we shall discuss the efficient computation of queue statistics.

4.3.5. The Basic Method

Let $c_n(\mathbf{i})$ denote the inverse of $C_n(\mathbf{r}_n \cdot \mathbf{Z})$; i.e., $c_n(\mathbf{i})$ is defined implicitly by

$$C_n(\mathbf{r}_n \cdot \mathbf{Z}) = \sum_{\mathbf{i} \geq 0} c_n(\mathbf{i}) Z_1^{i_1} Z_2^{i_2} \ldots Z_L^{i_L} \qquad (4.3.31)$$

where $\mathbf{i}$ is an L-dimensional index vector $\mathbf{i} = (i_1, i_2, \ldots, i_L)$. From the definition of the capacity function follows

$$c_n(\mathbf{i}) = a_n(|\mathbf{i}|) \frac{|\mathbf{i}|!}{i_1! i_2! \ldots i_L!} r_{n,1}^{i_1} r_{n,2}^{i_2} \ldots r_{n,L}^{i_L} \qquad (\mathbf{i} \geq 0) \qquad (4.3.32)$$

i.e., $c_n(\mathbf{i})$ is a multinomial distribution. Our goal is the calculation of

$$g(\mathbf{K}) = (c_1 * c_2 * \ldots * c_N) \qquad (\text{at } \mathbf{i} = \mathbf{K}) \qquad (4.3.33)$$

The convolution algorithn needs two storage arrays g and c with bounds $[-1:K_1, -1:K_2, \ldots, -1:K_L]$. The bordering (elements with negative indices) is introduced for convenience in the description of loops and could be omitted if so desired. The array g holds partial results of the convolution (4.3.33); the array c is used for storage of the coefficients $\{c_n\}$. We shall need the notation

$$K_+ = \sum_{l=1}^{L} K_l \qquad (4.3.34)$$

and

$$K_\times = \prod_{l=1}^{L} K_l \qquad (4.3.35)$$

The basic algorithm in a semiformal notation is given below.

Algorithm C

This is a convolution algorithm to compute the normalization constant, $g(\mathbf{K})$.

C1. [Initialize] $g \leftarrow 0$, $c \leftarrow 0$ (all elements); $n \leftarrow 1$.

C2. [Initialize g] $g(0, 0, \ldots, 0) \leftarrow 1$. Note that this step might look different if the network contains IS queues (see Section 4.3.8).

C3. [Convolve] Compute $c_n(\mathbf{i})$ for $0 \leq \mathbf{i} \leq \mathbf{K}$ and store result in c; compute partial result $g \leftarrow g * c$. Note that the details of this step may depend on the type of queue.

C4. [Loop on n] $n \leftarrow n + 1$; if $n \leq N$, go to C3, else stop. Upon completion, $g(\mathbf{K})$ is the corner element $g(K_1, K_2, \ldots, K_L)$.

Let us take a closer look at step C3. A naive evaluation of (4.3.32) would be very costly. Fortunately, the multinomial terms

$$\frac{|\mathbf{i}|}{i_1! i_2! \ldots i_L!} r_{n,1}^{i_1} r_{n,2}^{i_2} \ldots \,_{n,L}^{i_L} \qquad (4.3.36)$$

can be calculated more efficiently by a recursive scheme as follows:

Algorithm G

This algorithm is for expansion and convolution for a general queue. It is to be substituted for step C3 in Algorithm C.

G1. [Initialize] $c(0, 0, \ldots, 0) \leftarrow 1$.

G2. [Loop on k] For $k = 1, 2, \ldots, K_+$ (in this order), perform G3.

G3. [Loops are l and $i_1, i_2, \ldots, i_L$] $c(\mathbf{i}) \leftarrow \sum_{l=1}^{L} r_{n,l} c(\mathbf{i} - \mathbf{e}_l)$ for all $\mathbf{i}$ such that

$$|\mathbf{i}| = k \quad \text{and} \quad \mathbf{i} \leq \mathbf{K}$$

G4. [Loop on k] For $k = 1, 2, \ldots, K_+$, perform G5.

G5. [Loops on $i_1, i_2, \ldots, i_L$] $c(\mathbf{i}) \leftarrow a_n(k)c(\mathbf{i})$ for all $\mathbf{i}$ such that

$$|\mathbf{i}| = k \quad \text{and} \quad \mathbf{i} \leq \mathbf{K}$$

Now $c_n(\mathbf{i})$ is stored in the c-array.

G6. [Loops on $i_1, i_2, \ldots, i_L$] For $i_1 = K_1, K_1 - 1, \ldots, 0$; $i_2 = K_2, K_2 - 1, \ldots, 0$; $\ldots$; and $i_L = K_L, K_L - 1, \ldots, 0$ (in this order), perform G7.

G7. [Loops on $j_1, j_2, \ldots, j_L$]

$$g(\mathbf{i}) \leftarrow \sum_{0 \leq \mathbf{j} \leq \mathbf{i}} g(\mathbf{i} - \mathbf{j})c(\mathbf{j})$$

Step G3 is the recursive evaluation of (4.3.36). Step G7 is the definition of the L-dimensional convolution. An important detail is the fact that the loops in step G6 run backwards. Another storage array would otherwise have been necessary.

The operations count is $O(K_\times)$ for the computation of c and $O(K_\times^2/2^L)$ for the convolution. The latter is a rather high effort. Its reduction for some special but practically important queues will be the object of subsequent sections.

4.3.6. Fixed Rate Servers

We denote by $G_{(n)}(\mathbf{Z})$ the nth partial result; i.e., $G_{(n)}(\mathbf{Z}) = \prod_{i=1}^{n} C_i(\mathbf{r}_i \cdot \mathbf{Z})$. Then for a queue n with a fixed rate server, we have

$$G_{(n+1)}(\mathbf{Z}) = \frac{1}{1 - \mathbf{r}_n \cdot \mathbf{Z}} G_{(n)}(\mathbf{Z}) \tag{4.3.37}$$

or

$$G_{(n+1)}(\mathbf{Z}) = (\mathbf{r}_n \cdot \mathbf{Z})G_{(n+1)}(\mathbf{Z}) + G_{(n)}(\mathbf{Z}) \tag{4.3.38}$$

The inversion of (4.3.38) is easily seen to be

$$g_{(n+1)}(\mathbf{i}) = g_{(n)}(\mathbf{i}) + \sum_{l=1}^{L} r_{n,l} g_{(n+1)}(\mathbf{i} - \mathbf{e}_l) \tag{4.3.39}$$

Equation (4.3.39) is the basis for the efficient recursive computation of the convolution in

Algorithm F

This is a fixed rates server. This algorithm substitutes for step C3 in Algorithm C.

F1. [Loop on k] For $k = 1, 2, \ldots, K_+$ (in this order), perform F2.

F2. [Loops on $i_1, i_2, \ldots, i_L$] $g(\mathbf{i}) \leftarrow g(\mathbf{i}) + \sum_{l=1}^{L} r_{n,l} g(\mathbf{i} - \mathbf{e}_l)$ for all $\mathbf{i}$ such that

$$|\mathbf{i}| = k \quad \text{and} \quad \mathbf{i} \leq \mathbf{k}$$

The operation count of Algorithm F is only $O(LK_x)$, a substantial saving over $O(K_x^2/2^L)$. Note also that the storage array c is not needed. A computation diagram of Algorithm F is given in Figure 4.3.4.

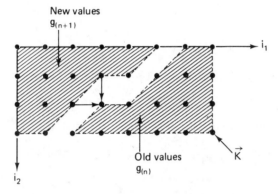

Figure 4.3.4. Computation diagram of algorithm F for the case $L = 2$.

4.3.7. Limited Queue-Dependent Server

In the case of a queue n with a limited queue-dependent server, we have

$$G_{(n+1)}(\mathbf{Z}) = \gamma_n(\mathbf{r}_n \cdot \mathbf{Z}) \frac{1}{1 - \mathbf{r}_n \cdot \mathbf{Z}} G_{(n)}(\mathbf{Z}) \tag{4.3.40}$$

We calculate $G_{(n+1)}$ in two steps, viz.,

$$1. \quad G^*(\mathbf{Z}) = \frac{1}{1 - \mathbf{r}_n \cdot \mathbf{Z}} G_{(n)}(\mathbf{Z}) \tag{4.3.41}$$

$$2. \quad G_{(n+1)}(\mathbf{Z}) = \gamma_n(\mathbf{r}_n \cdot \mathbf{Z}) G^*(\mathbf{Z}) \tag{4.3.42}$$

We evaluate (4.3.41) by algorithm F and (4.3.42) by Algorithm G. However, if $d < K_+$, the loops in steps G2 and G4 need only extend over $k = 1, 2, \ldots, d - 1$; similarly, the loops of G7 range over $i_1 - d < j_1 \leq i_1, i_2 - d < j_2 \leq i_2, \ldots, i_L - d < j_L \leq i_L$. Therefore, the operations count is only $O(LK_x) + O(K_x d^L)$, which may be significantly less than $O(K_x^2/2^L)$ especially if $d \ll K_+$, a condition often satisfied in practice (note that limited queue-dependent servers arise from the representation of multiserver queues $d =$ number of servers).

4.3.8.   Infinite Server Queues

The convolution for IS queues does not simplify. However, there is one degree of freedom which we have not exploited yet, namely the ordering of queues. In Algorithm C we have initialized $g \leftarrow$ {unit sequence} and then started the successive convolutions. Clearly, convolution with the unit sequence is a superfluous operation, and we could initialize $g \leftarrow \{c_1\}$ and then continue with $n = 2, 3, \ldots, N$. In this fashion, we can avoid one convolution, preferably of course the hardest one to do. We can, therefore, avoid most of the effort as follows:

- Combine the capacity functions for all IS queues in the network, i.e.,

$$C_0(r_0 \cdot \mathbf{Z}) = \prod_{\text{all IS queues}} \exp{(r_n \cdot \mathbf{Z})} = \exp{(r_0 \cdot \mathbf{Z})} \qquad (4.3.43)$$

with

$$r_0 = \sum_{\text{all IS queues}} r_n \qquad (4.3.44)$$

- Initialize g with (4.3.43).

The initialization is done by

Algorithm I

This algorithm is for IS queues. It is to be substituted for step C2 in Algorithm C.

I1.   [Initialize] $g(0, 0, \ldots, 0) \leftarrow 1$. If $\mathbf{r}_0 = \mathbf{0}$, skip steps I2 and I3.

I2.   [Loops on l and i] $g(i\mathbf{e}_l) \leftarrow r_{0,l}g((i - 1)\mathbf{e}_l)/i$ for $l = 1, 2, \ldots, L$ and $i = 1, 2, \ldots, K_l$ (in this order).

I3.   [Loops on $i_1, i_2, \ldots, i_L$]

$$G(\mathbf{i}) = \prod_{l=1}^{L} g(i_l \mathbf{e}_l) \qquad \text{for } \mathbf{0} \leq \mathbf{i} \leq \mathbf{K}$$

The operations count is $O(2K_x)$. Clearly, savings are substantial. Assume, for example, that $L = 2$, $N_0 = 2$, $K_1 = 20$, and $K_2 = 50$. For this case, Algorithm I requires 1140 operations as compared to 1,070,000, roughly an improvement of a factor of 1000.

4.3.9.   Efficient Computation of Queue Statistics

So far we have only dealt with the computation of the normalization constant $g(\mathbf{K})$. Of equal importance, however, is the computation of queue statistics such as throughput, mean queue size, and utilization factors. They are defined by sums which are structurally similar to the sum in (4.3.19) which defines $g(\mathbf{K})$. This has led to Theorem 3, Theorem 4, and Corollary 1 where the g.f.s of the queue statistics are related to $G(\mathbf{Z})$, the g.f. of $g(\mathbf{K})$.

These theorems provide the basis for an efficient computation of the desired statistics. The general idea is to convolve $\{g\}$ with a suitably chosen sequence $\{c\}$. The fact that Algorithm C computes simultaneously the normalization constants for all networks with populations $\{\mathbf{K}: 0 \leq \mathbf{K} \leq \mathbf{K}\}$ is now an essential advantage.

- The *throughput* of queue m is obtained at negligible computational effort from

$$\theta_m(\mathbf{K}) = \frac{\theta_m g(\mathbf{K} - \mathbf{e}_{l(m)})}{g(\mathbf{K})} \qquad (4.3.45)$$

  where $l(m)$ denotes the chain to which class m belongs.

- *The mean queue size of an IS queue* follows from (4.3.28) in a way analogous to (4.3.45).

- *The mean queue size of a fixed rate server queue* is related to $G_{(m^+)}$ by (4.3.27). We compute $g_{(m^+)}(\mathbf{K})$ by invoking once more Algorithm I with parameter $\mathbf{r}_m$. Thus $O(LK_\times)$ operations are required. Once $g_{(m^+)}$ is computed, q_m, the mean queue size of class m, follows from

$$q_m(\mathbf{K}) = \frac{\rho_m g_{(m^+)}(\mathbf{K} - \mathbf{e}_{l(m)})}{g(\mathbf{K})} \qquad (4.3.46)$$

- All *other quantities* such as mean queue size of queues with queue-dependent servers, utilization factors, and marginal queue size distributions require $g_{(m^-)}$, the inverse of $G_{(m^-)}(\mathbf{Z})$. Its computation is discussed below.

Clearly, $g_{(m^-)}$ can be obtained from Algorithm C by simply omitting the convolution with $\{c_m\}$ (i.e., by skipping step C3 if $n = m$). However, this requires a large computational effort. It is tempting to compute $g_{(m^-)}$ in one step by the inverse convolution $g_{(m^-)} = \{c_m^{-1}\} * \{g\}$ where $\{c_m^{-1}\}$ is defined by $\{c_m\} * \{c_m^{-1}\} = \{\text{unit sequence}\}$. It turns out, however, that this inverse convolution tends to be numerically unstable as $\mathbf{K}$ becomes large. It would also, in general, require Algorithm G with its high operations count. Therefore, the gain of having to perform just one convolution may be offset by the fact that this convolution requires $O(K_\times^2)$ operations. If all the remaining queues are simple, Algorithm C may be faster. Therefore, it is in most cases advantageous to use Algorithm C for the computation of $g_{(m^-)}$.

There is one important exception, however, namely, the case when queue m has a fixed rate server. In this case, $g_{(m^-)}$ may be obtained very efficiently by means of

Algorithm F⁻¹

This is the inversion of Algorithm F. It computes $g_{(m^-)}$ for a fixed rate server m.

F⁻¹1. [Loops on $i_1, i_2, \ldots, i_L$]

$$g_{(m^-)}^{(i)} \leftarrow g(\mathbf{i}) - \sum_{l=1}^{L} r_{m,l} g(\mathbf{i} - \mathbf{e}_l) \qquad \text{for } \mathbf{0} \leq \mathbf{i} \leq \mathbf{K}$$

The operations count is again $O(LK_\times)$. Note that $g_{(m^-)}$ can be stored conveniently in the c-array or in the g-array itself (in which case the loops must run backwards). *Algorithm F⁻¹ is stable if queue m is not the slowest queue.* For the bottleneck queue, it is advisable to use Algorithm C instead. For a discussion of numerical stability, see Section 4.3.11.

Often the whole sequence $\{g_{(m^-)}\}$ is not needed. The utilization of a fixed rate server m, for example, is obtained in negligible effort as follows:

$$U_m(\mathbf{K}) = \sum_{l=1}^{L} \frac{r_{m,l}\, g(\mathbf{K} - \mathbf{e}_l)}{g(\mathbf{K})} \tag{4.3.47}$$

Finally, one can take advantage of the fact that $\{g_{(N^-)}\}$ for the last queue ($n = N$) is always a by-product of the computation of g. Therefore, one should arrange queues such that, if possible, queue N is a variable rate queue. Also, if storage of intermediate results is feasible, the computation of $\{g_{(m^-)}\}$ for various queues m can be accelerated. The best such scheme requires $3N$ convolutions to obtain all $\{g_{(n^-)}: n = 1, 2, \ldots N\}$.

A signal flow diagram of the computation of the normalization constant and of various queue statistics is given in Figure 4.3.5.

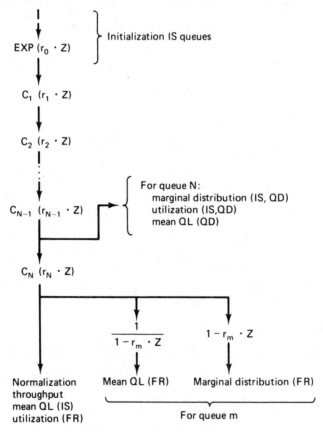

Figure 4.3.5. Signal flow diagram of the computation of $g(\mathbf{K})$ and of queue statistics. The abbreviations are DIST for distribution, QL for mean queue length, IS for infinite servers, QD for queue dependent servers, and FR for fixed rate servers.

4.3.10. Scaling

In Section 4.3.3 we have seen that the parameters $\{\lambda_l\}$ of conditioned chains $l(l = 1, 2, \ldots, L)$ are undetermined. Their choice, however, grossly affects the behavior of $g(\mathbf{K})$ as a function of the position $\mathbf{K}$. Some typical curves $g(K)$ vs. K are given in Figure 4.3.6. Asymptotically $g(\mathbf{K})$ grows or decays geometrically. If $\{\lambda_l\}$ is not chosen properly, floating point overflow or floating point underflow may easily occur, ever for moderately large values of $\mathbf{K}$ (< 50, say). We call scaling the proper choice of $\{\lambda_l\}$ to prevent floating point overflow.

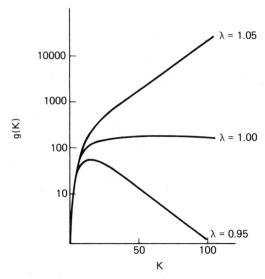

Figure 4.3.6. $g(\mathbf{K})$ versus $\mathbf{K}$ for a network with one closed chain ($L = 1$).

The following scaling rule is based on the fact that $G(\mathbf{1})$ is the sum of all $g(\mathbf{i})$ for $\mathbf{i} \geq 0$, viz.,

$$G(\mathbf{1}) = \sum_{\mathbf{i} \geq 0} g(\mathbf{i}) = \prod_{n=1}^{N} C_n(|\mathbf{r}_n|) \qquad (4.3.48)$$

Clearly, overflow is prevented if we choose $\boldsymbol{\lambda} = (\lambda_1, \lambda_2, \ldots, \lambda_L)$ such that

$$\prod_{n=1}^{N} C_n(\boldsymbol{\lambda} \cdot \mathbf{r}_n) < \beta \qquad (4.3.49)$$

where β is some suitably chosen threshold (e.g., $\beta = 10^{75}$ for IBM computers). Equation (4.3.49) does not uniquely determine $\boldsymbol{\lambda}$. We want to treat indivivual chains as equitably as possible. Therefore, we require additionally

$$\lambda_1 \max_n \{r_{n,1}\} = \lambda_2 \max_n \{r_{n,2}\} = \ldots = \lambda_L \max_n \{r_{n,L}\} \qquad (4.3.50)$$

Equations (4.3.49) and (4.3.50) lead to

Scaling Rule S

This rule is used to prevent overflow in Algorithm C.

S1. $\lambda_l \leftarrow 1/\max_n \{r_{n,l}\}$ for $l = 1, 2, \ldots, L$.

S2. Chose λ such that $\prod_{n=1}^{N} C_n(\lambda[\lambda \cdot \mathbf{r}_n])^{-1} > \beta^{-1}$. Note that this is a non-linear equation for λ. The crudest solution is good enough (e.g., obtained by a simple search loop).

S3. [Redefine $\{r_{n,l}\}$] $r_{n,l} \leftarrow \lambda \lambda_l r_{n,l}$ for $n = 1, 2, \ldots, N; l = 1, 2, \ldots, L$.

This scaling rule is essential for the development of general-purpose queueing software.

4.3.11.   Error Analysis

The normalization constant was obtained as the convolution of N strictly positive sequences. We would expect this operation to be numerically stable. In fact, Reiser (1976b) derived the following error theorem.

Theorem 5

- The relative error of $g(\mathbf{K})$ as calculated by Algorithm C is bounded by

$$|\epsilon(\mathbf{K})| < \epsilon[(L+3)N + (L+1)K_+] \qquad (4.3.51)$$

  where ϵ is the (relative) machine precision.

- The error in $g_{(m^-)}(K)$ as computed by Algorithm F^{-1} is bounded by

$$|\epsilon_{(m^-)}(\mathbf{K})| < \epsilon(\mathbf{K}) + \epsilon(2L+1)\frac{g(\mathbf{K})}{g_{(m^-)}(\mathbf{K})} \qquad (4.3.52)$$

The error bound (4.3.51) grows proportionally with the population size. For all practically relevant values of K_+, $\epsilon(\mathbf{K})$ remains totally negligible. Equation (4.3.52) allows an a posteriori error check of Algorithm F^{-1}. It is not difficult to prove that $g(\mathbf{K})/g_{(m^-)}(\mathbf{K})$ remains bounded for all queues m but the slowest one (i.e., largest work intensity). Theorem 5 is the result of a worst-case error analysis; i.e., the assumption is made that an error of maximum magnitude is generated after each machine operation.

4.3.12.   On Fast Convolution Algorithms

Algorithm G is based on the elementary definition of the discrete convolution. One might suspect that fast convolution algorithms (such as FFT or some number theoretical transforms) could bring significant improvements in efficiency. However, the domain of parameters covering computer modeling problems is such that the advantage of fast convolution methods seems marginal in most cases. The following are some reasons which lead to this conclusion:

- The fast convolution methods show their remarkable efficiency only for one-dimensional problems (i.e., $L = 1$). They require a highly divisible K (e.g., a power of 2) and *padding*, i.e., extra storage (storage requirements double).

- The asymptotic operations counts of the basic definition (Algorithm G), the recursive scheme (Algorithm F), and FFT are

$$\frac{1}{2}K^2: \quad \text{basic definition, general rate function}$$
$$Kd: \quad \text{basic definition, limited queue-dependent server}$$
$$K: \quad \text{recursive scheme, fixed rates}$$
$$\frac{3}{2}K \log_2 K: \quad \text{FFT algorithm}$$

These figures lead to the conclusion that Algorithm F is always the optimal choice for fixed rate servers. In the case of a limited queue-dependent server, there is a break-even point $d*$ such that for $d < d*$ the basic method beats FFT. We find $d* = \frac{3}{2} \log_2 K$. For example, $d* = 12$ for $K = 256$, a rather high value in practice.

- In our domain of application, we expect most queues to have fixed rates or limited queue-dependent rates with small d (e.g., multiservers). Also, the population size is mostly small to intermediate (e.g., < 128), so that the FFT efficiency does not yet really pay off.

- In the case of very large populations, the problem can usually be reduced to an equivalent open network with negligible computational effort.

4.3.13. Application of Regenerative Techniques to the Design of Simulation Experiments and to the Analysis of Simulation Output

Output statistics calculated from a simulation experiment are random variables. Each independent replication of the simulation experiment of the simulation experiment will, in general, yield a different outcome. To make a statement about the accuracy of simulation results one has to estimate the distribution of an estimator and one has also to establish by theoretical means the fact that this distribution becomes asymptotically centered about the true value. Neither one of these questions can be answered with certainty in the case of finite simulation time.

The traditional method is to make a large number of independent runs, each one long enough to make negligible the bias introduced by the initial conditions. One can then invoke a central limit theorem to fit a normal distribution to the data and to obtain confidence intervals, i.e., calculate a confidence interval width $\hat{\delta}$ such that the true value of q of a statistic falls into the interval $[\hat{q} - \hat{\delta}, \hat{q} + \hat{\delta}]$ with probability α, where $\hat{q}$ is the sample value of q obtained from the simulation. The problem with this approach is that a large number of long runs are required.

The regeneration point method is another way to obtain confidence intervals. It has great theoretical appeal and practical advantages. Since Chapter 2 provides a detailed account of the theory, we shall restrict the discussion here to some practical aspects. The regeneration point method makes use of the fact that many queueing systems have embedded a sequence of renewal epochs $T_j, j = 0, 1, \ldots$, such that the time evolutions between successive epochs are independent of each other and statistically independent. Time points T_j are called regeneration points; the evolution between regeneration points is called a tour or a cycle. In Figure 4.3.7 we portray a simple queueing process $X(t)$, where $X(t)$ measures the queue length at time t. The regeneration points are defined by arrivals to an empty system.

Tours define statistically independent samples. Let us assume that we are interested in the mean queue size, which can be obtained as a long-term time average, i.e.,

$$q = \lim_{t \to \infty} \frac{\int_0^t X(\tau)\, d\tau}{t} \qquad (4.3.53)$$

which we can estimate by using a fixed value for t. We introduce the following variables defined over a tour:

$$Y_j = \int_{T_{j-1}}^{T_j} X(\tau)\, d\tau \qquad (4.3.54)$$

and

$$Z_j = T_j - T_{j-1} \qquad (4.3.55)$$

Y_j is simply the area under $X(t)$ for tour j; Z_j is the length of tour j (see Figure 4.3.7). We now introduce the following ratio estimators:

$$\hat{q}(n) = \frac{\bar{Y}}{\bar{Z}} = \frac{\sum_{i=1}^{n} Y_i}{\sum_{i=1}^{n} Z_i} \qquad (4.3.56)$$

where n is the number of simulated tours and $\bar{Y}$, $\bar{Z}$ are sample means of $\{Y_j\}$, $\{Z_j\}$, respectively. It can be shown that under some mild restrictions on $X(t)$ the quantity $\hat{q}(n) - q$ becomes normally distributed as $n \to \infty$. There results a confidence interval

$$\alpha = \Pr\{\hat{q}(n) - \delta(n) \leq q \leq \hat{q}(n) + \delta(n)\} \qquad (4.3.57)$$

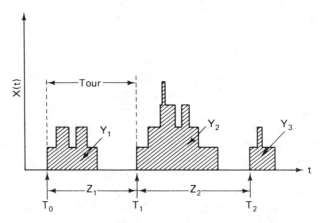

Figure 4.3.7. A simple queue length process with regeneration points $\{T_j\}$. Y_j is the area under $X(t)$ for tour j. Z_j is the length of tour j.

where $\delta(n)$ can be estimated by

$$\delta(n) = \gamma(\alpha)\left[\frac{V(n)}{n}\right]^{1/2} \frac{1}{\bar{X}} \tag{4.3.58}$$

with $\gamma(\alpha)$ being a constant which depends on α via the error function and $V(n)$ is a measure for the variance in $\{X_j\}$ and $\{Y_j\}$, viz.,

$$V(n) = S_{Y^2} - 2\hat{q}(n)S_{YZ} + \hat{q}(n)^2 \, S_{Z^2} \tag{4.3.59}$$

where S_{Y^2}, S_{YZ}, and S_{Z^2} are standard unbiased estimators for the sample variance and sample covariance.

There are two practical problems in applying the regeneration point method, namely

- How to choose the regeneration point sequence, and

- How many tours have to be simulated for the asymptotic theory to become valid.

The regeneration points may be conveniently defined through a regeneration state such that each time the system moves out of that state defines a regeneration point. In a Markovian system, each state may serve as a regeneration state. Note that a network in $\mathbb{Q}$ is Markovian if interarrival time distributions, service time distributions, and work demand distributions are of stage type [Cox (1955)]. We shall give preference to a regeneration state which is easy to define and which occurs frequently. There is empirical evidence that for a given amount of simulated time, t_0, say, the results obtained by a frequently occurring regeneration state are closer to the asymptotic limit than those for a less frequently occurring regeneration state. Note that in the limit $n \rightarrow \infty$ the confidence intervals become independent of the regeneration state [Crane and Iglehart (1974b)]. For a general network in $\mathbb{Q}$, a unique state may be fairly complicated to describe. The following are components of such a state:

- The time until the next arrival from each source in the network. In the special case of exponential interarrival distributions, we may note the *memoryless* property and not consider the time until the next arrival. In the special case of distributions consisting of several exponential stages [Cox (1955)], we need only identify the current distribution stage.

- The current population of the network.

- The placements of jobs in the network. Note that many network elements such as set gates, fission gates, split gates, etc., perform their functions instantaneously. The only elements which jobs may visit for nonzero amounts of time are classes, allocate gates, and fusion gates.

- Distinctions among jobs at classes, allocate gates, and fusion gates. For example, different jobs within a class may possess different numbers of tokens, or have may different values of their job variable, or may differ in being related or not related to other jobs. The same distribution aspects of interarrival times may also apply to service times on overhead periods. Similarly, jobs at an allocate gate may differ in the number of tokens requested.

- Interrelationships among jobs at classes or allocate gates or among jobs at a collection of classes or allocate gates (an active or a passive queue)—in particular, the order in which jobs will be served or allocated to if there is such an order or more than one order (with the processor sharing queueing discipline, order is irrelevant; with priority disciplines there may be only one possible ordering).

- The current number of tokens if that number may fluctuate due to destroy and create gates.

To date, no automatic way to select an optimal regeneration state is known. Another unanswered question is to what extent one can use *fuzzy* regeneration states. A fuzzy regeneration state is a set of states with a sufficiently strong common attribute. In RESQ, we do in fact use such fuzzy regeneration points which are defined by the population vector alone. The way the user defines such a state is shown in Figure 4.4.12. There is limited empirical evidence that this procedure works satisfactorily.

As important a problem as the choice of an appropriate regeneration state is the question of how many tours one has to simulate for the asymptotic theory to become valid. Depending on the system, an appropriate value of n may vary widely (e.g., less than 100 to more than 10,000). We must be concerned to simulate long enough so that the confidence intervals are valid, that is, so that they contain the true value the right number of times as the sample of observations becomes large. Again, there is a lack of an exact theory. There is evidence that if one simulates long enough for the confidence intervals to be usefully narrow, then one obtains the expected coverage [Moeller and Sauer (1977)]. This observation suggests a sequential technique to decide when to stop the simulation. We define two parameters, a number N_0 of tours and a threshold δ_0 for the confidence interval width. We start to simulate N_0 cycles and then calculate the confidence interval. If its width is less than δ_0, we spop; otherwise, we continue for another N_0 tours and repeat the procedure. Lavenberg has recently shown that this procedure is asymptotically valid as $\delta_0 \longrightarrow C$. We have implemented this sequential testing rule in RESQ.

Finally, we wish to address once more the question of the reliability of simulation results. We must always keep in mind that running a simulation is a statistical experiment and that there is inherent variability in the results. Statistical analyses, such as determining confidence intervals, are very important, but confidence intervals are never guaranteed to cover the true value. In addition to determining confidence intervals on a single experiment, it is often desirable to replicate the experiment using different random number streams.

Special problems may also arise with ill-defined networks. It may, for example, take a long time until a potential deadlock is realized. In such a case, one might interpret transient solutions as having reached a steady state. Note that such solutions may look quite stationary until the deadlock is actually realized.

4.4. PROGRAM IMPLEMENTATION AND EXAMPLES

The goals of a software package for modeling of computer systems are as follows:

- Improve quality and accuracy of modeling.
- Bring expertise which is not otherwise available to bear in the methods of solution.
- Free the modeler from having to write his own solution programs; make more of his time available for the task of modeling.
- Provide standards for terminology and output formats within a modeler community. Allow for a more meaningful comparison of results.

Of critical importance is the choice of the model class Q. This class should be rich enough in systems and work-load features to allow meaningful modeling, it should force the modeler to a certain level of abstraction. The choice is made easy in the case of the algebraic method of solution. Clearly, one would want to implement the full class Q^* of separable queueing networks (see Section 4.3.1). The very versatility of simulation as a method of solution, however, makes the choice of a suitable Q far from self-evident. We have decided on the class of queueing networks of Section 4.2. This class still allows a relatively simple *parameterized* description. A derivation to more general classes of stochastic models would in our view open the Pandora's box of yet another simulation language.

For a software package to meet the stated objectives, the following requirements should be met:

- Ease of use, efficiency.
- Provision for an interactive definition evaluation and alteration of models.
- Provision for interfacing with user-written programs to create and document permanent models.
- Indication of method of solution and of the accuracy of the results.

In our opinion, the last item is of special significance. The notion of accuracy depends on the method of solution. First we wish to distinguish clearly between the inaccuracy of modeling and the error or the uncertainty introduced by the method of solution. It is the second kind of error which concerns us. In the case of a numerical solution of an algebraic system of equations, the error can be analyzed by methods from numerical analysis. The nature of simulation results, however, is entirely different. The outcome of a simulation run is a realization of a stochastic process. A performance measure such as a mean queue length, for example, becomes a random variable. To make a statement about such a performance measure, one first has to extimate by statistical techniques its distribution. Then provided that one can assure by theoretical means that this distribution is at least asymptotically centered around the true value one can make a statement that with a given probability the performance measure falls within a certain interval (called the *confidence interval*). We feel strongly that such confidence intervals should always be part of simulation output. In summary, the following can be said about the accuracy of various methods of solutions:

- Results obtained by the convolution algorithm for separable networks are, for all practical purposes, error free.

- So far, little is known about the accuracy of approximate solutions such as forced decomposition and diffusion approximation. This lack of a theoretical foundation makes these methods less attractive for inclusion in a general software package. Output should always be clearly labeled as being of unknown accuracy.

- Confidence intervals can be computed automatically by the regeneration point method (see Section 4.3.13).

The remainder of this section is devoted to a description of the design and of the implementation of a program package called RESQ (for research queueing analyzer). The overall structure has already been given in Figure 4.1.1.

RESQ is the synthesis of previously developed program packages for the three methods of solution (i.e., QNET4 for separable queueing networks [Reiser (1975b, 1976a)], IQNA for approximate analytic solutions [MacNair (1976)] [method of Chandy et al. (1975b))], and APLOMB for simulative solution of general networks [Sauer (1975, 1977)]). The interactive part and the subroutine interface follow a design similar to that of QNET4.

4.4.1. Routing Description Language

The description of a queueing network in Q is straightforward but for the definition of the routing in Section 4.2.3, we have defined a formal notation to describe routing rules. This notation provides the basis of the routing description language of RESQ. To reduce the effort necessary to complete the routing of a network, we shall introduce the following extensions:

- A set of transitions $\{i_1 \rightarrow j_1; p_1, i_2 \rightarrow j_2; p_2, \ldots, i_m \rightarrow j_m; p_m\}$ can be described in parallel as follows:

$$i_1, i_2, \ldots, i_m \rightarrow j_1, j_2, \ldots, j_m; p_1, p_2, \ldots, p_m \qquad (4.4.1)$$

If all probabilities are unity, (4.4.1) reduces to

$$i_1, i_2, \ldots, i_m \rightarrow j_1, j_2, \ldots, j_m$$

- A set of transitions converging at a node j, $\{i_1 \rightarrow j; p_1, i_2 \rightarrow j; p_2, \ldots, i_m \rightarrow j; p_m\}$, can be combined into

$$i_1, i_2, \ldots, i_m \rightarrow j; p_1, p_2, \ldots, p_m \qquad (4.4.2)$$

or if all probabilities are equal to unity,

$$i_1, i_2, \ldots, i_m \rightarrow j \qquad (4.4.3)$$

- Routing statements of the form (4.2.2) to (4.2.5) and (4.4.1) to (4.4.3) can be chained together such that each "to part" serves as the "from part" of the next arrow. An example of chaining is given in Figure 4.4.1.

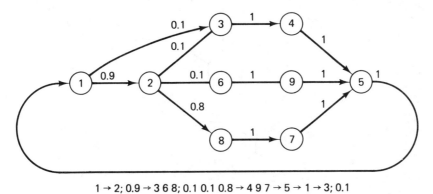

$$1 \to 2; 0.9 \to 3\ 6\ 8; 0.1\ 0.1\ 0.8 \to 4\ 9\ 7 \to 5 \to 1 \to 3; 0.1$$

Figure 4.4.1. Chaining of routing description statements. Each "to part" serves as "from part" of the next arrow.

It is also useful to distinguish the forks corresponding to fission and split gates from the normal choice rules [e.g., (4.2.2) to (4.2.5)]. If node i is a split gate (fission gate), then we write

$$i \longrightarrow j_1, j_2, \ldots, j_n; \textit{split} \tag{4.4.4}$$

and

$$i \longrightarrow j_1, j_2, \ldots, j_n; \textit{fission} \tag{4.4.5}$$

respectively. Note that predicates can only be given at forks, as discussed in Section 4.2.3.

As a first example, Figure 4.4.2 shows the description of the routing of the network given in Figure 4.2.6. We made the additional assumption that the fork at node 3 is probabilistic with 0.3 being the probability to leave and 0.7 being the probability to return to node 1.

A second example is furnished in Figure 4.4.3, where we portray a simple

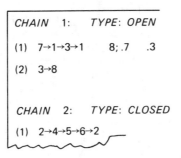

Figure 4.4.2. Routing definition for the network of Fig. 4.2.6.

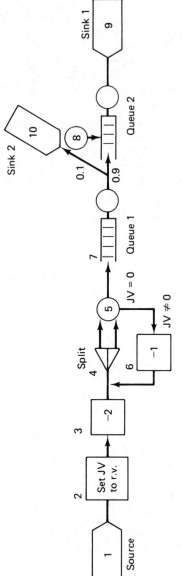

Figure 4.4.3. Sample network with batch arrivals.

queueing network consisting of one chain, a source which generates batch arrivals of random size, and two queues in series. This example also shows how set and split gates can be used to obtain a source with batch arrivals. Note that set and split gates introduce zero delay; hence the subnetwork before queue 1 generates a set of jobs instantaneously at the time points when the source generates jobs. The routing of the network in Figure 4.4.3 is given in Figure 4.4.4.

$$CHAIN \quad 1: \quad TYPE: OPEN$$

(1) $1 \rightarrow 2 \rightarrow 3 \rightarrow 4 \rightarrow 5 \quad 5; SPLIT$

(2) $5 \rightarrow 6 \quad 7; JV \neq 0 \quad JV = 0$

(3) $6 \rightarrow 4$

(4) $7 \rightarrow 8 \quad 10; .9 \quad .1$

(5) $8 \rightarrow 9$

Figure 4.4.4. Routing definition for the network of Fig. 4.4.3.

4.4.2. User Interfaces

RESQ provides an interactive dialogue interface and a subroutine interface. The dialogue interface is built around four parameter free commands, namely,

- *SETUP*:   To define a network.
- *EVAL*:   To provide parameters, which depend on the method of solution, and to evaluate results.
- *CHANGE*:   To change network structure and parameters.
- *LIST*:   To list parameters.

Each of the commands leads the user through a question and answer protocol. The design of such a protocol should be guided by human factors such as the need for conciseness and responsiveness and the avoidance of redundant or superfluous questions. A compromise must be made between the tutorial content of a question and its speed of appearance on the terminal. We have chosen to use brief questions whose meanings are not always self-evident. To help the novice user, each question may be answered by *HOW*. The *HOW* function then provides a detailed explanation of the meaning of the question and of the required input format. The comment is then followed by a second chance for the user to input the required parameter. Extensive checking of the validity and consistency of the data is another important requirement. Errors should be reported at the earliest possible moment, and a chance to correct the error should be given immediately. An example of a protocol with error messages and with the use of the *HOW* function is given in Figure 4.4.5.

Except for the routing (which we discussed in the previous section), the protocol for the description of a network is straightforward. Some examples of complete pro-

```
                            SETUP
          METHOD: SIMULATION
          ERROR:  CODE
          METHOD: HOW
          CHOOSE A METHOD OF SOLUTION. ENTER
          QNET4   FOR EXACT ANALYTIC SOLUTION OF
                      SEPARABLE QUEUING NETWORKS,
          IQNA      FOR APPROXIMATE ANALYTIC SOLUTION,
          APLOMB FOR SIMULATION.
          TRY AGAIN: APLOMB
          COMMENT:  EXTENDED CENTRAL SERVER MODEL
          NUMBER OF:
                  .
                  .
                  .
```

Figure 4.4.5. *SETUP* protocol with error message
and the use of the *HOW* function.

tocols are found in Section 4.4.4. Of interest here is the comment feature (which can be turned off if so desired). Providing comments describing the resources greatly enhances the readability of protocols and should also facilitate model documentation.

Besides the dialogue mode, there is a set of subroutines to interface RESQ with user programs. These subroutines are organized into four groups as follows:

- Declarative subroutines, e.g.,
  ENV: To define a RESQ environment,
  DEFCH: To define a routing chain.

- Subroutines to set or change parameters, e.g.,
  SETAR: Arrival rates,
  SETPR: Processing rate of a server.

- Function to invoke a method of solution,
  SOLV: To activate QNET4, IQNA, or APLOMB.

- Functions to return (as an argument) selected results, e.g.,
  PO: Population size,
  RT: Response time,
  QD: Queue size distribution,
  TP: Throughput, etc.

It is not our intention to give here a full account of all subroutines and their detailed syntax. It is important to note, however, that these subroutines also provide error and consistency checking to as great an extent as possible. More details are found in Reiser (1975).

4.4.3. On the Program Implementation

As already mentioned, RESQ is the combination of QNET4, IQNA, and APLOMB. The original QNET4 program is written in APL, IQNA is written in PL/1, and APLOMB is written in FORTRAN. We decided not to rewrite the programs. The interactive RESQ interface uses the APL system; the RESQ subroutine interface is an PL/1. A PL/1 version of QNET4 has also been added. The communication between the APL system and the batch languages is via files. In the VM/370 environment the swapping of systems can be automated and hidden from the user, who needs not be aware that APL has been suspended and a batch system entered. In the actual program implementation, some further restrictions have to be imposed on the class of networks, $\mathcal{Q}$. In the sequel, we shall discuss briefly some of these additional restrictions.

The algorithms for the evaluation of separable networks, as given in Section 4.3, leave the number of closed chains free. Practical programming languages, however, require a fixed number of indices. This limitation will impose an upper bound on L, the number of closed chains. We chose $L = 2$ in APL QNET4 and $L = 5$ in PL/1 QNET4. One should note that storage limitations set a practical limit on L, which will be quite low in any event. In APL, the use of indices should be minimized. This has led to a separate treatment of the cases $L = 1$ and $L = 2$. Array operators could then be substituted for explicit loops, which led to a significantly enhanced performance. The APL system may, in fact, be viewed as a *parallel* computing system with array processing. Some performance figures for an APL CMS system running on a 370/168 computer are summarized in Tables 4.4.1 and 4.4.2.

Table 4.4.1. CPU Times (sec) of APL QNET4 for the Case $L = 1$ (370/168, APL/CMS) [N = number of queues, K = population (all queues fixed rates)]

N \ K	100	1000
100	0.17	1.4
500	0.38	3.6

Table 4.4.2. CPU Times (sec) of APL QNET4 for the Case $L = 2$, $K_2 = 50$ (370/168, APL/CMS)

N \ K_1	0	25	50
100	5.0	10.5	32
500	24.2	73.3	158

APLOMB is implemented as a conventional event-driven simulation. Its two distinguishing features are that it is specifically tailored to the class of networks defined in Section 4.2 and that it has the regenerative confidence interval techniques built in. The regenerative technique and some practical aspects of it have been introduced in Section 4.3.13. The concepts of fuzzy regeneration states and the sequential stopping rule are realized is APLOMB.

APLOMB makes certain implementation restrictions on the class of networks, Q. In particular the queueing disciplines are limited to FCFS, PS, LCFS, priority, priority with preemption, cyclic polling of classes, and first fit. (First fit is a version of FCFS modified for passive resources. When tokens become available, they are allocated to the first customer waiting whose request can be satisfied, even if some other customer has been waiting longer.) It is possible for experienced users to define their own queueing disciplines by supplying appropriate FORTRAN subroutines. APLOMB also limits the distributions to a parameterized class consisting of discrete distributions, a generalized Erlang distribution, and a uniform distribution. Other forms can be added, but these three have been found to be sufficient for a wide variety of models which can be realized by a network of exponential stages.

The generalized Erlang distribution is especially important because

- It is especially appropriate to regenerative techniques.
- It includes practically important mixtures of exponential distributions such as the hyperexponential distribution and the classical Erlang distribution.
- It can approximate other distributions well when sufficiently many stages are used.

In many practical modeling applications, the user does not have a complete characterization of the distributions and can be satisfied with specifying only a few parameters, such as mean and variance, for example. APLOMB provides a two-parameter family of distributions specified by the mean and coefficient of variation. Special cases of the generalized Erlang distribution are used. However, when the coefficient of variation is small, then many stages are required and simulation will be slowed down. Therefore we substitute a uniform distribution whenever the number of stages becomes greater than a certain thseshold (typically four). In RESQ, we have decided to use the two-parameter family of distributions (mean and coefficient of variation) for all continuous distribution. Whether this choice is sufficiently general must first be borne out in practice. Clearly, the addition of other distributional forms does not pose serious difficulties. We use the following square bracket notation,

$$WORK\ DEMAND\ DISTR.:\ [5, 1.5]$$

which denotes a distribution with a mean of 5 and a coefficient of variation of 1.5.

4.4.4. Examples

We shall subsepuently give three examples: a central server model, its extension, and a communication line with pacing. The examples are all somewhat idealized since their only purpose is to illustrate the use of RESQ.

As a first example, we consider an interactive terminal subsystem, as shown in Figure 4.4.6. For simplicity, we assume that the batch work load does not interfere

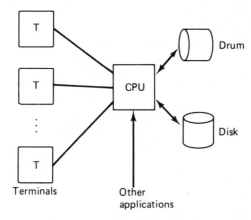

Figure 4.4.6. A simple terminal oriented subsystem.

with the interactive subsystem (i.e., the subsystem takes preemptive priority over the other applications). The following parameter values are given:

- Number of terminals: 20.
- Effective MIPS rate of CPU (after subtraction of supervisor overhead): 0.1.
- Path length between I/O requests: 2000 instructions.
- Total path length of job (mean): 40,000 instructions.
- Percentage of I/O to disk: 20%.
- Maximum number of storage resident jobs: 4.
- I/O transfer time disk (mean): 50 msec.
- I/O transfer time drum (mean): 8 msec.

We are interested in response times, device utilizations, and throughput.

First we assume that there are always exactly four jobs in storage. There results a closed central server model [Buzen (1971b)], as shown in Figure 4.4.7. The central server model provides an estimate for a jobs residency time in the hardware. It also provides an upper bound on throughput. The central server model is in Q* and can therefore be solved algebraically. *SETUP* and *EVAL* protocols are given in Figures 4.4.8 and in 4.4.9.

The central server model does not take into account the queueing of jobs for storage and hence is not capable of providing meaningful response time figures. A more complete model is portrayed in Figure 4.4.10, where storage is introduced as a passive resource.

The *SETUP* protocol for the extended central server model of Figure 4.4.10 is given in Figure 4.4.11. Although analytic or approximate techniques are available for

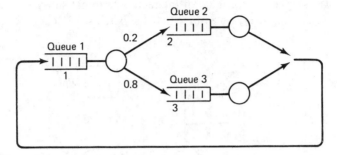

Figure 4.4.7. The central server model (queue 1 : CPU ; queue 2 : disk ; queue 3 : drum).

```
                        SETUP

METHOD:     QNET4
COMMENT:    SIMPLE CENTRAL SERVER MODEL

NUMBER OF:
    CHAINS:    1
    QUEUES:    3
    CLASSES:   3
    SOURCES:   0

CHAIN 1:   TYPE:   CLOSED
(1)   1→2   3;.2   .8→1
(2)
CHAIN POPULATION:  4

QUEUE 1:   TYPE: PS
COMMENT: CPU
RATE:        .1
WORK DEMAND DISTR: .002

QUEUE 2:   TYPE:  FCFS
COMMENT: DISK
STIME DISTR: .05

 QUEUE 3:   TYPE: FCFS
COMMENT:  DRUM
STIME DISTR:    .008

END OF SETUP.
```

Figure 4.4.8. SETUP protocol for the central server model of Fig. 4.4.7. The parameter given for the service time distributions is the mean service time. If no coefficient of variation is given the value one is assumed (i.e., exponential distribution).

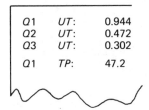

Q1	UT:	0.944
Q2	UT:	0.472
Q3	UT:	0.302
Q1	TP:	47.2

Figure 4.4.9. Results for the central server model (UT: utilization; TP: throughput).

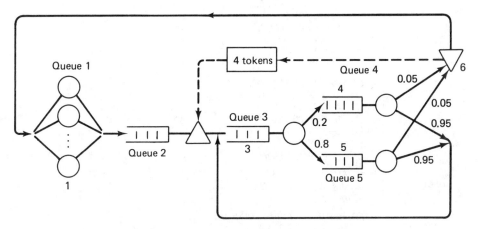

Figure 4.4.10. Extended central server model of the system portrayed in Fig. 4.4.6. (Queue 1: terminals; queue 2: storage; queue 3: CPU; queue 4: disk; queue 5: drum).

systems similar to the one of Figure 4.4.10 [Reiser and Konheim (1976)], we shall use simulation as our method of solution. Simulation-dependent parameters are furnished in the *EVAL* command as shown in Figure 4.4.12. Initial state and regeneration state are both defined as all jobs at the terminals. Initial state and regeneration state are both defined by giving a list of numbers which are population sizes in order of increasing node numbers. The simulator will sequentially sample each time the model has regenerated 20 times or changed state 200,000 times. When the width of confidence interval for the queueing time at queue 2 is less than 15% of the point estimate, the simulation will stop. (This queueing time is our measure of response time). 65539 will be used to determine the starting values for all of the (pseudo-) random number streams.

Excerpts from RESQ output are given in Figure 4.4.13. This output shows that the basic central server model did well in indicating utilizations and throughput. The mean response time, including queueing for storage, was about 3.6 seconds.

We must be cautious in interpreting simulation output. Although we are given 95% confidence intervals, there will still be times when the intervals do not cover the

```
                    SETUP

METHOD:     APLOMB
COMMENT:    EXTENDED CENTRAL SERVER MODEL

NUMBER OF:
     CHAINS:    1
     QUEUES:    5
     CLASSES:   4
     ALLOCATE GATES:    1
     RELEASE GATES:     1
     CREATE GATES:      0
     DESTROY GATES:     0
     SET GATES:         0
     FISSION GATES:     0
     FUSION GATES:      0
     SPLIT GATES:       0
     SOURCES:           0

CHAIN 1:  TYPE:   CLOSED
(1)  1→2→3→4  5; .2  .8
(2)  4→6 3; .05 .95
(3)  5→6 3; .05 .95
(4)  6→1
(5)
CHAIN POPULATION: 20

QUEUE 1:    TYPE: IS
COMMENT:    TERMINALS
STIME DISTR:  5

QUEUE 2:    TYPE: PASSIVE
COMMENT:    STORAGE
TOKENS:     4
QDSPL:      FCFS
ALLOCATE GATES: 2
     AMOUNT:    1
RELEASE GATES:   6

QUEUE 3:    TYPE:  PS
COMMENT:    CPU
RATE:       1
WORK DEMAND DISTR:  .002

QUEUE 4:    TYPE: FCFS
COMMENT:    DISK
STIME DISTR:  [.05, 1]

QUEUE 5:    TYPE: FCFS
COMMENT:    DRUM
STIME DISTR:  [.008,1]

END OF SETUP.
```

Figure 4.4.11. SETUP protocol of the extended central server model.

160

```
                        EVAL

INITIALIZE: 20 0 0 0 0 0
REGEN     : 20 0 0 0 0 0
SEQUENTIAL SAMPLING LIMITS:
    CYCLES: 20
      STATE CHANGES:   200000
CONFIDENCE LEVEL:      95
CHECK QUEUE:           2
       RELATIVE PCT. INTERVAL WIDTH: 15
SEED: 65539

            .
            .
            .
```

Figure 4.4.12. Simulation dependent parameters given in the *EVAL* command.

```
SIMULATED TIME: 858
NUMBER OF STATE CHANGES: 8.12E4
NUMBER OF CYCLES: 20
CORRELATION OF CYCLE LENGTHS: 0.327
```

Q2	UT−:	0.959	Q1	QL−:	11.6
	UT:	0.961		QL:	12
	UT+:	0.97		QL+:	12.4
Q3	UT−:	0.917	Q2	QL−:	7.58
	UT:	0.924		QL:	7.98
	UT+:	0.931		QL+:	8.37
Q4	UT−:	0.46	Q3	QL−:	2.61
	UT:	0.47		QL:	2.65
	UT+:	0.48		QL+:	2.7
Q5	UT−:	0.291	Q4	QL−:	0.765
	UT:	0.294		QL:	0.791
	UT+:	0.297		QL+:	0.818
			Q5	QL−:	0.391
				QL:	0.395
				QL−:	0.4
Q2	TP−:	2.34			
	TP:	2.36			
	TP+:	2.39			
Q3	TP−:	45.7	Q2	QT−:	3.19
	TP:	46.2		QT:	3.37
	TP+:	46.6		QT+:	3.56

Figure 4.4.13. Excerpts from the output which corresponds to the simulation parameters of Fig. 4.4.12. Lower bounds of the confidence intervals are indicated with a minus sign, upper bounds with a plus sign. Unsigned codes are point estimates. The codes are UT: utilization; TP: throughput; QT: queueing time (including service time).

161

expected value. It would be desirable to find a regeneration point that would occur more frequently so that we could have more faith in the asymptotic assumptions made in calculating confidence intervals. From the output of our first run we can try to choose a more frequently occurring regeneration point. A choice which seems promising is the state with 12 jobs at the terminals, 8 jobs in storage or waiting for storage, and all 4 jobs in storage using the CPU. This state is close to the mean values of Figure 4.4.13, and hence we expect it to occur more frequently than the state defined in Figure 4.4.12. Figure 4.4.14 shows RESQ input for the choice. We choose the other parameters so that the simulation will be as similar as possible to the previous run, and we can compare the effect of the regeneration point on the confidence intervals produced. Simulation output for this new choice is given in Figure 4.4.15. We conclude that

```
                        EVAL

INITIALIZE: 12 8 0 0 0 0
REGEN     : 12 8 4 0 0 0
SEQUENTIAL SAMPLING LIMITS:
        CYCLES: 9999
        STATE CHANGES: 82000
CONFIDENCE LEVEL: 95
CHECK NODE: 2
        RELATIVE PCT. INTERVAL WIDTH: 100
SEED: 65539
```

Figure 4.4.14.   Definition of a more frequently occurring regeneration point.

```
SIMULATED TIME: 847
NUMBER OF STATE CHANGES: 8.12E4
NUMBER OF CYCLES: 1.96E3
CORRELATION OF CYCLE LENGTHS: 0.0067
```

Q2	UT−:	0.937	Q2	TP−:	2.29
	UT:	0.967		TP:	2.36
	UT+:	0.996		TP+:	2.43
Q3	UT−:	0.921	Q3	TP−:	46
	UT:	0.928		TP:	46.3
	UT+:	0.935		TP+:	46.7
Q4	UT−:	0.462			
	UT:	0.472	Q2	QT−:	3.15
	UT+:	0.482		QT:	3.41
				QT:	3.67
Q5	UT−:	0.291			
	UT:	0.295			
	UT+	0.298			

Figure 4.4.15.   Output for the regeneration point of Fig. 4.4.14.

indeed the definition of the regeneration point had little effect on the confidence intervals. Repeating the run with a different seed of 314159 shows more of an effect on point estimates and confidence intervals (see the results in Figure 4.4.16 for this case).

SIMULATED TIME: 851
NUMBER OF STATE CHANGES: 8. 12E4
NUMBER OF CYCLES: 1.75E3
CORRELATION OF CYCLE LENGTHS: −0.0353

Q2	*UT−*:	0.93	Q2	*TP−*:	2.18
	UT:	0.963		*TP*:	2.26
	UT+:	0.996		*TP+*:	2.34

Q3	*UT−*:	0.92	Q3	*TP−*:	46.1
	UT:	0.93		*TP*:	46.6
	UT+:	0.94		*TP+*:	47.1

Q4	*UT−*:	0.447			
	UT:	0.458	Q2	*QT−*:	3.34
	UT+:	0.469		*QT*:	3.67
				QT+:	4

Q5	*UT−*:	0.291
	UT:	0.295
	UT+:	0.3

Figure 4.4.16. Output for a seed of 314159 (same regeneration point as in Fig. 4.4.15).

Our second example will be a model of a communication line between a computer and a terminal. We shall consider a pacing protocol which might be used to prevent the terminal from receiving more data than it can handle. Messages of 250 characters will be sent to the terminal. After one message has been sent, the host must wait until the terminal notifies it that another message may be sent. Let us assume that the message is broken into two packets of 125 characters, that the pacing response from the terminal consists of a single character packet, and that each packet has a header of 8 characters. Also assume that the line is half-duplex with a speed of 30 characters per second and that the messages arrive from the host with an exponential interarrival time of mean 12.5 seconds. A diagram of our model is given in Figure 4.4.17.

We use the passive resource to effect the pacing protocol, fission and fusion gates for the packetizing of the data message, and a split gate to produce the pacing response. The model works as follows:

1. When the terminal is ready to receive data, a message arrives at fission gate 2 and becomes two packets.

2. One of the packets has its job variable set to 1 (instead of 0) to indicate that it should produce a pacing response.

3. Both packets acquire a token from the passive resource, leaving no tokens available for subsequently arriving messages.

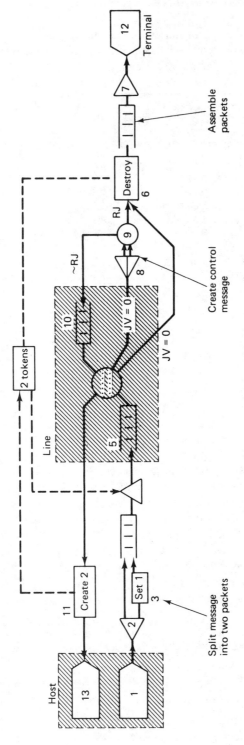

Figure 4.4.17. RESQ model for the communication line with pacing.

164

```
                    SETUP

METHOD:      APLOMB
COMMENT:     COMMUNICATION LINE WITH PACING

NUMBER OF:
      CHAINS:     1
      QUEUES:     2
      CLASSES:  2
      ALLOCATE GATES:  1
      RELEASE GATES:   0
      CREATE GATES:    1
      DESTROY GATES:   1
      SET GATES:       1
      FISSION GATES:   1
      FUSION GATES:    1
      SPLIT GATES:     1

CHAIN 1:  TYPE: OPEN
(1)  1→2→4 3; FISSION
(2)  3→4→5→6 8; JV = 0 JV≠0
(3)  6→7→12
(4)  8→9 9; SPLIT
(5)  9→6 10; RJ  ~RJ
(6)  10→11→13
(7)

SOURCES:  1
COMMENT: HOST COMPUTER
INTERARR. TIME DISTR:   [12.5,1]

QUEUE 1:   TYPE: PASSIVE
COMMENT: PACING CONTROL
TOKENS:     2
QDSPL:      FCFS
ALLOCATE GATES: 4
      AMOUNT:       1
DESTROY GATES:   6
CREATE GATES:    11
      AMOUNT:       2

QUEUE 2:   TYPE: FCFS
COMMENT: HALF DUPLEX LINE
CLASSES:              5                10
STIME DISTR:   [(125+8)÷30,0]  [(1 + 8) ÷ 30, 0]

LIST OF SET GATES:   3
      SET VALUES:       1

LIST OF FUSION GATES: 7

END OF SETUP.
```

Figure 4.4.18. SETUP protocol for the system of Fig. 4.4.17.

165

4. The packets are transmitted through the line.

5. The marked packet produces a pacing response.

6. The data packets destroy their tokens and are assembled into the message again and are received by the terminal.

7. The pacing response is transmitted back through the line and generates new tokens.

8. If a data message has been blocked waiting for a passive resource, it may now proceed.

In Figure 4.4.17 we have used the create and destroy gates, which were briefly mentioned in Section 4.2. A job passing through the create gate generates two tokens which replenish the pool. A job passing the destroy gate has its token count set to zero (the tokens are considered destroyed). The predicate RJ is true if the job has been generated by a fission gate; ~RJ is the negation of RJ. The *SETUP* protocol is given in Figure 4.4.18. One should note how expressions are substituted for numbers in the definition of the service time distribution of queue 2. In fact, expressions (or functions) can be given everywhere (except in the definition of the routing). At this point, we are not interested in a quantitative discussion of the results of the model given in Figure 4.4.17. We therefore do not provide listings of its output. The main purpose of the last example is to demonstrate the versatility of the class of networks in Q and to exhibit the power and conciseness of the RESQ input processor.

4.5. CONCLUSION

In this chapter we have presented our views on the design an implementation of queueing network software. While at the time of this writing RESQ was quite new, we have gained considerable experience with the QNET4 package. QNET4 has been widely accepted throughout IBM's development projects. Its success is due to the fact that the objectives set forth in Section 4.4 have largely been met. The user-oriented front end and the astonishing efficiency have been especially vital factors. QNET4 has been applied to different problem areas such as the performance evaluation of storage hierarchies and mass storage systems; the performance evaluation of small business systems; the modeling of parts of telecommunication networks; the evaluation of multiprocessor environments, including storage interference and software locks; and the evaluation of a virtual personalized computing system. The spectrum of problems ranges from hardware to software. So far the most use occurred in development groups, although there has been increased interest in marketing and field engineering divisions recently.

The major stumbling block in the application of QMET4 is the lack of priority disciplines and limited access to subsystems. The hierarchical decomposition technique is, so far, the only way out, unless one is willing to resort to simulation, the primary area addressed by RESQ.

We feel that a more or less definitive state has been reached in the area of separable queueing networks, both with respect to the class of models and to their numerical solution. Obtaining analytic results beyond that class is hard and computationally severely limited. Nevertheless, we feel it worthwhile to pursue further research into the numerical solution of balance equations. Having a rich enough set of such solutions serves the purpose of a standard against which approximate methods and simulation can be validated.

Finally, it would be very desirable to obtain a theoretical foundation for approximation techniques which to date are mostly of a heuristic nature. This, again, is a very hard problem, and we do not expect too much progress in the near future.

ACKNOWLEDGMENT

We are grateful to the many contributions of Ed MacNair to the design and implemention of the RESQ interface. We also deeply appreciate the many discussions we had with Steve Lavenberg.

CHAPTER 5

GRAPH MODELS

IN

PROGRAMMING SYSTEMS

J. L. BAER
Department of Computer Science
University of Washington
Seattle, Washington

5.1. INTRODUCTION

In this chapter we shall illustrate the use of directed graph models in programming systems. The two principal reasons behind the development of such models are that, first, they provide an excellent descriptive vehicle for a variety of problems arising in many areas of computer science, and that, second, the use of graph theoretic analytical techniques supplies implementors with tools for proving the correctness or improving the performance of systems.

The main feature of a directed graph from the modeling standpoint is that it indicates precedence constraints. If two nodes A and B are linked by an arc from A to B, this implies that the actions, e.g., computational tasks, happening at node A must precede those of node B. The constraint can be related to time, for example, loading must precede execution, or to control flow, for example, when A and B are two consecutive statements in a program. This key idea has found numerous applications, and it is not the purpose of this chapter to review them all exhaustively. Very generally one can see three situations in which directed graphs have been widely used for modeling purposes:

1. Program Flowcharts. The idea of representing the logical flow of a program by flowcharts is as old as programming itself. Nodes (or boxes) model (groups of) statements, while arcs show the flow of control. If the nodes contain a complete description of the computational tasks, i.e., if the graph is totally interpreted, we have not only an excellent documentation of the program but also a framework on which code optimization or program parallelization techniques can be applied. If we suppress some, or all, of the interpretation, then we can look to the flowchart as, for example, a schema to yield rules of structured programming or as a sequence of weighted tasks which have to be partitioned into independent or fixed-sized units for segmentation or pagination purposes. If we extend the flowchart to allow interpretation on the logical flow, then we can model parallel computations. Some of these applications will be explained in more detail in subsequent sections.

2. Task Scheduling. The representation of job-shop problems by directed acyclic graphs is very natural. Timing constraints couched in such unelegant statements as "operation i_1 of job j_1 must precede operation i_2 of job j_2" are depicted easily by a graph. The PERT models (nodes are events, and arcs are necessary activities leading to the achievement of an event) have been widely used in industry. More importantly, the graph representations often allow for the determination of optimal or suboptimal schedules, with their bounds in the latter case, through the use of nonenumerative algorithms. Of particular importance are those algorithms which are not too *hard*, i.e., which run with a number of steps not growing exponentially with the size of the graph.

3. State Graph Diagrams. The representation of the potential dynamic evolution of a system is often realized by showing the state diagram as a directed graph. Each node in the graph represents one of the finite number of states that the system might reach, while a path in the graph represents a series of transitions (possibly infinite) leading from state to state. Among the many applications of state diagrams one can list the description of the control of automata such as Turing machines or finite state automata, obtaining the reachability graph of some models for parallel computation, and the study of deadlocks in operating systems.

Rather than stepping from one application to another, we shall organize the remainder of this chapter as follows. In Section 5.2 we shall give the definitions relative to graph theory needed for the sequel, show alternative computer representations of directed graphs, and present a (small) number of classical graph algorithms that will be useful in subsequent sections. Directed acyclic graph models will then be presented in Section 5.3, with the emphasis being on deterministic scheduling. In Section 5.4 we shall deal mainly with program measurement, segmentation, optimization, and parallelization. The last topic will introduce us to models for parallel computation, treated more completely in Section 5.5. Finally, in a short conclusion we shall point out areas that will have been purposely overlooked.

5.2. DIRECTED GRAPHS

5.2.1. Definitions

There exists no standard terminology relative to graph theory. The reader is referred to Berge (1958), Harary (1969), and Deo (1974) for a sample of possible usages. We shall be concerned only with finite directed graphs.

A (finite) *directed graph* $G(X, \Gamma)$ (abbreviated digraph) consists of a (finite) set of *nodes* (or vertices) X and the function Γ mapping X into 2^X, the set of all subsets of X. An equivalent definition is $G(X, U)$, where U is the set of *arcs* $u_k = (x_i, x_j)$ with $x_i, x_j \in X$ and $x_j \in \Gamma x_i$. In figures the nodes will be represented by circles and the arcs by lines joining nodes with an arrow indicating the arc's direction.

If $u_k = (x_i, x_j) \in U$, then x_i is an *immediate predecessor* of x_j and x_j is an *immediate successor* of x_i. We shall note that $x_i \, \alpha \, x_j$. The α precedence relation is neither symmetric, nor reflexive, nor transitive. If $x_i \, \alpha \, x_j$ and $x_j \, \alpha \, x_k$, we note that $x_i \, \underline{\alpha} \, x_k$ and say that x_i is a *predecessor* of x_k and that x_k is a *successor* of x_i. The relation $\underline{\alpha}$ is transitive.

A *path* is a sequence of nodes linked by arcs, i.e., $p = \{x_i, x_j, x_k, \ldots, x_m, x_n\}$ is a path if all pairs $(x_i, x_j), (x_j, x_k), \ldots, (x_m, x_n)$ are arcs. The *path length* is the number of arcs in the path.

Example 1

Consider $G_1 = (X_1, U_1)$, where

$$X_1 = \{x_1, x_2, x_3, x_4\}$$
$$U_1 = \{(x_1, x_2), (x_1, x_3), (x_3, x_2), (x_3, x_4)\}$$

G_1 is shown in Figure 5.1. x_1 is an immediate predecessor of x_2, x_1 is a predecessor of x_4, and $p_1 = (x_1, x_3, x_4)$ is a path.

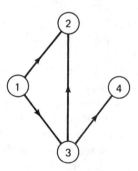

Figure 5.1. Graph G_1.

A *circuit* (or *elementary cycle*) is a path such that the initial and terminal nodes are the same and no other two nodes are the same. An elementary circuit with only two nodes, the initial and the terminal ones, which are necessarily the same, is called a *loop*. A *cycle* is a path formed by one or more circuits.

Example 2

Consider $G_2 = (X_2, U_2)$, where

$$X_2 = X_1 \quad \text{and} \quad U_2 = U_1 \cup \{(x_4, x_1), (x_2, x_2)\}$$

G_2 is shown in Figure 5.2. $p_1 = (x_1, x_3, x_4, x_1)$ is a circuit, $p_2 = (x_2, x_2)$ is a loop, and $p_3 = (x_1, x_3, x_4, x_1, x_3, x_4, x_1)$ is a cycle.

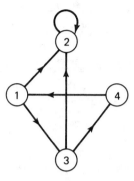

Figure 5.2. Graph G_2.

A *directed acyclic graph* (or *dag*) is a digraph without cycles (e.g., G_1 in Example 1). In a digraph, a node x_i is *reachable* from x_j if there exists a path from x_j to x_i. A node x_i is *isolated* if it is not reachable from any x_j and no x_j is reachable from x_i ($x_j \neq x_i$). A *digraph* is *connected* if it has no isolated node and *strongly connected* if any two different nodes x_i, x_j are always linked by two paths, one with x_i as initial node and one with x_j as initial node.

Example 3

Neither G_1 nor G_2 is strongly connected (note that a dag can never be strongly connected). Consider $G_3 = (X_3, U_3)$, where $X_3 = X_1$ and $U_3 = U_2 \cup \{(x_2, x_4)\}$. G_3, shown in Figure 5.3, is strongly connected.

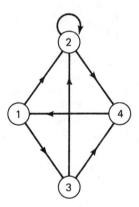

Figure 5.3. Graph G_3.

Let $G(X, U)$ be a digraph, $W \subseteq X$ be a subset of the node set, and $R \subseteq U$ be a subset of the arc set. Then $G'(W, W \times W \cap U)$ is a *subgraph* of G, and $G''(X, R)$ is a *partial* graph of G. One can also extend these definitions to that of a partial subgraph.

Example 4

Consider G_2 as shown in Figure 5.2, and let $W = \{x_1, x_3, x_4\}$. Then $G_2'(W, U')$ with $U' = \{(x_1, x_3), (x_3, x_4), (x_4, x_1)\}$ is a subgraph of G_2. Now let $R = \{(x_1, x_3), (x_3, x_4), (x_4, x_1)\}$. $G_2''(X_2, R)$ is a partial graph of G_2. Note that x_2 is an (isolated) node of G_2''.

A *maximally strongly connected subgraph* (MSCG) of a digraph $G(X, U)$ is a partial subgraph $G'(W, W \times W \cap U)$, $W \subseteq X$, such that G' is strongly connected and there exists no $x_i \in X$, $x_i \notin W$ such that x_i can be reached by some $x_j \in W$ and x_i can reach some $x_j \in W$.

Example 5

In G_2 (cf. Figure 5.2) there are two MSCG's, $G_2^1 = (X_2^1, U_2^1)$ with $X_2^1 = \{x_2\}$ and $U_2^1 = \{(x_2, x_2)\}$ and $G_2^2 = G_2'(W, U')$, as defined in Example 4. G_3 is an MSCG, and in G_1 all individual nodes are MSCG's (as in all dag's).

The *indegree* (resp. *outdegree*) of a node is the number of arcs incident in (out of) the node. A node without predecessors (successors) has indegree (outdegree) 0.

A *tree* T is a set of one or more nodes such that there exists one specially designated node called the *root* of the tree and all remaining nodes are partitioned into m (m nonnegative integer) disjoint sets $T_1, \ldots, T_m$ and each T_i is in turn a tree. A nonrecursive equivalent definition is to say that a tree is a dag, with the root being a node without successors and being a successor of all other nodes and such that if $x_i \underline{\alpha} x_j$ and $x_i \underline{\alpha} x_k$, then either $x_j \underline{\alpha} x_k$ or $x_k \underline{\alpha} x_j$. All nodes of the tree have outdegree 1 (but the root of outdegree 0). A node of indegree 0 is a *leaf*. The *level* of a node is one for the root and equal to the level of its immediate successors plus one otherwise. The *height* of a node is one for a leaf and equal to the maximum height of its immediate predecessors plus one for the others. The concept of level can be easily extended to dag's. A *forest* is a set of 0 or more disjoint trees.

Example 6

Figure 5.4 shows a tree $T = \{x_1, x_2, x_3, x_4, x_5, x_6, x_7\}$ of root x_1. x_2, x_5, x_6, x_7 are leaves. x_1 is of level 1, x_2, x_3, x_4 of level 2, and x_5, x_6, x_7 of level 3. An extension of the concept of level to G_1 yields x_2, x_4 of level 1, x_3 of level 2, and x_1 of level 3.

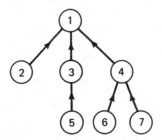

Figure 5.4. Tree T.

In the following, we shall consider trees only as special cases of dag's. Important applications of trees can be found in Knuth (1968) and Knuth (1973); they fall outside the scope of this chapter.

5.2.2. Computer Representation of Directed Graphs

In the sections to follow we shall present some algorithms which massage the graph structures. It is therefore important to have an efficient representation of these graphs. Three main data structures can be used. In the three cases we shall assume that the nodes are numbered from 1 to n. The problem is then to represent arcs, paths, cycles, etc.

1. Sequential List Representation. Arcs are listed in some prespecified order, e.g., in ascending order of their initial node. With each node we associate an index indicating where in the list is the first arc for which it is an initial node as well as the number of its immediate successors, i.e., its outdegree. The internal representation of the arc need only be the terminal node since its initial node is implicitly defined. A second list of the same format can be used for immediate predecessors.

The advantages of such a representation are that it takes little space and that retrieval of basic relationships is fast. Unhappily it is quite inflexible; i.e., any dynamic construction of the graph involving incremental addition to successor or predecessor lists has to be ruled out. Therefore its applications are quite limited.

Example 7

Figure 5.5 shows the sequential list representation of the graph $G_2(X_2, U_2)$ of Figure 5.2. A four-dimensional array or equivalently four vectors of dimension[1] $|X_2| = 4$ contain for each node i its indegree, its outdegree, an index in the list of immediate predecessors, and an index in the list of immediate successors. Two vectors of dimension $|U_2| = 6$ list terminal and initial nodes, respectively. For example, there are two immediate successors to x_3 (OUTDEGREE (3) $= 2$)

INDEGREE	OUTDEGREE	IPRED	ISUC	PARC	SARC
1	2	1	1	4	2
3	1	2	3	1	3
1	2	5	4	2	2
1	1	6	6	3	2
				1	4
				3	1

Figure 5.5. Sequential representation of G_2.

[1]We note that $|X|$ is the cardinality of the set X.

found at locations SARC (ISUC (3)) (i.e., node 2) and SARC (ISUC (3) + 1) (i.e., node 4).

2. Linked List Representation. With each node we associate a header containing information such as indegree and/or outdegree. This header also contains pointers to the next node header, a linked list of immediate predecessors, and/or a linked list of immediate successors.

Admittedly this representation is more space-consuming than the previous one. It might even be more time-consuming to search for particular items. But its flexibility, mainly the ease with which one can create or delete subgraphs, makes this method more attractive.

Example 8

A linked list representation of $G_2(X_2, U_2)$ is shown in Figure 5.6. Each list of immediate predecessors or successors is a linked stack.

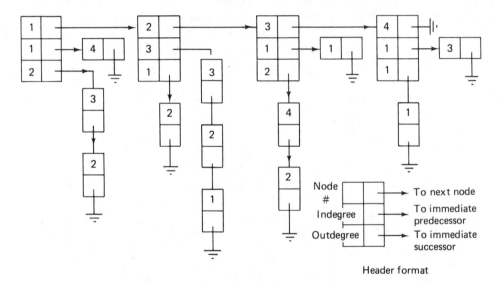

Figure 5.6. Linked list representation of G_2.

3. Boolean Matrix Representation. The presence or absence of an arc between two nodes x_i and x_j can be encoded by a single bit (or Boolean variable). Hence a square Boolean matrix M of $|X| \times |X|$ elements can represent the graph $G(X, U)$ with $M_{i,j} = 1$ if $(x_i, x_j) \in U$. In a given row (resp. column) i of the matrix all elements of value 1 represent immediate successors (resp. predecessors). Such a matrix is called the *connectivity* (or adjacency) matrix of the graph.

One advantage of such a representation is its compactness. For a graph of n nodes and a computer word of w bits, $n \cdot \lceil n/w \rceil$ words[2] are needed. This has to be com-

---

[2] $\lceil x \rceil$ is the smallest integer larger than or equal to x. Similarly, $\lfloor x \rfloor$ is the largest integer smaller than or equal to x.

pared with $cn + da$ for a linked list representation, where a is the number of arcs (a varies from n to n^2), c is a constant (in general between 3 and 6), and d is also a constant (between 2 and 4). If the graph is sparse, that is, a is $0(n)$ instead of $0(n^2)$, the list representation[3] is more advantageous for large n. If the graph is not sparse or if n and w are of the same order of magnitude, then the Boolean matrix approach is attractive. Furthermore, there exist some algorithms which use the Boolean matrix representation in an efficient way.

Example 9

The connectivity matrix of G_2 is shown in Figure 5.7. For example, the immediate successors of x_2 are found in row 2 (i.e., x_2 itself) and its immediate predecessors in column 2 (i.e., x_1, x_2, and x_3).

$$\begin{array}{c} \\ 1 \\ 2 \\ 3 \\ 4 \end{array} \begin{array}{cccc} 1 & 2 & 3 & 4 \\ \left[\begin{array}{cccc} 0 & 1 & 1 & 0 \\ 0 & 1 & 0 & 0 \\ 0 & 1 & 0 & 1 \\ 1 & 0 & 0 & 0 \end{array}\right] \end{array}$$

Figure 5.7. Connectivity matrix of graph G_2.

It is worthwhile to note that the connectivity matrix space requirements depend only on the number of nodes, while those of list representations vary with the number of arcs. An interesting exception is the case of trees. Knuth (1968) shows how general trees can be mapped into binary trees (trees with two distinguishable sons) whose representation takes cn words (c being 2 or 3 depending on the implementation). A generalization of this concept to arbitrary graphs has been attempted by Pfaltz (1975), but in order to be successful some extra nodes might have to be introduced.

5.2.3. Some Basic Algorithms

The detection of certain important properties of directed graphs are required to make use of the models that will be introduced further on. Among these properties one can list, for example, the ordering of nodes according to various criteria, shortest and longest path detection, determination of circuits, and MSCG's. The basic algorithms described below have been selected because they are executed frequently during the analysis and evaluation of the models.

Two distinct techniques are useful when implementing graph algorithms. In the breadth-first method, when a node is "visited" its immediate successors are entered in a first-in-first-out (FIFO) queue and "visited" in that order. In other words, the graph is traversed in "level order" if we allow a rather broad generalization to our definition of level. In the depth-first method, the immediate successors are pushed onto a last-in-first-out (stack) queue. Hence the traversal tends to follow one path as deeply as possible and then backtrack to an unvisited node of level lower than the last one reached. This difference in approach will become clear in the examples to follow.

---

[3] x is $0(n^\alpha)$ if x is a polynomial in n of highest term cn^α, where c is a constant.

Currently the trend is to design depth-first algorithms because they are, in general, more efficient. This last term is explained now.

In recent years, the concept of time complexity (see Chapter 6) has emerged as a potential work measure for the efficiency of an algorithm. It is linked to the number of steps that it takes to solve a given problem. For example, in our case, enumerative techniques have a tendency to grow exponentially with the size of the graph. If we claim that we have devised, or that we are using, an efficient algorithm, we have to show that its running time is less than exponential, e.g., that it is $0(n^\alpha)$, where n is the number of nodes in the graph and α is a constant. This can often be done by direct analysis, and we shall use this approach whenever possible. But it might happen that the algorithm belongs to a class of problems, called NP-complete, for which only conjectures can be made. More precisely, the conjecture is that they are not of polynomial running time if run on a deterministic model of a computer (e.g., a deterministic Turing machine), while it is known that they run in polynomial time on a non-deterministic machine. In other words, it is thought but not proven that they are of exponential running time. For example, the test to see if a digraph $G(X, U)$ has a circuit containing every node of X (a Hamiltonian circuit) belongs to the class of NP-complete problems. The reader is referred to Chapter 6 for a detailed discussion.

We shall now present some basic algorithms.

1. Topological Sort. Given a directed acyclic graph $G(X, U)$, label the nodes $x_i \in X$ in such a way that if x_i is a predecessor of x_j, label $(x_i) <$ label (x_j). The breadth-first algorithm is as follows. Let $n = |X|$, and let LABEL (x_i) be an integer between 1 and n. The other arrays and variables have self-evident meanings.

```
Comment Initialize COUNTS and QUEUE of nodes to relabel ;
         For i = 1 step 1 until n do
             begin COUNT (i) :=INDEGREE (i) ;
                 if COUNT (i) = 0 then enter (i,QUEUE) ;
             end ;
             j := 1 ;
Comment Relabel 1st element of queue and decrement Count of its
         immediate sucessors. Loop until the queue is empty ;
         while QUEUE not empty do
         begin i := front (QUEUE) ;
             LABEL (i) := j ; j := j +1
             For k ∈ ISUC (i) Comment This loop is executed OUTDEGREE(i) times do
             begin COUNT (k) := COUNT (k) − 1 ;
                 If COUNT (k) = 0 then enter (k, QUEUE) ;
             end
         end ;
```

Since every node and every arc are traversed once, the running time of this algorithm is $0(c_1 n + c_2 a)$, where a is the number of arcs (max $(a) = [n(n − 1)]/2$; i.e., the running time has a maximum of $0(n^2)$).

To change this breadth-first to a depth-first algorithm, we can use a stack instead of a queue. It is apparent that there may exist many different topological sorts of a given dag. A program to list them all can be found in Knuth and Szwarcfiter (1974).

Example 10

Consider the graph $G_4(X_4, U_4)$ of Figure 5.8(a). A breadth-first algorithm yields the relabeling of Figure 5.8(b), assuming that the arcs incident out from a given node are listed in ascending order of their terminal node. Under the same assumption a depth-first algorithm yields the relabeling of Figure 5.8(c).

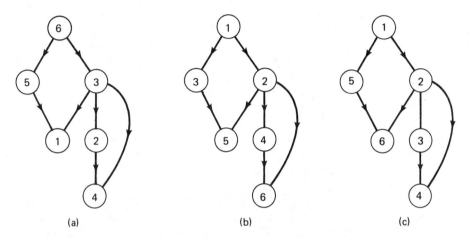

(a)   (b)   (c)

Figure 5.8. Examples of topological sorts.

2. Longest Paths in a Dag. Given a dag $G(X, U)$ such that $x_i \in X$ is a predecessor of all nodes $x_j \in X (i \neq j)$ and such that a weight w_k is associated with each $u_k \in U$, find the longest path from x_i to all $x_j \in X$. The longest path is defined as that path $(x_i, \ldots, x_j)$ such that the sum of the weights of the arcs leading from x_i to x_j is maximum. Finding the longest path for a dag is just a variation on the topological sort algorithm. Starting with LONGEST-PATH $(x_i) = 0$ for all $x_i \in X$, we modify the statement "enter (k,QUEUE)" as follows:

begin <u>For</u> m $\in$ IPRED(k) <u>Comment</u> This loop is executed INDEGREE (i) times <u>do</u>
    LONGEST-PATH (k) = max [LONGEST-PATH (k), LONGEST-PATH (m) +
                                   WEIGHT (m,k)] ;
    enter (k,QUEUE) ;
<u>end</u>

As in the topological sort, each node is visited once, but now arcs are visited twice. However, the order of magnitude of the running time stays the same. It is not difficult to modify the algorithm to the case where weights are carried by nodes instead of arcs.

Example 11

Consider $G_4(X_4, U_4)$ as in Figure 5.8(a) but with the weights on arcs shown in Figure 5.9(a). Applying the algorithm yields the LONGESTPATH shown in Figure 5.9(b).

3. Shortest Paths (Single Source). The description of the problem is similar to the one above, replacing longest by shortest, but we shall now consider directed

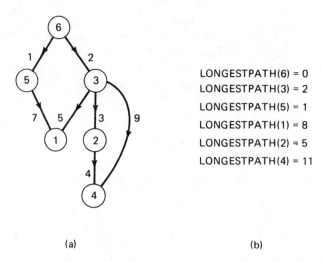

$$\begin{aligned}
\text{LONGESTPATH(6)} &= 0 \\
\text{LONGESTPATH(3)} &= 2 \\
\text{LONGESTPATH(5)} &= 1 \\
\text{LONGESTPATH(1)} &= 8 \\
\text{LONGESTPATH(2)} &= 5 \\
\text{LONGESTPATH(4)} &= 11
\end{aligned}$$

(a)   (b)

Figure 5.9.   Example of longest paths algorithm.

cyclic graphs. As before we consider nonnegative weights being carried by the arcs. In this case the following solution due to Dijkstra (1959) is the most efficient known. The basic idea is to start by giving to all immediate successors x_j of the source x_i a temporary SHORTPATH value equal to the weight of the arc (x_i, x_j) and to the others an infinite SHORTPATH. That is, the initialization step is

$$\text{SHORTPATH } (x_j) = \text{WEIGHT } (x_i,x_j) \text{ with WEIGHT } (x_i,x_j) = \infty \text{ if } (x_i,x_j) \notin U, x_i \neq x_j$$

Then we successively select the node of minimal SHORTPATH, mark it, and give to all unmarked nodes a new temporary SHORTPATH in a manner similar to the previous longest path algorithm. More precisely, we have (in letting the source have label 1)

```
Mark (1) ; SHORTPATH (1) := 0 ;
For j ∈ X − {1} Comment This loop is executed (n−1) times do
        SHORTPATH (j) := WEIGHT(1,j) ;
While There is an unmarked node Comment This loop is executed (n−1) times do
        begin Choose the unmarked node  of minimal SHORTPATH ;
            Comment This is an 0(n) process ;
        Mark (j) ;
        For each unmarked node k do
            SHORTPATH(k) := min [SHORTPATH(k), SHORTPATH(j) + WEIGHT(j,k)] ;
        Comment This loop takes also 0(n) ;
        end
```

From the comments we can see that the running time is $0(n^2)$.

Example 12

Consider $G_2(X_5, U_5)$ of Figure 5.10 and associated weights. The marking and assignment of SHORTPATH is done as follows:

	SHORTPATH (i)					
Marked Nodes	1	2	3	4	5	6
1	0	7	2	1	∞	∞
1, 4	0	5	2	1	∞	∞
1, 4, 3	0	5	2	1	6	5
1, 4, 3, 2	0	5	2	1	6	5
1, 4, 3, 2, 6	0	5	2	1	6	5
1, 4, 3, 2, 6, 5	0	5	2	1	6	5

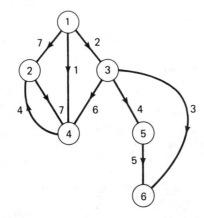

Figure 5.10. Graph G_5 for shortest-path examples.

Let us prove the correctness of the above algorith. Let M be the set of marked nodes. The proof is by induction on the cardinality of M, the induction hypothesis being

(a) For each $i \in M$, SHORTPATH(i) is the shortest path from node 1 to node i.

(b) For each $j \notin M$, SHORTPATH(j) is the shortest path from node 1 to node j with all nodes on the path being in M except for j.

The induction hypothesis holds for $|M| = 1$ since node 1 is the only once marked, SHORTPATH(1) $= 0$ (cf. first line of the algorithm), and the only noninfinite other SHORTPATH are those for which $(1, i) \in U$, thus satisfying hypothesis (b).

Assume now that node m, $m \notin M$, is the next unmarked node to be chosen. If SHORTPATH(m) is not the shortest path from node 1 to node m, there exists another path P, of shorter length, with one or more nodes not belonging to M (in addition to node m) linking node 1 to node m. Let n be the first node on that path such that $n \notin M$. Evidently SHORTPATH(n) $<$ SHORTPATH(m), and since all nodes from 1 to n lie in M except node n, n should have been selected instead of m. This contradiction implies that there is no shorter path P, and SHORTPATH(m) corresponds to induction hypothesis (a). Induction hypothesis (b) is conserved when the cardinality of M is incremented by 1 because of the min operation performed on all unmarked nodes.

The shortest path technique does not carry over to longest paths in cyclic graphs since the longest path between two nodes in a same cycle is infinite.

4. Transitive Closure and Associated Algorithms. Given the digraph $G(X, U)$, find the digraph $G^*(X, V)$ such that $(x_i, x_j) \in V$ if and only if there exists a path from x_i to x_j in G. There exist some algorithms more efficient than the $0(n^3)$ one that we present below [see, e.g., Munro (1971) for an $0(n^{2.81})$ algorithm based on the Strassen (1968) matrix multiplication scheme], but our choice is dictated by the numerous by-products that are available through this implementation. The algorithm due to Warshall (1962) is based on the Boolean matrix representation. Starting from G's connectivity matrix C, G^*'s connectivity matrix P, also called G's *precedence* matrix, is generated as follows:

```
Comment Initialize P to C ;
    For i :=1 step 1 until n do
        For j := 1 step 1 until n do
            P[i,j] := C[i,j] ;
Comment Traverse column by column
    For k = 1 step 1 until n do
            Comment If k has predecessor i, i.e. P[i,k]=1, then all of k's
                        successors are also i's ;
        For i := 1 step 1 until n do
            For j := 1 step 1 until n do
                P[i,j] := P[i,j] ∪ (P[i,k] ∩ P[k,j])
```

Proof of correctness of Warshall's algorithm [cf. Warren (1975)]: First it is immediate that $P[i, j]$ will be 1 only if there exists a path from i to j since when processing column j, only arcs linking immediate predecessors of j to immediate successors of j will be added. (Note, however, that the original graph gets an increasing number of arcs.)

The remainder of the proof, done by induction on the length of the path from i to j, shows that $P[i, j]$ is 1 if there exists a path from i to j.

If the length is 1, $P[i, j]$ will be 1 since $C[i, j]$ was 1 (cf. initialization) and no bit with value 1 is ever changed to 0. Assume now that the induction hypothesis is true for all paths of length less than m. Let x_i be linked to x_j through a path of length m. Let x_k be the lowest numbered node which lies on the path from x_i to x_j ($k \neq i, k \neq j$). Let the path of length m be $(x_i, \ldots, x_{k^-}, x_k, x_{k^+}, \ldots, x_j)$, where x_{k^-} and x_{k^+} are, respectively, an immediate predecessor and an immediate successor of x_k. Warshall's algorithm is going to introduce an arc (x_{k^-}, x_{k^+}), and the new path $(x_i, \ldots, x_{k^-}, x_{k^+}, \ldots, x_j)$ has length less than m. By the induction hypothesis $P[i, j]$ will then be set to 1.

Example 13

Applying Warshall's algorithm to the connectivity matrix of G_2 (cf. Figures 5.2 and 5.7) yields the precedence matrix of Figure 5.11(a) corresponding to the transitive closure $G^*(X, V)$ of Figure 5.11(b).

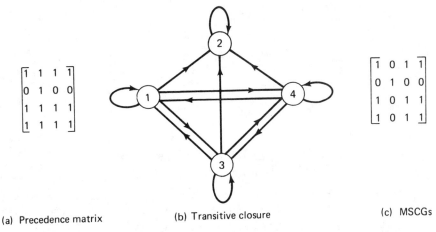

$$\begin{bmatrix} 1 & 1 & 1 & 1 \\ 0 & 1 & 0 & 0 \\ 1 & 1 & 1 & 1 \\ 1 & 1 & 1 & 1 \end{bmatrix}$$

$$\begin{bmatrix} 1 & 0 & 1 & 1 \\ 0 & 1 & 0 & 0 \\ 1 & 0 & 1 & 1 \\ 1 & 0 & 1 & 1 \end{bmatrix}$$

(a) Precedence matrix   (b) Transitive closure   (c) MSCGs

Figure 5.11. Transitive closure of G_2.

In addition to the description of the transitive closure of a digraph, the precedence matrix contains information which can be useful during the modeling process. While rows and columns of the connectivity matrix indicate, respectively, immediate successors and predecessors, i.e., the relation α, those of the precedence matrix show successors and predecessors, i.e., the relation $\underline{\alpha}$. If one considers the intersection, element by element, of P and its transpose P^T, then the resulting (symmetric) matrix will show for any given row i those nodes which are at the same time predecessors and successors of i. In other words, we have a means to detect the MSCG's of G [for more details, the reader is referred to Ramamoorthy (1966)]. One should not, however, deduce from the above that this is the most efficient method to find the MSCG's. An alternative method is described in Munro (1971).

Example 14

$R = P \cap P^T$ for G_2 is found in Figure 5.11(c). The two MSCG's have node sets $\{1, 3, 4\}$ and $\{2\}$. (Compare with Example 5.)

A simple modification to Warshall's algorithm yields the shortest paths between all pairs of nodes. With the same convention as before, i.e., infinite weights for non-existent arcs, and initializing the distance matrix D with the weights, we replace the Boolean operations in the inner loop by

$$D[i, j] = \min (D[i, j], D[i, k] + D[k, j])$$

Example 15

Figure 5.12(a) shows the initial distance matrix for G_5. The first and second iterations through the outer loop do not change it. In the third iteration $D[1, 5]$ and $D[1, 6]$ are set up to their final values [Figure 5.12(b)]. At the fourth iteration $D[1, 2]$ is changed [Figure 5.12(c)], and the last two iterations do not modify D. The first row of D is to be compared with the results of Example 12.

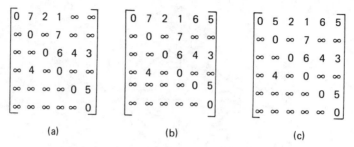

$$
\text{(a)} \quad
\begin{bmatrix}
0 & 7 & 2 & 1 & \infty & \infty \\
\infty & 0 & \infty & 7 & \infty & \infty \\
\infty & \infty & 0 & 6 & 4 & 3 \\
\infty & 4 & \infty & 0 & \infty & \infty \\
\infty & \infty & \infty & \infty & 0 & 5 \\
\infty & \infty & \infty & \infty & \infty & 0
\end{bmatrix}
\quad \text{(b)} \quad
\begin{bmatrix}
0 & 7 & 2 & 1 & 6 & 5 \\
\infty & 0 & \infty & 7 & \infty & \infty \\
\infty & \infty & 0 & 6 & 4 & 3 \\
\infty & 4 & \infty & 0 & \infty & \infty \\
\infty & \infty & \infty & \infty & 0 & 5 \\
\infty & \infty & \infty & \infty & \infty & 0
\end{bmatrix}
\quad \text{(c)} \quad
\begin{bmatrix}
0 & 5 & 2 & 1 & 6 & 5 \\
\infty & 0 & \infty & 7 & \infty & \infty \\
\infty & \infty & 0 & 6 & 4 & 3 \\
\infty & 4 & \infty & 0 & \infty & \infty \\
\infty & \infty & \infty & \infty & 0 & 5 \\
\infty & \infty & \infty & \infty & \infty & 0
\end{bmatrix}
$$

Figure 5.12. Illustration of shortest-path multiple source algorithm.

5. *Elementary Circuits of a Diagraph.* As we shall see in the following sections, important aspects of the modeling process and of the analysis of the models are based on the cyclic structure of the graph. We have just shown how MSCG's could be found. If one wants more refined information on the cyclic structure, one has to detect and/or list the circuits, or elementary cycles, of the graph:

- Is the graph acyclic? Warshall's algorithm provides an immediate (and costly) answer. A faster method is to see if a topological sort will succeed. If the algorithm terminates, the graph is acyclic; otherwise there exists at least one cycle. The first cycle so encountered can be identified by modifying slightly the original algorithm as shown in Knuth (1968).

- Is there a circuit passing through node x_i? Again a true-false answer can be provided by Warshall's algorithm. But it is more efficient to use a modification of Dijkstra's algorithm, which will not only provide the answer to the question but which will also list the nodes belonging to the circuit(s) passing through x_i.

- List all circuits of the graph $G(X, U)$. For example, in the graph of Figure 5.13(a) these circuits are $(1, 2, 4, 1)$, $(1, 3, 4, 1)$, $(4, 5, 7, 4)$, $(4, 6, 7, 4)$, $(7, 8, 10, 7)$, and $(7, 9, 10, 7)$. This question is certainly more complex since the number of elementary circuits in a digraph of n nodes can grow faster than 2^n. We present first a solution due to Tiernan (1970) and show how it can be improved.

Tiernan's solution can be summarized as follows. Starting with node 1, each node is considered in turn, in the natural order, as a starter of a possible elementary circuit. The path building process is constrained by three conditions, as stated below. Let p be the elementary path with starter node i, and let us suppose that we try to expand $p = \{i, \ldots, h, j\}$ with k one of the immediate successors of j. Now k will be part of p if and only if

(a) $k > i$ (so that each elementary circuit will be considered only once).

(b) $k \notin p$ (necessary condition for an elementary path).

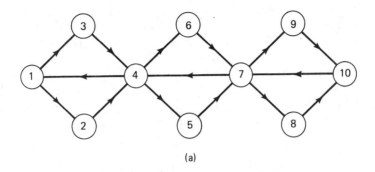

(a)

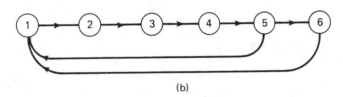

(b)

Figure 5.13. Graph G_6.

(c) The arc (j, k) has not already been considered for an elementary circuit with
     i as a starter node. If it has been done before, k is said to be "closed to j."
     This will ensure that each elementary path is considered at most once.

If a k exists such that the path can be extended, then the process is called again
with $p = \{i, \ldots, h, j, k\}$. If no k can be included in p, then either

  • One of the immediate successors of j is i itself; then p extended with i is
     an elementary circuit. It is recorded so.

or

  • The path $p = \{i, \ldots, h, j\}$ cannot lead to an elementary circuit.

After this circuit confirmation process, the "closeness of j relative to h" for i as
a starter node is recorded, j is deleted from p, and the process is started again unless
p has become empty. In this case the path building is reinitialized with $i + 1$ as a possible starter node until all nodes have been considered as possible starters.

Although each circuit is traversed only once the worst-case running time is
exponential in the size of the graph as well as exponential in the number of circuits.
The major inefficiency stems from the fact that many unnecessary elementary paths
are traversed. To remedy this, Tarjan (1973) reduces the backtracking through a
marking process. When some node v lies in the current elementary path p of starter
node s, it becomes marked. It stays so as long as v stays in p or it is known that every

path leading from v to s intersects p at a node other than s. The modification to the path building process is that once v has been used in p once, it can be reused (with the same restrictions as before) only when it is unmarked. The latter happens when v might lie on an elementary circuit which is an extension of p.

The detailed algorithm uses a "path-stack" containing the current p and a "mark-stack" for marked nodes. Initially each node is unmarked. Then, as in Tiernan's algorithm, all nodes are considered as starters and the recursive procedure TRACE is called with each node as an argument; i.e., the main program is

```
Unmark all nodes;
For s:=1 step 1 until n do
begin TRACE (s, flag) ;
        Unmark and pop all nodes in the mark-stack;
end
```

The TRACE procedure is

```
procedure TRACE (v,f) ;
begin logical g ;
      f := false ; Push (v,mark-stack) ; Mark(v) ; Push (v,path-stack) ;
      For w ∈ ISUC (v) do
      If w < s then begin ISUC (v) : = ISUC (v) − w ;
                    Comment This is Tiernan's condition (a) ;
              end
      else if w = s then begin output circuit given by path-stack;
                            f : = true ;
                    end
      else if unmark (w) then begin Trace (w,g) ;
                                  f : = f ∪ g ;
                            end ;
      Comment f = true if the path-stack is an elementary circuit;
      If f = true then
          begin while Top (mark-stack) ≠ v do
          Unmark and pop nodes in the mark-stack;
          Unmark and pop v from mark-stack;
      end ;
      pop (v, path-stack) ;
end TRACE ;
```

Example 16

Consider the digraph G_6 of Figure 5.13. With 1 as a starter node, Tiernan's algorithm will generate the elementary paths

$$p_1 = (1, 2, 4, 5, 7, 8, 10)$$
$$p_2 = (1, 2, 4, 5, 7, 9, 10)$$
$$p_3 = (1, 2, 4, 6, 7)$$
$$p_4 = (1, 2, 4, 6, 7, 9, 10)$$

while discovering that $(1, 2, 4, 1)$ is a circuit. In Tarjan's modification, after the generation of p_1, p_2 will be limited to $p'_2 = (1, 2, 4, 5, 7, 9)$ because 10 is marked. Then p_3 is further reduced to $p'_3 = (1, 2, 4, 6)$ (7 is still marked). There is no equivalent to p_4 since 6 is already marked.

It is proven in Tarjan (1973) that the running time of this algorithm is $0[ae(c + 1)]$, where c is the number of circuits, or alternatively $0[a(s + a)]$, where s is the sum of the length of all circuits.

But Tarjan's algorithm can still be improved. Johnson (1975) gives an $0[(n + a)(c + 1)]$ algorithm which is based on Tiernan's and Tarjan's but now each node in the graph is considered at most twice between the selection of two distinct elementary circuits. [This is obviously not the case for Tarjan's algorithm in the graph of Figure 5.13(b).] The new twist is that a node v is blocked, i.e., not available for reuse, as long as every path from v to the starter node s intersects p at a node other than s, and furthermore a node becomes a starter only if it is the smallest, labelwise, in an elementary circuit. This implies the computations of MSCG's for subgraphs of the original graph, a process less time-consuming than the overall path searching.

As stated earlier, the presentation of these basic algorithms is necessarily limited. However, it should be sufficient to proceed with the description of some modeling techniques.

5.3. DIRECTED ACYCLIC GRAPH MODELS

5.3.1. Deterministic Scheduling

As already mentioned in our introductory remarks, dag's are mostly useful to model precedence constraints introduced by timing considerations. This section on dags is then mostly devoted to the modeling technique known as deterministic scheduling. Job-shop studies in operations research furnished an early impetus in this discipline [cf. Conway et al. (1967)] and now the advent of multiprocessing computer systems and of networks continues to justify this type of study. An example of its application is the evaluation or prediction of performance of a system. The denomination deterministic is there to differentiate this aspect of scheduling theory from its stochastic, or probabilitic, counterpart for which the analysis is done mostly through queueing theory or by Markov chains.

Our goal here is not to review extensively deterministic scheduling. Because there are many possible variations on the models used and goals sought for, we shall voluntarily restrict ourselves. Our main purpose will be to demonstrate the use of dag's, and of algorithms operating on them, to yield some interesting properties of schedules. The reader interested in more details should consult Coffman and Denning (1973) and Coffman (1976).

The practical importance of deterministic scheduling should not be overemphasized. The approach is quite abstract, and no real system, or program, can realistically be faithfully represented via a model like the one we are presenting now. However, the analytical results given below provide guidelines on how to exploit parallelism in multitasking environments or in networks of computers. Bounds on the speed-up that one can expect, worst-case analysis, and heuristics evaluation should be known to implementors of dispatchers in operating systems. Potential anomalies that can result from "random" scheduling can be avoided, and this could be of certain interest in the control and scheduling of real-time processes. Moreover, an idealized evaluation of performance can be attained by this modeling technique.

We shall use a dag to model the users' input, or tasks. These tasks are to be executed on a multiprocessor system. The order of execution will be determined by a scheduling algorithm whose goal will be to optimize some specific function related to the tasks. The dag will show the precedence constraints (partial order) between the tasks. Some variations on the topological sort algorithm will generally be used to generate priorities in the scheduling algorithm. The dag structure itself will be used in some cases to yield bounds on the results that scheduling algorithms can obtain. To be more precise, we shall now describe the different components of the model.

The *tasks system* is represented by a dag $G(T, U)$ with nodes $T_i \in T, 1 \leq i \leq m$, being tasks and arcs showing the precedence constraints. With each task will be associated attributes such as timing considerations or memory requirements. We shall use only a single attribute, the expected execution time $\mu(T_i)$ or weight. In job-shop problems tasks are split into operations which have to be executed, in some prespecified order, on different machines. Our interest here is more directed to tasks running as a whole on a system consisting of $n(n \geq 2)$ *processors* which are not necessarily identical. In the latter case we shall indicate the relative speeds of the processors. The assignment of tasks is performed by a *scheduling algorithm*. One has to distinguish between *nonpreemptive* algorithms, i.e., once a task is assigned on a processor it has to run to completion, and *preemptive* algorithms. We shall deal mostly with the former. Moreover, the scheduling algorithms are *priority driven* (also called list scheduling); that is, the tasks are ranked before any scheduling is attempted according to a *labeling algorithm*. This labeling takes into account the precedence constraints shown in the graph. The goal of the scheduling algorithm is to be *optimal* with respect to some function which will here be the minimization of the completion time of all tasks.

Since the set of tasks T is finite, we can always find an optimal schedule. If one wants to apply some of the results of deterministic scheduling studies to the design of dispatchers in operating systems, then the algorithms at hand have to be computationally practical. Hence, for practical as well as for theoretical reasons, only polynomial time algorithms are of interest. As we shall see below, the number of known polynomial-time optimal scheduling algorithms is very limited. Therefore, another important aspect of the theory is to yield bounds on the performance of algorithms known to be nonoptimal. Again for reasons of practicality, those algorithms whose labeling is such that if level $(T_i) <$ level (T_j), then T_i has priority over T_j (i.e., *level algorithms*) are worth studying since they model rather realistically what could happen in a real situation (tasks further from completion have a higher probability of entering earlier in the input queue).

To summarize, the major components of the model are the dag showing the precedence constraints, the attributes (time) of the tasks, the priority list, and the number and characteristic (speed) of the processors. A skeleton of the scheduling process is

Phase 1.   Input dag and attributes;
            Perform the labeling algorithm;
            Output the priority list.

Phase 2.   Input priority list, task attributes, and system characteristics.

> While priority list not empty <u>do</u>
> <u>begin</u> Find first available processor P_i
>   Search priority list for first candidate T_j.
>   Assign candidate T_j on P_i
> end

Phase 1 will be discussed in more detail in the remainder of this section. To visualize phase 2 it is convenient to associate a clock C_i with each P_i and to look at the process like an event-driven simulation with a current-time indicator t. Initially all clocks and t are set to 0. At time t a processor P_i is available if $C_i = t$. If at time t a processor is available to find the first candidate T_j (if any), we search the priority list (in order) until we find a T_j which has not yet been assigned and whose all immediate predecessors have completed their execution by time C_i. Assigning T_j on P_i increases C_i by $\mu(T_j)$. After assigning candidates at time t, two situations are possible. Either there is no available processor and then we set t to min (C_i), which will make P_i available (and maybe other processors if there were ties), and we repeat the assignment process, or we have one (or more) available processors but no candidate. In this case we set t to min (C_k) for $C_k > t$ and set all clocks less than this new t to t. Since at least one more task has completed by then, we can repeat the search for a task candidate. The process terminates when all tasks have been assigned and the completion time is max (C_i).

Two warnings are necessary at this point. First, serious anomalies might happen when deterministic scheduling is used. A complete and thorough treatment of this topic can be found in Graham (1972). For some task system $G(T, U)$ scheduled on n identical processors the author shows that if we vary singly either of the four main parameters by

- Using a new labeling algorithm, leaving $G(T, U)$, $\mu(T_i)$, and n unchanged;
- Relaxing the precedence constraints (i.e., suppress some arcs from U), leaving the labeling algorithm, $\mu(T_i)$, and n unchanged;
- Decreasing the weights $\mu(T_i)$, leaving the other three parameters unchanged;
- Increasing the number of processors, without affecting the task system;

then the total completion time can increase. We shall illustrate the latter case with the following example.

Example 17

Consider the task system G_7 shown in Figure 5.14(a). The notation $T_{i/j}$ means task T_i of weight j. Assume a labeling algorithm yielding the priority list $(T_1, T_2, T_3, T_4, T_5, T_6, T_7)$. Then phase 2 of the scheduling algorithm with two identical processors yields the timing diagram (or Gantt chart) of Figure 5.14(b), i.e., a completion time of 6 time units. With three identical processors, we have the completion time of 7 time units [cf. Figure 5.14(c)].

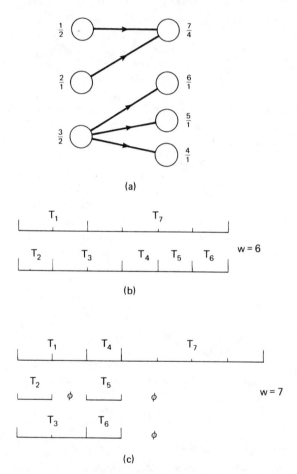

(a)

(b)

(c)

Figure 5.14. Anomaly in deterministic scheduling.

In fact Graham gives a precise bound on the ratio of the total completion times w'/w, where w is the result of applying a scheduling algorithm on $G(T, U)$, with $\mu(T_i)$ attributes, n identical processors, and a labeling algorithm L and w' is the resulting completion time for $G'(T, U')$ with $U' \subseteq U$, $\mu'(T_i) \leq \mu(T_i)$ for all $T_i \in T$, and another labeling L' and n' processors. Then $w'/w \le 1 + (n-1)/n'$ (and this bound is the best possible). If $n = n'$, then $w'/w \le 2 - 1/n$. An important conclusion which can be drawn from the latter formula is that for given tasks and a given multiprocessor system no schedule will turn out to be worse than twice the optimal one. It is also worthwhile to remark that one does not need to concoct unrealistic examples in order to achieve this bound. It can be done with all $\mu(T_i)$ equal to 1.

The second warning is relative to the difficulty in obtaining efficient (in the sense of the last section) optimal algorithms. The two apparently simple problems,

- Find an optimal schedule on two identical processors for n independent tasks T_i [i.e., the dag $G(T, U)$ has an empty arc set], with all $\mu(T_i)$ being integers;
- Find optimal schedules on any k processors for a task system $G(T, U)$ with all $\mu(T_i) = 1$ (i.e., find a labeling algorithm which subsequently yields an optimal schedule independent of the number of processors);

are both in the class of NP-complete problems [Ullman, 1973]. In fact, polynomial time optimal scheduling algorithms are more the exception than the rule. We shall devote our next subsection to some of them.

5.3.2. Some Optimal Scheduling Algorithms

In this subsection we shall consider all time attributes to be 1 unless otherwise stated. With this restriction it is evident that a trivial algorithm yields an optimal schedule if all tasks are independent. But, as stated above, the general problem is polynomial-complete. There are some cases between these two extremes which are of interest.

1. The Dag Is a Tree. In this case if the labeling algorithm ranks the tasks by levels, i.e., a longest path algorithm, then an optimal schedule is obtained independently of the number of (identical) processors. This "cutting of the longest queue" procedure, due to Hu (1961), is now illustrated.

Example 18

Consider the tree of Figure 5.15(a). Hu's labeling yields the list $(T_1, T_2, \ldots, T_9)$ and the optimal schedule of Figure 5.15(b) on two processors. Note that not all topological sorts give optimal schedules. A breadth-first one would yield the labeling $(T_1, T_2, T_3, T_7, T_8, T_4, T_5, T_6, T_9)$ and the schedule (nonoptimal) of Figure 5.15(c).

Hu's algorithm is expressed in a very simple manner. However, a proof of its optimality requires some care.

Let L be the maximum number of levels in the tree (with the root at level 1), let m be the number of processors, and denote by $P(j)$ the set of tasks of level greater than

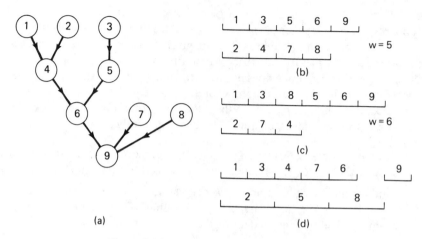

Figure 5.15. Examples of schedules on trees.

or equal to j. L is an obvious lower bound on the total execution time. Similarly, $\lceil |P(1)|/m \rceil$, and in fact by looking at all integer intervals between 1 and L we have a lower bound for the completion time W_c:

$$W_c \geq \max_{0 \leq j \leq L} \left[j + \left\lceil \frac{|P(j+1)|}{m} \right\rceil \right] \tag{5.1}$$

We note also that

$$W_c = L \tag{5.2}$$

if there are less than m leaves in the tree since we need at least L units of times [from (5.1)] and at each unit (i) of time we can assign all the tasks at level $(L + 1 - i)$.

Assume, now, more than L leaves ($L > 1$), and let us show that $t = W_c = \max [j + \lceil |P(j+1)|/m \rceil]$, where t is the completion time following Hu's algorithm, $0 \leq j \leq L$.

Let N_i be the set of tasks executed during the first i units of time, and let P be the earliest time for which a processor is not busy; i.e., $|N_{p+1} - N_p| < m$, $|N_p| = pm$.

If $p = 0$, we are done [from (5.2)]; hence let $0 < p < t$. Let r_j be the maximum level of the tasks left to be scheduled after $j + 1$ units of time. At time $j + 1 = p + 1$, r_p is such that $P(r_p + 1) \subseteq N_{p+1}$ (evident from the definition of p), and it is relatively easy to show that $P(r_{p+1}) \neq N_p$, for if the equality were to hold, during the interval $p + 1$ we would have scheduled the tasks at level r_p (and all of them since $|N_{p+1} - N_p| < m$), and hence we would have $P(r_p) \subseteq N_{p+1}$, which contradicts the definition of r_p.

Now the completion time t is composed of the first $p + 1$ units of time plus the longer path of the remaining subtree [cf. (5.2)]; i.e.,

$$t = p + 1 + r_p = r_p + \left\lceil \frac{|N_{p+1}|}{m} \right\rceil$$

We shall now consider three cases.

(a)   The tasks scheduled on the first p units of time are all of level greater than r_p. Then

$$\left\lceil \frac{|N_{p+1}|}{m} \right\rceil = \left\lceil \frac{|P(r_{p+1})|}{m} \right\rceil$$

and

$$t = r_p + \left\lceil \frac{|P(r_{p+1})|}{m} \right\rceil \le \max_{0 \le j \le L} \left\{ j + \left\lceil \frac{|P(j+1)|}{m} \right\rceil \right\}$$

(b)   There is at least one task of level r_i or less scheduled during the first i units of time, $1 \le i \le p$. It is then easy to show that $t = L$.

(c)   During the first s $(1 \le s < p)$ limits of time all tasks scheduled are of level greater than r_s [i.e., $N_s \subseteq p(r_{s+1})$] and s is the largest such integer. Then

$$t = r_p + (p - s) + \left\lceil \frac{|P(r_s + 1)|}{m} \right\rceil$$

But between s and p, one level is assigned, and hence $r_p + (p - s) = r_s$ and

$$t = r_s + \left\lceil \frac{P(r_{s+1})}{m} \right\rceil \le \max_{0 \le j \le L} \left\{ j + \left\lceil \frac{P(j+1)}{m} \right\rceil \right\}$$

Hu's algorithm can be extended to the case of heterogeneous processors. If there are two of them of speed ratio 2/1, then Hu's labeling is still optimal [cf. Figure 5.15(d) for an example]. If the speed ratio is now 3/1, one can still find a polynomial time algorithm for an optimal schedule, but it involves many special cases. A straightforward application of Hu's procedure yields a schedule which is at most one unit of time longer than the optimal [cf. Baer (1974)].

2. The Number of Processors Is Limited to Two. The longest path labeling algorithm (i.e., the extension of Hu's algorithm) does not result in a priority list for a subsequent optimal schedule. A counterexample for two processors is shown below.

Example 19

Consider the dag G_7 of Figure 5.16(a). Hu's labeling algorithm will yield the list $(T_6, T_5, T_4, T_3, T_2, T_1)$ and the schedule of Figure 5.16(b). An optimal schedule (shorter by one unit of time) is shown in Figure 5.16(c).

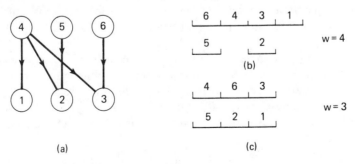

Figure 5.16. Scheduling on two processors.

A refinement of the longest path algorithm, due to Coffman and Graham (1972), yields an optimal schedule for the case of two identical processors (recall that the case of any k processors is NP-complete). The algorithm discriminates among tasks with the same longest path length, or level, by comparing their (immediate) successors. In particular, an important property of the labeling is that if T_i and T_j are independent and if the set of successors of T_i is properly contained in the set of successors of T_j, then T_j has priority over T_i.

The algorithm involves the comparison of decreasing sequences of integers. We say that $N = \{n_1, n_2, \ldots, n_s\}$ is smaller than $N' = \{n'_1, n'_2, \ldots, n'_t\}$ if either

(1) $n_j = n'_j, 1 \leq j \leq i - 1$ and $n_i < n'_i$ for some $i \geq 1$, or

(2) $s < t$ and $n_i = n'_i, 1 \leq i \leq s$.

Now, for a given task T_i, let $N(T_i)$ be the decreasing sequence of the labels of its successors. The labeling algorithm is

(1) Label the nodes without successors as $1, 2, \ldots, m$.

(2) Assume that $k - 1$ nodes have been labeled. Consider all unlabeled tasks $T_{i_1}, \ldots, T_{i_n}$ which have all their successors in these $k - 1$ nodes. Let $N(T_{i_1}), \ldots, N(T_{i_n})$ be the decreasing sequences corresponding to the respective labels of their successors. Label k that T_{i_j} for which $N(T_{i_j})$ is minimal. Repeat step 2 until all tasks have been labeled.

(3) The priority list is by decreasing label order.

Example 20

This algorithm applied to the task system of Figure 5.16(a) yields the labeling $(T_4, T_5, T_6, T_3, T_2, T_1)$ and the (optimal) scheduling on two processors of Figure 5.16(c).

The Coffman-Graham algorithm is not directly extendable to either the case of three processors, or two processors of different speeds, or of tasks with unequal weights even if these weights are only 1 or 2. The last problem is NP-complete, there is a strong conjecture that the second one could be solved in polynomial time, and the first problem still remains an open question.

3. Preemptive Scheduling. We shall now consider the case where a task T_i can be interrupted and resumed later on, possibly on a different processor. We make no more restrictions on the time attributes except that they are mutually commensurable; i.e., for our purposes we consider all weights to be integers. Scheduling independent tasks becomes a trivial problem, and the optimal schedule has a completion time (for an n processor system) of

$$w = \max \left\{ [\max \mu(T_i)], \frac{1}{n} \sum_{i=1}^{m} \mu(T_i) \right\}$$

The duals of Hu's algorithm, i.e., optimal schedules on any number of processors in the case of a tree, and that of Coffman and Graham, i.e., optimal schedule on two processors in the case of a dag, do exist in the case of preemptive scheduling. The algorithm due to Muntz and Coffman (1969) can be explained as follows.

When a task T_i has a weight $\mu(T_i)$ larger than 1, we expand it into $\mu(T_i)$ tasks, $T_{i_1}, T_{i_2}, \ldots, T_{\mu(T_i)}$ such that $T_{i_1} \alpha T_{i_2} \alpha \cdots \alpha T_{i_{\mu(T_i)}}$. This is done for all $T_i \in T$. We now build a priority list on the new task system according to the longest path (level) labeling algorithm. We consider all tasks at the highest level. Say that there are k of them and n processors. We assign them as a set of independent tasks. If $k > n$ and $k \bmod n \neq 0$, then we must preempt some tasks and reschedule them during the k/n time period so that no processor is idle (see Example 21 below). We continue in this fashion level by level until all tasks are assigned.

Example 21

Consider the dag in Figure 5.17(a), and its transform in Figure 5.17(b). The optimal schedule on two processors, without preemption, is shown in Figure 5.17(c) (it was not obtained by a known scheduling algorithm), and the preemptive optimal algorithm is in Figure 5.17(d). Notice that tasks $T_{1.2}$, $T_{2.2}$, and $T_{4.1}$ "share" $1\frac{1}{2}$ time units.

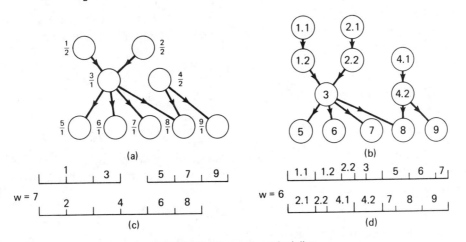

Figure 5.17. Preemptive scheduling.

Muntz and Coffman's algorithm is not extendable to the case of a dag and more than two processors.

Because of all the limitations on optimal algorithms, it is necessary to study some bounds on the behavior of nonoptimal algorithms.

5.3.3. Bounds on Schedules

Graham's bound, as introduced at the beginning of this section, can be sharpened in two different ways. First, bounds can be devised for a given dag; second, the performance of a particular scheduling algorithm can be assessed. We shall look at these two options in turn.

1. Bounds on a Given Dag. The minimum completion time for a given dag is the length of the longest path (with nodes carrying the weight attributes) from a node of indegree 0 to a node of outdegree 0. We shall denote it w_c (c is for completion as well as for critical—or longest—path). An obvious lower bound for the minimum number of processors (LBP) required to process the dag in w_c is

$$\text{LBP}_1 = \left\lceil \frac{\sum_{i=1}^{m} \mu(T_i)}{w_c} \right\rceil$$

Let us now consider two simpleminded scheduling algorithms, assuming that we have as many processors at our disposal as we wish. The first one is to schedule tasks at the latest possible time. If we transform our dag into one with all weights equal to 1, as we did in the preemptive case, but this time we do not change the labels of the nodes, this schedule is a level-by-level schedule. Now an upper bound on the number of processors needed to obtain a completion time w_c is

$$\text{UBP}_1 = \max_{\forall i} |L_i|$$

where L_i is the set of tasks at level i. The second option is to schedule tasks at the earliest possible time (or by heights if we extend that definition originally restricted to trees). We obtain similarly

$$\text{UBP}'_1 = \max_{\forall j} |E_j|$$

where E_j is the set of tasks at height j. But since the number of heights and levels are the same, we have

$$\text{UBP}_2 = \min (\max_{\forall i} |E_i|, \max_{\forall} |L_i|)$$

If now we denote $E_i(L_i)$ the set of nodes scheduled at time i according to the earliest (latest) strategy, the minimum number of processors necessary to complete within w_c is

$$\text{LBP}_2 = \max_{\forall i} (|L_i \cap E_i|)$$

But now if we look back at LBP_1, it can easily be seen that it can be sharpened by looking at all possible (integer) intervals between 1 and w_c so that

$$\text{LBP}'_1 = \max_{\forall i} \left(\left\lceil \frac{1}{i} \sum_{i=1}^{w_c} |L_i| \right\rceil \right)$$

and combining this with the previous bounds, Ramamoorthy et al. (1972) devised the following:

$$\text{LBP} = \max \left[\max_{\forall i} (|L_i \cap E_i|), \max_{\forall i} \left(\left\lceil \frac{1}{i} \sum_{i=1}^{w_c} |L_i| \right\rceil \right) \right]$$

$$\text{UBP} = \min_{\forall i} (\max |L_i|, \max_{\forall i} |E_i|)$$

Example 22

Consider the dag G_7 of Figure 5.18(a). The critical path is shown with double arrows. All weights are 1 except for nodes T_3, T_6, and T_{14}. Figures 5.18(b) and (c) show the dag with latest and earliest levels. The critical path is $w_c = 8$; LBP = 3 (obtained at time unit 5), and UBP = 5 [obtained at time unit 6 on the earliest graph, Figure 18(c)]. The complete schedules according to the latest or earliest strategies are shown in Figures 5.18(d) and (e).

The lower bound can be sharpened even further. Instead of looking only at w_c intervals as in LBP$_1'$, we can look at all intervals (θ_1, θ_2) (θ_1 and θ_2 integers, $0 \le \theta_1 < \theta_2 \le w_c$). For each such interval (θ_1, θ_2) in a given schedule, let us look at the multisets,[4] or bags, of scheduled tasks during that period. Let $\bar{L}$ denote the multisets corresponding to the latest schedule and $\underline{E}$ those corresponding to the earliest schedule. Then, as devised by Fernandez and Bussell (1973), the improved bound is

$$\text{LBP}_3 = \left\lceil \max_{\substack{(\theta_1, \theta_2) \\ 0 \le \theta_1 < \theta_2 \le w_c}} \frac{1}{\theta_2 - \theta_1} |\bar{L} \cap \underline{E}| \right\rceil$$

Example 23

Consider the dag G_7 and its latest and earliest schedules in Figures 5.18(d) and (e). During the interval $(4, 6)$, $\bar{L} = \{6, 7, 8, 9, 10, 11, 12, 13\}$, $\underline{E} = \{6, 7, 8, 9, 10, 11, 12, 14\}$, $\bar{L} \cap \underline{E} = \{6, 7, 8, 9, 10, 11, 12\}$, $|\bar{L} \cap \underline{E}| = 7$, and LBP$_3 = \lceil 7/2 \rceil = 4$.

Although the latter bound is better than the previous ones, it has the major inconvenience that one has to compute $0(w_c^2)$ multiset intersections instead of $0(w_c)$ set intersections as in the other cases.

The same technique can be used to find a lower bound on the minimum time to execute a schedule on a dag, given n processors. Fernandez and Bussell (1973), extending the work of Hu (1961) and Ramamoorthy et al. (1972), have shown that the lower bound has the form

$$w_1 = w_c + \lceil q \rceil$$

where

$$q = \max_{\substack{(\theta_1, \theta_2) \\ 0 \le \theta_1 < \theta_2 \le w_c}} \left| -(\theta_2 - \theta_1) + \frac{1}{n} |\bar{L} \cap \underline{E}| \right|$$

i.e., the minimum time increase over w_c in the interval (θ_1, θ_2).

2. Bounds for a Given Scheduling Algorithm. Graham's bound, i.e., $2 - 1/n$ for the ratio

$$\frac{\text{completion time for any list algorithm}}{\text{optimal completion time}}$$

---

[4]A multiset, or bag, is a set where repeated elements are accepted. The union and intersection of multisets are straightforward extensions of the same concepts for sets. For example, if $A = \{a, a, b\}$ and $B = \{a, b, c\}$, $A \cup B = \{a, a, a, b, b, c\}$ and $A \cap B = \{a, b\}$.

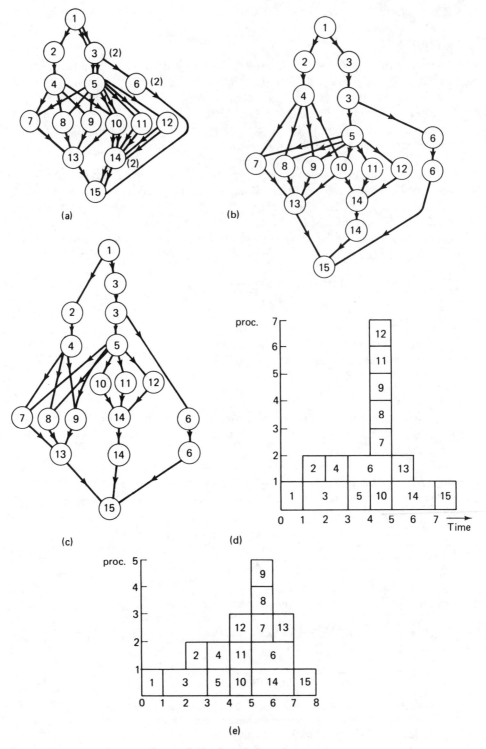

(a)

(b)

(c)

(d)

(e)

Figure 5.18. Bounds for a given graph.

was for all possible list schedulings. It is not surprising that it should be sharpened in more restricted situations. We shall now consider several such cases.

As shown in Figure 5.16, the longest path priority rule is not optimal. In fact the case of Figure 5.16 is the worst for two processors (4/3). It was thought for some time that a direct generalization of it, that is, an alternation of units of time where all processors were busy and units where all but one of the processors were idle, was the worst possible. This situation is shown for four processors in Figure 5.19(a) (we indicate nodes by points to avoid cluttering the figure). It can readily be seen that for n processors the worst schedule has for completion time $2n$ [Figure 5.19(b)] and the optimal one $n + 1$ [Figure 5.19(c)], yielding a bound of

$$\frac{2n}{n + 1} \quad \text{or} \quad 2 - \frac{2}{n + 1}$$

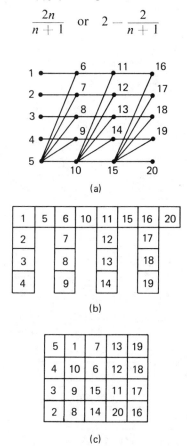

(a)

(b)

(c)

Figure 5.19. Longest path scheduling (erroneous bound).

Although this is in fact the worst case for $n = 2$ and $n = 3$ [cf. Chen and Liu (1974)], Chen (1975) has shown that the true bound is larger, namely $2 - [1/(n - 1)]$ for $n \geq 4$. Intuitively this can be explained by the fact that the last "column" of time where a single processor is busy in a repeated subgraph can be imbricated with the first column of the next repetition. Figure 5.20 makes this process clear for the case of four processors.

The bound on Coffman and Graham's algorithm can be obtained in a somewhat similar manner. The worst case for the case of three processors is shown in Figure 5.21 (4/3). Lam and Sehti (1974) have generalized to the case of n processors, obtaining the bound $2 - (2/n)$. Baer (1974) has studied the behavior of the same algorithm on two processors of speed ratio 2/1 and has found a worst case of 6/5. The interesting aspect here is that in order to obtain the optimal algorithm one has to delay a task which was a candidate (cf. Figure 5.22). This can also happen in the longest path method. Kohler (1975) gives such an example, although it is not a worst case.

The longest path algorithm and Coffman and Graham's labeling can also be adapted to the cases where the $\mu(T_i)$ are unequal (and mutually commensurable). One constructs the dag as in the preemptive scheduling study. But now once T_{i_1} (in

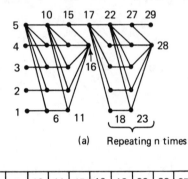

(a)   Repeating n times

1	5	6	10	11	15	16	18	22	23	27	28
2		7		12		17	19		24		29
3		8		13			20		25		
4		9		14			21		26		

(b)   Repeating n times

5	1	7	13	16	19	25	28
4	10	6	12	22	18	24	
3	9	15	11	21	27	23	
2	8	14	17	20	26	29	

Repeating n times

(c)

Figure 5.20. Longest path scheduling (correct bound).

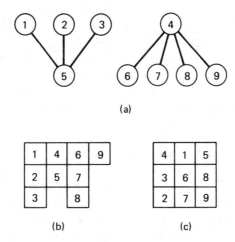

(a)

(b)   (c)

Figure 5.21. Coffman-Graham algorithm's worst case for three processors.

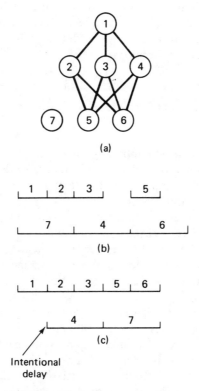

(a)

(b)

(c)

Intentional delay

Figure 5.22. Coffman-Graham algorithm's worst case for two processors of different speed.

the chain $T_{i_1}, \ldots, T_{i_{\mu(T_i)}}$) has been assigned to a processor, all its successors in the chain corresponding to T_i are assigned to the same processor in the $\mu(T_i) - 1$ following units of time. For the case of two processors, Kaufman (1974) has shown that the bound is 5/4 for the extended Coffman-Graham algorithm.

There are certainly many more variations on this theme. We have presented some of the solutions which rely more heavily on the modeling by directed graphs. An appraisal of the performance of these algorithms is necessary to justify the theoretical studies.

5.3.4. Heuristics and a More Realistic Model

How far from optimal are those methods mentioned above? Of course we know a general bound, $2 - (1/n)$, for the worst case. But two other questions, of less theoretical importance but with more practical impact, can be raised, namely, which algorithm should be chosen in order to obtain "good" results, and how far from optimality are these results in the "random" case (good and random are to be defined in this context). Several studies have been conducted in an attempt to obtain some insights.

To rank the various scheduling disciplines one has to generate test vehicles, i.e., random graphs. The randomness is present in the dag structures, for example, number of nodes and arcs and their relationship, and also in the time attributes. The graph structures and time attributes could be drawn from existing programs. However, this requires two main assumptions:

- The program does not have loops; i.e., the graph is acyclic.

- The program does not take any decisions; i.e., there is no branching on predicates.

We can deal with the first assumption by considering all MSCG's as single nodes. This cyclic-acyclic transformation will be explained in more detail further on. A model to take care of the second assumption will be presented after reviewing the success of the heuristics on our original task system.

One possible way to generate a random dag is the procedure described by Adam et al. (1974). The input consists of the minimum and maximum number of levels, the minimum and maximum number of nodes per level, the average outdegree of a node, and the average weight. Then a random node can be connected to its immediate successors, at lower levels, using these parameters. Weights can be drawn from specific distributions.

Once a dag has been generated, we might want to compare the results of schedules obtained from different heuristics with the optimal schedule. Therefore, we need to know the latter. As stated earlier, this is a time-consuming (exponential) proposition. Dynamic programming and branch-and-bound approaches have been considered by Ramamoorthy et al. (1972) and Kohler (1975). However, according to Adam et al. (1974), the Fernandez and Bussell (1973) bound, as presented in Section 5.3.3, is sufficiently tight to be able to replace the computations of the optimal schedules.

From the preceding discussion, some scheduling disciplines appear immediately as good candidates. The most prominent are those related to the longest path algorithm, namely, the one building the priority list according to the longest path taking into account the weights of the tasks (LPW), and the one using the longest path assuming that all the weights are the same (LPL). Two other candidates would be priority lists built following the early set strategy with the same distinction on weights as above (ESW and ESL). Finally, strategies built around Coffman and Graham's algorithm, and purely random lists could also be envisioned.

Example 24

The four heuristics above applied to the dag of Figure 5.18(a) yield the priority lists and completion times (on two processors)

$$LPW = (1, 3, 2, 4, 5, 10, 11, 12, 6, 7, 8, 9, 14, 13, 15),$$
$$W = 10 \text{ (optimal)}$$

$$LPL = ESW = ESL = (1, 2, 3, 4, 5, 6, 7, 8, 9, 10, 11, 12, 13, 14, 15),$$
$$W = 11$$

These heuristics have been extensively tested, in preemptive and nonpreemptive environments, by Adam et al. (1974). The main result is that the LPW heuristic is best and gives schedules close to optimality. The other three are about as efficient and are not near-optimal. The near optimality of LPW has been confirmed experimentally by Kohler (1975).

We return now to the assumption regarding branching nodes. We can modify our task system $G(X, U)$ in such a way that for some nodes called branching or EOR nodes—we call the others AND nodes—only one out of their immediate successors will be executed for some input data set. If x_i is a branching node, then the arcs $u_k = (x_i, x_j)$ incident out from it carry probabilities $q_{i,j}$ such that

$$\sum q_{i,j} = 1$$
$$u_k = (x_i, x_j) \in U$$

The complete cyclic model, known as the UCLA or bilogic graph model, will be considered in the next section.

Because the nodes which are going to be executed for different inputs are not necessarily the same subsets of the dag node set, the concept of optimal schedule does not make sense. There exist optimal schedules for each partial subgraph composed only of AND nodes and the arcs incident out of them and of EOR nodes with a single arc incident out from them. For each such subgraph $A(Y, V)$, called an AND-type subgraph, we associate a probability P_A, which is the product of the probabilities of the arcs belonging to V incident out of the EOR nodes belonging to Y. For such an AND-type subgraph there exists an optimal schedule. Martin and Estrin (1969) introduced the concept of (optimal) mean path length, i.e., the sum over all AND-type subgraphs $\sum_{A \in G} P_A O_A$, where O_A is the optimal schedule for the AND-type subgraph A. One can expand this definition to nonoptimal schedules.

Example 25

Consider the dag of Figure 5.23(a). The notation $*$ is for AND, and $+$ is for EOR. The arc probabilities are $q_{2,3} = \frac{1}{3}$ and $q_{2,4} = \frac{2}{3}$. The two AND-type subgraphs are shown in Figure 5.23(b), and the optimal mean path length assuming an unlimited number of processors (in fact, two suffice) is

$$\mu_1 + \tfrac{1}{3} \max (\mu_2 + \mu_2 + \mu_5 + \mu_6) + \tfrac{2}{3} \max (\mu_2 + \mu_4 + \mu_5 + \mu_6) + \mu_7 = \tfrac{31}{3}$$

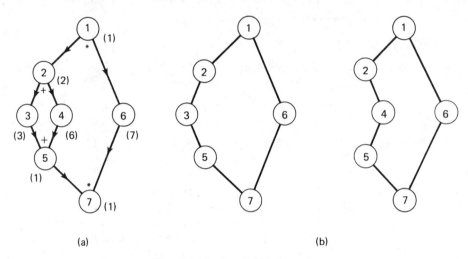

(a)   (b)

Figure 5.23. Acyclic bilogic graph.

Evidently, computing optimal schedules (an exponential process) on an exponential number of AND-type subgraphs is not practical. A modification to the longest path algorithm can, however, be applied on a bilogic acyclic graph, yielding an optimistic value of the mean path length, when the number of processors is unrestricted, that is, when we allow maximum parallelism. Let p_i be the probability of ever reaching x_i from an initial node x_1 assumed unique. We have to differentiate between nodes called AND-input logic nodes, which will be candidates when all their immediate predecessors have terminated (i.e., they all belong to the same AND-type subgraph), and the EOR-input logic nodes, which have only one immediate predecessor in a given AND-type subgraph. Baer et al. (1970), building on Martin's work, have shown that

$$p_i = \sum_{j=1}^{m} p_j \cdot q_{j,i}, \qquad \text{where } (x_j, x_i) \in U, x_i \text{ is EOR-input}$$

$$p_i = \min_j (p_j \cdot q_{j,i}), \qquad \text{where } (x_j, x_i) \in U, x_i \text{ is AND-input}$$

To obtain the mean path length, we modify the longest path algorithm, replacing the longest path calculation by

$$\text{MEANPATH(i)} = \text{WEIGHT(i)} + \max_{j \in \text{IPRED(i)}} (\text{MEANPATH(j)}) \text{ if } x_i \text{ is AND-input}$$

or

$$\text{MEANPATH(i)} = \text{WEIGHT(i)} + \frac{1}{p_i} \sum_{j \in \text{IPRED(i)}} p_j\, q_{j,i}\, \text{MEANPATH(j)}$$

$$\text{if } x_i \text{ is EOR-input.}$$

Martin and Estrin (1969) proved that the mean path length computed this way is never larger than the mean path length as originally defined.

Example 26

This procedure applied to the dag of Figure 5.23(a) yields

$$p_1 = p_2 = p_5 = p_6 = p_7 = 1, \qquad p_3 = \tfrac{1}{3}, \qquad p_4 = \tfrac{2}{3}$$

MEANPATH(1) = 1 ; MEANPATH(2) = 3, MEANPATH(3) = (3+3)x = 2 ;
MEANPATH(4) = (2+6)·x = 6 ; MEANPATH(5) = (2+6) + 1 = 9
MEANPATH(6) = 1+7=8 ; MEANPATH(9) = max (8,9) + 1 = 10

This last result is to be compared with that of Example 25.

This optimistic result allows for the computation of an expected lower bound on the number of processors needed to obtain an optimal mean path length, namely,

$$\left\lceil \frac{\text{MEANPATH}(k)}{\sum_{i=1}^{|X|} \mu_i} \right\rceil$$

where k is assumed to be the unique node without successors. An upper bound can be detected directly on the graph by finding the maximum number of nodes which are processable concurrently and are not mutually exclusive, i.e., which can never be in the same AND-type subgraph. A polynomial time algorithm which disregards both the time attributes and the probabilities is described in Baer and Estrin (1969).

One can again test heuristics based uniquely on the graph structure or on the mean path length. Experiments have shown that policies based on time attributes behave more efficiently.

Some work has also recently been started regarding the *deterministic* assumption in the model. That is, instead of considering that the time attributes are known, Chandy and Reynolds's (1975) approach is to take these attributes from random distributions. It should be noted, first, that Graham's general bound is still valid if one considers expected completion times. But very few other results (i.e., few optimal algorithms) carry over to the stochastic studies when the time attributes are unknown. An exception is Hu's algorithm when applied to trees, two identical processors, and tasks having exponential (independent) time attributes with equal mean (the memory-less property of the exponential distribution is a requirement for the proof to hold). However, the most important conclusion of the study is that LP heuristic schedules perform (on the average) better in a stochastic environment than in a deterministic one.

5.3.5. Other Dag Models

Directed acyclic graph models can also be used in other contexts. The two examples which follow represent only a small sample geared toward the improvement of performance in parts of the computing system.

1. Straight-Line Code Optimization.   One can represent as a dag what is commonly called a block of assignment statements. Nodes of the dag represent computations, at the machine instruction level, and arcs show the sequencing of the instructions. Following Aho and Ullman (1973), a block is a triple (P, I, O), where

- P is a set of statements $S_1, S_2, \ldots, S_n$ (or instructions), where S_i is of the form (in reverse polish notation) $A \leftarrow \theta_i B_1 B_2 \ldots B_r$ (θ_i is the operator; the B_j's are the operands).
- I is a set of input variables.
- O is a set of output variables.

The oriented dag representing the block is constructed in the following manner. For each variable $A \in I$, create a node with label A. This node becomes the last definition of A. For each statement S_i, $A \leftarrow \theta_i B_1 \ldots B_r$, create a node of label θ_i, with arcs numbered from 1 to r from that node to the nodes which are the last definitions of $B_1 B_2 \ldots B_r$. The node of label θ_i becomes the last definition of A. After all elements of P have been considered the last definitions of the output variables are called distinguishable.

Example 27

The straight-line program

$$X = (A+B) * (B + C)$$
$$Y = (A+B) * (A+C)$$

is transformed into the block (P, I, O) with $I = \{A, B, C\}$, $O = \{X, Y\}$, and P.

$$S_1: \quad T_1 \leftarrow A+B$$
$$S_2: \quad T_2 \leftarrow B+C$$
$$S_3: \quad X \leftarrow T_1 * T_2$$
$$S_4: \quad T_3 \leftarrow A+B$$
$$S_5: \quad T_4 \leftarrow A+C$$
$$S_6: \quad Y \leftarrow T_3 * T_4$$

The corresponding dag is shown in Figure 5.24(a) (x_i represents S_i). The distinguishable nodes are circled twice.

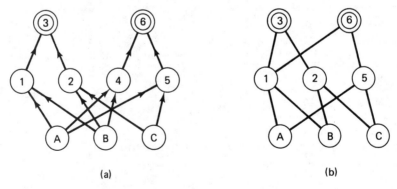

(a)   (b)

Figure 5.24. Elimination of common instructions in straight-line programming.

With the dag representation it is easy to perform two steps of the optimization process. One is to suppress all instructions which are useless. This is performed by looking at nodes without successors. If they are not distinguishable, they can be suppressed, and the procedure can be called again on the reduced graph until all nodes of outdegree 0 are distinguishable. The second is to eliminate common subexpressions, i.e., statements which compute the same expression. If one considers the dag as the representation of the state diagram of a finite state automaton (FSA), we can use known algorithms to reduce its number of states to the final minimal FSA. Eliminating states is equivalent in our case to eliminating redundant instructions.

Example 28

The dag of Figure 5.24(a) can be reduced to that of Figure 5.24(b), saving one computation of $A+B$.

Since this process can be done in $0(n \log n)$, for n statements, we have an efficient means of optimizing code at that level. Unhappily, it does not include algebraic rules such as commutativity, associativity, and distributivity. If in Example 27 we had had $T_1 \leftarrow B+A$, then we could not have eliminated $T_3 \leftarrow A+B$.

Any topological sort on the dag will yield an acceptable program. From our studies of deterministic scheduling, we are not surprised that there is no efficient algorithm to find the optimal sort when optimality is with respect to some criterion such as the length of the generated program (e.g., minimizing fetches and stores). Heuristics are discussed by Aho and Ullman (1973).

2. Minimizing the Control Memory of a Microprogrammable Computer. The control section of a microprogrammed computer can be viewed as a vector of control words. Each word contains two basic fields: the B field encoding the operations to be done and the M field indicating the address of the next microword. In the horizontal approach to microprogramming, several operations can be performed in parallel and have to be encoded in the B field. The optimization problem at hand is to minimize the length of B for a given instruction set, assuming that we want to have as few microwords as possible. The instruction set can be represented by a forest of connected dag's, each dag corresponding to an instruction sequence. Labeled nodes represent microevents. The same label can appear on two different nodes in the same dag. Nodes which are not linked by a precedence relationship in a dag represent microevents which can be executed concurrently. Two obvious realizations of B are

- Reserve a bit for each of the m possible microevents (label).
- Give a special encoding to each event. Then $B = \lceil \log_2 m \rceil$. But then we have a vertical microprogramming approach, i.e., no parallelism.

Several investigators [for a bibliography, see Montangero (1974)] have proposed grouping events by levels in each dag in such a way that for a given instruction the number of microwords is equal to the length of the longest path in that dag. What remains is to assign those microevents not on the critical path(s) such that the width of B is minimized. It appears that at this point only heuristic procedures are possible.

5.4. CYCLIC GRAPH MODELS BASED
ON FLOWCHARTS

Many aspects of program and system optimization are based on structural properties which can be easily depicted by flowcharts or flowgraphs, that is, digraphs. In this section we shall consider three specific areas where the analysis of flowcharts results in performance improvements for the programs under study.

5.4.1. Frequency of Execution of Program
Statements

It is often strongly suggested that all compilers should insert probes in source programs so that programmers can be aware of where most of the time is spent during execution. One of the first FORTRAN systems of that type, implemented by Russell and Estrin (1969), has three components: a preprocessor, the FORTRAN compiler, and a postprocessor. The preprocessor inserts probes at specific points, to be detailed later, in the source programs. These probes are statements of the form CALL EMIT (i), where i corresponds to the ith counter for the module being compiled (main program, subroutine, or function). The FORTRAN compiler itself is not modified. The postprocessor gathers the statistics, i.e., the contents of each counter, and computes the frequency of execution of each statement.

Since this early implementation, many other systems of that type have been built for several high-level languages, both in industrial and academic environments. In all cases, one has to decide where probes should be inserted. Russell and Estrin (1969) describe in detail the instrumentation of FORTRAN programs based on a digraph representation of the program $G(X, U)$. Evidently, if there exists an arc $(x_i, x_j) \in U$ such that OUTDEGREE (x_i) = INDEGREE (x_j) = 1, then the frequency of execution of x_j is the same as that of x_i. Translated in terms of FORTRAN programs, only statements which influence the flow of control (IF, DO, etc., . . .) and those which can be accessed from more than one other statement (labeled statements) are of importance. Thus in the remainder of the discussion, we shall assume that a reducing procedure has been called, collapsing those arcs and nodes which have no influence on the flow of control. Furthermore, we shall consider only digraphs with a single node of indegree 0, i.e., the *initial node* x_1, and a single node of outdegree 0, i.e., the *terminal node* x_n. From a flowcharting viewpoint there is no loss of generality. What remains is a directed graph such as the one shown in Figure 5.25(a), and the problem at hand is to insert the minimum number of probes such that all node frequencies can be computed. This minimalization reduces the artifact generated at run time by the calls to the EMIT routines.

For analytical purposes, we add an arc linking the terminal node to the initial node. Let $G(X, U)$ be the digraph F_i be the frequencies of $x_i \in X$, and $F_{i,j}$ be the frequencies of $u_k = (x_i, x_j) \in U$.

First, $G(X, U)$ must be strongly connected. Otherwise there would be statements reachable from x_1 which would never reach x_n, that is, either infinite looping or abnor-

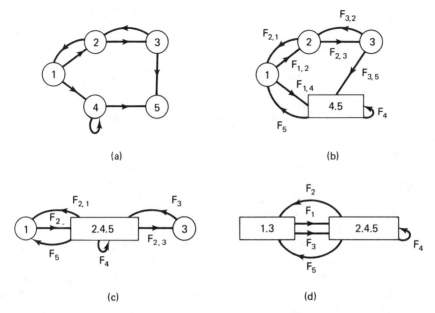

Figure 5.25. Optimal insertion of probes.

mal termination, or statements not reachable from x_1, that is, useless statements because they would never be executed. Second, knowledge of the $F_{i,j}$'s implies that of the F_i's, since we can apply Kirchhoff's first law:

$$\sum_{j \in \text{IPRED}(i)} F_{j,i} = F_i = \sum_{k \in \text{ISUC}(i)} F_{i,k}$$

Knuth (1968) shows that if there are n nodes and m arcs, we need to measure only $m - n + 1$ arc frequencies to determine all F_i's and $F_{i,j}$'s. Although this is an interesting theoretical result, it does not help in practice since the probes are inserted within a node and not on arcs. A construction due to Knuth and Stevenson (1973) shows how to transform the digraph so that now node frequencies are going to be measured. The basic idea is to replace nodes x_i and x_j such that $(x_k, x_i) \in U$ and $(x_k, x_j) \in U$ by a single node x_{ij} and transform the digraph and the arc frequencies accordingly. The procedure is best explained by the example found in the above reference.

Example 29

Consider the digraph of Figure 5.25(a) to which an arc (x_5, x_1) of frequency $F_{5,1} = F_5$ (Kirchhoff's law) has been added. Since (x_4, x_4) and (x_4, x_5) are arcs, we lump the nodes x_4 and x_5 in the (super) node $x_{4,5}$ as shown in Figure 5.25(b). The arcs incident out from x_4 are lumped into $(x_{4,5}, x_{4,5})$ of frequency $F_{4,5,4,5} = F_{4,4} + F_{4,5} = F_4$ (again Kirchhoff's law on the original graph). Looking now at Figure 5.25(b), (x_1, x_2) and $(x_1, x_{4,5})$ are arcs, yielding a supernode $x_{2,4,5}$ and Figure 5.25(c). The new arc $(x_1, x_{2,4,5})$ has frequency $F_{1,2,4,5} = F_{1,2} + F_{1,4,5} = F_{1,2} + F_{1,4} = F_1$. Similar computations are done for the other arcs. Finally nodes x_1 and x_3 can be collapsed, yielding the final graph of Figure 5.25(d). From the latter we see that $F_1 + F_3 = F_2 + F_5$ so that probes have to be inserted at x_4 and three nodes out of (x_1, x_2, x_3, x_5).

Knuth and Stevenson prove the optimality of this procedure. If instead of FORTRAN we use a programming language such that the source code is composed of the concatenation of structured statements (e.g., compound, If-then-else, case, while, etc.), we can apply the optimal procedure to each template. In fact at this point the results become rather obvious unless we allow GO_TO statements and recursive procedures.

Once one has detected the most often executed or the most time-consuming parts of the program, code optimization techniques can be applied or rewriting in assembly language can be done to render the program more efficient.

A drawback of this instrumentation method is the overhead involved in the preprocessor and the postprocessor (the execution time artifact is generally insignificant). An estimate of the node frequencies could be obtained if one knew the probability of the branches out of a node with more than one immediate successor. In terms of the same digraph model as previously, this would result in the a priori knowledge of arc probabilities $q_{i,j}$ instead of frequencies $F_{i,j}$. If we assume that the branching decisions are all independent, our digraph is the representation of a regular Markov chain. It is then possible to compute the expected number of times a given node will be executed by solving for the limiting probability vector of the regular transition matrix $Q = \{q_{i,j}\}$. Unhappily the Markovian approach is not directly applicable for constructs such as DO loops with premature exists in languages such as FORTRAN. A detailed analysis of this case can be found in Baer and Caughey (1972).

It is interesting to remark that once the frequencies of nodes have been computed, one can remove the arcs forming cycles to get a dag. If the original flowchart was also showing the potential parallelism, then the resulting dag would correspond to the acyclic bilogic graph that we introduced ealier (cf. Section 5.3.5). This cyclic-acyclic transformation, following Baer and Caughey (1972) and Martin and Estrin (1967), can be done in mean-path-length-preserving fashion.

5.4.2. Segmentation

The segmentation of programs in almost independent modules, or in blocks of equal size, arises in the management of the memory hierarchy of medium- to large-sized computers. We shall now present three approaches to this problem based on the digraph representation of programs. Their sophistication increases with the amount of information present in the model.

1. Determination of the Overlay Structure. Consider a computer system which does not have a virtual memory component. Programs which are too large to fit into main memory have to be split before run time into smaller partitions or overlay segments. If we consider each segment as a supernode, the resulting graph has to be a tree in order for communication between segments to be handled in an efficient fashion. The maximum size to be allotted to the program is then the value of the longest path, where node weights are the size of each overlay segment that they represent. To transform the cyclic digraph into a tree, the easiest way is first to lump all MSCG's into supernodes as suggested in Ramamoorthy (1966a). If the longest path computed on the resulting dag is within the memory constraint, the overlay structure is simply the dag transformed into a tree by suppressing trivially some arcs. Otherwise supernodes have to be decomposed according to, e.g., the frequency of execution of the nodes comprising them, as discussed in the preceding section. But then more information than is readily available at compile or load time is necessary. A more attainable node attribute is the memory size that each node is going to occupy. The next approach uses this information.

   2. Packing of Nodes To Fit Blocks or Pages of Equal Size. In this application, the goal is to pack code in pages (blocks of equal size) in such a way that the number of interpage transitions due to instructions is reduced in comparison with the compiler's usual memory allocation technique. Here again the only information available is that which can be derived at compile time, namely, the digraph and the memory size or weight attributes for each node. Also given is the page size.

   Although no frequency of execution is known, a fair assumption is to pack first those statements which are in the most nested cycles. Therefore, the first phase of the modeling procedure will be to detect elementary cycles in the graph $G(X, U)$, the reduced representation, in the sense of Section 5.4.1, of the original program model. Once the cycles have been detected, we can construct a dag $H(Y, V)$ such that each node $y_i \in Y$ corresponds to an elementary cycle $(x_{i_1}, x_{i_2}, \ldots, x_{i_n})$ of G and $(y_i, y_j) \in V$ if all nodes x_k in y_j are also in y_i. In other words, $(y_i, y_j) \in V$ if cycle y_j is embedded in cycle y_i. But we are mostly interested in strict embeddedness, that is, if $(y_i, y_j) \in V$ and $(y_j, y_k) \in V$, we do not want to keep the redundant information that $(y_i, y_k) \in V$. That is, we further transform $H(Y, V)$ into $H'(Y, V')$, its transitive reduction. The latter dag is now used for packing purposes.

   The embeddedness property leads to a (heuristic) packing algorithm, as found in Baer and Caughey (1972). The latter reference includes a bibliography for other methods. To pack first those nodes corresponding to the most nested cycles, we could sort the dag breadth first by level. However, it is beneficial to keep, as much as possible, the image of the structure of the source program (e.g., to minimize the number of transfer instructions to be added). A possible way of doing this is to transform the dag into a tree by suppressing all but one of the arcs incident into a node y_i of indegree larger than 1. The arc (y_j, y_i) kept is the one emanating from the node y_l of highest height, i.e., of deepest embeddedness. Now the resulting tree can be traversed in a variation of inorder; i.e.,

 • Order the sons of the root r by decreasing heights, say $(r_1, r_2, \ldots, r_k)$.

 • Traverse the subtrees of root $r_1, r_2, \ldots, r_k$ in that order.

   When a subtree is composed of only a single node, its root is traversed. During this traversal one can compute the weight of each cycle from its original components and pack it in such a way that no node corresponding to an original statement is split between two pages unless it is greater than the page size. The procedure is completed by considering that the whole program itself is a cycle.

Example 30

Consider the tree of Figure 5.26(a), where each node y_i is a cycle. These cycles contain nodes x_i of weights w_i as follows [notation (x_i/w_i)]:

$$y_1 = (x_1/4, x_2, x_3, x_4, x_5, x_6, x_7, x_8/2)$$
$$y_2 = (x_2/7, x_3, x_4)$$
$$y_3 = (x_5/4)$$
$$y_4 = (x_6/4, x_7/2)$$
$$y_5 = (x_3/6, x_4/6)$$

The page size is $p = 8$. First cycle y_5 is packed on pages p_1 and p_2. Then cycle y_2, i.e., x_2, the only statement left in that cycle, is assigned page p_3. The procedure continues until the packing of Figure 5.26(b) is obtained. A straightforward packing would have yielded $\lceil w_i/p \rceil = 5$ pages instead of 6, but some cycle such as $y_3 = (x_5)$ would have been split between two pages. This would have probably increased the number of page faults since when executing that portion of code two pages would have had to be resident instead of one.

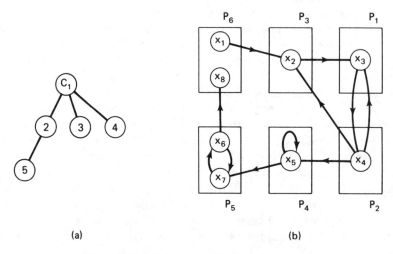

(a)   (b)

Figure 5.26. Packing algorithm based on cycle embeddedness.

The packing can be improved by looking at sets of pages which are partially empty and trying to fit them together. Additional heuristics are discussed in Baer and Caughey (1972). At this point it is more interesting to discuss an optimal packing algorithm.

3. Optimal Packing. We keep the same digraph model and weight attributes but we add transition frequencies between nodes of the digraph. In essence, we add some run time information. The goal now, as before, is to partition the graph into subsets, or supernodes, of size less than the page size p, still minimizing the frequency of interpage transitions. However, as opposed to the previous method, we do not allow for the distortion of the layout of the code; that is, if we number the nodes as integers from 1 to n in the order that the usual compiler would have done, pages contain only nodes of consecutive numbers. With this additional constraint, Kernighan (1971) devised an optimal algorithm for the page partitioning which runs in $0(a)$ $(a = |U|)$. The method is of particular interest because it is a form of dynamic programming which yields a polynomial time algorithm. A few supplementary definitions are necessary and are illustrated in Figure 5.27(a).

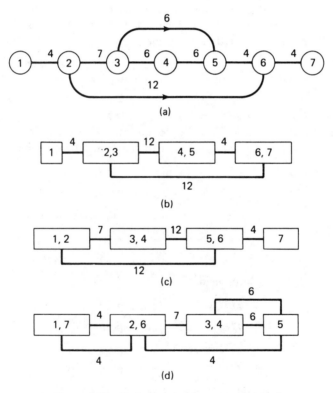

Figure 5.27. Optimal and other sequential partitions.

All nodes will have labels, i.e., $X = \{1, 2, \ldots, n\}$ (here $n = 7$). If $(i, j) \in U$ and $(j, i) \in U$, we keep only (i, j) with a frequency $F_{i,j} = F_{i,j} + F_{j,i}$ (e.g., $F_{3,4} = 6$). Now our digraph has become a dag. The distance between two nodes i and j is $d_{i,j} = \sum_{k=1}^{j} w_k$, where w_k is the size attribute of node k (e.g., $d_{2,4} = 3$ if $w_2 = w_3 = w_4 = 1$).

A partition, or page, is a set of consecutive nodes $(i, i + 1, \ldots, j)$ such that $d_{i,j} \leq p$. The first node of a partition is called a break point. If x is a break point, we note $C(x) = \sum_{i < x \leq j} F_{i,j}$; i.e., $C(x)$ is the sum of the costs of the arcs cut by a break point at x (e.g., if 3 is a break point, $C(3) = F_{2,3} + F_{2,6} = 19$). At break point x, the minimal partial cost is $T(X) = C(x) + T(y)$ such that $d_{y,x-1} \leq p$ and $T(y)$ is minimal for all possible y allowed by the last inequality. (If more than one y is possible, we choose the smallest.) Also one has to be careful not to include the cost of an arc in both $C(x)$ and $T(y)$. We compute $T(x)$ for all nodes 0 to $n + 1$, with $w_0 = w_{n+1} = 0$, $F_{0,1} = F_{n,n+1} = 0$, remembering at each computation of $T(x)$ which node played the role of y. When node $n + 1$ is reached, i.e., the minimal cost $T(n + 1)$ has been reached, the last break point was node k such that $d_{k,n} \leq p$ and $T(k)$ was minimal. Now, we can go back at $T(k)$, find the previous y which defined the previous break point, and so forth until x_0 is reached.

It is not difficult to show the optimality of the method. In addition Kernighan (1971) has proved that the number of pages needed is minimal over all optimal partitions. Also each arc is considered twice in the computations of the $T(x)$—hence an $0(a)$ algorithm.

Example 31

Consider the dag of Figure 5.27(a). Assume that all weights are 1 and that $p = 2$. Hence for each node x we have to compute two costs, one corresponding to $y = x - 1$ and one to $y = x - 2$. For the particular dag, we have

$$T(1) = 0; \qquad T(2) = F_{1,2} = 4$$
$$T(3) = \min [F_{2,3} + F_{2,6} + T(2), F_{2,3} + F_{2,6} + T(1)]$$
$$= F_{2,3} + F_{2,6} + T(1) = 19 \qquad \text{(break point is 1)}$$
$$T(4) = \min [F_{3,4} + F_{3,5} + T(3), F_{2,6} + F_{3,4} + F_{3,5} + T(2)]$$
$$= F_{2,6} + F_{3,4} + F_{3,5} + T(2) = 28 \qquad \text{(break point is 2)}$$

Continuing in this fashion yields

$$T(5) = 31 \qquad \text{(break point is 3)}$$
$$T(6) = 32 \qquad \text{(break point is 4)}$$
$$T(7) = 35 \qquad \text{(break point is 5)}$$
$$T(8) = 32 \qquad \text{(break point is 6)}$$

Retrieving our break points with a minimal cost of 32 yields the partitions (1), (2, 3), (4, 5), and (6, 7), as shown in Figure 5.27(b). The ordinary compiler allocation would have given the partitions (1, 2), (3, 4), (5, 6), and (7) of cost 35 [Figure 5.27(c)]. If we assume that (3, 4, 5) is a cycle embedded in (2, 3, 4, 5, 6), then the algorithm of the previous section packs the nodes as in Figure 5.27(d) of cost 31. (Of course the constraint of the code sequentiality is not met.)

5.4.3. Improvement and Parallelization of Code

We have already seen how dags can be used in the optimization of straight-line programs. Methods to detect the parallelism within an assignment statement have also been thoroughly investigated [see, e.g., Baer (1973) for a survey]. In this section we are interested in cyclic graphs. Optimization or parallelization algorithms are not possible anymore because it is not possible to decide whether two programs are equivalent in any worthwhile sense. Bernstein (1966) has shown, for the parallelization case, how this is related to the Turing machine halting problem. But there exist some transformations which, if not optimal, at least improve the code or discover some of the parallelism. Two general approaches are valid for code amelioration.

1. Code Improvement Via Control Flow Analysis. As in the previous section, our interest is centered on the most often executed portions of code, i.e., the cycles of the digraph modeling the program. Among the improvements that one wishes to achieve are the elimination of redundant expressions and the removal from a cycle of those computations which are invariant during the cycle.

Our model is the digraph presented before where each node is a block of assignment statements. Sequential blocks are collapsed under the criterion of Section 5.4.1 with unique initial, x_1, and terminal, x_n, nodes. A useful relation between two blocks, or nodes, is that of *dominance*. Node x_i dominates node x_j if all paths from x_1 to x_j contain x_i. A node x_i is an *immediate predominator* of x_j if it dominates x_j, and if there exists a x_k dominating x_j, then x_k also dominates x_i. Finding the (immediate) dominance relations in a digraph can be done efficiently through a repeated application of a slight modification of Dijkstra's algorithm for shortest path.

The dominance relation has been used extensively by Lowry and Medlock (1969) in optimizing FORTRAN compilers. For example, the elimination of redundant computations can be performed as follows. If x_i and x_j compute the same subexpressions, and x_i dominates x_j, and no variable used in the computation is redefined on any of the paths between x_i and x_j, then the computation in x_j can be removed.

Example 32

Consider the digraph of Figure 5.28(a). x_1 (immediately) dominates x_2, x_3, and x_4. The expression $B + C$ has the same value at nodes x_1, x_3, and x_4. Then at node x_1 we can insert the additional statement $T \leftarrow A$, leave the node x_3 empty, and transform x_4 as shown in Figure 5.28(b).

Although this example might appear to be trivial, it is quite realistic if one views it in the context of a compiler generating intermediate code of the form

result   operand 1   operator   operand 2.

Then one can imagine a number of lines between x_1 and x_3 which involve neither A, B, nor C, as, for example, the computation of other unrelated expressions.

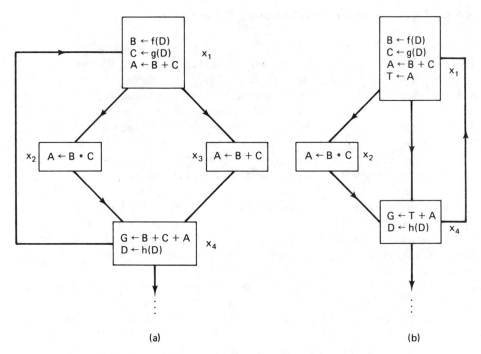

Figure 5.28. Elimination of common subexpressions.

As already seen in the previous section, an important place to improve the code is within cycles. The more nested the cycles, the more gain will occur if we can remove some code out and place it in a less often executed part of the program. The dominance relation can be used if one restricts oneself to cycles, or MSCG's, with a single entry point. This is the case of all DO loops in FORTRAN or of the looping constructs in structured programming. Now if some code is invariant in the cycle, with a single entry node, we can move it out of the cycle and place it in the immediate predecessor(s) of the entry node. In terms of dominance, the cycle, or MSCG, has a single entry point x_i if and only if there exists x_j such that (x_j, x_i) is an arc and x_i dominates x_j or is x_j [for a proof, see Aho and Ullman (1973)].

Example 33

In the FORTRAN program represented in Figure 5.29(a),

```
            DO  1000    I = 1,10       (1)
              DO    100   J = 1,25      (2)
                  DO  10   K = 1,5   (3)
     10               X(I,J,K) = A+B+C  (4)
     100        C = ...                 (5)
     1000  A      = ...                 (6)
```

one can see several instances of code motion.

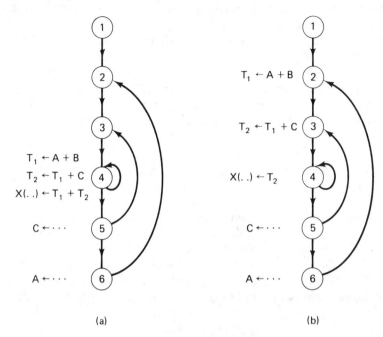

Figure 5.29.   Code motion.

First, {4}, {3, 4, 5}, and {2, 3, 4, 5, 6} are cycles with a single entry point, respectively {4}, (4 plays the role of x_i and x_j), {3} (3 is x_i and 5 is x_j), and {2}. In the innermost cycle {4} A+B+C is invariant, and we place its computation in its immediate predecessor, i.e., node 3. In node 3, A+B is invariant, and we place its computation in node 2. The optimization process results in the following program [cf. Figure 5.29(b)]:

```
          DO   1000  I = 1,10
                T₁ = A+B
          DO   100   J=1,25
                T₂ = T₁ + C
                DO  10   K = 1,5
    10                X(I,J,K) = T₂
    100         C = −
    1000  A      = − −
```

2. Code Improvement Via Data Flow Analysis.   The control information available through the analysis described above might not show all the opportunities of code improvement. To detect useless operations and constant propagations one can use the knowledge of the set of nodes where a variable was last defined before reaching some node x_i or conversely of the nodes where variables used in x_i were last defined. This will permit also the detection of undefined variables.

Hence, basic to this analysis is the knowledge of the set of variables and of their last definitions which are available in a block. Allen and Cocke (1976) extensively review investigations of this type and propose adequate procedures for data flow analysis. The sequel is a brief summary of their work.

Given a variable v, we note v_i its definition and/or its use in block (node) x_i. A *locally available definition* of v is the last definition of v in the block. LD_i is the set of all locally defined variables in block x_i. If v is not defined locally in x_i, then the set of all its definitions which can reach x_i are members of P_i, the *preserved* set of x_i. We note AV_i the set of *available* (not necessarily locally) definitions at x_i and R_i the set of definitions which *reach* x_i. We say that a definition d in x_k reaches x_i if either

(a) $d \in LD_i$

or (b) n_i is a successor of n_k and there is at least one path from n_k to n_i which preserves d.

The knowledge of R_i is paramount to the optimization process. If we define U_i as the set of those variables v in block x_i which are *used* and not preceeded in that block by their definition, or which are used in x_k such that x_i is a predecessor of x_k and there is no definition of v in the path from x_i to x_k, then the *live* definitions are $L_i = R_i \cap U_i$. It is on this set L_i that the optimization operations take place.

The difficulties reside in obtaining the sets R_i and U_i. From the definitions we can see that

$$R_i = \cup AV_p \qquad x_p \in \text{IPRED}(x_i)$$
$$AV_i = (R_i \cap P_i) \cup LD_i$$

Example 34

In the digraph of Figure 5.28(a) [assuming that the arc (x_4, x_1) is removed] we have five variables A, B, C, E, and G. Denoting A_i the definition of variable A in node x_i, the sets LD_i and P_i are

$$LD_1 = \{A_1, B_1, C_1\} \qquad P_1 = \{D_4, G_4\}$$
$$LD_2 = \{A_2\} \qquad P_2 = \{B_1, C_1, D_4, G_4\}$$
$$LD_3 = \{A_3\} \qquad P_3 = \{B_1, C_1, D_4, G_4\}$$
$$LD_4 = \{D_4, G_4\} \qquad P_4 = \{A_1, A_2, A_3, B_1, C_1\}$$

and the computations of R_i and A_i are

$$R_1 = \varnothing \qquad AV_1 = \{A_1, B_1, C_1\}$$
$$R_2 = \{A_1, B_1, C_1\} \qquad AV_2 = \{A_2, B_1, C_1\}$$
$$R_3 = \{A_1, B_1, C_1\} \qquad AV_3 = \{A_3, B_1, C_1\}$$
$$R_4 = \{A_2, A_3, B_1, C_1\} \qquad AV_4 = \{A_2, A_3, B_1, C_1, D_4, G_4\}$$

If the digraph is a dag, a direct application of the above formulas yields the result. But in case of cycles, we have to iterate until there is no change in the R_i and AV_i sets (it can be proven that such an iteration converges). It can also be done through the detection of subgraphs, called *intervals*. The interval of a given node x_i, of $G(X, U)$, called the header, is the subgraph I_i constructed as

1. $x_i \in I_i$.
2. If x_j is not in I_i, $x_j \neq x_i$, and all arcs $(x_k, x_j) \in U$ are such that $x_k \in I_i$, than add x_k to I_i.
3. Repeat step 2 until no node can be added to I_i.

Example 35

In the digraph $G(X, U)$ of Figure 5.29(a), we have

$$I_1 = (x_1); \qquad I_2 = (x_2); \qquad I_3 = (x_3); \qquad I_4 = (x_4, x_5, x_6)$$

It is important to note that the intervals partition the set of nodes, and that if a cycle exists in the interval, the header is part of the cycle, the header dominates all members of the interval, and for a given header the interval is unique and independent of the order in which nodes were selected in its construction. This uniqueness property allows us to collapse $G(X, U)$ into $H(Y, V)$, where $y_i \in Y$ is an interval and $(y_i, y_j) \in V$ if there is an arc $(x_i, x_j) \in U$ such that $x_i \in y_i$ and x_j is the header of y_j. Now intervals of H can be constructed and the collapsing construction can be repeated. If this sequence terminates with a graph of a single node, the digraph is said to be *reducible*.

Because of the above properties, the detection of the R_i can be done more easily. The two-phase process starts from the outside in, i.e., computes LD and R sets for the intervals in the original graph and then reduces the graph and combines these sets until no reduction can occur. Then the R sets are computed from the inside out using the previous phase. Details and implementation hints are found in Allen and Cocke (1976).

3. Parallelization of Programs at the Interstatement Level.

We shall now consider the digraph model of a program before its reduction; i.e., each node represents a (simple) statement of the original program. Several systems have been built which automatically detect some of the parallelism present in the program. Bernstein (1966) was the first to give the rules which allow two statements (or blocks) x_i and x_j originally scheduled to be executed sequentially before some statement x_k to be initiated in parallel.

Variables which are referenced during the execution of x_i can be partitioned into four sets: W_i (read only), X_i (stored only), Y_i (first read, then stored), and Z_i (first stored, then read). If the processors which are going to execute x_i and x_j share a common memory, then

1. Locations which are read during the execution of x_i, i.e., $W_i \cup Y_i \cup Z_i$, must not be destroyed by the storing, $X_j \cup Y_j \cup Z_j$, done during the execu-

tion of x_j, i.e.,

$$(W_i \cup Y_i \cup Z_i) \cap (X_j \cup Y_j \cup Z_j) = \varnothing$$

and by symmetry

$$(W_j \cup Y_j \cup Z_j) \cap (X_i \cup Y_i \cup Z_i) = \varnothing$$

2. When initiating the execution of x_k the state of the memory must be independent of the order of execution of x_i and x_j. This implies that the locations which are first read by x_k, $W_k \cup Y_k$, must be independent of the storing performed in x_i and x_j. Or

$$(W_k \cup Y_k) \cap (X_j \cup Y_i \cup Z_i) \cap (X_j \cup Y_j \cup Z_j) = \varnothing$$

which can be reduced to

$$(W_k \cup Y_k) \cap X_i \cap X_j = \varnothing$$

Then if with each node x_i of the digraph we associate sets I_i (input variables) and O_i (output variables), x_i and x_j are independent if

$$I_i \cap O_j = I_j \cap O_i = O_i \cap O_j = \varnothing$$

Based on these relations, the detection of cycles, the Boolean matrix representations of graphs, and the analysis of flow of control as in Section 5.4.1, that FORTRAN and ALGOL 60 programs have been analyzed. The resulting graph could be a directed cyclic bilogic graph (recall the acyclic bilogic graph of Section 5.3.5). However, this representation is not powerful enough to model some synchronization aspects which appear during the concurrent processing of programs.

5.5. GRAPH MODELS FOR PARALLEL COMPUTATIONS AND SYSTEMS

5.5.1. Petri Nets

In previous parts of this chapter we have seen how a model for parallel computations could be developed (program parallelization), simplified (cyclic-acyclic transformation), and analyzed (scheduling studies). Certainly this model is adequate to represent concurrency of operations. But a major component of the behavior of parallel processes, namely the means to represent the synchronization of the concurrent activities, is not representable in a straightforward manner within this framework. We need additional elements in the graph which allow for modeling primitives such as the semaphores introduced by Dijkstra (1968) and for representing the concept of critical sections.

The descriptive power of the graph model should not prohibit the proof of formal properties or the detection, via efficient graph-oriented algorithms, of interesting behavioral or structural qualities of the system under scrutiny. Therefore, rather than settling for one model, we might want to introduce a hierarchy of models built upon the same basic primitive entities. The levels in the hierarchy will correspond to levels of interpretation in a manner similar to what we did for flowcharts in Section 5.4. For example, total interpretation can be used to describe a multiprogrammed operating system. The determinacy of an algorithm can be checked in a partial interpreted model, and an uninterpreted graph is sufficient for detecting potential deadlocks.

Among many possible graph models [see Baer (1973) for a survey] we have chosen to present Petri nets because they are the most prevalent nowadays. Subsets as well as generalized and extended Petri nets have also been used, and other systems for representing parallel activities, not necessarily graph oriented, often use Petri nets as a convenient frame of reference. Our presentation at this point is not so formal as it could be, and some details are purposely skipped.

A *Petri net* is a triple $PN = (X, A, M_0)$ where

1. $X = P \cup T$ is a finite set of nodes with $P = \{p_1, p_2, \ldots, p_n\}$ being a finite set of *places* and $T = \{t_1, t_2, \ldots, t_m\}$ being a finite set of *transitions*.

2. $A = I \cup O$ is a finite set of (weighted) arcs where $I: P \times T \rightarrow \mathbb{N}$ are the (weighted) input arcs and $O: T \times P \rightarrow \mathbb{N}$ are the (weighted) output arcs ($\mathbb{N}$ is the set of nonnegative integers).

3. $M_0: P \rightarrow \mathbb{N}$ is an initial *marking*, or state of the net.

Graphically, the net is represented as a bipartite graph, i.e., a graph with nodes partitioned into two sets, with places being circles, transitions being bars, elements of I (and O) being arcs from (to) input (output) places to (from) transitions with their associated weights, and the initial marking being *tokens* on places. A place holding one or more tokens is said to be full.

A transition is *firable* if its input places are full and each input place holds as many tokens as the weight of the arc linking it to the transition. The firing of a transition generates a new marking by removing tokens from the input places and adding tokens to the output places according to the weights of the input and output arcs. Sequences of transition firings are called *execution sequences*.

Places represent conditions, and transitions model events. Hence, a full place shows the holding of a condition, and when all conditions prior to an event are holding, then the event can occur (the transition is firable). An execution sequence represents a simulation of the system being modeled, with the initial marking being the initial conditions.

A Petri net is *safe* if a place cannot hold more than one token at any time (extension of this definition to *k*-safe is immediate). A marking M' is *reachable* from marking M if there exists an execution sequence which starts from initial state M and terminates with the state M'. The set of all reachable markings from M is denoted $r(M)$. A transition t_i is *live* for a marking M if for all markings $M' \in r(M)$ there exists an execution sequence which reaches a marking M'' where t_i is firable. A Petri net is live if all its transitions are live. The firable transitions t_i and t_j are in *conflict* if they share a common input place.

Example 36

Figure 5.30(a) represents a Petri net and its initial marking. Either transition t_1 or t_2 is firable. Figure 5.30(b) shows the net and its marking after firing of transition t_1. This Petri net is not live. For example, if t_2 fires instead of t_1, no more firing will occur. The Petri net is 2-safe. Transitions t_1 and t_2 are in conflict over place p_1. If the weight of (p_1, t_1) were 1 and the initial marking $M_0 = (1, 0, 0, 0, 0)$, the net would be neither live nor safe.

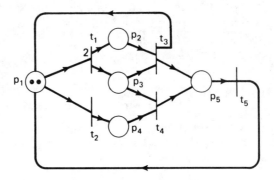

(a) Initial marking $M_0 = (2, 0, 0, 0, 0)$

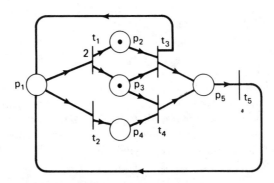

(b) Marking $(0, 1, 1, 0, 0)$. Transition t_1 has fired

$$PN = (X, A, M_0)$$

$$X = P \cup T$$

$$P = \left\{ p_1, p_2, \ldots, p_5 \right\}$$

$$T = \left\{ t_1, t_2, \ldots, t_5 \right\}$$

$$A = I \cup O$$

$$I = \left\{ (p_1, t_1)^2, (p_1, t_2), \ldots, (p_5, t_5) \right\}$$

$$O = \left\{ (t_1, p_2), (t_1, p_3), \ldots, (t_5, p_1) \right\}$$

$$M_0 = (2, 0, 0, 0, 0)$$

Figure 5.30. Example of a Petri net.

The liveness property is related to the absence of deadlock and that of safety to the boundedness in the use of resources, and conflicts are used to model synchronization constraints as well as predicates. As we shall see below, it is not possible for Petri nets to test for the exact number of tokens on a place and in particular for the emptiness of a place. Extensions to Petri nets which allow for such tests through either inhibitors or Boolean expressions on the contents of (input) places have been proposed. The price to be paid will be the undecidability of many formal properties.

5.5.2. Modeling with Petri Nets

The usual programming language constructs are easily depicted by Petri nets. It is sufficient to introduce a transition on each arc of a flowchart and let the nodes be places to obtain a Petri net representing a sequential program. But the basic interpretation of the roles of transitions and places is not followed. In general, the modeling will be performed in such a way that all transitions will correspond to executable statements and places will act as deciders besides having their usual meaning of condition holders.

Example 37

The programming constructs DO-WHILE and IF-THEN-ELSE are shown in Figure 5.31. Notice that the IF predicate is shown as a place, as well as the test for the loop termination.

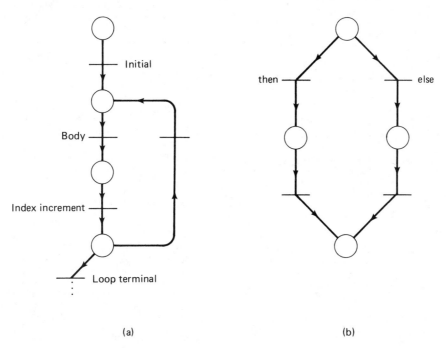

(a)   (b)

Figure 5.31. Petri net representation of DO-WHILE and IF-THEN-ELSE.

To model more faithfully events by transitions and to be closer to the flowchart terminology, some modifications to the firing rule have been proposed. The most common one is to introduce branching transitions, i.e., transitions which upon firing place a token on only one of their output places, and OR-input transitions, i.e., transitions which are firable when one of their input places is full. Petri nets allowing these rules are direct descendants of the bilogic graphs of Section 5.4.3. Predicates can now be modeled by transitions.

Example 38

Figures 5.32(a) and (b) correspond to Figures 5.31(a) and (b) with the additional firing rules noted with a + at either the input or the output of the transitions they affect. Figure 5.32(c) shows how to transform a Petri net with branching and OR-input transitions to a regular Petri net.

In addition to the sequential constructs, parallel operations are modeled elegantly by Petri nets. The FORK-JOIN assembly language instructions and the PARBEGIN-PAREND high-level language equivalent correspond to the activation and termina-

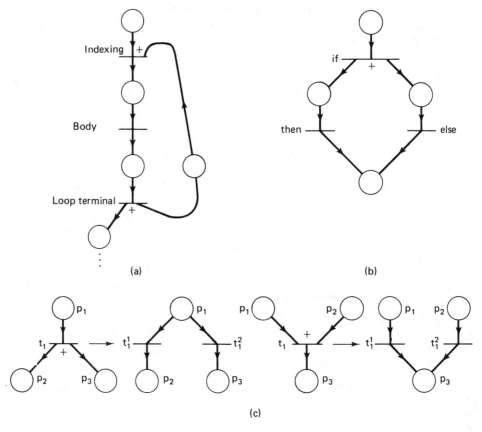

Figure 5.32. A first extension to Petri nets.

tion of concurrent execution sequences. That is, if a block is enclosed by the brackets PARBEGIN_PAREND instead of BEGIN_END, it indicates that the statements in the block (separated by semicolons as usual) can be processed in parallel.

Example 39

The following parallel-ALGOL-like program is modeled by the Petri net of Figure 5.33:

```
PARBEGIN
    S1:  PARBEGIN
                S1.1:  BEGIN ... END ;
                S1.2:  BEGIN ... END ;
          PAREND ;
    S2:  BEGIN ... END ;
    S3:  BEGIN ... END .
PAREND
```

The application of these constructs is not limited to the modeling of programs. Figure 5.34 shows how the instruction cycle of a uniprocessor with a single accumu-

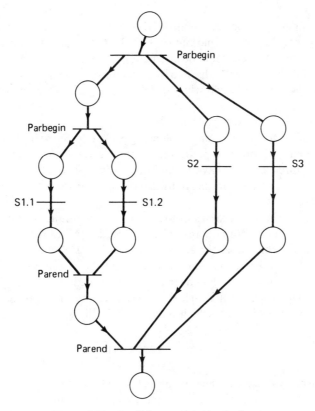

Figure 5.33. Parallelism modeled by Petri nets.

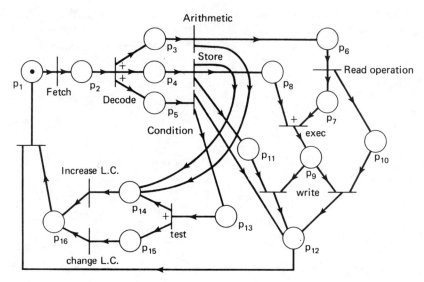

Figure 5.34. Instruction cycle modeled by Petri nets.

lator arithmetic unit could be represented. If, following Patil and Dennis (1972), we show, via a data graph, the internal registers of the CPU—i.e., the accumulator, the memory data, and address registers, the instruction register, and the location counter— as well as their interaction with the Petri net, we have a clear view of the dynamic behavior of the system. It is worthwhile to remark that the net of Figure 5.34 is live and safe.

Modeling of sharable subprograms, procedures, or co-routines as well as the modularization of Petri nets are more challenging problems. Some initial investigations have shown that either more interpretation has to be given to the graph or additional concepts, e.g., colored tokens, have to be introduced. But on the other hand, Petri nets are extremely valuable for the representation of process synchronization and mutual exclusion.

A typical situation which arises in the design of operating systems is to prevent two processes sharing a common resource to access this resource simultaneously. The part of the code which does the accessing is called a *critical section*. For example, one process can be a reader, the other a writer, and the resource a common buffer. Numerous solutions to this problem have appeared in the literature. Dijkstra's (1968) introduction of *semaphores* is a classical approach to the problem. Semaphores are nonnegative integer variables on which only two indivisible operations,

$$V(S) : S \leftarrow S+1 \; ;$$
$$P(S) : L: \text{ If } S=0 \text{ then go to } L$$
$$\text{else } S \leftarrow S-1 \; ;$$

can be performed. By enclosing the critical sections of the reader and writer processes within a *P* and a *V* operation on a common semaphore, simultaneous access to the buffer can be prohibited. In terms of Petri nets, a semaphore is modeled as a conflicting place between the transitions representing the critical sections. Figure 5.35 is a representation of the reader-writer problem with an unbounded buffer in Petri net form (there are other possibilities, but this net is safe—not live, but properly terminating a property which will be discussed later). Place p_s is in conflict with t_r (read) and t_w (write), hence enforcing the mutual exclusion of accessing the buffer.

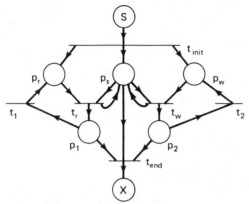

Figure 5.35. Modeling mutual exclusion via Petri nets.

Let us consider now a slight extension of this problem. There are three resources, e.g., a card reader, a line printer, and a tape drive, and three processes, *A*, *B*, and *C*. To proceed, *A* requires the use of the card reader and line printer, *B* the use of the line printer and tape drive, and *C* that of the card reader and tape drive. (This is commonly referred to as Patil's three smokers problem.) If each process retains one of the resources, we have a deadlock. Hence we need to synchronize the access to the resources. Figure 5.36 shows the Petri net solution to the problem, which is conceptually as simple as that in Figure 5.35. All transitions are firable, but once one has fired, the other two are not firable any more (i.e., the net is not persistent). In programming language terms, however, the solution requires extensions to the *P* and *V* primitives either through arrays of semaphores or generalized *P*'s and *V*'s which can test more than one semaphore in an indivisible operation [cf. Presser (1975) for a sur-

Card reader   Line printer   Tape drive

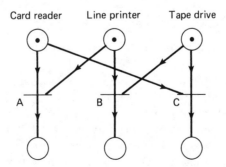

Figure 5.36. Patil's three smokers problem.

vey]. The interesting point here is that the Petri net solution leads to a simple programming language solution if these generalized constructs are allowed.

But the power of representation of Petri nets is limited since we cannot test for the exact number of tokens resident on a place. The following problem due to Kosaraju (1973) illustrates the situation well. Two producers P_1 and P_2 produce items and deposit them, respectively, in buffers B_1 and B_2. When consumer C_1 is activated, it accesses the first element of buffer B_1, removes it from the buffer, and deactivates itself. The activation is of course possible only if the buffer is not empty. Let consumer C_2 follow the same routine with buffer B_2. The synchronization problem is that the consumers cannot access the buffers simultaneously because they are on the same device. Stated in these terms, it is evident that a slight modification of Figure 5.35 would be a satisfying answer. We now add the constraint that C_1 has priority over C_2; i.e., C_2 can be activated only when B_1 is empty. If one allows unbounded buffer queues (i.e., unsafe nets), Kosaraju shows that Petri nets cannot model this situation. In fact, most priority problems become unrepresentable because of the same inability to model adequately predicates on token counts.

This lack of descriptive power is a handicap which can be removed by allowing the firing rule to be extended. Agerwala and Flynn (1973) have introduced inhibitors (noted by a dashed arc in figures) which allow testing of whether a place is empty. Now the priority probelm is solved easily, as shown in Figure 5.37. The arc (B_1, t_2) is an inhibitor which indicates that t_2 can fire only when B_1 is empty and of course B_2 and C_2 full.

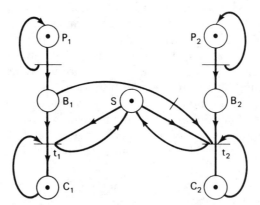

Figure 5.37. Use of inhibitors for priority rules.

Instead of an inhibitor which represents a NOT condition, we can restrict the OR firing rule discussed previously to make it an exclusive-OR (EOR) condition; that is, a transition t_i with EOR-input can fire if and only if one of its input places is full. Choosing between EOR rules or inhibitors, or choosing both, is a matter of convenience for the modeler. What is certainly important to discuss is the impact of such extensions on the formal properties which can be tested on the net.

5.5.3. Formal Properties of Petri Nets

It is not our intention to review theorems and proofs relative to the properties of Petri nets. Our aim is to show the main lines of reasoning behind two techniques which have been used in connection with Petri nets or equivalent models. The power of Petri nets as a formal model of computations will not be discussed except for a short review of known results.

The first approach, introduced by Karp and Miller (1969) and extended by Keller (1972), is to consider Petri nets as a representation of a transition system. As already mentioned, a marking, or state, can be represented as a vector of size $|P|$, the number of places, with each coordinate representing the number of tokens in a given place. In Keller's *vector replacement system* (VRS) the firing of a transition t_i with input places $p_{i_1}, \ldots, p_{i_k}$ and output places $p_{j_1}, \ldots, p_{j_m}$ is represented by a pair of vectors U_i, V_i, where U_i, the test vector, has for coordinates the weights of the arcs leading from p_{i_n} to t_i (or 0 if there is no such arc) and V_i, the replacement vector, has for coordinates the weights of the arcs leading from t_i to p_{j_n}. If M is a marking, t_i can fire if the vector $(M - U_i)$ has all its coordinates nonnegative and the new marking becomes $(M - U_i + V_i)$.

Example 40

The VRS representation of the Petri net of Figure 5.30 is

$$U_1 = (2, 0, 0, 0, 0) \qquad V_1 = (0, 1, 1, 0, 0)$$
$$U_2 = (1, 0, 0, 0, 0) \qquad V_2 = (0, 0, 1, 1, 0)$$
$$U_3 = (0, 1, 1, 0, 0) \qquad V_3 = (1, 0, 0, 0, 1)$$
$$U_4 = (0, 0, 1, 1, 0) \qquad V_4 = (0, 0, 0, 0, 1)$$
$$U_5 = (0, 0, 0, 0, 1) \qquad V_5 = (1, 0, 0, 0, 0)$$

With an initial marking of $M = (2, 0, 0, 0, 0)$, $(M - U_1)$ and $(M - U_2)$ are nonnegative and t_1 and t_2 are firable.

With the VRS formalism one can construct a *reachability tree* of the net, i.e., a state diagram, which permits detection of whether the Petri net is safe. The reachability tree gives a procedure for determining if given some initial marking M_0, there exists a reachable marking M larger, coordinate by coordinate, than some marking M' but does not answer the specific question whether M' can be reached. Hack (1974) has shown that the reachability and the liveness problem are equivalent, and it is still unknown at this time if they are "decidable" problems.

We shall give below the reachability tree construction. The tree will have four types of nodes representing markings. All nodes created during the tree's construction are first labeled working. They become leaf nodes when they are dead, i.e., there is no firable transition; they become internal nodes if they have successors, i.e., if there exists at least one transition which can fire at the marking they represent; finally, they become loop nodes if their marking is the same as the marking of one of their predecessors. If some marking M is larger than some predecessor marking M', i.e., all coordinates $m_i \geq m'_i$, we mark by * those coordinates which are strictly larger. This implies that they can grow infinitely by the repetition of the execution sequence which led from M' to M. Given n transitions and associated vectors U_i and V_i of dimension m and an initial marking M_0, the algorithm is

1. [Initialization]. Let the root be labeled M_0. Set M_0 to be a working node.

2.
    > While there exists a working node M_i do
    > If there exists no j such that $(M_i - U_j) \geq$ then set M_i to be a leaf
    > Else begin set M_i to be internal;
    > X = {$M_j \mid M_j$ is a predecessor of M_i} $\cup$ {M_i}
    > For each j such that $(M_i - U_j) \geq 0$ do
    >   begin $M_k \leftarrow M_i U_j + V_j$; (M_i, M_k) becomes an arc of the tree ;
    >   if $M_1 \in X$ s.t. $M_1 = M_k$ then set M_k to be a loop
    >   else begin For each $M_1 \in X$ do
    >   For each coordinate p do
    >   If coordinate $(M_1) <$ coordinate (M_k)
    >   then coordinate $(M_k) \leftarrow *$;
    >   Set M_k to be working ;
    >   end
    >   end
    > end

Example 41

This construction applied to the Petri net of Figure 5.30 yields the tree of Figure 5.38. Since no node has a coordinate larger than 2, the net is 2-safe.

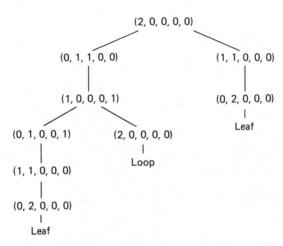

Figure 5.38. Reachability tree construction.

Evidently the reachability tree construction also determines if the number of markings is finite (as, e.g., in Example 40), and in that latter case the liveness condition is of course decidable.

More graph-oriented algorithms have been used for liveness and safety in subsets of Petri nets. For example, if one restricts node to have their indegrees and outdegrees to be 1, then Commoner et al. (1971) show that these "marked graphs" are live if and only if the token count of every circuit is positive and they are safe if and only if every place in the net is in a circuit with token count 1 (the token count of a circuit is the sum of the tokens found on the places belonging to the circuit).

One inconvenience of the reachability tree method is that the procedure is slow since a complete state diagram (loops excepted) has to be generated and for each new node a whole path has to be retraced and tested. On the other hand, the reduction procedure approach of Gostelow et al. (1972) is going to reduce (as its name implies) the state diagram of the system. The basic idea is to associate with each transition a rewriting rule of the form

$$p_{i_1} \cdots p_{i_k} \longrightarrow p_{j_1} \cdots p_{j_m}$$

where the left-hand side corresponds to input places and the right-hand side to output places. If the right-hand side of transition t_i is a superset (in the multiset sense seen of Section 5.3) of the left-hand side of transition t_j, then we can suppress transition t_j and replace the part of the right-hand of t_i corresponding to t_j by the right-hand side of t_j. This replacement is allowed if and only if it can be done simultaneously for all t_i which are supersets of t_j and if no place which was part of the left-hand side of t_j remains in the rewriting rules of the reduced system. The goal of such a reduction is to test if starting from some initial state M_0 we can reach a final state M_f, i.e., if the final reduction rule is of the form

$$M_0 \longrightarrow M_f$$

or if this cannot be achieved by the reduction procedure, it can be seen from the reduced state graph. This property, called proper termination, is closely related to some graph-theoretic procedures for the prevention of deadlocks as investigated by Holt (1972).

Example 42

The Petri net of Figure 5.35 has the following rewriting rules:

$$S \longrightarrow p_r p_s p_w \qquad (t_{\text{init}})$$
$$p_r p_s \longrightarrow p_1 p_s \qquad (t_r)$$
$$p_w p_s \longrightarrow p_2 p_s \qquad (t_w)$$
$$p_1 \longrightarrow p_r \qquad (t_1)$$
$$p_2 \longrightarrow p_w \qquad (t_2)$$
$$p_1 p_2 p_s \longrightarrow X \qquad (t_{\text{end}})$$

Applying the reduction procedure to it does not yield any reduction! However, if $M_0 = \{S\}$ and $M_f = \{X\}$, it can be seen (by drawing the state diagram) that it is properly terminating if one disallows infinite looping.

The reduction procedure can be applied to extended Petri nets also.

Example 43

The (extended) Petri net of Figure 5.34 has the following rewriting rules:

$$p_1 \longrightarrow p_2; \quad p_2 \longrightarrow p_3; \quad p_2 \longrightarrow p_4; \quad p_2 \longrightarrow p_5; \quad p_5 \longrightarrow p_6 p_{14};$$
$$p_4 \longrightarrow p_8 p_{11} p_{14}; \quad p_5 \longrightarrow p_{12} p_{13}; \quad p_6 \longrightarrow p_7 p_{10}; \quad p_7 \longrightarrow p_9; \quad p_8 \longrightarrow p_9;$$
$$p_9 p_{10} \longrightarrow p_{12}; \quad p_9 p_{11} \longrightarrow p_{12}; \quad p_{13} \longrightarrow p_{14}; \quad p_{13} \longrightarrow p_{15}; \quad p_{14} \longrightarrow p_{16};$$
$$p_{15} \longrightarrow p_{16}; \quad p_{12} p_{16} \longrightarrow p_1$$

The reduction of p_2 yields

$$p_1 \longrightarrow p_3; \quad p_1 \longrightarrow p_4; \quad p_1 \longrightarrow p_5; \quad p_3 \longrightarrow p_6 p_{14}; \quad \text{etc.}$$

After reducing p_3, p_4, and p_5 we would have

$$p_1 \longrightarrow p_6 p_{14}; \quad p_1 \longrightarrow p_8 p_{11} p_{14}; \quad p_1 \longrightarrow p_{12} p_{13}; \quad p_6 \longrightarrow p_7 p_{10}; \quad \text{etc.}$$

Further reductions would yield

$$p_1 \longrightarrow p_9 p_{10} p_{16}; \quad p_1 \longrightarrow p_9 p_{11} p_{16}; \quad p_1 \longrightarrow p_{12} p_{16}; \quad p_9 p_{10} \longrightarrow p_{12};$$
$$p_9 p_{11} \longrightarrow p_{12}$$

At this point the reduction stops, although human insight rapidly discovers that one could go to $p_1 \longrightarrow p_1$ through the state diagram.

An interesting property of properly terminating nets is that no token is left hanging in places if M_0 and M_f are the same. Then the net can be used as the model of a pipeline stage.

If one associates a symbol, a member of a finite alphabet, to the firing of a transition, it is interesting to try to classify the set of languages generated by execution sequences. Because of the finiteness of states, it is not surprising that properly terminating nets are equivalent to regular languages. Hack (1975), among others, has shown that Petri nets can generate a subset of the context-sensitive languages (and this subset does not contain all context-free languages) and that Petri nets with inhibitors have the same computational power as Turning machines. This last result implies that liveness and safety are undecidable for these nets. This is not a sufficient reason to eliminate them from the arsenal of useful models, but one has to be wary of the difficulties that can be encountered.

5.6. CONCLUSION

In this chapter we have reviewed some graph-theoretical models used for the improvement and evaluation of programming systems. Their applications have ranged from abstractions of computer systems (e.g., in deterministic scheduling) to engineering-oriented techniques used in production facilities (e.g., probe insertion for program instrumentation). The algorithms used have been either straight applications of classical graph algorithms or variations on some well-known themes. We have stressed the efficiency of these algorithms since this quality is a requirement when one deals with performance improvement.

As stated in the introduction, we have not tried to be complete. We have not touched on a number of areas for which graph models have been used. Among the most prominent of those we can list

- Data bases. One of the most important representations of data schemes which has been introduced lately is the network model of the data base task group. Relationships between groups and subgroups are modeled via a cyclic directed graph.

- Program testing and fault-tolerance studies. These topics are related to the flowchart modeling techniques presented in Section 5.4.

- Network protocols. Graph models of computations similar to Petri nets and techniques like the reduction procedure of Section 5.5 have been used to describe and prove the correctness of network protocols.

- Deadlock in computer systems. Several graph techniques have been extensively used for the prevention, detection, and recovery of deadlock in operating systems and data base systems.

Certainly graph models will still be used in these and other contexts. The dual advantage of a graphic representation and of possible analysis makes them a natural area of study.

CHAPTER 6

COMBINATORIAL PROBLEMS

AND

APPROXIMATION SOLUTION*

C. L. LIU and DONALD K. FRIESEN
Department of Computer Science
University of Illinois at Urbana–Champaign
Urbana, Illinois

6.1. INTRODUCTION

In this chapter we shall examine some aspects of the design and evaluation of computing algorithms, using problems from several different areas as illustrative examples. Two of the most important aspects about a computing algorithm we wish to consider are its accuracy and its efficiency. Indeed, these are frequently the criteria used to choose among algorithms.

By the accuracy of an algorithm, we mean how good the result produced by the algorithm is. In many cases, there is associated with each solution to a problem a cost which we wish to minimize or maximize. For example, in a traveling salesman problem we wish to determine a tour with minimum cost, and in a job scheduling problem we wish to maximize throughput. Clearly, a best possible solution is one that minimizes or maximizes the cost, and it is most desirable to have algorithms that produce best possible solutions. On the other hand, there is the possibility of employing algorithms that produce results which are good but might not be best possible. Such a possibility becomes particularly attractive when other aspects, such as efficiency, of algorithms are taken into consideration. Algorithms that produce results that may not be best possible are known as approximation algorithms, and we shall study some of these in detail in Sections 6.3 and 6.4.

By the efficiency of an algorithm we mean how economically resources are utilized to produce a result. The most commonly used criteria to measure the efficiency of an algorithm are the time and the space required by the algorithm to deter-

*Supported in part by the National Science Foundation under Grant NSF MCS 73-03408-A01.

mine an acceptable solution. Needless to say, it is highly desirable to be able to design efficient computing algorithms. However, as our intuition would immediately suggest, accuracy and efficiency are two conflicting requirements of computing algorithms that we must balance in choosing a method. We shall discuss in Section 6.2 more precisely the notion of efficient algorithms in terms of computation time.

In evaluating the performance of an algorithm, we can consider either its average performance or its worst-case performance. Since an algorithm works on different sets of input data, the performance of an algorithm can either be measured by its expected performance on the basis of a given statistical distribution of the input data or by its performance corresponding to the most unfavorable (with respect to the algorithm) set of input data. Our discussion in this chapter will be restricted to worst-case performance of algorithms.

6.2. CLASSIFICATION OF DIFFICULT PROBLEMS

We shall investigate in this section the problem of measuring the efficiency of algorithms. Among all criteria used for measurement, computation time is certainly a most meaningful and significant one. Thus, we would say that an algorithm is efficient if it produces an acceptable solution in a "short time" and inefficient if it requires a "long time" to produce such a solution. Clearly, we must be more precise about what we mean by "long" and "short" time.

We note first that the computation time of a given algorithm is usually a function of the size of the problem. In most problems, there is an obvious quantity which determines the amount of input to our algorithm, e.g., the number of variables in an equation, the number of vertices or edges in a graph, or the number of jobs to be scheduled. Clearly, we expect that if these numbers are larger, our algorithm will require more time. What we would like is for the time needed to run the algorithm to grow as slowly as possible as the amount of input increases.

For example, many algorithms are known for sorting lists. The time required by a *bubble sort* is proportional to the square of the number of items on the list, while the fastest algorithms require time proportional to $n \log n$ to sort n items. Sorting algorithms can be applied to very long lists since the function $n \log n$ does not grow very rapidly compared to n. However, there are a great many interesting problems for which no known algorithm performs well enough to compute its result in time which is polynomial in the amount of input.

Intuitively, we can consider a problem "easy" if there exists an "efficient" algorithm for solving it and "hard" if no such algorithm exists. In the literature, a problem is called *tractable* if it can be solved by an algorithm in time which is bounded by a polynomial function of the "amount" of input. If there is no such algorithm, then the problem is called *intractable*. We should be more precise about what we mean by amount, but to avoid getting into the technical details, we shall simply use "the length of a reasonable representation of the input." For example, the input to a sorting algorithm could be the numbers to be sorted in decimal (or binary) form, and the input data to a scheduling algorithm could be the execution time of the jobs represented in decimal (or binary) form together with a (0–1)-matrix representation of the precedence relation.

To show that a problem is tractable, we only need to exhibit an algorithm operating in polynomial time which produces the desired result. Thus any of the usual algorithms for sorting can be used to show that this problem is tractable. However, it is not a simple matter to show that a problem is intractable. Examples of such problems, and a proof of their intractability, can be found in Chapter 11 of Aho et al. (1976).

A fascinating problem in computational complexity is to determine if a certain collection of problems for which no known polynomial algorithm exists is in fact intractable. This class of problems, called NP-complete problems, was first formally described by Cook (1971). A great many famous problems have been shown to be in this class [see Karp (1972), for example], including the traveling salesman problem, the graph colorability problem, the general integer linear programming problem, and the satisfiability problem for Boolean expressions. These problems are classified together because it has been shown that if there is a polynomial algorithm for any one of them, then each of them has a polynomial algorithm.

To understand this relationship more fully we must introduce the notion of *polynomial transformability*. A problem P_1 is *polynomially transformable* into problem P_2 if there is an algorithm, operating in time bounded by a polynomial function of the input, which will convert an arbitrary input of length n for P_1 into a suitable input for P_2 of length bounded by a polynomial $p(n)$ so that the solution to P_2 with this input determines the solution to P_1 with the original input. Thus, if P_1 is polynomially transformable to P_2, then a polynomial algorithm for P_2 could be used to obtain a polynomial algorithm for P_1.

We can use the class of NP-complete problems as a point of reference to classify problems according to their difficulty, since any NP-complete problem is known to be polynomially transformable to any other. A problem is said to be NP-hard if any one of the NP-complete problems is polynomially transformable to it (and thus all NP-complete problems are transformable to it). Intuitively, an NP-hard problem is not easier than an NP-complete problem. A problem is said to be NP if it is polynomially transformable to any (and thus all) of the NP-complete problems. Intuitively then, an NP problem is not harder than an NP-complete problem. According to these definitions, a problem is NP-complete if it is both NP and NP-hard.

To show that a particular problem is NP-hard, we can choose any NP-complete problem we wish as a problem for comparison. For our first example, 3-colorability of graphs, we will use *3-satisfiability* of Boolean expressions. In general, the problem of determining if an arbitrary Boolean expression is satisfiable, i.e., whether there is an assignment of true or false to the variables for which the expression is true, is an NP-complete problem. It is easy to show that any Boolean expression can be converted to an equivalent one in conjunctive normal form with exactly three literals in each disjunction. Thus 3-satisfiability, determining if an arbitrary Boolean expression in conjunctive normal form with three literals in each disjunction, is also NP-complete.

The 3-colorability problem can be stated as determining whether each of the vertices of a graph can be labeled with one of three colors, call them 1, 2, and 3, so that no two vertices of the same color are connected by an edge. We shall prove in the following theorem that 3-satisfiability of Boolean expressions can be polynomially transformed into a problem of determining the 3-colorability of graphs.

Theorem 6.2.1

The 3-colorability problem for graphs is NP-hard.

Proof: We assume that we are given a Boolean expression E in the variables $u_1, u_2, \ldots, u_n$ in conjunctive normal form with three literals in each disjunction. From this we shall construct a graph G which can be colored with three colors if and only if E is satisfiable. Before giving the complete construction, we shall examine a graph H which will be a subgraph of G. The graph H, shown in Figure 6.2.1, possesses two important properties:

(i) In any 3-coloring of H, if a, b, c are all the same color, then d must also be that color.

(ii) In any 3-coloring of H, if a, b, and c are colored with two colors, say 2 and 3, then d can be colored either 2 or 3 by choosing the colors of the intermediate vertices appropriately.

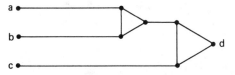

Figure 6.2.1 The graph H.

These facts can be verified easily and will be used in the subsequent proof.

We now associate a graph G with the Boolean expression E. We begin with two vertices t_1, t_2 which are joined by an edge $\{t_1, t_2\}$. Corresponding to each variable u_i there are a pair of vertices $u_i, \bar{u}_i$ which are connected by an edge $\{u_i, \bar{u}_i\}$. Each of these vertices is connected to t_1 by edges $\{u_i, t_1\}, \{\bar{u}_i, t_1\}$. Corresponding to each disjunction $u_p^* \vee u_q^* \vee u_r^*$ of E, where we use u_i^* to denote either u_i or $\bar{u}_i$, there will be a subgraph isomorphic to H, with a, b, and c being u_p^*, u_q^*, and u_r^*, respectively, and with d connected to t_2.

The following example may clarify the construction. Let

$$E(u_1, u_2, u_3, u_4) = (u_1 \vee \bar{u}_2 \vee u_3) \wedge (\bar{u}_1 \vee \bar{u}_2 \vee u_4)$$

Then G would be as shown in Figure 6.2.2.

We first observe that if E is satisfiable, then the graph G that we construct from it is 3-colorable according to the following scheme.

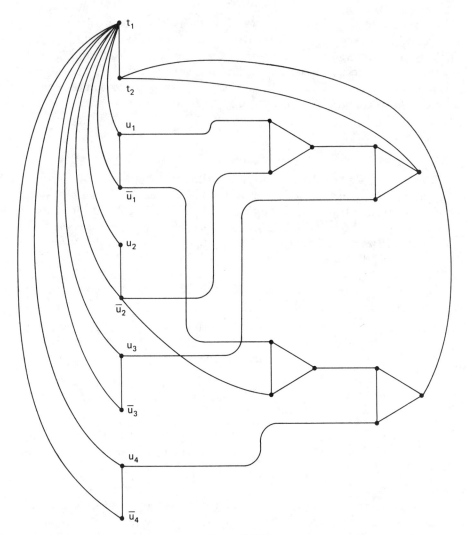

Figure 6.2.2

We select a color, say 1, for vertex t_1 and another color, say 2, for t_2. The vertices u_i, $\bar{u}_i$ must be colored 2 and 3; we choose u_i to be colored 3 and $\bar{u}_i$ to be colored 2 if in the assignment satisfying E, u_i is set to be true; otherwise u_i is colored 2 and $\bar{u}_i$ is colored 3. For each copy of H we can choose colors so that the vertex corresponding to d is colored 3 since we cannot have a, b, c all colored 2. This is a 3-coloration of G.

Conversely if we have a 3-coloration of G, we can assume t_1 and t_2 are colored with colors 1 and 2, respectively. Then vertices u_i, $\bar{u}_i$ are again colored 2 or 3, and from (i) and (ii) above we can assume d in each copy of it is colored 3. (It cannot be colored 2, and if it were colored 1, we could modify the other colors inside the copy of H to change it to 3 without affecting the color of any

u_i, $\bar{u}_i$ vertices.) Since d is never colored 2, it is impossible that any a, b, c be all colored 2, and hence assigning a variable u_i the value true if it is colored 3 in this coloration gives an assignment in which any disjunction has at least one literal with value true.

What we have accomplished so far is to show that if we are given a Boolean expression E in conjunctive normal form with 3 literals in each disjunction we could determine if it is satisfiable by checking 3-colorability of the associated graph G. Since the number of vertices of G is 2 plus twice the number of variables of E plus 6 times the number of disjunctions, we can construct G in time which is linear in the length of the expression. If we had a polynomial time algorithm for 3-colorability of G, we could determine satisfiability of E in polynomial time. Thus we are justified in saying that 3-colorability is as hard as 3-satisfiability, that is, NP-hard.

A frequently asked question, once a problem has been shown to be NP-hard, is whether special cases are equally difficult. For example, we now know that 3-colorability of an arbitrary graph is NP-hard. One might wonder whether 3-colorability of a planar graph is also NP-hard. (Note that the graph G in our construction is not in general planar.) As it turns out, it can be shown that the answer to this question is affirmative.

The idea of the proof is to show that if we are given an arbitrary graph G we can construct a planar graph $\hat{G}$ which can be 3-colored if and only if G can. Intuitively the idea is simple. For each vertex x of G, we shall have a set of vertices $\{x_1, \ldots, x_m\}$ in G such that in any 3-coloration of $\hat{G}$, all x_i must be colored the same. For each pair of adjacent vertices x and y of G we want some pair x_i and y_i to be adjacent in $\hat{G}$. [The actual construction of the configuration $\{x_i, \ldots, x_m\}$ and its interconnection with $\{y_1, \ldots, y_m\}$ is somewhat complicated, but it is described in detail in Stockmeyer (1973).]

The idea of showing that simplifications are still NP-hard can be carried still further. For example, in Garey, et al. (1974) it is shown that even if each vertex of the planar graph has degree ≤ 4, determining 3-colorability is still an NP-hard problem.

6.3. THE TRAVELING SALESMAN PROBLEM

In the solution of optimization problems, to be able to obtain a best possible result is, from a mathematical point of view, an ultimate goal that one always tries to reach. From a practical point of view, however, a best possible result would invariably mean a decrease in efficiency or an increase in cost. In this section and in Section 6.4, we shall consider several examples to illustrate some of the concepts concerning algorithms that produce results which are not necessarily best possible but which, to various degrees, approximate optimal solutions.

There are many instances in which although it is possible to find the best possible solution, to do so might be prohibitively expensive or time-consuming. A simple example is the case in which there are only a finite number of ways to perform a certain task. Clearly, we can always examine all possible ways to perform the task and then pick the one that yields the best result. However, exhaustively examining all possible ways of performing the task might not be a practical proposition at all. Consequently, in many instances one might wish to settle for algorithms that produce only sub-optimal results. Indeed, settling for something short of the very best is a very attractive idea, as will be illustrated in our subsequent discussion.

The well-known traveling salesman problem will provide further insight into the idea of efficiency of algorithms and its relation to approximation algorithms. The problem can be formulated in the following way. Let G be a complete graph of n vertices. To each edge $\{i, j\}$ a positive real number, denoted $w(i, j)$ and called the distance between i and j, is assigned. We wish to determine a tour, or Hamiltonian circuit (see Chapter 5), such that the sum of the distances w for the edges on the tour is a minimum. For a tour T, we shall denote the sum of the distances of the edges in T by $w(T)$.

A proof for the following theorem can be found in Karp (1972).

Theorem 6.3.1

The traveling salesman problem is NP-hard.

A somewhat more surprising result is that finding a "good" approximation algorithm is also NP-hard, as shown by the following result due to Gonzales and Sahni (1976).

Theorem 6.3.2

The problem of determining a tour T for the traveling salesman problem such that

$$\frac{w(T)}{w(T_o)} \leq r$$

where T_o is an optimal tour and r is any positive constant, is NP-hard. We shall refer to T as an r-suboptimal tour.

The proof will be carried out by transforming the problem of determining the existence of a Hamiltonian circuit in a graph, which is known to be NP-hard [Karp (1972)], to the problem of finding an r-suboptimal tour. Suppose we are given a graph with n vertices, $G = (V, E)$. We construct a traveling salesman problem by defining a complete graph on V with the distance function

$$w(i, j) = \begin{cases} 1 & \text{if } \{i, j\} \in E \\ \lceil nr \rceil & \text{otherwise} \end{cases}$$

Clearly the cost of a tour T consisting of only edges from E is n while if at least one edge is not from E,

$$w(T) \geq n - 1 + \lceil nr \rceil$$

If the cost of an r-suboptimal tour is less than nr it must consist of only edges from E. Therefore G has a Hamiltonian circuit if and only if the corresponding traveling salesman problem has an r-suboptimal tour of length less than or equal to nr.

Since the construction of the traveling salesman problem can easily be done in polynomial time, we would have a polynomial time algorithm for the Hamiltonian circuit problem if we could find an r-suboptimal tour in polynomial time.

We have seen that not only is the problem of determining an optimal traveling salesman tour in an arbitrary complete graph NP-hard but also that that of determining an approximation solution is NP-hard. For most practical situations, the distance function defined on the graph satisfies a constraint, known as the triangle inequality, namely, for any three vertices i, j, and k,

$$w(i, k) \leq w(i, j) + w(j, k)$$

Curiously enough, although the problem of determining an optimal tour in a complete graph with a distance function satisfying the triangle inequality is still NP-hard Papadimitriou (1977), that of determining an approximate solution no longer is. We shall present two algorithms for determining an approximation tour in a complete graph satisfying the triangle inequality. We present two algorithms for the purpose of comparison. One of these has a worst-case behavior bound that is a function of the size of the problem, while the other has a worst-case behavior bound that is a constant.

The first algorithm, called the *nearest neighbor method*, uses a very simple heuristic to construct a tour. In this method we start with an arbitrarily chosen vertex and then find the vertex which is closest to the starting vertex, forming an initial path of one edge. We successively add edges to our path by selecting that unchosen vertex which is closest to the last vertex selected until all vertices are included. Adding the edge from the last vertex chosen to the starting vertex yields a tour which we analyze in the following theorem.

Theorem 6.3.3

Using the nearest neighbor method on a graph with n vertices satisfying the triangle inequality, we obtain a tour T such that

$$\frac{w(T)}{w(T_o)} \leq \frac{1}{2}(\lceil \log_2 n \rceil + 1)$$

Proof: Let T denote the tour obtained according to the nearest neighbor method. Let the length of the edges in decreasing order be $l_1, l_2, \ldots, l_n$. Thus $w(T) = \sum_{i=1}^{n} l_i$. We shall prove the following inequalities:

$$w(T_o) \geq 2l_1 \tag{6.3.1}$$

$$w(T_o) \geq 2 \sum_{i=k+1}^{2k} l_i, \qquad 1 \leq k \leq \left\lceil \frac{n}{2} \right\rceil \tag{6.3.2}$$

$$w(T_o) \geq 2 \sum_{i=\lceil n/2 \rceil + 1} l_i \tag{6.3.3}$$

[Note that if n is even, (6.3.3) is included in (6.3.2).] Once we have proved these inequalities the proof of the theorem is easy. Summing the inequalities (6.3.2) using $k = 1, 2, 4, \ldots, 2\lfloor \log_2 n \rfloor - 1$, we get

$$(\lfloor \log_2 n \rfloor - 1)w(T_o) \geq 2(\sum_{i=2}^{2^{\lceil \log_2 n \rceil - 1}} l_i) \tag{6.3.4}$$

From (6.3.3), since $\lceil n/2 \rceil + 1 \leq 2^{\lceil \log_2 n \rceil - 1} + 1$ for $n > 1$, we get

$$w(T_o) \geq 2 \sum_{i=2^{\lceil \log_2 n \rceil - 1} + 1}^{n} l_i \qquad (6.3.5)$$

Adding (6.3.1), (6.3.4), and (6.3.5) yields

$$(\lceil \log_2 n \rceil + 1)w(T_o) \geq 2 \sum_{i=1}^{n} l_i = 2w(T)$$

and the result follows.

The proof of (6.3.1) follows almost immediately from the triangle inequality. Suppose the longest edge in T is $\{x, y\}$. Then the triangle inequality implies that the length of any path between x and y is at least l_1. Since any Hamiltonian circuit of G can be broken up as two paths between x and y, (6.3.1) must be true.

Let a_i denote the vertex to which the ith longest edge in T was added in our construction by the nearest neighbor algorithm. For a fixed k, $1 \leq k \leq \lfloor n/2 \rfloor$, let H be the complete subgraph of G containing the vertices a_i, $1 \leq i \leq 2k$. Let C be the Hamiltonian circuit in H that visits the vertices in H in the same circular order as a minimum Hamiltonian circuit visits the vertices in G, ignoring vertices in G that are not in H. If the length of C is t, we have, by the triangle inequality,

$$d_o \geq t$$

Let $\{a_i, a_j\}$ be an edge in C. If in our construction according to the nearest neighbor algorithm vertex a_i was added before a_j, then $w(a_i, a_j) \geq l_i$. If a_i was added after a_j, then $w(a_i, a_j) \geq l_j$. Thus, we have

$$w(a_i, a_j) \geq \min(l_i, l_j)$$

Summing these inequalities for all edges $\{a_i, a_j\}$ in C, we obtain

$$t \geq \sum_{\{a_i, a_j\} \in C} \min(l_i, l_j) \geq 2(l_{2k} + l_{2k-1} + \cdots + l_{k+1})$$

$$= 2 \sum_{i=k+1}^{2k} l_i$$

Since d_o was at least as large as t, (6.3.2) follows immediately.

The proof of (6.3.3) is similar to the preceding proof and will be omitted.

Recently better bounds have been obtained for other algorithms [see, for example, Lewis, et al. (1977)]. The best known so far is due to Christofides (1977). He discovered the following algorithm for a graph G satisfying the triangle inequality.

(i) Determine a minimum spanning tree S for G.

(ii) Let $\hat{G}$ denote the complete subgraph of G which contains the vertices of G which have odd degree as vertices of S. (The reader should show that $\hat{G}$ must have an even number of vertices.) Determine an optimal matching $\hat{M}$ of $\hat{G}$, i.e., a set of edges $\hat{M}$ such that every vertex in G is incident on exactly one edge in $\hat{M}$ and so that the sum of the weights of the edges in $\hat{M}$ is minimized. Since $\hat{G}$ is a complete subgraph with an even number of vertices, it is always possible to find a set of edges $\hat{M}$ so that every vertex in G is incident on exactly one edge in $\hat{M}$.

(iii) Let H be the union of S and $\hat{M}$, with edges occurring in both included twice.

(iv) Since every vertex of H has even degree, we can select an Eulerian circuit $C = (v_{i_1}, v_{i_2}, \ldots, v_{i_j})$ of H. (In an Eulerian circuit every vertex must be visited at least once, whereas in a Hamiltonion circuit every vertex must be visited exactly once.)

(v) Scan the vertices of C from left to right, and delete any reappearance of a vertex in the sequence except that $v_{i_1} = v_{i_j}$. The result is the Hamiltonian circuit T of G. Due to the triangular inequality, the cost of T cannot exceed that of C.

The method is exemplified by Figures 6.3.1(a) through (f). Christofides' algorithm yields the optimal tour in this case. We leave it to the reader to construct an example where the algorithm is not optimal.

Christofides proves that the resulting tour T satisfies the inequality of the following theorem.

Theorem 6.3.4

If $G = (V, E, w)$ is a complete graph with distance function w satisfying the triangle inequality and $|V| = n$, then in time proportional to n^3 a tour T can be constructed such that

$$\frac{w(T)}{w(T_o)} \leq \frac{3}{2}$$

Proof: The time for the algorithm described above is $0(n^3)$ since the most time-consuming portion of the algorithm is (iii), which can be done in times at most $0(n^3)$. Lawler (1977) gives an $0(n^3)$ algorithm for finding a minimum matching. Many efficient algorithms are known for finding a minimum spanning tree, and the remaining steps can be done in linear time.

To see that the inequality is satisfied we note that by deleting any edge of the optimal tour T_o, we obtain a spanning tree of G. Hence

$$w(S) \leq w(T_o)$$

Let $\hat{T}_o$ be an optimal tour of $\hat{G}$. Since the triangle inequality is satisfied,

$$w(\hat{T}_o) \leq w(T_o)$$

However, from $\hat{T}_o$, by taking alternate edges, we obtain two matchings of $\hat{G}$. The smaller of these matchings can have total distance at most $\frac{1}{2}w(\hat{T}_o)$. Since the minimum matching, $\hat{M}$, can be no longer than this,

$$w(\hat{M}) \leq \tfrac{1}{2}w(\hat{T}_o) \leq \tfrac{1}{2}w(T_o)$$

By the triangle inequality, steps (iv) and (v) can only reduce the length and we obtain

$$w(T) \leq w(\hat{M}) + w(S) \leq \tfrac{3}{2}w(T_o)$$

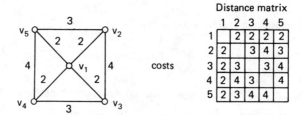

Distance matrix

	1	2	3	4	5
1		2	2	2	2
2	2		3	4	3
3	2	3		3	4
4	2	4	3		4
5	2	3	4	4	

costs

(a) Find minimum cost tour in the above graph G

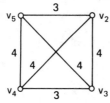

Cost = 8

(b) Minimum spanning tree S for G

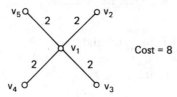

(c) Complete subgraph $\hat{G}$ of vertices of odd degree in S

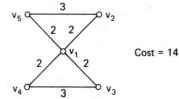

Cost = 6

(d) Minimum matching M in $\hat{G}$

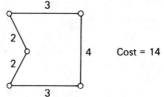

Cost = 14

(e) H, the union of S and M, Eulerian circuit C = $(v_1, v_4, v_3, v_1, v_2, v_5, v_1)$

Cost = 14

(f) A Hamiltonian circuit T obtained by deleting an occurrence of v_1 in C

Figure 6.3.1

242

6.4. JOB SCHEDULING PROBLEMS

We saw in the last section that, in some cases, there is a pitfall in searching for approximation algorithms, namely that any approximation algorithm for a particular problem may also be inefficient. However, as in the traveling salesman problem when the distance function satisfies the triangle inequality, it is often the case that a "good" approximation can be found in much less time than the optimal solution. [In fact, for sample problems, Kim (1977) and Lewis et al. (1977) contain some empirical results on the performance of approximation algorithms for the traveling salesman problem which are better than worst case bounds.] It is, therefore, a worthwhile goal to look for approximation algorithms for hard problems.

We now turn to the question of designing approximation algorithms. Unfortunately, our understanding of approximation algorithms has not reached a point where we can talk about general methodology for designing such algorithms; however, we shall try to identify some general ideas and concepts in connection with their design. In particular we shall draw examples from a problem concerning deterministic job scheduling in multiprocessor computing systems.

We shall describe first a general model of a computing system which can be specialized in various ways to include most of the results in the literature on job scheduling. We begin with the following assumptions.

1. A computing system consists of two classes of resources, *dedicated* and *shared*. In each class, there are different *kinds* of resources.

2. There are a certain number of units of dedicated resources of each kind. The execution of a job requires an integral number of units of each kind (including zero units as a possibility). The execution of a job completely occupies a unit, and no other jobs can be executed on the same unit concurrently. Examples would be processors, I/O devices, etc.

3. There is one unit of shared resources of each kind (there is no loss of generality in normalizing each kind of shared resources to one unit). The execution of a job requires a fraction of the unit of each kind of shared resource, again including zero as a possibility. Concurrent execution of a number of jobs might share the same unit of a shared resource, provided the sum of the fractions of the unit they share does not exceed 1. Examples could be core memories, magnetic disks and drums, etc.

4. The units of each kind of dedicated resource need not be idenitcal. It may be the case that the execution time for a job will depend on which units it is using or that a job can only be done on certain units. Since the execution of a job in general requires more than one unit of each kind, the execution of a job is said to be completed when execution of all units is completed.

5. The unit of each kind of shared resource is considered to be uniform. A job will release its fraction of shared resources when its execution on all units of dedicated resources is completed.

Let $J = \{J_1, J_2, \ldots, J_i, \ldots\}$ be a set of jobs, and let $<$ be a precedence relation on J. That $J_k < J_l$ means the execution of job J_l cannot begin until the execution of job J_k has been completed. J_k is called a *predecessor* of J_l, and J_l is called a *successor* of J_k. A set of jobs is said to be *independent* if the precedence relation $<$ is empty.

The set of jobs J with the precedence relation $<$ can be conveniently represented as an acyclic directed graph, as in Figure 6.4.1.

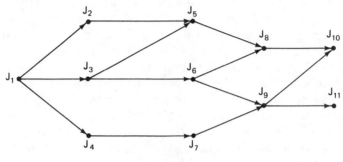

Figure 6.4.1

By a schedule of a set of jobs on a computing system we mean a specification at each moment of time of what work is to be done on each resource. This specification must not violate the precedence relation, or allow more than one job to use a unit of a dedicated resource simultaneously, or allow more than 100% of each kind of shared resource to be used at any time. A *scheduling algorithm* is a procedure that produces a schedule for every given set of jobs. ˙

By a *preemptive* scheduling discipline we mean allowing the interruption of the execution of jobs in a schedule. Most of our discussion will refer to *nonpreemptive* schedules where a job must continue execution to completion once its execution begins.

Although the description of a schedule is, in general, quite complicated, schedules for the execution of jobs on computing systems with one kind of dedicated resource can be specified rather compactly by one-dimensional *timing diagrams*. For example, Figure 6.4.2 shows a schedule for the execution of a set of jobs $\{J_1, J_2, \ldots, J_6\}$ on a computing system with three units of one kind of dedicated resource, where each horizontal axis is marked off to show the time intervals on each of the units within

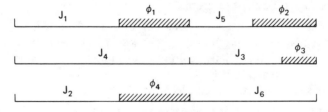

Figure 6.4.2

which jobs in the set are executed. We use $\phi_1, \phi_2, \ldots$ to denote *idle periods* during which a unit is left idle.

Different criteria can be used to measure how good a schedule is. The most common one is the *completion time* of a schedule, that is, the total time it takes to complete the execution of a set of jobs according to the schedule. Clearly, for a given set of jobs, a "good" schedule is one with "short" completion time, and an *optimal* schedule is one with the shortest possible execution time. The accuracy of a scheduling algorithm is measured by how good the schedules it produces are. One might wish to consider the worst-case performance of a scheduling algorithm, or one might wish to consider the average-case performance of a scheduling algorithm. Most of the current works are concerned with the worst-case performance analysis of scheduling algorithms. As mentioned above, we shall make an attempt to identify some of the general features of scheduling algorithms whose accuracy will be measured by the completion time of the schedules they produce.

1. There are algorithms that produce optimal schedules. Clearly, optimal schedules and algorithms that produce optimal schedules are of significant interest. Unfortunately, very little is known about "efficient" algorithms that produce optimal schedules for arbitrary computing systems and arbitrary sets of jobs. As a matter of fact, efficient algorithms thet produce optimal schedules are known only for the following cases:

(i) Jobs having unit execution times with the precedence relation over them being a forest are to be scheduled on a computing system with identical processors.

(ii) Jobs having unit execution times are to be scheduled on a computing system with two identical processors.

We shall describe an algorithm due to Hu (1961) which produces an optimal schedule for case (i). We shall introduce first the concept of a demand scheduling algorithm. A schedule is called a *demand schedule* if, according to the schedule, no resource is left idle intentionally, that is, if there is a job which could be executed on it. For example, the set of jobs shown in Figure 6.4.3(a) is to be executed on a system with two identical processors. Two schedules are shown in Figures 6.4.3(b) and (c). The schedule in Figure 6.4.3(b) is a demand schedule, while the schedule in Figure 6.4.3(c) is not. Note that in the schedule in Figure 6.4.3(c) processor P_2 is left idle for one unit of time (between the ninth and tenth units), although J_3 is executable during that time. As a matter of fact, the schedule in Figure 6.4.3(c) is a *best possible* schedule, illustrating the point that demand schedules are too restrictive to be optimal in all cases. On the other hand, a moment of reflection reveals that for jobs with unit execution time, there always exists an optimal schedule that is a demand schedule.

A particularly simple class of demand scheduling algorithms is the class of *list scheduling algorithms*. A list scheduling algorithm assigns distinct priorities to jobs and allocates resources to jobs with highest priorities among those executable at any time instant.

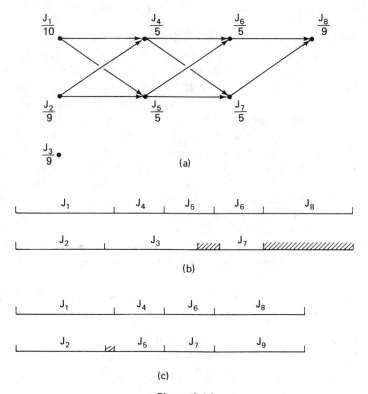

Figure 6.4.3

Hu's algorithm is a list scheduling algorithm. First we define the notion of *level* of a job:

(1) The level of a job that has no successor is defined to be 1.

(2) The level of a job that has one or more successors is defined to be 1 plus the maximum level of its successors.

In Hu's algorithm, priorities are assigned to jobs according to their levels such that jobs of higher levels will have higher priorities. (Assignment of priorities to jobs of the same level is arbitrary.)

For example, for the set of jobs shown in Figure 6.4.4(a), the levels of jobs J_1, J_2, and J_3 are 4, the levels of jobs J_4 and J_5 are 3, the levels of jobs J_6, J_7, J_8, and J_9 are 2, and the level of job J_{10} is 1. Consequently, a possible assignment of priorities, in decreasing order, is $J_1, J_2, J_3, J_4, J_5, J_6, J_7, J_8, J_9, J_{10}$. The corresponding schedule for the execution of this set of jobs on a computing system with two identical processors is shown in Figure 6.4.4(b). Hsu (1966) contains a simple proof that Hu's algorithm produces optimal schedules for case (i).

Fujii et al. [1971] and Coffman and Graham (1973) discovered algorithms that

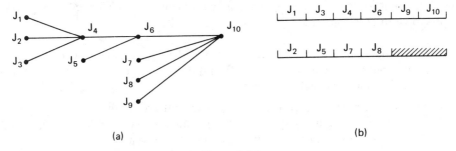

(a)   (b)

Figure 6.4.4

produce optimal schedules for case (ii). We present here Coffman and Graham's algorithm, which also is a list scheduling algorithm. In Coffman and Graham's algorithm, priorities are assigned to jobs as follows:

(1) Starting with 1, the lowest priority, distinct and consecutive priorities are assigned to jobs that have no successors arbitrarily.

(2) Priorities are assigned to jobs with one or more successors recursively:
   (a) A job whose successors have all been assigned priorities will be labeled with the priorities of its successors $(i_1, i_2, \ldots)$ in decreasing order.
   (b) Compare the labels of all labeled jobs according to lexicographical order. Starting with the lowest unassigned priority, distinct and consecutive priorities are assigned to the labeled jobs such that jobs with larger labels will be assigned higher priorities.

For example, Figure 6.4.5 shows a set of jobs $\{J_1, \ldots, J_9\}$. jobs J_6 and J_9 have no successors and so are assigned priorities 1 and 2. Then jobs J_7 and J_8 are labeled $(2, 1)$ and (2). By the lexicographic ordering, J_8 is assigned priority 3 and J_7 is assigned 4. Continuing, J_4 is labeled (4) and J_5 is labeled $(4, 3)$. In this way, the priorities in decreasing order are $J_2, J_3, J_1, J_5, J_4, J_7, J_8, J_9, J_6$,

For many years our inability to discover efficient algorithms that produce optimal schedules has been a rather frustrating experience. In view of the recent results concerning NP-hard problems, it appears doubtful that efficient algorithms for optimal

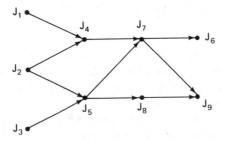

Figure 6.4.5

schedules exist for most interesting scheduling problems. Among the scheduling problems shown to be NP-hard are

(i) To determine whether a set of independent jobs can be scheduled on a computing system with two identical processors so that the completion time is less than or equal to a given ω.

(ii) To determine whether a set of jobs with unit execution times can be scheduled on a computing system with n identical processors, for any n, so that the completion time is less than or equal to a given ω.

(iii) To determine whether a set of independent jobs with unit execution times can be scheduled on a computing system with three identical processors and one kind of shared resource so that the completion time is less than or equal to a given ω.

The complexity of scheduling problems was first studied by Ullman (1973). See also Brucker et al. (1977) and Garey and Johnson (1975).

We should point out that there is a large body of literature on obtaining optimal schedules by the methods of complete enumeration, mixed integer and nonlinear programming, and dynamic programming. Note that in these approaches the computation time required to produce an optimal schedule will be an exponential function of the number of jobs to be scheduled. We refer the reader to Lenstra (1976) and Rinnooy Kan (1974). See also Horowitz and Sahni (1977) and Sahni (1976).

2. Realizing that in most cases it is too difficult to find an optimal schedule, we would like to examine various approaches to determining suboptimal schedules and to determine how far from optimal they are. [As general references to the area of approximation algorithms, see Johnson (1974) and Garey and Johnson (1977).] If we make no priorities at all in an n identical processor system, assigning jobs arbitrarily, the following result, due to Graham (1966, 1969, 1972), shows that we shall never use more than twice the time required by an optimal schedule.

Theorem 6.4.1

For a computing system with n identical processors, let ω denote the completion time of a schedule for a given set of jobs produced by an arbitrary list scheduling algorithm and let ω_0 denote the shortest possible completion time. Then

$$\frac{\omega}{\omega_0} \leq 2 - \frac{1}{n}$$

For $n = 2$, the ratio ω/ω_0 in Theorem 6.4.1 is upperbounded by the constant $\frac{3}{2}$. That is, in terms of the completion time a schedule produced by any list scheduling algorithm is not worse than an optimal schedule by 50%. When the number of processors in the system increases, although the comparison becomes less favorable, the suboptimal schedule is never worse than an optimal schedule by 100%.

The proof of Theorem 6.4.1 is fairly easy.

Consider the timing diagram for the execution of the set of jobs according to the arbitrary priority list L. We first make two observations: (1) The termination of any idle period on one processor coincides with the completion of a job on another processor, and (ii) if any job begins execution on any processor during an idle period of another processor, a job that precedes it must have completed on some processor at that time. Figure 6.4.6 illustrates these points. Notice that J_{12} must precede J_{22} and

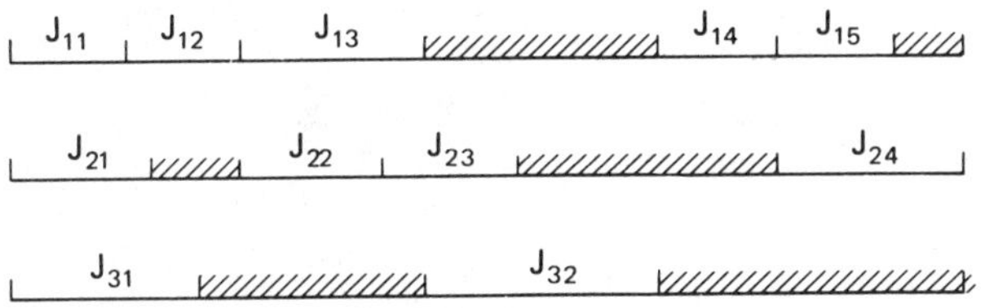

Figure 6.4.6

$J_{13}, J_{22} < J_{23}, J_{13} < J_{32} < J_{14}$, and $J_{14} < J_{15}, J_{14} < J_{24}$. The idea of the proof of the theorem can be illustrated by noting that the jobs $J_{12}, J_{13}, J_{32}, J_{14}$ and J_{24} provide a chain which must be executed, sequentially, so that no matter what priority list is used, the total time must be at least the sum of the lengths of these jobs. Consequently the schedule shown in Figure 6.4.5 differs from an optimal schedule by, at most, the time used for execution of job J_{11}.

More precisely, if we let $\phi_1, \phi_2, \ldots, \phi_n$ denote periods of time during which at least one processor is idle, then during each block ϕ_i we can find a chain $J_{i1} < J_{i2} < \cdots < J_{il_i}$ such that each J_{ij} overlaps ϕ_i. This observation follows from (ii) above since some job must be executing at the termination of ϕ_i. If it was begun during ϕ_i, by (ii), its start must have coincided with the completion of some job which preceded it. By continually applying (ii) in this way, we reach a job J_{i1} which began at least as soon as ϕ_i. We would like to find a single chain of jobs which "covers" all idle periods. To accomplish this, we begin with a chain for ϕ_k. Each job begun after the termination time T of ϕ_{k-1} must be a successsor of some job being executed or completed at time T. We use this job as $J_{k-1, l_{k-1}}$ and obtain a chain for ϕ_{k-1} and continue this process, obtaining a chain of jobs

$$J_{11} < J_{12} < \cdots < J_{1l_1} < J_{21} < \cdots < J_{kl_k}$$

such that one of the jobs is executing at each instant that any processor is idle. Hence, even for an optimal schedule,

$$\omega_0 \geq \sum_{i=1}^{k} \sum_{j=1}^{l_i} \mu(J_{ij}) \tag{6.4.1}$$

where $\mu(J_{ij})$ denotes the execution time of J_{ij}.

Since there are n processors, ω_0 must also satisfy

$$\omega_0 \geq \frac{1}{n} \sum_{\text{all jobs}} \mu(J) = \frac{1}{n} [\sum_{J \in \mathcal{G}} \mu(J) + \sum_{J \in \mathcal{C}} \mu(J)] \tag{6.4.2}$$

where $\mathcal{C}$ is the set of jobs in the chain and $\mathcal{G}$ is the remainder of the jobs.

It is also clear that for our arbitrary schedule

$$\omega \leq \sum_{J \in \mathcal{C}} \mu(J) + \frac{1}{n} \sum_{J \in \mathcal{J}} \mu(J) \tag{6.4.3}$$

Combining (6.4.1), (6.4.2), and (6.4.3), we can obtain our result. We consider two cases depending on which of the two inequalities (6.4.1) and (6.4.2) is stronger. For convenience of notations, let

$$A = \sum_{J \in \mathcal{C}} \mu(J), \qquad B = \sum_{J \in \mathcal{J}} \mu(J)$$

If

$$A \geq \frac{1}{n}(A + B)$$

we have

$$\omega \leq A + \frac{1}{n} B = \frac{n-1}{n} A + \frac{1}{n}(A + B) \leq \frac{n-1}{n} A + A = \frac{2n-1}{n} A$$

Since $\omega_0 \geq A$ according to (6.4.1), we have

$$\frac{\omega}{\omega_0} \leq 2 - \frac{1}{n}$$

If $A < (1/n)(A + B)$, then

$$\omega \leq A + \frac{1}{n} B = \frac{n-1}{n} A + \frac{1}{n}(A + B)$$

$$\omega_0 \geq \frac{1}{n}(A + B) \geq A$$

Thus

$$\frac{\omega}{\omega_0} \leq \frac{[(n-1)/n]A + (1/n)(A + B)}{(1/n)(A + B)} = \frac{[(n-1)/n]A}{(1/n)(A + B)} + 1 \leq \frac{[(n-1)/n]A}{A} + 1$$

$$= 2 - \frac{1}{n}$$

This completes the proof of Theorem 6.4.1.

Theorem 6.4.1 can be extended immediately to

Theorem 6.4.2 [Liu and Liu (1974)]

For a computing system with n_1 processor of speed b_1, n_2 processors of speed $b_2, \ldots, n_k$ processors of speed b_k, where $b_1 > b_2 > \cdots > b_k \geq 1$, we have

$$\frac{\omega}{\omega_0} \leq \frac{b_1}{b_k} + 1 - \frac{b_1}{\sum\limits_{i=1}^{k} n_i b_i}$$

As an illustration of the result in Theorem 6.4.2, let us consider a computing system with one processor of speed 10 and ten processors of speed 1. According to Theorem 6.4.2, we have the bound

$$\frac{\omega}{\omega_0} \leq \frac{10}{1} + 1 - \frac{10}{20} = \frac{21}{2}$$

When we compare this bound with that in Theorem 6.4.1 for a computing system with twenty identical processors (using ten processors of speed 1 for the processor of speed 10), $2 - \frac{1}{20}$, we note that determining a close-to-optimal schedule is more crucial for heterogeneous computing systems.

Garey and Graham (1975) and Yao (1974) studied list scheduling algorithms for computing systems with shared resources. For example, similar to Theorems 6.4.1 and 6.4.2, we have

Theorem 6.4.3 [Garey and Graham (1975)]

For a computing system with n identical processors and one kind of shared resource, we have

$$\frac{\omega}{\omega_0} \leq n$$

Theorem 6.4.4 [Garey and Graham (1975)]

For a computing system with two or more processors and q kinds of shared resources and for a set of independent jobs, we have

$$\frac{\omega}{\omega_0} \leq \min\left(\frac{n+1}{2}, q + 2 - \frac{2q-1}{n}\right)$$

3. In general we would expect to get better results if we assign priorities in some meaningful way. One way to do this is to look at the algorithms producing optimal solutions in special cases and to try to implement them in a more general setting where they may no longer be optimal.

For example, Hu's algorithm is optimal when the set of jobs with precedence relations is a forest. We could apply this algorithm even if the resulting graph is not a forest. The following theorem, due to Chen (1975), states the result.

Theorem 6.4.5

When Hu's algorithm is applied to schedule a set of jobs with unit execution times on a computing system with n identical processors, then

$$\frac{\omega}{\omega_0} \leq \frac{4}{3} \qquad n = 2$$

$$\frac{\omega}{\omega_0} \leq 2 - \frac{1}{n-1}, \qquad n \geq 3$$

We shall illustrate the algorithm for the example in Figure 6.4.7(a). Since J_4, J_5, and J_6 have the same level, J_1, J_2, and J_3 also have the same level, and a possible list in order of decreasing priorities is $J_2, J_3, J_1, J_4, J_5, J_6, J_7$. (We remind the reader that ties are broken arbitrarily in Hu's algorithm in assigning priorities to jobs of the same level.) A corresponding schedule when this set of jobs is executed on a computing system with two identical processors is shown in Figure 6.4.7(b). An optimal schedule is shown in Figure 6.4.7(c).

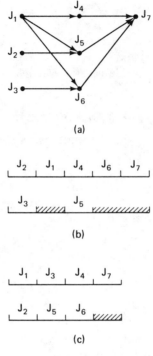

(a)

(b)

(c)

Figure 6.4.7

We note that the worst-case behavior bound $2 - [1/(n - 1)]$ in Theorem 6.4.5 is superior to the bound $2 - (1/n)$ in Theorem 6.4.1, which is for the case of assigning priorities in a completely arbitrary manner.

Similarly, although Coffman and Graham's algorithm yields an optimal schedule only for the scheduling of jobs with unit execution times on a computing system with two identical processors, one might wish to apply the algorithm to obtain a suboptimal schedule even when there are more than two processors in the computing system. We have

Theorem 6.4.6 [Lam and Sethi (1977)]

When Coffman and Graham's algorithm is applied to schedule a set of jobs with unit execution times on a computing system with n identical processors, then

$$\frac{\omega}{\omega_0} \leq 2 - \frac{2}{n}$$

Again, we note that the worst-case behavior bound $2 - (2/n)$ in Theorem 6.4.6 is superior to the bound $2 - (1/n)$ in Theorem 6.4.1.

Kaufman (1974) extended Hu's algorithm to the scheduling of jobs with unequal execution times on a computing system with n identical processors where the precedence relation over the jobs is a forest. By defining the level of a job to be the length of the chain between the job and the root of the tree it is in (including the execution time of the job itself), Kaufman has shown that

Theorem 6.4.7

In the extended Hu's algorithm described above

$$\omega \leq \omega_p + k - \frac{k}{n}$$

where ω_p is the completion time when the jobs are executed according to an optimal preemptive schedule and k is the execution time of the longest job in the set.

For example, in Figure 6.4.8(a), jobs J_1, J_2, J_3, and J_4 have level 5, and jobs J_5, J_6, and J_7 have level 4. For a two-processor system, Figure 6.4.8(b) shows a schedule resulting from Kaufman's algorithm, while Figure 6.4.8(c) shows an optimal schedule. Note that the upper bound of Theorem 6.4.7 is met in this example, $\omega = 10 = 8 + 4 - \frac{4}{2}$.

4. There are algorithms that perform a certain amount of computation in order to produce good schedules. For example, consider the problem of scheduling a set of independent jobs on a computing system with n identical processors. If we sort the jobs according to their execution times and assign high priorities to jobs with long execution times, we can upperbound the worst-case behavior of such a list scheduling algorithm by

Theorem 6.4.8 [Graham (1969)]

For the scheduling algorithm described above,

$$\frac{\omega}{\omega_0} \leq \frac{4}{3} - \frac{1}{3n}$$

Extensions of the idea of assigning high priorities to jobs with long execution times to computing systems with nonidentical processors have been carried out by Gonzales et al. (1975) and Ibarra and Kim (1975).

5. There are scheduling algorithms which give preferential treatments to some of the jobs to be scheduled. As an example, we shall consider the following algorithm for scheduling a set of independent jobs on a computing system with n identical processors: We pick out the k longest jobs in the set and schedule them in such a way that the total execution time (for the execution of these k jobs) is minimum. The remaining jobs will be scheduled according to the rule that whenever a processor is free an arbitrarily chosen job will be executed on that processor. Graham (1969) has shown that

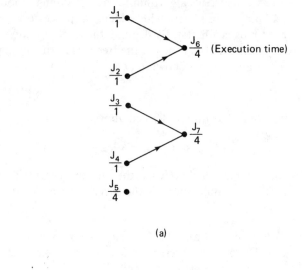

(a)

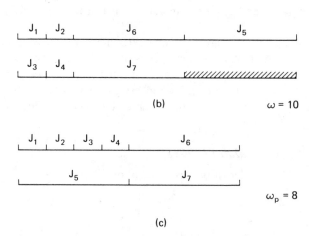

(b) $\omega = 10$

(c)

Figure 6.4.8

Theorem 6.4.9

For the scheduling algorithm described above,

$$\frac{\omega}{\omega_0} \leq 1 + \frac{1 - (1/n)}{1 + \lfloor k/n \rfloor}$$

6. One can consider algorithms that produce schedules which are as close to optimal shcedules as desired at the expense of computation time. An algorithm is said to be an *ϵ-approximation algorithm* if for a given ϵ the algorithm will yield a schedule such that the ratio $(\omega - \omega_0)/\omega_0$ is less than ϵ. Sahni (1976) studied the

problem of scheduling a set of independent jobs on a computing system with n identical processors and obtained an ϵ-approximation algorithm whose complexity is $O[m(m^2/\epsilon)^{n-1}]$, where m is the number of jobs in the set.

In this section we have looked at several problems in scheduling with the aim of illustrating the role of approximation algorithms. We have not attempted to be exhaustive and consequently have omitted many large areas of importance such as scheduling to meet deadlines, scheduling to minimize mean flow time, and preemptive scheduling. General references such as Baer (1973), Baker (1974), Coffman (1976), Coffman and Denning (1973), and Conway et al. (1967) can provide the interested reader with information on these and other areas.

CHAPTER 7

SYSTEM DEADLOCKS

A.N. HABERMANN
Computer Science Department
Carnegie-Mellon University

7.1. THE DEADLOCK PHENOMENON

7.1.1. Let Us Play a Game

We shall illustrate the deadlock phenomenon by describing a game that mirrors a class of resource allocation problems in operating systems. This game will give us some feeling for estimating the likelihood that a system deadlock will occur. Moreover, later in this chapter some fundamental theorems about avoiding deadlocks will be based on an extended version of the game.

The elements of the game are a pair of dice, m identical objects which we call *resource units* ($m \geq 12$), and a bank which has an infinite supply of money. All players start with an equal amount of money in their bank accounts, and all the resource units are initially owned by the bank. Players increase and decrease the amount of money in their bank accounts by buying and selling resource units from the bank. The players decide when the game is to terminate. The winner is the player ending with the largest amount of money in his account.

A player uses his first turn to determine how many units he is going to collect in the near future. We call this number his *goal*. It is determined by throwing the dice.

When his goal has been set, a player uses his subsequent turns to buy resource units until he has reached his goal. After reaching his goal, he starts selling his resource units back to the bank until all the units he possesses are sold. A player loses his turn when he is supposed to buy resource units but there are none left in the bank. A player is not permitted to possess more resource units than his goal indicates.

The dice are also thrown when resource units are bought or sold. The number shown on the dice determines the current price for buying or selling one resource unit. For each unit bought from (sold to) the bank, a player pays (receives) the current price. That is, a player who buys (sells) X units pays (receives) X times the current price shown on the dice.

A player may buy (if he has not yet reached his goal) or sell (after reaching his goal) any number of units in one turn, provided he does not exceed his goal or credit.

The resource units needed to reach one's goal may be bought all at once or in smaller quantities in subsequent turns.

A buyer must use his turn to buy at least one resource unit (if he can). Likewise, a seller may sell several or all of his resource units at the current price, but he must sell at least one unit. If a player sells his last resource unit, he must use his next turn to determine a new goal so that he may start buying and selling resource units again.

7.1.2. Game Analysis

The rules of the game state that m, the number of resource units, must be greater than or equal to 12. This is obviously related to the fact that 12 is the highest number one can throw with a pair of dice. A player's goal is determined by a throw of the dice. Therefore, the goal always falls in the range [2:12]. If $m < 12$, it would be possible for a player to set a goal greater than the total number of resource units. Obviously, a player is not able to reach such a goal.

If we start with a given number of resource units m, the game should only permit players to set goals in the range [1:m] so that the goal can be reached. This brings us to the first condition for playing a realistic game:

$$1 \leq \text{goal}_i \leq m \qquad (1)$$

for all players P_i, where m is the number of resource units.

A player's goal determines when he changes from buyer to seller. Therefore a player is not permitted to buy more resource units than his goal indicates. This rule of the game is expressed by

$$0 \leq \text{alloc}_i \leq \text{goal}_i \qquad (2)$$

for all players P_i. The quantity alloc_i represents the number of resource units in P_i's possession (that is, the number of resources allocated to P_i).

Another rule of the game states that a player loses his turn when he is supposed to buy, but there are no resource units left in the bank. This rule amounts to saying that the players together cannot buy more resource units from the bank than the bank initially possesses. As a result, the sum of all units bought cannot exceed the total number of resource units.

Let $S(n) = \sum_{i=1}^{n} \text{alloc}_i$, where n is the number of players and alloc_i is as defined before. The fact that all the players together cannot possess more than the total number of resource units is expressed by

$$S(n) \leq m \qquad (3)$$

If "rem" represents the number of units left in the bank, condition (3) can be written as a conservation law: The equality

$$S(n) + \text{rem} = m \qquad (4)$$

is true at all stages of the game, where $S(n)$ and rem are both nonnegative.

The rules of the game have been stated so that conditions (1), (2), and (3) are satisfied. This gives us a minimal assurance that playing the game is not totally impossible.

7.1.3. Deadlock States

Suppose four players A, B, C, and D set their goals, respectively, at 3, 5, 7, and 9, and suppose they buy, respectively, 2, 3, 3, and 3 resource units. If $m = 12$, rem $= 1$. We describe this state of the game by the matrix

	bank	A	B	C	D
goal:	12	3	5	7	9
alloc:	1	2	3	3	3

We call this state a *realizable* state, because it satisfies the three conditions of the preceding section: All players possess less resource units than their goals indicate, all goals are less than the total number of resource units, and the conservation law is satisfied.

Suppose player D buys the last resource unit from the bank. The resulting state is described by the matrix

	bank	A	B	C	D	
goal:	12	3	5	7	9	(5)
alloc:	0	2	3	3	4	

This state is also a realizable state. (In fact, all states we shall consider will be realizable states.) However, this state has the awkward property that all players must indefinitely skip their turns, because no one has reached his goal but there are no resource units left in the bank. We say that a player who will never be able to reach his goal runs into a *deadlock*.

The deadlock in this example could easily have been avoided. If player A buys the last resource unit from the bank instead of player D, the resulting state is free of deadlocks. In that case the state matrix is

	bank	A	B	C	D	
goal:	12	3	5	7	9	(6)
alloc:	0	3	3	3	3	

Players B, C, and D may lose several turns, but player A has reached his goal and will start selling his resource units back to the bank. These resource units suffice for player B to reach his goal. The resource units sold to the bank by player B suffice for player C to reach his goal. Likewise, the resource units sold back to the bank by player C suffice for player D to reach his goal. Thus, players B, C, and D may lose several turns, but they will be able to play sometime and reach their goals. Therefore, the state is free of deadlocks. In the preceding example either all players ran into a deadlock or none of them did. It is also possible that some players run into a deadlock, while others do not.

Example

	bank	A	B	C	D
goal:	12	3	3	10	10
alloc:	2	2	2	3	3

Players *A* and *B* can reach their goals and will sell six resource units back to the bank. This number is not sufficient to enable either player *C* or player *D* to ever reach his goal.

> *Definition:* A state of the game contains a *deadlock* if it can be shown that, no matter in which order the players take their turns, some players will never reach their goals. We call such a state a *deadlock state* for short.

7.1.4. Relevance of the Game

Almost all general-purpose operating systems running on medium size or large machines are multiprogramming systems. This means that several user programs are executed concurrently. Processors and primary memory space are allocated to a user program for short periods of time so that all ready-to-run programs receive a fair share of these resources. This has the effect that it seems to users as if all programs run in parallel, although in fact the number of running programs at any given instant is limited by the actual number of processors.

On the other hand, most of the resources available to the user programs are serial devices: They can be used by only one program at a time. For instance, peripheral devices can process only one command at a time; a memory cell can be read or written into by only one processor at a time; a processor can execute only one instruction at a time; etc. Serial devices cause contention to arise in a multiprogramming system, because such a resource can be used by only one user at a time. This contention is resolved by allocation and deallocation rules which are enforced by the operating system.

We distinguish between two kinds of resources: preemptible and nonpreemptible resources. A preemptible resource can be temporarily deallocated without affecting the logic of the program using the resource. When the resource is deallocated, a description of the current state of the user and resource is preserved. This description makes it possible to restore the state when the resource is reallocated. Central processors and memory space are typical examples of preemptive resources. Allocation and deallocation of preemptive resources are entirely controlled by the operating system up to the extent that user programs may not even be aware of temporary deallocations.

A nonpreemptible device cannot be deallocated from its user without affecting the user's state. Therefore, the user should decide when he can release a nonpreemptible device. The monitoring system should deallocate a nonpreemptible resource only in abnormally awkward circumstances, such as a user holding on to a resource longer than he promised. I/O devices are a typical example of nonpreemptible resources. A line printer, for example, processes one command for printing a line at a time. The composition of an output page requires a sequence of such commands. The output lines of one program should, of course, not get mixed with those of another. Thus, when a user's output is being printed, the line printer should remain reserved for this user until the entire output is printed.

The rules for managing nonpreemptible resources are very similar to those of the game discussed in the preceding sections. Buying and selling resource units from and to the bank correspond to receiving and returning nonpreemptible resources from and to the operating system. Throwing the dice in order to determine a goal reflects the arrival of a new competing program. Such programs have varying needs for resource units, unknown to the operating system. Throwing the dice when units are bought or sold mirrors the fact that programs request and return their resource units in variable quantities.

Allocation and deallocation of nonpreemptible resource units differ in two respects from the game. First, the programs do not request and release resource units in a fixed order as players of a game usually do. Second, a program does not first request, then release, all of its resource units in the rigid order done in the game. On the other hand, when a program requests a resource which is not available, it will, like the player in the game, wait until it can get the resource. Therefore, useful results may be derived from the game model only if we do not rely on the order of the players (which has not been fixed in the rules anyway).

One may question whether an operating system knows the goals of the programs it serves. In case of peripheral devices, this information is in all likelihood known in advance. If memory space is treated as a nonpreemptible resource, information about the goals may be provided by a compiler or may be derived from the program's behavior at run time. It is not unreasonable to ask that a programmer provide information about the resources his program needs. We shall see further on that without such information system deadlocks cannot be entirely ruled out.

7.1.5. The Occurrence of Deadlocks

Intuitively one feels that deadlocks will not occur if the players won't set their goals too high and if there are plenty of resource units in the bank. In this section we shall discuss exactly how the occurrence of deadlocks depends on these figures and the number of players.

Suppose the range in which goals can be set is $[1:G]$, where G is the largest possible goal. We can easily prove

Theorem 1

No deadlock can occur if the largest possible goal, G, the total number of resource units, m, and the number of players, n, satisfy the relation

$$n * G \leq m \qquad (7)$$

Proof: Partition the set of resource units into the subsets $S_1, S_2, \ldots, S_n$, each containing exactly G units, and place the remaining units in subset S_{n+1}. We reserve subset S_i for player P_i. That is, every resource unit bought by P_i will be taken from S_i and every unit sold will be placed in S_i. If player P_i possesses x resource units, subset S_i contains $G - x$ units. This number is sufficient for player P_i to reach his goal, because goal$_i \leq G$ for all players. Since this reasoning applies at all times to all players, every player is always able to reach his goal.

Corollary

There is no purpose in having more than $n * G$ resource units, because those in excess of $n * G$ are never used.

In Section 7.1.2 we reasoned that $G \leq m$ must be true or else a player could set himself an unreachable goal. Thus, if we assume that n and G are given, m should be chosen in the range $[G : n * G]$.

Corollary

No deadlocks can occur if the game is played by one player. We assume $n > 1$.

A refinement of Theorem 1 is

Theorem 2

A deadlock can occur if and ony if the largest possible goal, G, the total number of resource units, m, and the number of players, n, satisfy the inequality

$$m \leq n * (G - 1) \tag{8}$$

Proof: Suppose $m = n * (G - 1) - x$, where $x = a * n + b$, $a \geq 0$, $b \in [0 : n - 1]$. Consider the state

$$\text{goal}_i = G \qquad \text{for all } i \in \{1, \ldots, n\}$$
$$\text{alloc}_i = G - 1 - a \qquad \text{for all } i \in \{1, \ldots, n - 1\}$$
$$\text{alloc}_n = G - 1 - a - b$$

In this state

$$S(n) = \sum_{i=1}^{n} \text{alloc}_i = n * (G - 1) - n * a - b = m$$

Thus, all resource units have been bought. But no player has reached his goal. Hence, no player will ever reach his goal, because there are no units left in the bank. This proves that if $m \leq n * (G - 1)$, deadlocks may occur.

Suppose $m > n * (G - 1)$, and assume players $P_1, \ldots, P_p$ ran into a deadlock. The bank will never have enough resource units to satisfy any of these p players. In other words,

$$\text{goal}_i - \text{alloc}_i \geq \text{rem} + 1 \tag{9}$$

for all deadlocked players, no matter how the others play. Relation (9) must hold even if the other players sell all their resource units. In that case

$$S(p) = S(n) = m - \text{rem} \tag{10}$$

Since $\text{goal}_i \leq G$ for all players, we find, using (9) and (10),

$$p * G \geq \sum_{i=1}^{p} \text{goal}_i \geq S(p) + p * (\text{rem} + 1) \geq m + (p - 1)\text{rem} + p$$

$$\geq n(G - 1) + 1 + (p - 1)\text{rem} + p$$

Thus,

$$(n - p)(G - 1) + (p - 1)\text{rem} + 1 \leq 0 \tag{11}$$

This inequality is false, because $1 \leq p \leq n$ and $(G - 1)$, rem ≥ 0. Hence, the assumption that p players ran into a deadlock when $m > n * (G - 1)$ is false.

Theorem 1 states that deadlocks cannot occur if m is chosen equal to the upper bound of its domain $[G : n * G]$. Theorem 2 splits the domain into a subdomain $[G : n * (G - 1)]$ for which deadlocks may occur and the remaining domain $[n * (G - 1) + 1 : n * G]$ for which no deadlocks can occur.

If m is chosen equal to the upper bound $n * G$, players will never lose a turn, because there are always enough resource units left in the bank. The smaller m is chosen, the larger is the chance that players have to skip a turn. This seems to be an additional argument in favor of choosing m somewhere in the upper part of the domain. On the other hand, it may not be wise to choose m so large for the following reason. The varying price of resource units makes it advantageous for players to buy or sell units in quantities smaller than their goals indicate. A player will buy as little as possible when the current price is high, and he will sell as little as possible when the current price is low. This strategy has a very interesting result. The sum of the resources possessed by the players, $S(n)$, is in general less than the sum of their goals, because many players will possess fewer units than their goals indicate. Thus, we may expect that usually

$$S(n) < \sum_{i=1}^{n} \text{goal}_i \leq n * G \tag{12}$$

Since $S(n)$ is the number of resource units really needed by the players, the closer m is chosen to the upper bound $n * G$, the more units will be rarely used. On the other hand, selecting m in the lower domain is justified only if deadlocks can easily be avoided.

We must face the problem of avoiding deadlocks for situations other than those for which we wish to keep m as small as possible. The problem must also be solved in case the upper bound of the goals cannot be fixed or if the number of players may grow. The first step toward avoiding deadlocks is being able to detect them.

7.1.6. Deadlock Detection

A game state contains a deadlock if we can show that some players are unable to reach their goals. That is, no matter in which order the players are going to take their turns, some players will never reach their goals.

The difficulty in detecting a deadlock is that we must prove something about all possible ways in which the players may proceed from a given state of the game. In this section we shall show that (fortunately) it won't be necessary to consider all possible combinations. The state matrix contains sufficient information to determine the presence or absence of deadlocks.

The m by m grid of Figure 7.1 plots the goals of all players. The players are ordered by descending goals. Players with equal goals are put in descending order of number of allocated resource units. The picture shows three players: two with goals of five resource units and one player with a goal of three units.

The heavily shaded squares represent the allocated resource units. Allocated units are plotted from the top of the goal downwards. A player has reached his goal when he reaches the bottom line of the grid. The game state corresponding to the picture of Figure 1.1 is described by the matrix

$$
\begin{array}{lcccc}
 & \text{bank} & A & B & C \\
\text{goal:} & 8 & 5 & 5 & 3 \\
\text{alloc:} & 2 & 3 & 1 & 2
\end{array}
\qquad (13)
$$

It is obvious that a picture like that of Figure 7.1 can be drawn for every state of the game.

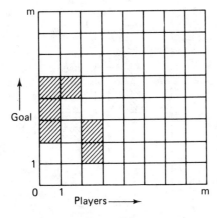

Figure 7.1

The presence or absence of deadlocks can be determined by counting the heavily shaded squares (representing the allocated resource units) in a particular way. This is done as follows. Choose one of the horizontal lines, $y = k$, of the grid. This line divides the grid into an upper and a lower rectangle. Count the total number of allocated units in the upper rectangle and the total number of allocated units in the lower rectangle. Let these number be U_k and L_k. All the allocated units are counted exactly once and are added either to U_k or to L_k. Thus

$$
U_k + L_k = S(n) \qquad (14)
$$

This counting procedure is repeated for all horizontal lines of the grid. It results in assigning values to the elements of two arrays $U[0:m]$ and $L[0:m]$ Applied to the picture of Figure 7.1, we find

$$U_0 = 6 \qquad L_0 = 0$$
$$U_1 = 6 \qquad L_1 = 0$$
$$U_2 = 5 \qquad L_2 = 1$$
$$U_3 = 3 \qquad L_3 = 3$$
$$U_4 = 2 \qquad L_4 = 4$$
$$U_k = 0 \qquad L_k = 6 \qquad \text{for } 5 \le k \le m.$$

The picture is, of course, no more than an aid to facilitate the computation of arrays U and L. The values can be derived directly from the matrix of the given state by the formulas (see Figure 7.2)

$$U_k = \sum_{i=1}^{n} \max (k, \text{goal}_i) - \sum_{i=1}^{n} \max (k, \text{goal}_i - \text{alloc}_i) \tag{15}$$

$$L_k = \sum_{i=1}^{n} \min (k, \text{goal}_i) - \sum_{i=1}^{n} \min (k, \text{goal}_i - \text{alloc}_i) \tag{16}$$

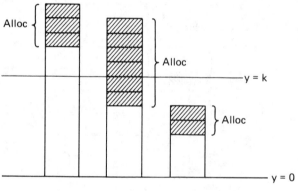

Figure 7.2

The following theorem tells how the arrays U and L can be used to detect deadlocks.

Theorem 3

A game state contains a deadlock if and only if there is a $k \in \{0, \dots, m\}$ such that

$$U_k > m - k \tag{17}$$

or

$$k > \text{rem} + L_k \tag{18}$$

Proof: The inequalities (17) and (18) are equivalent, because $m = S(n) + \text{rem}$ [see (4)] and $U_k + L_k = S(n)$ [see (15)].

Assume (17) is true, for $k = k_0$, but there is no deadlock. Divide the set of players into two subsets D and F. Subset D contains all players P_i such that

$goal_i > k_0$ and subset F the players P_i such that $goal_i \leq k_0$. Subset D cannot be empty, because if so, $U_k = 0$ and this makes (17) false for $k = k_0$. Let P_i be the first player of subset D to reach his goal. None of the players in subset D has sold his resource units back to the bank. Player P_i possesses exactly k_0 resource units that are not counted in U_{k_0}. Thus,

$$S(n) \geq U_{k_0} + k_0 > (m - k_0) + k_0 = m \qquad (19)$$

This inequality is false, because the number of allocated resource units does not exceed the total number of units [see (3)]. Hence, the assumption that there are no deadlocks in (17) is false.

Assume $U_k \leq m - k$ for all $k \in \{0, \ldots, m\}$. Partition the set of players in the subsets $S_0, S_1, \ldots, S_m$ such that subset S_j contains those players who need an additional number of j resource units to reach their goal. The absence of deadlocks is proved if we show that there is a way of continuing the game so that all players reach their goals. Consider the following way of continuing the game. Each player gets two turns in a row. In the first of these two turns he buys all the resource units he needs and in the second he sells all the units he possesses back to the bank. The order in which the players take their two turns is such that all players in subset S_k go before all players in S_l for $0 \leq k < l \leq m$. Players in S_0 are not deadlocked, because they have reached their goals. Assume that, when player P_i in S_k takes his turn, all players in $S, S_1, \ldots, S_{k-1}$ have already returned their units to the bank. Since all players in $S_k, S_{k+1}, \ldots, S_m$ are at least k resource units away from their goals, we find

$$L_k = 0 \quad \text{or} \quad U_k = S(n) \qquad (20)$$

Using the assumption and (4), we find

$$U_k = S_k(n) = m - \text{rem} \leq m - k \qquad (21)$$

Thus, rem $\geq k$. This means that there are enough resources available for player P_i to reach his goal. All the players of subset S_k are able to reach their goals in turn. Hence we have proved the induction hypothesis that all players in $S_0, \ldots, S_k$ are able to reach their goals if the players in $S_0, \ldots, S_{k-1}$ can reach their goals. Hence, all players can reach their goals, and the absence of deadlocks has been shown.

Corollary

A game state is deadlock-free if and only if

$$U_k \leq m - k \qquad (22)$$

for all $k \in \{0, \ldots, m\}$.

Corollary

A game state is deadlock-free if and only if

$$k \leq \text{rem} + L_k \qquad (23)$$

for all $k \in \{0, \ldots, m\}$.

7.1.7. Deadlock Avoidance

If deadlocks are possible under the current rules of the game, the obvious approach to avoiding them is by modifying the rules. Players who cause a deadlock should not be allowed to buy. This additional rule means that a player may have to skip his turn in order to avoid a deadlock, although the number of resource units he wants to buy may be available. The additional rule is enforced by testing the new state that results if resource units are bought. Using Theorem 3, we design an algorithm for detecting deadlock in a given state. The new game state is described by the variables m, rem and the arrays goal$[1:n]$ and alloc$[1:n]$. The deadlock detection algorithm builds the array $U[0:m]$ out of the given arrays goal and alloc. If assigning to an element U_k results in a value $> m - k$, the presence of a deadlock is reported. The new state is deadlock-free if the algorithm terminates and no deadlock was reported.

Assigning to an element U_k is based on the following observation. A player whose goal$_i$ is greater than k contributes to U_k the amount of min (alloc$_i$, goal$_i - k$) (see Figure 7.3). Thus, the following program adds the contribution of player P_i to all elements of array U and tests for deadlocks on the way.

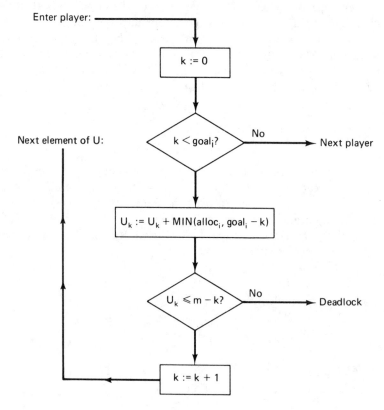

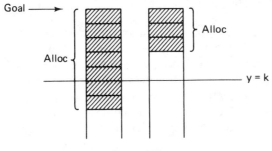

Figure 7.3

Next, we need a driver program that executes "enter player" for each player so long as no deadlock is detected. This driver program initializes all elements of array U to zero and enters the players one after another. If it succeeds in entering all players without a deadlock being reported, it reports that the state is deadlock-free. The driver program is

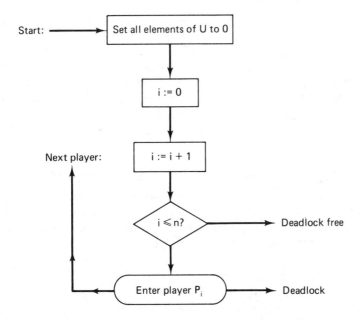

The driver program is classified as a *linear program*, because the number of iterations it requires is proportional to n, the number of players. This classification is denoted by $O(n)$. The program that enters a player is linear in m, the number of resource units. Since "enter player" is executed once in each iteration of the driver program, the deadlock detection algorithm as a whole is a $O(nm)$ program.

7.1.8. Incremental Deadlock Avoidance

In the preceding section we designed an algorithm for detecting a deadlock in a given state. The deaclock avoidance rule that we added to the game can make use of this algorithm. Permission to buy depends on the outcome of applying the algorithm to the new state which would result if the requested number of units were allocated.

This way of enforcing the deadlock avoidance rule is very inefficient. The inefficiency is caused by the fact that the information we have about the current state is not utilized. Instead of testing a given (new) state, we ought to test whether the *transition* from a deadlock-free state into some other state introduces a deadlock. The objective of the deadlock avoidance rule is to stay within deadlock-free states and avoid the transition into a deadlock state.

Testing a transition rather than a state can be done if we preserve the computed values of the array U. Let U represent the value of the array in the current state and U' the value in the new state that would result if the requested resource units were allocated. The current state is deadlock-free, so

$$U_k \leq m - k \qquad \text{for all } k \in \{0, \dots, m\}$$

Testing the transition amounts to computing U' from U and the requested resource units and checking that

$$U'_k \leq m - k \qquad \text{for all } k \in \{0, \dots, m\}$$

A state transition takes place as the result of one player P_i taking his turn. Let req_i be the number of resource units that player P_i wants to buy (the requested resource units in Figure 7.4). We observe that

$$U'_k = U_k \qquad\qquad \text{for } k \geq goal_i - alloc_i \tag{24}$$

and

$$U'_k = U_k + req_i \qquad \text{for } 0 \leq k < goal_i - alloc_i - req_i \tag{25}$$

The increment of U_k for the remaining values of k depends on the number of requested resource units that lie above the line $y = k$. When k runs from $goal_i - alloc_i - req_i$ to $goal_i - alloc_i$, the increment is one smaller in every step until the upper bound is reached. A program that computes the new values of array U for given

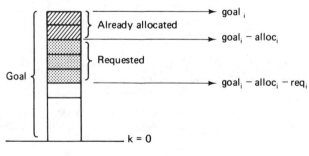

Figure 7.4

req_i consists of two successive loops. The first loop updates the elements U_k for $k = 1, 2, \ldots, (\text{goal}_i - \text{alloc}_i - \text{req}_i - 1)$, the second loop for $k = (\text{goal}_i - \text{alloc}_i - \text{req}_i), \ldots, (\text{goal}_i - \text{alloc}_i - 1)$. Updating the remaining elements is unnecessary, because they do not change [see (24)].

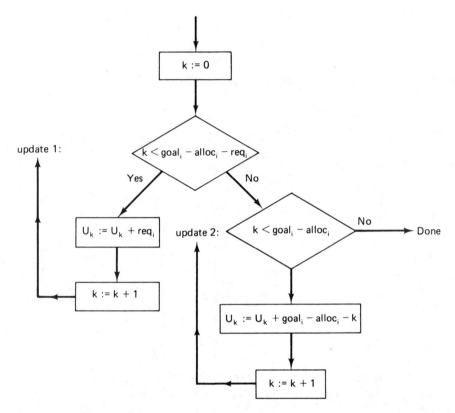

If a player wants to buy, the new state must first be checked for deadlocks before the elements of array U are updated by this program. A variation of this program can be used as a deadlock detection program. The new state is deadlock-free if and only if (22) is satisfied for all k. This is true if $U'_k = U_k + \text{req}_i \leq m - k$ for $k = 0, \ldots, \text{goal}_i - \text{alloc}_i - \text{req}_i - 1$ and $U'_k = U_k + (\text{goal}_i - \text{alloc}_i - k) \leq m - k$ for $k = \text{goal}_i - \text{alloc}_i - \text{req}_i, \ldots, \text{goal}_i - \text{alloc}_i - 1$. It is not necessary to check the elements U_k for $k = \text{goal}_i - \text{alloc}_i, \ldots, m$ because of (24).

The deadlock detection program has the same control structure as the updating program. The only difference is that the program performs the deadlock test instead of the assignments to the elements U_k.

If this program runs to completion without detecting a deadlock, the new state is deadlock-free, because it satisfies (22). In that case array U is updated by subsequent execution of the updating program. Deadlock states can more efficiently be avoided with this program than with that of the preceding section. The number of iterations in

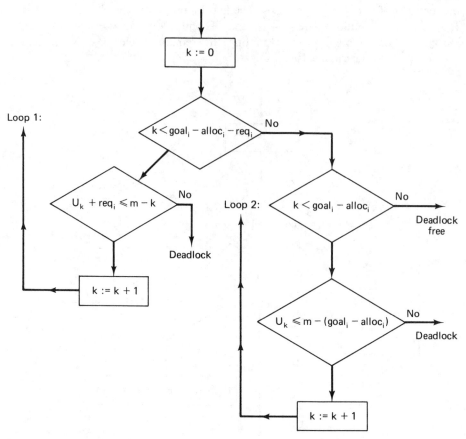

the two successive loops of this program is proportional to the number of resource units, m. That is, it is a $O(m)$ program, compared to a $O(mn)$ program for the preceding section.

7.1.9. Deadlock Detection in Relation to Goals

The deadlock detection algorithms of the preceding sections do not take into account the upper bound of the goals. If we do that, it is possible to construct an algorithm even better than the one of the preceding section. In Section 7.1.5 we found that no deadlock can occur if $m \leq n * (G - 1)$ (see Theorem 2). In that case the deadlock avoidance test is entirely superfluous. In this section we shall investigate how deadlock detection algorithms can be shortened if they depend on knowledge about the goals.

Figure 7.5 represents the goals of three players without showing their allocated resources. The players are ordered by descending goal. We apply to the goals a counting procedure similar to that for allocated resources in Section 7.1.5. A horizontal line $y = k$ divides the m by m grid into two rectangles, an upper rectangle

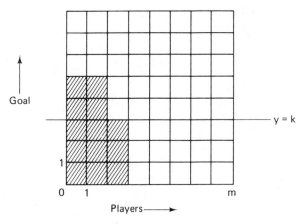

Figure 7.5

and a lower rectangle. We count the number of shaded squares in each rectangle and store these numbers in the variables V_k and M_k. Counting the shaded squares in the upper and lower rectangle for every horizontal line $y = k$ results in two arrays, $V[0:m]$ and $M[0:m]$, respectively. For a given state, the elements of the two arrays are determined by the formulas

$$V_k = \sum_{i=1}^{n} \max(0, goal_i - k) \tag{26}$$

$$M_k = \sum_{i=1}^{n} \min(goal_i, k) \tag{27}$$

It follows from (15) and (26) that

$$U_k \le V_k \tag{28}$$

and from (16) and (27) that

$$L_k \le M_k \tag{29}$$

for all $k \in \{0, 1, \dots, m\}$.

Combining (28) and (22) leads to the interesting conclusion that all states for which

$$V_k \le m - k \qquad \text{for all } k \in \{0, 1, \dots, m\} \tag{30}$$

are deadlock-free (see Figure 7.6).

The step function in Figure 7.6 represents $f(k) = m - k$. The vertical lines represent the values of array V. Inequality (30) is satisfied when V does not cross the step function.

The state of the given example does not satisfy inequality (30). This implies that there are game states for this set of goals that contain deadlocks. If we plot array U in the same way as array V, we see that a state contains a deadlock if and only if array U crosses the step function [see (17)]. The latter is possible if V crosses the step function. On the other hand, if a particular element V_k does not exceed $m - k$, the corresponding element U_k is also less than or equal to $m - k$ [see (28)]. In the

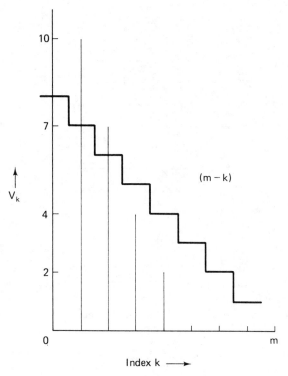

Figure 7.6

given example this is true for $k = 3, 4, \ldots, m$. This implies that there is no need to check the element U_k so long as V_k does not change (that is, so long as players buy or sell resource units but do not increase their goals).

It is not a matter of coincidence that in the given example not only $V_3 \leq m - 3$, but also $V_k \leq m - k$ for $k = 4, \ldots, m$.

Theorem 4

If there is a $k \in \{0, 1, \ldots, m\}$ such that $V_k \leq m - k$, then

$$U_j \leq m - j \qquad \text{for all } j \in \{k, \ldots, m\}$$

Proof: We shall show that $V_j \leq m - j$ for all $j \in \{k, \ldots, m\}$ if $V_k \leq m - k$. Let $x(k)$ be the number of players whose goals exceed k. The upper rectangle of $y = k$ in Figure 7.5 contains exactly $x(k)$ more shaded squares than the upper rectangle of line $y = k + 1$. Thus,

$$V_k = V_{k+1} + x(k) \qquad \text{for } k = 0, 1, \ldots, m - 1 \tag{31}$$

If $x(k) = 0$, then $V_k = V_{k+1} = 0$, because no goal exceeds k. In that case, $V_k \leq m - k$ and $V_{k+1} \leq m - (k + 1)$ are both true.

If $x(k) \neq 0$, then $x(k) \geq 1$. Suppose $V_{k+1} > m - (k + 1)$. In that case

$$V_k = V_{k+1} + x(k) \geq V_{k+1} + 1 > m - (k + 1) + 1 = m - k \tag{32}$$

Thus, if V_{k+1} crosses the step function, then V_k exceeds the step function also.

Hence, $V_{k+1} \leq m - (k + 1)$ if $V_k \leq m - k$. It follows (by induction) that

$$V_j \leq m - j \quad \text{for } j = k, \ldots, m \qquad \text{if } V_k \leq m - k$$

Since $U_k \leq V_k$ for all $k \in \{0, 1, \ldots, m\}$, we find that

$$U_j \leq m - j \quad \text{for } j = k, \ldots, m \qquad \text{if } V_k \leq m - k$$

Corollary

If there is a $k < m$ such that $V_k \leq m - k$, it is not necessary to test all elements U_k when resource units are bought. The test can be limited to the elements $U_0 \ldots U_{k-1}$.

Corollary

Let k_0 be the *smallest index* such that $V_{k_0} \leq m - k_0$. The deadlock test can be restricted to the elements $U_0, \ldots, U_{k_0-1}$.

The deadlock avoidance rule of the game is now enforced in the following manner. If a player changes his goal, array V is updated by the update algorithm of the preceding section applied to V instead of to U. As a side effect of this algorithm, we determine the smallest index k_0 such that $V_{k_0} \leq m - k_0$. When resources are sold, array U is updated with that same algorithm. When resources are bought, array U is updated as usual. During the updating, the elements $U_0, \ldots, U_{k_0-1}$ are tested for deadlocks as in the last program of the preceding section, but the elements U_k for $k = k_0, \ldots, \text{goal}_i - \text{alloc}_i$ are not tested. Although some time is gained, the improvement is not substantial, because it is still necessary to update all the elements of U and V in order to be able to use them when k_0 changes. Our next objective is to find a way of avoiding the updating of array V and the elements $U_{k_0}, \ldots, U_m$.

7.1.10. Admission

A more interesting application of the results of the preceding section is a deadlock test with a fixed testing upper bound. Instead of computing the smallest index k_0 for which deadlock cannot occur, we treat this index as a system parameter and fix its value. This means a number k_0 is chosen for which we require that $V_{k_0} \leq m - k_0$ is true at all times.

Fixing the index k_0 has the advantage that the elements $U_{k_0}, \ldots, U_m$ and $V_{k_0+1}, \ldots, V_m$ become entirely superfluous! Moreover, when a user modifies his goal, it is not necessary to update the whole array V. It suffices to update element V_{k_0} and test that $V_{k_0} \leq m - k_0$ remains true after the goal modification.

But what should be done if a player determines his new goal and the result is that $V_{k_0} > m - k_0$? We propose adding the rule that the player must skip his turn until his new goal does not have this undesirable effect.

This new rule works like an admission test. It forbids a player to start buying resource units if adding his goal would make the condition $V_{k_0} \leq m - k_0$ false. Introducing the admission test is motivated and justified as follows. The admission test limits the number of players that compete for the resource units. This has two advantages. First, the deadlock test that must be applied when resource units are bought can be reduced to testing elements $U_0, U_1, \ldots, U_{k_0-1}$, and, more importantly, the elements $U_{k_0}, \ldots, U_m$ and all the elements of array V, except V_{k_0}, can be omitted entirely. The overhead of deadlock testing is greatly reduced this way. Second, the admission test limits the number of players with large goals but does not affect the players with small goals. This has a beneficial effect on the game, because it is easier for players with large goals to cause a deadlock than for players with small goals to do so.

Applying the admission test seems to have two disadvantages. First, not all the states for given $V_{k_0} > m - k_0$ are deadlock states. Thus, the admission test has the effect of ruling out some deadlock-free states. However, applied to resource allocation policies in a computer, this disadvantage is small compared to the important advantage of smoother resource allocation. The operating system would soon be overcommitted if many users with large goals were allowed to compete for the resource units.

Another disadvantage of applying an admission test is the occurrence of a phenomenon called *permanent blocking* or, a more colorful name, *starvation*. The admission rule forces a player to skip his turn if his new goal would cause $V_{k_0} > m - k_0$. It is in principle possible that this player would never be admitted if this inequality happens to be accidentally true every time he takes his turn.

Starvation must be prevented by scheduling the order in which players are admitted. There are many different scheduling algorithms used in operating systems to prevent starvation. The simplest is the one that does not permit any player to start if another player has been waiting to start for a longer time. A discussion of such scheduling algorithms falls outside the scope of this chapter.

Let k_0 be the chosen index for which $V_{k_0} \le m - k_0$ is enforced. The admission test is carried out as follows.

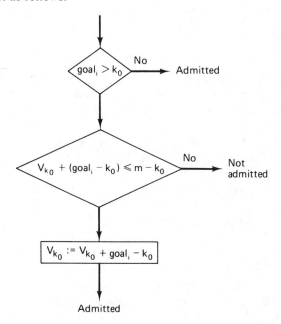

Array $U[0:k_0 - 1]$ is now tested for deadlocks by the following program.

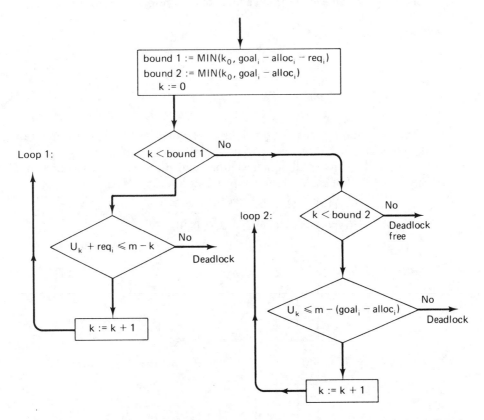

The updating program which is executed if the new state is deadlock-free has the same control structure as the adeadlock detection program. The difference is that the deadlock tests are replaced by assignments to U_k (see Section 7.1.7).

The programs can, of course, be further optimized if expressions such as ($goal_i$ — $alloc_i$) are computed only once instead of in every iteration. Such optimizations have not been incorporated for the sake of readability. The reader can judge for himself where the efficiency of the programs can be improved.

7.2. DIFFERENT TYPES OF RESOURCES

7.2.1. Dealing with Several Resource Types

In the second half of this chapter we shall consider the case of deadlocks involving several *different types* of resource units. In terms of the game, the bank has several sets of resource units, identical within one set but differing between sets. Translated into operating system terms, we look, for instance, at combinations such as file space divided into memory blocks on a secondary storage device and a set of tape units.

The players of the game have a goal for each type of resource. A state is now determined by the goals and allocated resource units of each resource type for each player.

Example

	bank	A	B	C
$goal_1$	12	10	5	5
$alloc_1$	2	4	3	3
$goal_2$	8	4	6	6
$alloc_2$	2	2	2	2

The total number of resource units of the first type is represented by the bank's $goal_1$ and that of the second type by the bank's $goal_2$. The numbers $alloc_1$ and $alloc_2$ in the bank column indicate the number of remaining resource units of each type. To test each resource type for deadlocks, we compute

$$U(type_1) = (10, 10, 10, 8, 6, 4, 4, 3, 2, 1, 0, 0, 0)$$

$$U(type_2) = (6, 6, 6, 5, 4, 2, 0, 0, 0)$$

(see Figure 7.7).

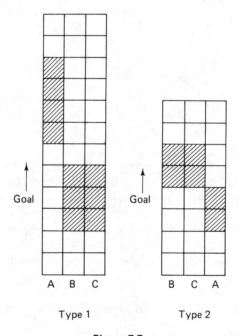

Type 1   Type 2

Figure 7.7

We find that for each resource type the inequality $U_k \leq m - k$ is true for all k. Thus it seems that the state is deadlock-free [see (22)].

This conclusion is, unfortunately, not correct. The given example contains a deadlock that is caused by the combined use of the two resource types. The deadlock occurs in the following manner. Although player A is allowed to buy resource units of type t_2, he may wish to buy units of type t_1 first. Similarly, players B and C are allowed to buy units of type t_1 but may currently be interested in buying units of type t_2. However, A cannot reach his goal of type t_2 resources if B and C don't release any. Players B and C won't do so until player A releases some units of type t_1 so that they can buy units of type t_1. A deadlock results. The example shows that the single-resource-type case does not extend simply to more than one resource type. The problem is caused by the fact that different players are allowed to buy resource units for different resource types in arbitrary order.

A possible solution to the problem is found in the additional rule that resource units must be bought in a fixed order, first the resources of type t_1, then the ones needed of type t_2, etc. In this manner a player is in fact competing for one resource type at a time. However, such a restriction may not suit the nature of the resource types and the use that the players make of those. In the case of tape units and file space, for instance, it is likely that a combination of these resources is used at one time. We consider such a restriction somewhat too stringent. Therefore, we shall investigate whether a deadlock avoidance strategy can be set up in the same spirit as in the first half of this chapter. It will not contain any additional restrictions on playing the game except for the deadlock avoidance rule introduced in the first half. (The deadlock avoidance rule forbids a player to buy if his purchase would cause a deadlock.)

7.2.2. Deadlock-Free States

Just as in the single-resource-type case, we restirct our discussion of several resource types to realizable game states. Let m_j be the number of resource units of type t_j, rem_j the number of resource units of type t_j that are left in the bank, and $goal_{ij}$ the goal of player P_i for resource type t_j. Let $alloc_{ij}$ be the number of resource units of type t_j allocated to player P_i and $S_j(n)$ the total number of resource units of type t_j in the possession of the n players. A realizable game state is characterized by

$$(a) \quad 1 \leq goal_{ij} \leq m_j \tag{33}$$

$$(b) \quad 0 \leq alloc_{ij} \leq goal_{ij} \tag{34}$$

$$(c) \quad S_j(n) + rem_j = m_j \tag{35}$$

for all $i \in \{1, \ldots, n\}$ and $j \in \{1, \ldots, t\}$, where t is the number of different resource types [see (1), (2), and (4)]. The readability is much improved by representing the different resource types by a vector notation. Let

$$\mathbf{m} = (m_1, m_2, \ldots, m_t) \tag{36}$$

$$\mathbf{rem} = (rem_1, rem_2, \ldots, rem_1) \tag{37}$$

$$\mathbf{goal}_i = (goal_{i1}, goal_{i2}, \ldots, goal_{it}) \tag{38}$$

$$\mathbf{alloc}_i = (alloc_{i1}, alloc_{i2}, \ldots, alloc_{it}) \tag{39}$$

$$\mathbf{S}(n) = (S_1(n), S_2(n), \ldots, S_t(n)) \tag{40}$$

A realizable state is then characterized by

$$\text{(a)} \quad \mathbf{1} \leq \mathbf{goal}_i \leq \mathbf{m} \tag{41}$$

$$\text{(b)} \quad \mathbf{0} \leq \mathbf{alloc}_i \leq \mathbf{goal}_i \tag{42}$$

$$\text{(c)} \quad \mathbf{S}(n) + \mathbf{rem} = \mathbf{m} \tag{43}$$

These relations in vector form mean that the equality or inequality holds for every vector component. The term *state* is always used in the sense of "realizable state."

To find out whether or not a given state contains a deadlock we try to find a way of letting the players take their turns so that each player can reach his goal. In the proof of Theorem 3 we tried the game strategy in which the players each take two turns in a row. In his first turn a player buys all the resource units of all types he needs, and in his second turn he sells all the units he possesses of the different types back to the bank. If we can show that this strategy works, the game contains no deadlock, because it is possible that each player will reach his goal at some time in the future. In the proof of Theorem 3 we let the players take their two successive turns in the order of increasing need (i.e., the player closest to his goal first). This strategy does not apply here, because the ordering by need is not the same for different resource types. Let us try the following approach.

Suppose there is a player who needs no more units of every resource type than what are left in the bank. Let this player be P_1 (the player indices can always be reassigned). If there is such a player, we have

$$\mathbf{goal}_1 - \mathbf{alloc}_1 \leq \mathbf{rem} \tag{44}$$

We let this player be the first to take his two turns, because we can be sure that he can buy the resource units of all the different types that he needs in order to reach his goal.

When player$_1$ has sold all the resource units he possesses back to the bank, the number of units in the bank has increased by $\mathbf{alloc}_1$ compared to the current state. Thus the bank will then have $\mathbf{rem}' = \mathbf{rem} + \mathbf{alloc}_1$. Suppose there is a player who needs at most $\mathbf{rem}'$ resource units of the various resource types. Let this player be P_2. If there is such a player, we have

$$\mathbf{goal}_2 - \mathbf{alloc}_2 \leq \mathbf{rem}' = \mathbf{rem} + \mathbf{alloc}_1$$

or

$$\mathbf{goal}_2 \leq \mathbf{rem} + \mathbf{alloc}_1 + \mathbf{alloc}_2 \tag{45}$$

If the sum $\mathbf{alloc}_1 + \mathbf{alloc}_2$ is represented by $\mathbf{S}(2)$, equation (45) reads

$$\mathbf{goal}_2 \leq \mathbf{rem} + \mathbf{S}(2) \tag{46}$$

Next, we look for a player P_3 who satisfies

$$\mathbf{goal}_3 \leq \mathbf{rem} + \mathbf{S}(3) \tag{47}$$

If we find one, we have a player P_3 who can reach his goals after players P_1 and P_2 have sold all their units back to the bank. We continue this ordering of the players and we search for a player P_i that satisfies

$$\mathbf{goal}_i \leq \mathbf{rem} + \mathbf{S}(i) \tag{48}$$

after having put players $P_1, \ldots, P_{i-1}$ in order. If we succeed in putting all players in order, the current state contains no deadlocks, because we have shown that it is possible for all players to reach their goals sometime in the future.

Corollary

A game state is deadlock-free if the players can be ordered such that inequality (48) is true for all players.

7.2.3. A Deadlock Detection Algorithm for Multitype Resources

The preceding section amounts to the simple observation that a given state is deadlock-free if the players can reach their goals in some order. We use this idea for constructing a deadlock detection program. The core of this program is an attempt to order the players such that (48) is true for all $i \in \{1, \ldots, n\}$. This sorting is done in the same way as in the preceding section.

Let the players be $P_1, \ldots, P_n$. First, a player P_j is sought who can reach all his goals using the remaining resources (described by **rem**). We exchange players P_1 and P_j so that (48) is satisfied for $i = 1$. When k players have been exchanged so that (48) is true for $i = 1, \ldots, k$, the algorithm searches for a player P_j in the range $[k + 1, \ldots, n]$ who can reach all his goals assuming that players $P_1, \ldots, P_k$ have returned all their units to the bank. The sorting terminates if all players have been put in order or if none of the remaining players satisfies (48).

To make the program readable, we maintain the vector notation introduced in the preceding section. An assignment of the form

$$\mathbf{u} := \mathbf{u} + \mathbf{v}$$

means that the assignment

$$u[j] := u[j] + v[j]$$

is executed for $j = 1, \ldots, t$, where t is the number of different resource types. (The vector notation is consistently used to represent the different resource types.) A comparison of the form

$$\mathbf{u} \leq \mathbf{v}$$

Is true if and only if

$$u[j] \leq v[j]$$

for all $j = 1, \ldots, t$.

In addition to assignment, addition, and comparison of vectors, we use an exchange operater "$\#$" for vectors. The statement

$$\mathbf{u} \, \# \, \mathbf{v}$$

means that the values of $u[j]$ and $v[j]$ are exchanged for all $j = 1, \ldots, t$.

A given realizable state is described by the vectors **m**, **rem**, **alloc**$_i$, and **goal**$_i$. The program uses two additional variables, i and k, and a vector **sum** (short for array sum$[1:t]$). Variable k is initialized to zero and indicates the progress of sorting the players. That is, the program has sorted the players $P_1, \ldots, P_k$ such that (48) is satisfied for $i = 1, \ldots, k$.

In the program, the variable i is used to search for one of the remaining players who satisfies (48). Therefore, i ranges in the program from $k + 1$ to n. Vector **sum** is initialized to **rem** and corresponds to $\mathbf{S}(k)$. When k players have been put in order, element sum$[j]$ is equal to the sum of all resources of type t_j allocated to players $P_1, \ldots, P_k$.

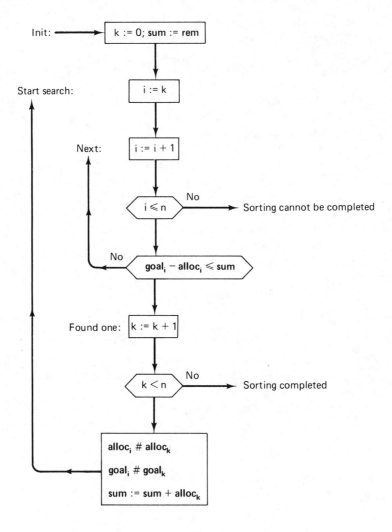

The program consists of two nested loops. In the inner loop (starting at the label "next") the range $[k + 1 : n]$ is tested for a player who can be added to the permutation under construction. If one is found, the permutation is extended by incrementing k (see the statement labeled "found one"). If k has reached n, all players have been put in order. In that case the program terminates successfully. Otherwise, the sorting is not yet complete. In that case, players P_i and P_k are exchanged so that (48) is true for P_1 up to the new P_k. After updating **sum**, the program starts searching for a player P_i that can be exchanged with player P_{k+1} (see Figure 7.8).

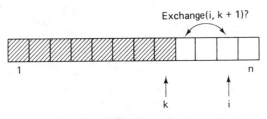

Figure 7.8

If none of the remaining players $P_{k+1}, P_{k+2}, \ldots, P_n$ can be exchanged with player P_{k+1}, the sorting is terminated unsuccessfully. This case is detected in the inner loop if the variable i exceeds the value n.

If the program is able to complete the sorting, we may conclude that the inspected state is deadlock-free, because it is not impossible that all players will reach their goals sometime in the future. However, what if the sorting program terminates unsuccessfully? It seems that all we can say is that this particular permutation of the players does not satisfy (48), but some other permutation may satisfy (48). It seems, therefore, necessary to try all permutations and see if there is one that satisfies (48). This could mean a lot of work, because there are $n!$ different permutations.

It turns out that the sorting program is much more effective than one is inclined to believe at a first glance. It is not necessary to inspect all $n!$ permutations, because we can prove that *none* of those satisfies (48) if the permutation constructed by the algorithm does not satisfy (48).

Theorem 5

If there is a permutation π and an index $k < n$ such that

$$\textbf{goal}_j \leq \textbf{rem} + \textbf{S}(j) \qquad \text{for } j = 1, \ldots, k$$

and

$$\textbf{goal}_j - \textbf{alloc}_j > \textbf{rem} + \textbf{S}(k)$$

for $j = k + 1, \ldots, n$, then no permutation π' exists such that

$$\textbf{goal}_j \leq \textbf{rem} + \textbf{S}'(j) \qquad \text{for all } j = 1, \ldots, n \tag{49}$$

Proof: Suppose such a permutation π' does exist. Let the players $P_1, \ldots, P_k$ in permutation π be painted green and the remaining players $P_{k+1}, \ldots, P_n$ red.

There is at least one red player, because $k < n$. In permutation π, all green players precede all red players. Permutation π' consists of the same set of players but in another order. That is, π' consists of a mixture of red and green players. Let Q be the leftmost red player in π'. In permutation π, Q is player P_i, where $k + 1 \le i \le n$. In permutation π', Q is player P'_l, where $1 \le l \le k + 1$, because all players to the left of Q in π' are green. Since $Q \equiv P_i$ in π,

$$\mathbf{goal}_Q - \mathbf{alloc}_Q > \mathbf{rem} + \mathbf{S}(k) \tag{49}$$

Since $Q \equiv P'_l$ in π,

$$\mathbf{goal}_Q - \mathbf{alloc}_Q \le \mathbf{rem} + \mathbf{S}'(l - 1) \tag{50}$$

assuming that (48) is true for π'. However,

$$\mathbf{S}'(l - 1) \le \mathbf{S}(k) \tag{51}$$

because $\mathbf{S}(k)$ is the sum of the resources allocated to *all* the green players and $\mathbf{S}'(l - 1)$ is the sum of the resources allocated to a *subset* of the green players. This shows that (50) conflicts with (49) and hence (50) is false. Thus, permutation π' does not satisfy (48), and consequently no permutation does.

Corollary

A permutation π satisfying (48) exists if and only if one is constructed by the sorting program.

We argue that the sorting program is in fact a deadlock detection algorithm. If it terminates successfully, the program has shown that it is not impossible for the players to reach their goals some time in the future. Thus, the state is deadlock-free. On the other hand, if a given state is deadlock-free, the players are able to reach all their goals in some order. That is, there must be at least one ordering of the players that satisfies (48). Theorem 5 implies that in that case the sorting program must terminate successfully. Thus, if the sorting program terminates unsuccessfully, the state is not deadlock-free.

Corollary

A given state is deadlock-free if and only if the sorting algorithm is able to construct a permutation that satisfies (48).

7.2.4. Analysis of the Sorting Algorithm

The sorting program consists of two nested loops. Both loops are linear in the number of players, n, because i ranges from $k + 1$ to n and k from 1 to n. Every comparison or vector updating is linear in t, the number of different resource types. Thus, the sorting program is of complexity $O(n^2 t)$. This figure is comparable to the complexity $O(mn)$ of the detection algorithm for $t = 1$ but worse than the complexity $O(m)$ of the avoidance algorithm for $t = 1$.

We already saw that the multitype resource case is inherently more difficult than the single-type case. It is therefore unlikely that there is an avoidance algorithm for the multitype case of complexity $O(nt)$. Such a simple algorithm may suffice if the rules of the game are restricted in other ways, such as fixing the order in which resource types can be bought. Without additional limitations, it is unlikely that a $O(nt)$ algorithm can be constructed.

On the other hand, an improvement over $O(n^2t)$ is not unlikely. It is well known that efficient sorting algorithms do much better than $O(n^2)$. For example, William's heapsort algorithm is of complexity $O(n \log n)$ [Williams *CACM* 64]. Another interesting algorithm is Hoare's quicksort. Its expected running time is $O(n \log n)$, although it needs $O(n^2)$ in the worst case. An excellent presentation and discussion of several sorting algorithms is found in Knuth and also in Hopcroft and Ullman.

An array $A[1:n]$ is a *heap*, arranged in ascending order, if

$$A[i / 2] \leq A[i] \qquad (52)$$

for $i = 2, 3, \ldots, n$. (The symbol / represents integer division.) If the array is represented as a binary tree with $A[1]$ at the root, the element $A[i/2]$ is the parent node of element $A[i]$. Heap order (52) means that the value of a parent node is less than or equal to that of its offspring (see Figure 7.9). The example in Figure 7.9 shows that a

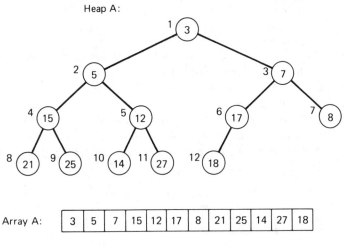

Heap A:

Array A: | 3 | 5 | 7 | 15 | 12 | 17 | 8 | 21 | 25 | 14 | 27 | 18 |

Figure 7.9

heap-ordered array is partially ordered but not necessarily totally ordered. We are interested in two operations on heaps:

(a) Adding an element at the end.

(b) Removing the root element (the first array element).

First we discuss adding an element at the end of a heap-ordered array. The new element disturbs the heap order if its value is less than that of its parent. To restore the heap property, we are going to "move the new element up" by exchanging it with its parent node until it has either reached the root or found a parent with smaller or

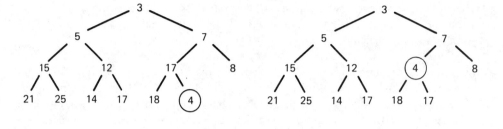

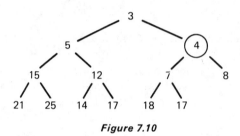

Figure 7.10

equal value. Figure 7.10 shows the states which array A of Figure 7.9 goes through when a new element with value 4 is added.

The *moveup* algorithm works as follows. The new element starts in position $k = n + 1$. If $k > 1$, element $A[k]$ has element $A[k / 2]$ as parent. If the parent has a larger value than the new element, the two are exchanged and the new position of the element is determined by replacing k by $k / 2$. This procedure is repeated until either the root is reached for $k = 1$ or the parent's value is not greater than that of the new element. The new element, initially placed in $A[n + 1]$, is represented by x.

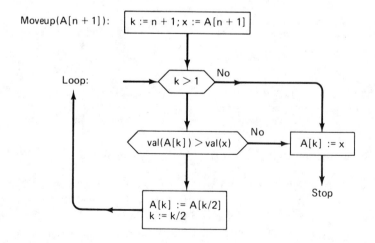

Note that this program also works if the array was empty before the new element was added (case $n = 0$). The second operation we wish to apply to a heap is that of removing the root element. The remainder consists of two disconnected heaps that we want to merge into one heap again. This is accomplished as follows. We act as if the root node were still there but its contents have been removed. In its place we substitute the contents of the last element and we delete the last node. The value of the new root is in all likelihood too large. If it is larger than that of one of its offspring, it is exchanged with the offspring that has the smallest value. This procedure is repeated until the former last element has either reached a leaf position or its value is smaller than or equal to its offspring's. Figure 7.11 shows the states which array A of Figure 7.9 goes through when its root is removed and its last element is "moved down" from the root.

In the following program we use the expressions *left offspring* and *right offspring* of element $A[k]$. The left offspring is element $A[2k]$, and the right offspring is element $A[2k + 1]$. After removing the last element, $A[n]$, from array $A[1:n]$, element $A[k]$ has a left offspring in the remaining tree if $2k \leq n - 1$ and two offsprings (a left and a right offspring) if $2k + 1 \leq n - 1$. If an element has two offsprings, their values are compared so that the smallest can be compared with the value that is moved down.

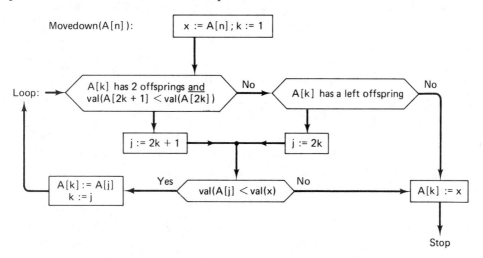

The program is constructed so that j points to the smallest offspring if there are two and to the left offspring if there is only one. The program terminates if x can be placed in element $A[k]$ and $A[k]$'s offsprings have values that are greater than or equal to the value of x or if x can be placed in a leaf node $A[k]$. Note that the program still works if the array has only one element (case $n = 1$).

The complexity of both procedures *moveup* and *movedown* is $O(\log_2 n)$, because the number of iterations in each of these two programs is less than or equal to the number of levels in the binary tree.

Instead of these heap operations we might consider inserting a new element into an ordered array. It is possible to determine the position where a new element should

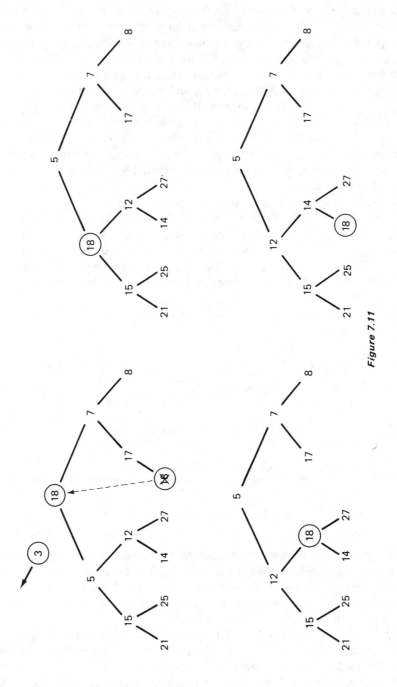

Figure 7.11

be inserted into an ordered array in O(log n) steps (for instance, by a binary search). However, putting the new element in its place requires O(n) steps, because all the array elements to the left (or to the right) of the selected position must be moved to make room for the new element. Working with linked lists is not any better, because finding the place of insertion requires O(n) steps. Thus, the heap operations are basically more efficient than inserting into a totally ordered array or list.

In the next section we shall use the heap operations for constructing an efficient deadlock detection algorithm. The algorithm partitions the players into subsets and wants to find the smallest element of each subset. Efficiency is gained by keeping each subset ordered as a heap. When a new element is added to a subset, the heap order is restored by moveup, and when the smallest element has been removed, the heap order is restored by movedown. We shall see that the new algorithm is of complexity O($tn \log n$).

7.2.5. An Efficient Deadlock Detection Algorithm

The basic idea of the faster detection algorithm is to build a heap for every resource type and let the players wander through all these heaps in a given order.

Let the heaps be represented by arrays $H_1[1:n]$, $H_2[1:n]$, ..., $H_t[1:n]$. The variable n_i is equal to the number of elements currently in heap H_i. We permit a heap H_i to be empty. This is indicated by $n_i = 0$.

The detection algorithm will be constructed so that players who travel through all the heaps are certain to reach all their goals. Let F be the set of all players that are certain to finish; these players will eventually sell all their resource units to the bank. Thus, the bank may count on having available

$$\textbf{sum} = \textbf{rem} + \sum_{P_j \in F} \textbf{alloc}[j] \qquad (53)$$

resource units of the various types when the players in F are done. When the detection algorithm starts, all heaps and the set F are empty (i.e., $n_i = 0$ for $i = 1, \ldots, t$). Thus, vector **sum** is initialized to **rem**. Every time the algorithm puts a player P_i in the finishing set F, his resource units (given by **alloc**$_j$) can be added to **sum**.

Let the vectors **need** $[1:n]$ be defined by

$$\textbf{need}[j] := \textbf{goal}[j] - \textbf{alloc}[j] \qquad (54)$$

Vector **need**$[j]$ determines the number of resource units of each type that player P_i still needs in order to reach all his goals. The heaps H_i will be ordered by increasing need for resource units of resource type t_i. This means that the value of a node in heap H_i is determined by its need for resource units of type t_i. That is, the need for resource units of type t_i of a heap element $H_i[k]$ is greater than or equal to its parent's need for resource units of type t_i, i.e.,

$$\text{need}_i[H_i[k]] \geq \text{need}_i[H_i[k \,/\, 2]] \qquad (55)$$

for $k = 2, \ldots, n_i$. This heap ordering places the player with the smallest need in the root node.

Next we construct a procedure for transferring elements from one heap to another. The procedure will transfer the top element of heap H_i to heap H_{i+1} if this top element can reach its goal for type t_i. That is, the top element $H_i[1]$ is transferred to H_{i+1} if

$$\text{need}_i[H_i[1]] \leq \text{sum}_i \qquad (56)$$

When the top element $H_i[1]$ has been transferred, the heap order in H_i is restored as described previously. Likewise, the transferred element is added to in H_{i+1}, and its heap order is restored. After transferring one element, heap H_i is one element shorter and heap H_{i+1} one longer. The transfer can be continued until either heap H_i is empty or the new root element in H_i does not satisfy (56). In the latter case none of the remaining elements in H_i satisfies (56), because the root has the smallest need for type t_i.

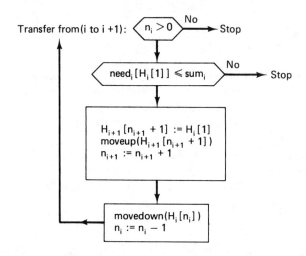

It is obvious that transfer from (i to $i + 1$) can be applied for $i = 1, \ldots, t - 1$ but not for $i = t$. For the latter case we construct a procedure that lets a player reach finish F after having passed through all heaps. The detection algorithm will be constructed such that a player passes through the heaps in the order $H_1, H_2, \ldots, H_t$. If players are moved from one heap to the next only by "transfer from (i to $i + 1$)," every player in heap H_i satisfies (56) for $k = 1, 2, \ldots, i - 1$, because each such player has been the root of each heap H_k at some time. Suppose the root element of heap H_t satisfies (56). If so, we have found a player that satisfies (56) for all $i = 1, \ldots, t$, that is, a player satisfying

$$\textbf{need}[j] \leq \textbf{sum} \qquad (57)$$

This player is able to reach all his goals. Thus, he can be placed in F, and his resource units can be added to **sum** [see (53)].

Let variable "fnshd" count the number of elements of F; fnshd is initialized to zero. Instead of "transfer from" we apply "finish" to heap H_t. This procedure tests the root element of H_t for (56), and if satisfied, removes this element from H_t and adds it to F. The procedure terminates if either H_t is empty or the root element does not satisfy (56).

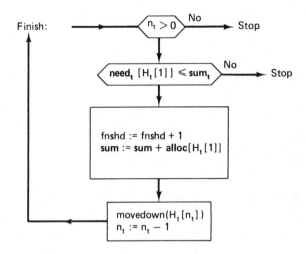

The detection algorithm starts with **goal**$[1:n]$, **alloc**$[1:n]$, **sum** = **rem**, fnshd = 0, and $n_i = 0$ for all $i = 1, \ldots, t$. The players are placed in array $H_1[1:n]$ in arbitrary order (for instance, by initializing $H_1[j]$ to its own index j). Observe that heap H_1 is still empty, although array $H_1[1:n]$ has been filled, because $n_1 = 0$. Array H_1 is heap-ordered by successively moving up its elements through heap H_1. The algorithm then starts its main loop, applying transfer to heaps $H_1, H_2, \ldots, H_{t-1}$ and finish to H_t. After some players have been added to F, **sum** has been incremented. The increased value of **sum** enables the algorithm to start transferring players from one heap to the next again.

If the algorithm succeeds in transferring all players to F, it has constructed a permutation of the players (determined by the order in which they reach F) that satisfies (48). In that case the given state is deadlock-free.

Another possibility is that the algorithm is not able to add any new players to F at the end of its main loop. This case is detected if, after transferring through all preceding heaps, the root element of heap H_t cannot be moved to F. In that case the algorithm constructed part of a permutation that satisfies (48) but is not able to complete this permutation. Theorem 5 states that in that case there is no permutation satisfying (48). Thus, the algorithm has detected a deadlock.

The program of the efficient deadlock detection algorithm follows:

```
init:  sum = rem; fnshd = 0; i := 0
init:  n_j = 0 for j = 1, ..., t
init:  H_1[j] = j for j = 1, ..., n
```

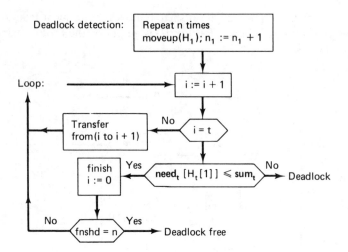

To analyze the complexity of this algorithm we observe that a player is in exactly one of the heaps or in F. That is,

$$\sum_{i=1}^{t} n_i + \text{fnshd} = n \tag{58}$$

is invariant. Next we observe that finish increments fnshd by one every time it executes movedown on H_t. Since fnshd starts at zero, the total number of times that movedown is applied to H_t by finish is n (or less if a deadlock is detected). The point is that this number is independent of the number of iterations of the detection program. Thus, repeated execution of finish contributes $O(n \log n)$ to the complexity of the whole program.

The number of times moveup and movedown are executed in repeated executions of transfer is also independent of the number of iterations for the following reason. Each player passes through all the heaps and is transferred to the next heap exactly once. Therefore, the operations moveup and movedown are executed exactly once for moving a player from one heap to the other. Thus, these operations are executed in total exactly $n * (t - 1)$ times, no matter how many times the inner loop is executed! Since the complexity of moveup and movedown is $O(\log n)$, the complexity of the whole algorithm is $O(tn \log n)$.

The presentation in this section suggests that the heaps $H_1, \ldots, H_t$ are implemented as arrays. Since a heap contains at most n elements, it suffices to declare each heap as an array $H_i[1 : n]$. This way the detection algorithm needs $O(tn)$ space. That is much worse than the straightforward $O(tn^2)$ algorithm, which only needs $O(n)$ space.

It is obvious that using $O(tn)$ space is very wasteful if we consider that the number of elements in use in the t arrays (of n elements each) is in total not more than n [see (58)]. It is, unfortunately, not possible to pack the heaps into one single array of n elements without losing in run-time efficiency. The efficiency of moveup and movedown is achieved by keeping the root node of a heap in a fixed place. If the heaps are packed into a single array, it may be necessary to shift heaps through the array when an element is transferred from one heap to the next. Shifting a heap is a linear operation that adds $O(n)$ time to the $O(\log n)$ execution time of moveup and movedown. This would bring the complexity of the whole algorithm up to $O(tn^2)$. (An exception is the case $t = 2$; in that case the two heaps H_1 and H_2 can be placed with their roots at either extreme of a single array $A[1:n]$.)

A space efficiency $O(t + n)$ can be achieved by another representation of the heaps. Each heap node is represented by a record of four fields. Since all the heaps together contain at most n elements, we reserve an array $P[1:n]$ of such records. In addition to this array P, we need an array ROOT$[1:t]$. Element ROOT$[i]$ points to the record in P that is the root element of heap H_i.

The four fields of a record describing a heap element are pred, parent, left, and right. The pred field indicates the predecessor of a heap element. The predecessor of the root of a heap H_i is the last element of this heap. The remaining three fields represent the heap connec.,ons. The parent of a root node points to itself. Likewise, the left field (right field) points to the record itself if this node has no left offspring (right offspring).

The procedures moveup and movedown must, of course, be reprogrammed for this new representation. This can be done in an obvious way. The result of reprogramming the procedures is that the space needed by the detection algorithm is reduced to $O(n + t)$, determined by the arrays P and ROOT. Since each element of P has four fields, reprogramming does not pay off for $t \leq 4$.

7.2.6. Deadlock Avoidance for Multitype Resources

The dramatic improvement achieved in the single-resource-type case by changing from deadlock detection to deadlock avoidance cannot be achieved for multiple resource types. The difficulty is that both detection algorithms for the multitype case are based on ordering the players, whereas the players can be arbitrarily ordered in the single-type case. If a given state is changed by allocating resource units to a player, the permutation that satisfied (48) may no longer do so after the change. Allocation to a player P_j decreases the right-hand side of (48) for all players $P_1, \ldots, P_{j-1}$ by the allocated amount, because this amount is subtracted from **rem** while $S(1), \ldots, S(j - 1)$ remain unchanged.

Nevertheless, some practical improvements are possible. We shall discuss some of these.

If a player wants to buy resources and he still needs less than **rem** units of all types together, it is not necessary to apply a deadlock avoidance test. In that case we can prove that the state after allocating the requested resources is deadlock-free provided that the original state is deadlock-free.

Theorem 6

If a given state is deadlock-free and a player P_j satisfies

$$\textbf{need}_j \leq \textbf{rem} \tag{59}$$

the state that arises after allocating **req** resource units to P_j (where **req** $\leq$ **need**$_j$) is also deadlock-free.

Proof: Let λ be the given deadlock-free state. We start building a permutation π that satisfies (48) and use player P_j as first element. Since P_j satisfies (59), he also satisfies (48), because

$$\textbf{goal}_j = \textbf{need}_j + \textbf{alloc}_j \leq \textbf{rem} + \textbf{S}(1)$$

[$\textbf{S}(1)$ consists of the units allocated to the player in the first position; thus $\textbf{S}(1)$ = **alloc**$_j$.] It follows from Theorem 5 that permutation π can be completed to a full permutation satisfying (48), because state λ is deadlock-free.

Permutation π also satisfies (48) in the new state, because

$$\textbf{rem}' + \textbf{S}'(j) = (\textbf{rem} - \textbf{req}) + (\textbf{S}(j) + \textbf{alloc}_j' - \textbf{alloc}_j)$$
$$= \textbf{rem} - \textbf{req} + \textbf{S}(j) + \textbf{req}$$
$$= \textbf{rem} + \textbf{S}(j)$$

This is true for all $j = 1, 2, \ldots,$ n, because player P_j takes the first position in permutation π. It follows from Theorem 5 that the new state is also deadlock-free.

It is conceivable that a system designer chooses a deadlock avoidance policy that allows allocation of resource units only to those users whose **need** does not exceed **rem**. This policy has the great advangage that applying a O($tn \log n$) deadlock detection is unnecessary. All that is needed is the simple check **need**$_j \leq$ **rem**. An alternative is the conservative policy that requires that the sum of all goals does not exceed the total number of resource units of all types. The conservative policy has the advantage that no test at all is necessary when resource units are requested, because all possible states are deadlock-free.

Theorem 7

If

$$\sum_{i=1}^{n} \textbf{goal}_i \leq \textbf{m} \tag{60}$$

where the components of vector **m** indicate the total number of resource units of the different resource types $t_1, t_2, \ldots, t_l$, then all realizable states are deadlock-free.

Proof: In a realizable state that satisfies (60), we have

$$\sum_{i=1}^{n} \textbf{alloc}_i \leq \sum_{i=1}^{n} \textbf{goal}_i \leq \textbf{m}$$

Thus,

$$\sum_{i=1}^{n} (\textbf{goal}_i - \textbf{alloc}_i) \leq \textbf{m} - \sum_{i=1}^{n} \textbf{alloc}_i = \textbf{rem} \tag{61}$$

Since **goal**$_i$ = **alloc**$_i \geq 0$ for all $i = 1, \ldots, n$, it follows from (61) that

$$\textbf{need}_i = \textbf{goal}_i - \textbf{alloc}_i \leq \textbf{rem}$$

for all $i = 1, \ldots, n$. This means that every player satisfies the condition of Theorem 6 in all states. Thus, a deadlock test is unnecessary.

The conservative policy has the disadvantage that it is wasteful of resources. If users do not need the number of resource units equal to their *goals* all the time, the difference

$$\sum_{i=1}^{n} \textbf{goal} - \sum_{i=1}^{n} \textbf{alloc} \leq \textbf{m} - \sum_{i=1}^{n} \textbf{alloc}$$

may be considerable. Such a waste can be avoided if $\sum \textbf{goal}$ is allowed to exceed $\textbf{m}$. The price one pays is some form of deadlock avoidance test which can be reduced to a $O(t)$ algorithm if we are willing to restrict allocation to users whose **need** is less than or equal to **rem**.

The following deadlock avoidance test is more elaborate than the one based on Theorem 6 but not so expensive as the $O(tn \log n)$ deadlock detection algorithm. When user P_j requests resources up to an amount of **req**, we determine the subset R of all users who satisfy

$$\textbf{need}_i \leq \textbf{rem} - \textbf{req} \tag{62}$$

R is the set of all users for whom the number of resource units remaining after allocating the requested units is sufficient for reaching their goals.

The requested resources are allocated to P_j if P_j satisfies

$$\textbf{need}_j \leq \textbf{rem} + \textbf{S}(R) \tag{63}$$

where $\textbf{S}(R) = \sum_{P_i \in R} \textbf{alloc}_i$. This deadlock avoidance policy works because of the following theorem.

Theorem 8

If a given state is deadlock-free and P_j requests **req** resource units and P_j satisfies (63) where

$$R = \{P_i \,|\, \textbf{need}_i \leq \textbf{rem} - \textbf{req}\}$$

then the state after allocating the requested resource units is also deadlock-free.

Proof: The number of resource units still available in the new state (after allocating the requested resources) is

$$\textbf{rem}' - \textbf{req} = \textbf{rem} \tag{64}$$

We build a permutation π for the old state that begins with all k member of R(in any order) followed by P_j. This part of π satisfies (48), because it follows from (62), (64), and $\textbf{alloc}_i \leq \textbf{S}(i)$ that

$$\textbf{goal}_i \leq \textbf{need}_i + \textbf{alloc}_i \leq \textbf{rem}' + \textbf{S}(i) \leq \textbf{rem} + \textbf{S}(i)$$

for $i = 1, 2, \ldots, k$, and from (63) it follows that

$$\textbf{goal}_{k+1} = \textbf{goal}(P_j) \leq \textbf{need}_{k+1} + \textbf{alloc}_{k+1} \leq \textbf{rem} + \textbf{S}(R) + \textbf{alloc}_{k+1}$$
$$= \textbf{rem} + \textbf{S}(k + 1)$$

Since the given state is deadlock-free, it follows from Theorem 5 that permutation π can be completed into one that satisfies (48) for all $i = 1, 2, \ldots, n$.

We now show that permutation π also satisfies (48) for the new state. For the first k elements of π the condition of the theorem implies

$$\mathbf{goal}_i \leq \mathbf{need}_i + \mathbf{alloc}_i \leq \mathbf{rem}' + \mathrm{S}(i)$$

The kth element is P_j. For this element we have.

$$\begin{aligned}
\mathbf{goal}_{k+1} &\leq \mathbf{need}_{k+1} + \mathbf{alloc}_{k+1} \\
&\leq (\mathbf{rem} + \mathrm{S}(R)) + (\mathbf{alloc}'_{k+1} - \mathbf{req}) \\
&\leq \mathbf{rem}' + \mathrm{S}(R) + \mathbf{alloc}'_{k+1} \\
&\leq \mathbf{rem}' + \mathrm{S}'(k+1)
\end{aligned}$$

For the remaining elements of π we have

$$\begin{aligned}
\mathbf{goal}_i &\leq \mathbf{rem} + \mathrm{S}(i) \\
&\leq \mathbf{rem} + \mathrm{S}'(i) + \mathbf{alloc}_{k+1} - \mathbf{alloc}'_{k+1} \\
&\leq \mathbf{rem} + \mathrm{S}'(i) - \mathbf{req} \\
&\leq \mathbf{rem}' + \mathrm{S}'(i)
\end{aligned}$$

Thus, permutation π also satisfies (48) in the new state. It follows from Theorem 5 that the new state is also deadlock-free.

A deadlock avoidance test based on Theorem 8 is of complexity $\mathrm{O}(nt)$. When **req** resource units are requested, the deadlock avoidance algorithm must compute **rem′** = **rem** − **req**, test all **need**$_i$ for (62), and compute $\mathrm{S}(R)$. Finally, **need**$_j$ must be tested for (63).

Instead of doing all the work when resource units are requested, part of the work can be done when resources are released. We keep around the set $R = \{P_i \mid \mathbf{need}_i \leq \mathbf{rem}\}$. When **req** resources are requested, we go through set R and determine the subset $R' = \{P_i \mid \mathbf{need}_i \leq \mathbf{rem} - \mathbf{req}\}$. This subset determines $\mathrm{S}(R')$, the amount used in test (63). If the requested resources can be allocated, set R' replaces R. When resources are released, the complement of R is scanned for members who now satisfy **need**$_i \leq$ **rem**. These elements are added to R. This way the deadlock avoidance algorithm does not have to search through the whole set of n elements (it looks only at members of R), but the remaining elements are scanned when resources are released. This may save some time if the deadlock avoidance test frequently disallows a request, because in that case every act of releasing resources corresponds to several preceding deadlock avoidance tests.

We now have five different deadlock avoidance policies:

1. The conservative policy which requires no deadlock test.

2. Allocation to P_j only if **need**$_j \leq$ **rem**; this policy requires a $\mathrm{O}(t)$ deadlock test.

3. Allocation to P_j only if $\textbf{need}_j \leq \textbf{rem} + \textbf{S}(R)$, where $R = \{P_i \,|\, \textbf{need}_i \leq \textbf{rem} - \textbf{req}\}$; this policy requires a O(tn) deadlock test.

4. The efficient deadlock detection test is applied every time resources are requested; this policy requires a O($tn \log n$) deadlock test.

5. The straightforward detection test is applied every time resources are requested; this policy requires a O(tn^2) deadlock test.

Each of the first three policies is contained in the next one down. This means that every state transition that is permitted by policy p_i also permitted by policy p_{i+1}, but there are state transitions permitted by policy p_{i+1} that are not permitted by p_i. In that sense the policies range from conservative to liberal, but no policy, including the most liberal, allows transition to a deadlock state.

The fourth and fifth policies have the same effect. These policies are the most accurate ones. They disallow a state transition only if the next state would be a deadlock state. The other policies are too protective. They disallow transitions that would do no harm for the sake of saving time checking for deadlocks.

Which of these policies is the most suitable one? Unfortunately, this question cannot be answered in general. It depends on several factors which are not inherent to the deadlock algorithms but to the circumstances under which they are applied. For instance, if the resource units are very cheap, the conservative policy is appropriate. It does not matter if such resources are permanently reserved. The conservative policy is also appropriate if the users need their *goals* all the time. The other policies work if the users need only part of their goals at one time. The importance of serving the user is also a factor. If the resources are expensive but the users have patience, it may still be possible to get away with policy 1 or policy 2. System designers should determine statistically which deadlock avoidance policy is most suitable in a given environment. It is likely that, after experimenting, the system designer will decide to apply several different deadlock policies in his system to different resource configurations.

7.2.7. Concluding Remarks

At the beginning of the chapter we listed three different ways to approach the deadlock phenomenon:

1. Take the risk and resolve a deadlock by brute force when it occurs.

2. Prevent the occurrence of deadlock states.

3. Avoid the transitions that lead to deadlock states.

We can afford to adopt policy 1 only if the cost of recovering from a deadlock state is not too high. The cost is too high if crucial information is lost, if a real-time controlling function is disturbed, or if it takes a considerable effort to reconstruct generated or modified data. We can never afford for part of the resources, such as

I/O devices or memory blocks, to be permanently blocked. It seems that the first approach is the right one only under very rare circumstances.

Deadlock prevention is primarily important for situations that are statically decidable. For example, if objects x and y are always needed as a pair, it is unwise to write in one program

$$- - - -get(x)\,;get(y)- - - -$$

and in another

$$- - - -get(y)\,;get(x)- - - -$$

If these programs can run simultaneously, the possibility of a deadlock state is apparent. It can easily be prevented by fixing the order of getting the objects or by introducing an operation that gets both at the same time. Another example is circularity. We write a program A so that it asks information from another program B and, depending on that information, A sends information to B. But program B is written similarly. It waits until it receives information from A before it generates and sends information to A. The communication between A and B gets into a deadlock when each is waiting to hear from the other. Such circularities can, of course, also be constructed for rings with more than two elements.

This type of deadlock should be prevented altogether. It is up to the system designer to prove that the concurrently running programs are deadlock-free. Of course, proving the absence of statically detectable deadlock in programs is not simple. Proof techniques for sequential programs have been developed in recent years but are applicable only to small programs. Research into proof techniques for concurrent programs has started only recently. Techniques for proving the correctness (including the absence of deadlocks) of large concurrent programs are practically nonexistent. In this chapter we focused primarily on deadlocks which could not be detected statically. These are of the kind that arise under dynamic conditions such as an operating system serving resource requests of user programs. We have seen that deadlock prevention in this case either leads to very restrictive rules for resource allocation or to poor resource utilization. Deadlocks are prevented by either placing limits on the concurrent users and their requests or by providing plenty of resources. In any case, the number of resources must be so large compared to what the users need that no deadlock states result from fluctuations in the number of allocated resources.

Applying a deadlock avoidance test may improve the resource utilization and increase the throughput because more programs can run concurrently. We discussed in the preceding section algorithms of increasing complexity to avoid transitions that lead to deadlock states. The beneficial effect that each of these algorithms produces depends on the characteristics of the environment in which it is applied. The accuracy of the algorithm increases with the complexity, but, unfortunately, the overhead does too. The latter may have such an impact that it defeats the purpose of applying a deadlock avoidance test. The avoidance tests discussed in this chapter are based on some minimal knowledge about the future need of user programs. It is, of course, conceivable that more information is available, such as the order in which resources are requested or the time profile of resource usage. Such cases have been studied, and special algorithms have been designed to exploit such additional information.

Deadlock avoidance policies have been discussed here independently of other policies that may interfere with them. The deadlock detection algorithms determine a permutation of the users. The users can be served in an order other than that specified by the permutation if the transition does not lead to a deadlock state. But the permutation indicates an order in which the processes can be served if need be. If resources are running scarce, the system can always fall back on that permutation. This ordering may interfere with priority rules that may not allow the user programs to be served in the order of the permutation. Under such circumstances the deadlock avoidance algorithms must build permutations that satisfy the externally defined priority rules. (It has been shown that such priority rules behave as an additional resource.)

Deadlock analysis has been applied in this chapter to nonpreemptible resources. In some cases the distinction between preemptible and nonpreemptible resources is not significant. It may be that preempting a resource is such an expensive operation that it should be applied only if there is no alternative. An example is the allocation of primary memory space to concurrently running user programs. It is possible in principle to let one user program steal space from another user program by copying the latter's data or program parts onto secondary memory. However, the user program that lost things it needed may do the same to another program. The result is a very time-consuming traffic between two memory levels. This may slow down the overall processing rate so much that it would have been better not to run so many programs together. If some information is available about the space needed by each program, it may be advantageous to treat primary memory as a nonpreemptible resource and apply deadlock avoidance algorithms. If the algorithms must frequently deny space requests, memory is apparently overcommitted.

It is, of course, not possible to discuss all the aspects of the deadlock phenomenon in one chapter. The issue of statically detectable deadlocks has only been mentioned. However, the essential tools for dealing with dynamically detected deadlocks have been presented. These should provide the interested reader sufficient background to study related problems and to determine the policy that best suits the characteristics of a given environment.

CHAPTER 8

OPTIMAL
MULTIPROGRAMMED
MEMORY MANAGEMENT*

PETER J. DENNING
Computer Science Department
Purdue University
West Lafayette, Indiana

Abstract

To attain its full work capacity, a computer system must regulate load and program resident sets to minimize each program's memory space time. Intuitions derived from the phase/transition model of program behavior and supported by experimental measurement, demonstrate that setting the working set policy parameter of a program to cause operation near its knee lifetime will minimize memory space time. Efficient procedures for measuring these lifetime functions are outlined in an appendix.

8.1. INTRODUCTION

In this chapter we shall discuss optimal load control in multiprogrammed computer systems with paged virtual memory. There is no difficulty in demonstrating that an optimum exists; the difficulty is in finding some practical optimal load control. When used with system behavior models, recent empirical advances in our understanding of program behavior enable us now to make strong claims about the (near) optimality of load controls based on working set memory management. The intuitions enunciated in 1968 now have firm empirical support [Denning (1968)].

In showing the connections between program behavior and computer system performance, I have emphasized models—of programs, of memory policies, and of multiprogrammed computer systems. All the model assumptions have firm empirical

*Supported in part by NSF Grant GJ-41289.

support. To spare you, dear reader, and me from a chapter of undue length, I have not included detailed discussions of data supporting my modeling assumptions, but I have indicated where in the literature you can find the data.

8.1.1. Overview of the Control Problem

Figure 8.1 illustrates the behavior of $T(n)$, which is the system *work rate* or *throughput* (transactions or jobs completed per second) as a function of n, the *load* or level of multiprogramming. This behavior has been observed in real systems since the middle 1960's; for example, Weizer and Oppenheimer (1969) saw it in the RCA Spectra/70, Rodriguez and Dupuy (1973) saw it in CP-67, and Sekino (1972) saw it in Multics. It has been observed in simulations and numerical studies of system models, for example Courtois (1975a) and Denning and Kahn (1975). An overview is given by Denning et al. (1976).

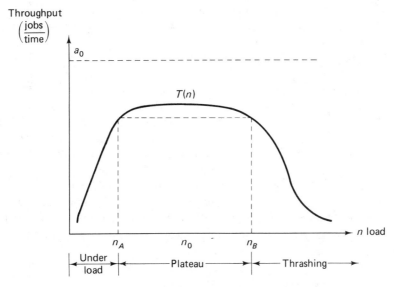

Figure 8.1.   Throughput as a function of the multi-programming level.

The curve $T(n)$ initially rises as the increasing load drives the system toward saturation; the highest possible work rate of a single processor system is denoted by a_0, where $1/a_0$ is the mean program execution time. However, the increasing load eventually reduces the memory space available to each program below the minimum required to sustain its working set, producing excessive paging and reducing the work capacity of the system. The *plateau* of $T(n)$ is an interval (n_A, n_B) of loads in which $T(n)$ is within some specified tolerance (e.g., 5%) of the optimal $T(n_0)$. If load exceeds n_B, the system is *thrashing*, while if it does not reach n_A, it is *underloaded*. (The latter condition is not often encountered in practice.)

Consider a system whose user community is of size N, where each user takes a mean time Z to submit a next transaction after the system returns his last. During an interval of constant load n, the mean response time W is approximated by

$$W = \frac{N}{T(n)} - Z \qquad (8.1)$$

See [Buzen (1976)] for a derivation and [Courtois (1975)] for a discussion of why this approximation is usually good. This formula shows that controlling the load to maximize $T(n)$ for a given user community tends to minimize the mean response time for a transaction. Since transactions progress in virtual time only if executing on the processor, the normalized throughput $T(n)/a_0$ is also the processor utilization $U(n)$ and is maximized at the optimal load.

The objective of a load controller is regulating the load so that throughput remains near optimal. The most direct control simply hunts, by varying n and observing $T(n)$, for a maximal throughput. [Badel et al. (1975) treat an example.] Unfortunately, such a direct control is often impractical; an estimate of $T(n)$, which depends on observing a series of recent transactions *departing* from the system, may not apply to the conditions *in* the system. A controller capable of reacting to current conditions must use measurements of system variables whose rates of change are considerably faster than the rate of user interactions with the system. In other works, a practical controller regulates throughput indirectly by regulating internal quantities.

A practical controller may require estimates of several internal quantities. As noted earlier, the measured processor utilization, $U(n)$, can serve as an estimate of normalized throughput $T(n)/a_0$. If we can identify additional quantities whose values indicate the effect on $U(n)$ of a proposed change in n, the controller can be made to locate an optimum without having to hunt for it. The additional quantities must be related to program behavior because changes in n are strongly correlated with changes in the memory space available to each program. Our purpose in this chapter is to show that a program's lifetime function (specifying mean virtual time between page faults at a given resident set size) contains enough information about program behavior to be the basis for practical optimal load controllers.

8.1.2. Memory Policies and Their Measures

The following definitions of memory policy behavior will be used throughout. For a given program and $t = 1, 2, \ldots, T$, let $r(t)$ denote the index of the page containing the address referenced at the tth virtual memory access; t is sometimes called *virtual time*. Let MP denote a memory policy with a single adjustable parameter (θ). A *resident set* of MP, denoted $M(t)$, is the set of pages of a given program which are present in main memory at virtual time t; $r(t)$ is a member of $M(t)$. Starting with an initial resident set $M(0)$, MP generates a sequence of resident sets for $t = 0, 1, \ldots, T$. This sequence is uniquely determined (i.e., reproducible) for a given reference string $r(1) \ldots r(T)$ and parameter θ. The size of $M(t)$ is defined as

$$|M(t)| = \text{number of pages in } M(t) \qquad (8.2)$$

and the *mean space demand s*, or *mean resident set size* (for given θ), is

$$s = \frac{1}{T} \sum_{t=1}^{T} |M(t)| \tag{8.3}$$

For any subset M of pages, define the indicator function,

$$H(M, i) = \begin{cases} 1, & i \in M \\ 0, & \text{otherwise} \end{cases} \tag{8.4}$$

so that the *hit rate* (for given θ) is

$$h = \frac{1}{T} \sum_{t=1}^{T} H(M(t-1), r(t)) \tag{8.5}$$

The *page fault rate* of MP is defined as

$$f = 1 - h \tag{8.6}$$

The *lifetime interval* of MP is defined as

$$g = \frac{1}{f} \tag{8.7}$$

The lifetime interval is usually used to estimate the mean time between page faults (for given θ). It is exact only when the final fault occurs at time T; however, for large T, the error between g and the true mean interfault time is not significant.

A pair (s, f) is called a *demand point* of MP. The piecewise linear graph connecting a set of such points expresses the trade-off between a space investment s and the resulting fault rate f. This graph is usually called the *faut rate function* of MP, and we write $f(s)$ as the fault rate for mean resident set size s. (The literature contains many examples of such graphs; for surveys, see [Denning and Graham (1975), Chu and Opderbeck (1976b), Spirn (1976, 1977)]). The related graph of points (s, g) is usually called the *lifetime function* of MP, and we write $g(s)$ as the lifetime interval for mean resident set size s. Figure 8.2 illustrates empirical lifetime functions measured by Graham (1976). (The policies WS, PFF, and LRU are explained below.) When the dependence of s, f, or g on the memory policy parameter θ is important, we shall write $s(\theta), f(\theta)$, or $g(\theta)$, respectively. [The distinction between $f(s)$ and $f(\theta)$ or $g(s)$ and $g(\theta)$ will be clear from the context.]

Associated with page i at time t is the *backward distance* $b(i, t)$ specifying the time since prior reference to page i: If $b(i, t) = u$, then $r(t - u)$ is the latest prior occurrence of i; $u = 0$ implies $r(t) = i$. If there is no prior reference, we consider $b(i, t)$ to be infinite.

The *least recently used* (LRU) memory policy interprest the integer parameter $\theta \geq 1$ as a fixed resident set size; its $M(t)$ comprises the θ (or fewer) pages of least (finite) backward distance. As soon as θ distinct pages have been referenced, $s = \theta$ for this policy. The list ordering the pages according to increasing backward distance is called the *LRU stack*, $S(t)$. The position of $r(t)$ in the stack $S(t - 1)$ is called the *stack distance*, $d(t)$; a page fault occurs at time t if and only if $d(t) > \theta$. The stack $S(t)$ is obtained from $S(t - 1)$ by moving the referenced page $[r(t)$, at position $d(t)]$ to the top and pushing the intervening pages down by one position. Efficient methods of

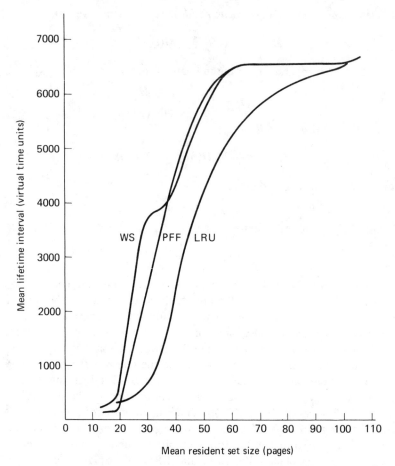

Figure 8.2. Lifetime functions of a program under different memory policies. (*From* Graham (1976, pp. 281–282).)

computing LRU demand points $(\theta, f(\theta))$ from empirical stack distance frequency distributions are known [Coffman and Denning (1973)].

The *working set* $W(t)$ is the set of pages i for which $b(i, t) \leq \theta$, where $\theta \geq 1$ is a fixed integer known as the *window*. The working set memory policy (WS) is the MP in which $M(t) = W(t)$ for all t. It generates variable resident set size. Efficient methods of computing WS demand points $(s(\theta), f(\theta))$ from empirical frequency distributions of interreference intervals are known; they are summarized in the Appendix [Coffman and Denning (1973), Denning and Schwartz (1972), Denning and Slutz (1976), and Slutz and Traiger (1974)].

The *page fault frequency policy* (PFF) was proposed in 1972 by Chu and Opderdeck (1972, 1976b). It is a variant of WS designed to make replacement decisions only at page fault times. Let $t - v$ and t be successives times at which a PFF page fault occurs. If $v \geq \theta$, PFF retains in residence only the pages whose usage bits are on; that is, PFF uses the working set at time t under window v to define $M(t)$. If $v < \theta$, PFF adds the faulting page to the resident set; that is, PFF sets $M(t) = M(t-1) + r(t)$. All usage bits, and the clock measuring interfault time, are reset at the page fault times. The premise is that $1/\theta$ represents a maximum desirable paging rate; if paging momentarily exceeds this rate ($v < \theta$), the resident is increased in order to reduce paging. The attraction of PFF is its allowing an approximation to WS which can be implemented, with minimal operating system overhead, in a machine having no working set hardware. [Morris (1972) discusses such hardware.] No efficient computational method for determining PFF demand points is known. Franklin et al. (1978) recently discovered anomalies in PFF behavior: For some reference strings, PFF may *increase* paging and *decrease* mean resident set size when θ is increased. Graham (1976) also observed *gap behavior*: For some reference strings, minute increases in θ can produce very large increases in mean resident set size. Neither LRU nor WS suffers from these peculiarities.

8.2. PROGRAM BEHAVIOR

8.2.1. Phases and Transitions

It has been known for a long time that programs refer to instructions and data in their address spaces in definite, nonrandom patterns [Denning (1972)]. These patterns arise from looping, sequential, and block-forming program control structures and from the normal grouping of related data into structures. They are referred to loosely as *locality of reference*. A common method of displaying them constructs a timing diagram, known as a *reference map*, which is a matrix whose rows correspond to pages and columns to successive Δ-intervals of virtual time; a mark is placed in square (i, j) whenever page i is referenced during the jth Δ-interval. An example is shown in Figure 8.3. [See [Hatfield and Gerald (1971), Chu and Opderbeck (1976b), and Kahn (1976)] for empirical examples of such diagrams.]

Reference maps reveal two distinct types of behavior:

1. *Stable, or phase, behavior.* Over extended periods. the program concentrates all references in small, fixed subsets of pages. Each maximal such period is called a *phase*; the associated pages constitute the *locality set* of the phase.

2. *Disruptive, or transition, behavior.* In the intervals between phases, the nicely localized phase patterns are broken; the reference pattern is discontinuous, unordered.

The phase-type behavior is typically observed to cover a heavy majority of virtual time. In one study, Batson (1976) and Madison and Batson (1976) observed that 90% of virtual time was covered by phases of at least 10^5 references. In another study, Kahn (1976) observed well over 98% of virtual time covered by phases. However, this does not mean that transition behavior is unimportant.

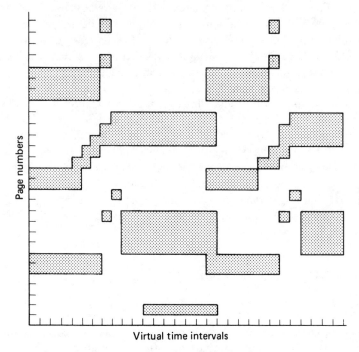

Figure 8.3. Sketch of a page reference map.

Working set memory management derives from this description of program reference patterns. The set of referenced pages in the jth Δ-interval is just the working set $W(t)$ with $t = j\Delta$ and window $\theta = \Delta$. This working set $W(t)$ is likely to predict $W(t + \Delta)$ with high probability if the interval $(t - \Delta, t + \Delta)$ is contained in a phase. During a transition, $W(t)$ is unlikely to predict $W(t + \Delta)$. For many programs the working set policy will produce little paging during phases; staccato paging will result primarily from transitions. This is why transition behavior cannot be ignored.

The published reference maps are formulated for address space pages rather than logical program segments. Striking direct evidence of phase/transition behavior in logical program structure has been reported by Madison and Batson (1976) and Batson (1976). Their definition of phases and transitions uses an LRU stack of program data segment names. For given k, a phase is a maximal interval of virtual time during which (a) the stack distances do not exceed k, (b) at least once the stack distance is k, and (c) k segments are referenced at least once each. The locality set of such a phase is the set of k segments at the top of the stack. For the data references of actual programs, they observed

1. This definition gives rise to a small set of distinct phases. Adjacent phases may have different k-values.

2. Phases of lower k-values are nested within phases of higher k-values. (The inner phases correspond to such program structures as inner loops or enclosed blocks.)

3. Outermost phases (the ones of largest observed k-value) seldom contain more than 20% of program data segments. Outer phases of length at least 10^4 references covered 97% of virtual time, while outer phases of length at least 10^5 references covered 90% of virtual time.

4. Adjacent outermost phases tend to have locality sets that differ by more than they match; large disruptions are common. The amount of disruption was not strongly dependent on the size of the locality sets of the adjacent phases.

Using a different approach, Kahn (1976) studied empirical phase/transition for paged programs. The page size was 64 words. The reference strings included both instruction and data addresses. He recorded the page fault sequence generated by the WS policy under various choices of window size. By locating bursts of unusually short lifetime intervals, he classified page faults as phase or transition faults. His major findings were the following:

1. Phases covered at least 98% of virtual time.

2. Paging rates in phases were 1/100 to 1/1000 of paging rates in transitions. However, transitions produced only 50% or less of the total numbers of page faults.

3. There was strong serial correlation between lifetime intervals within phases, but in transitions, lifetime intervals were nearly independent and exponentially distributed in length.

These experimental studies show that locality is an inherent property of logical program behavior, that phase behavior is dominant, and that, because it can generate sudden heavy demands on the system swapping devices, transition behavior definitely cannot be ignored.

If logical program segments are not apportioned carefully among pages, the inherent program locality can be masked off—the pages can appear to be referenced randomly even though the segments they contain are not. For this reason there has been considerable interest in distributing program segments among pages to preserve the phase/transition behavior in page reference patterns. See [Hatfield and Gerald (1971) and Ferrari (1974, 1975, 1976).]

8.2.2. Models

The most general program behavior models seek to describe the reference string $r(1) \ldots r(T)$ as a stochastic process; coupled with a memory policy, a model is used to evaluate the fault rate or the lifetime function. Simpler models attempt to describe only the resident set size and page fault arrival processes without accounting for resident sets themselves. Still simpler ones describe only the page fault arrival process.

The first model to be extensively analyzed is the *independent reference model* (IRM); it specifies that there is a fixed probability distribution $\{a_i, i = 1, \ldots, p\}$ over the program's pages and that a_i is the independent probability that each $r(t)$ is i. Expressions for demand points (s, f) have been derived in this model for many memory policies [Coffman and Denning (1973) and Smith (1976b)]. Because it fails to capture phase/transition behavior, this model makes gross errors in predicting working set fault rate curves when the a_i's are the observed reference densities of the program; various empirical studies have observed errors of at least 200% between predicted and actual WS mean resident set sizes [Spirn and Denning (1972)]. Baskett and Rafii (1976) showed a simple method of fitting the a_i's so that IRM agrees well (within 25% average relative error) with actual data; however, the fitted a_i's have no empirical interpretation.

If the model a_i's are to be empirically observable, the IRM has little value as a program model over long periods of virtual time. However, it may be useful for program reference activity within a phase.

Another model which has been subjected to extensive analysis and measurement is the *LRU stack model* (LRUSM) [Arvind et al. (1973), Coffman and Denning (1973), Shedler and Tung (1972), Spirn and Denning (1972), and Spirn (1976, 1977)]. This model specifies that there is a fixed probability distribution $\{a_i, i = 1, \ldots, p\}$ over the possible stack positions and that a_i is the independent probability that each distance $d(t)$ is i. Though this model is a better estimator than IRM of working set demand curves, it does make serious errors predicting page fault rates; average errors of 10% and maximum errors of 40% are typical [Arvind et al. (1973), Graham (1976), and Spirn and Denning (1972)]. Typical data show that the distance probabilities tend to decrease $(a_1 \geq a_2 \geq \ldots)$; see [Chu and Opderbeck (1972, 1976b) and Spirn (1976, 1977)]. Because this implies stability of reference toward the top stack positions, this model too is incapable of forecasting transitional behavior. In fact, if distance probabilities are decreasing, this model predicts that the lifetime curve of the LRU policy dominates that of the WS policy, contradicting measurements of most practical programs [Spirn (1976, 1977)]. The disruptions of transitions are needed to explain physical observations [Chu and Opderbeck (1972), Denning and Graham (1975), and Denning and Kahn (1975)]. A semi-Markov derivative of this model, reported by Chu and Opderbeck (1976a), can be used to describe the holding times in each resident set size of the PFF policy; however, this derivative is no more capable of capturing transition behavior than the LRUSM from which it is derived.

The models mentioned above have the common ability to describe the stable, predictable regimes of program activities. None is capable of describing the discontinuities at transitions. None is considered accurate enough to be a model of long-term program behavior. The initial attraction of these models was not only their simplicity but also the hope that the dominance of phase behavior would reduce the errors between them and the world. We know now in retrospect that the transition behavior is sufficiently disruptive that it must be modeled too.

A useful approach to modeling phase/transition behavior derives from the principle of *decomposability* for systems [Courtois (1975a) and Courtois and Vantilborgh (1976)]. The central observation is that if the rate of interactions within a given system is high compared with the rate of interactions between that system and its environment, then transient behavior of the system has no significant influence on the long-run dynamics of the environment. Under this assumption we can approximate the true behavior by assuming that the system is in equilibrium for the full duration of each interval between interactions with the environment. In other works, we can decompose the problem, studying first the system in its own right and then using just its equilibria to study the environment.

To employ this principle in program modeling, we decouple the phase and transition behaviors. We use a *macromodel* to describe the phase holding times and associated locality sets. We use a *micromodel* to describe the reference pattern within each phase determined by the macromodel. An example of a macromodel is a semi-Markov process whose states are specific locality sets, whose holding time distributions specify the phase lengths of each state, and whose state transition matrix specifies the probability that a given next locality set follows the current one. Examples of micromodels are the IRM and LRUSM; the probability distribution $\{a_i\}$ for a given macromodel state is restricted to the set of pages in the locality set of that state.

Simulation experiments show that even simple forms of a phase/transition model are capable of reproducing observed behaviors, such as WS lifetimes dominating LRU lifetimes, which are outside the pale of models such as the IRM or LRUSM [Denning and Kahn (1975)]. Experimental studies by Graham (1976) verify the hypotheses of such a model for actual programs. Using a simple filtering technique, Kahn (1976) classified page faults as transition or phase faults; he then showed how to use separate phase and transition data to construct a statistically justifiable two-state semi-Markov model for the page fault sequence. The Batson (1976) and Madison and Batson (1976) experiments also give ample evidence supporting this approach. Courtois and Vantilborgh (1976) have shown that the mathematical tools to be used for such models are straightforward.

8.3. WORKING SET MEMORY MANAGEMENT

Our objective in this section is studying working set memory management in order to determine what information about a program's behavior is contained in its working set lifetime curve and under what conditions and in what senses a working set policy is optimal. Recall that the working set $W(t)$ is the set of pages i whose backward distances satisfy $b(i, t) \leq \theta$.

8.3.1. Comparisons with Optimal Policy

Prieve and Fabry (1976) have defined an optimal policy, VMIN, for which the fault rate $f(s)$ at each mean resident set size s is minimal over all demand paging policies [also see Denning (1976)]. Smith (1976b) gives expressions for $f(s)$ under the IRM and LRUSM program behaviors. At each successive time t, VMIN decides either to retain $r(t)$ until its next reference or to remove it immediately from the resident set. The decision to retain or remove depends on an integer parameter $\theta \geq 1$. If $r(t)$ and $r(t + u)$ are successive references to the same page, VMIN retains $r(t)$ in the resident set during $[t, t + u]$ only if $u \leq \theta$; otherwise, VMIN removes it just before time $t + 1$. If $r(t)$ is the last reference to a page, VMIN removes it just before time $t + 1$.

Both VMIN and WS generate the same fault sequence, and fault rate, for each value of θ. Let $r(t)$ and $r(t + u)$ denote successive references to the same page. That $u > \theta$ implies that VMIN removes $r(t)$ just before time $t + 1$, which will produce a page fault at time $t + u$ and that WS will remove $r(t)$ just before time $t + \theta + 1$, also producing a fault at time $t + u$. Conversely, $u \leq \theta$ implies that $r(t)$ is still resident for both WS and VMIN at time $t + u$. Moreover, increasing θ increases the mean resident set size and decreases the paging rate, since the resident sets of both VMIN and WS satisfy an inclusion property:

$$M_\theta(t) \subseteq M_{\theta+\epsilon}(t), \qquad t = 0, \ldots, T, e > 0 \tag{8.8}$$

These ideas are illustrated in Figure 8.4. VMIN's fault rate curves are easy to compute from working set statistics; see the Appendix.

Figure 8.5 compares resident set sizes of VMIN and WS in the vicinity of a transition at time t from a locality of a pages to one of b pages phaving c pages in common. [Time plots, showing the transient behavior of WS size for real programs, are given by

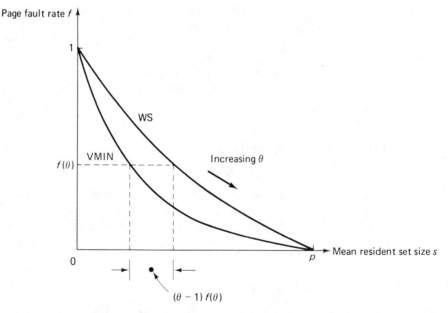

Figure 8.4. WS and VMIN fault rate curves for a p-page program.

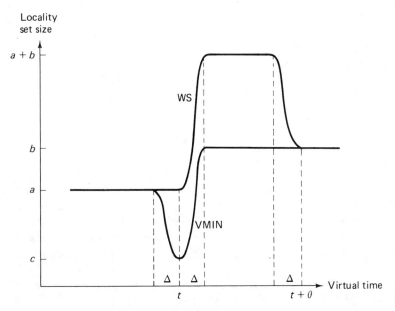

Figure 8.5. Policy behavior for transition at time t.

Smith (1976a).] The figure is drawn for the idealization that every locality set page is referenced within every Δ-interval. We assume that θ is larger than Δ but less than every phase holding time. Under these conditions, the resident sets of both policies are identical beginning θ time units after the phase begins and until Δ time units before the phase ends, and there is no paging during phases. Consider a series of such transitions at times $\{t_j, j = 1, \ldots, J + 1\}$ spanning J phases. At the jth transition the number of faults is the number of entering pages, e_j. (If $t = t_j$ in Figure 8.5, then $e_j = b - c$.) The fault rate observed over these J phases is

$$f = \frac{1}{t_{J+1}} \sum_{j=1}^{J} e_j = \frac{J}{t_{J+1}} \frac{1}{J} \sum_{j=1}^{J} e_j = \frac{E}{H} \tag{8.9}$$

where H is the observed mean holding time per phase and E is the mean number of pages entering at a transition [Denning and Kahn (1975)]. The mean lifetime of both WS and VMIN for the given $\theta(\Delta < \theta < H)$ in an ideal phase/transition program is therefore

$$g = \frac{H}{E} \tag{8.10}$$

Equation (8.10) is an approximation for real programs. If it is not true that every locality set page is referenced in every θ-interval within a phase, then WS (and VMIN) will generate an average of $D > 0$ faults in a phase, and the observed lifetime will be

$$g = \frac{H}{D + E} \tag{8.11}$$

Most of the reference strings analyzed by Kahn (1976) had the ratio $D : E$ in the range $1 : 1$ to $3 : 1$; however, a significant number had this ratio exceeding $15 : 1$.

The mean resident set size of WS exceeds that of VMIN, owing primarily to behavior near transitions. At the beginning of a page's forward reference interval exceeding θ—i.e., after the last reference to that page in a phase—WS retains the page $\theta - 1$ time units longer than VMIN. Since each such interval produces a page fault, the number of such intervals in a reference string is $f(\theta) \cdot T$. Since each such interval accounts for a contribution of $(\theta - 1)/T$ to the mean excess of WS over VMIN, we obtain as an estimate of the mean space difference at the given θ

$$s_{\text{WS}} - s_{\text{VMIN}} \simeq (\theta - 1)f(\theta) \tag{8.12}$$

This has been indicated in Figure 8.4. The only way to cause WS and VMIN to be more alike is to structure the program to have as few transitions as possible. Because phase/transition behavior is inherent, much of this difference may be irremovable.

This discussion suggests the possibility of clipping off the spatial excess of WS by temporarily reducing the value of θ near transitions. Smith (1976a) proposed a second window, $\theta' < \theta$, and a special decision at each page fault: The faulting page replaces the WS page of largest backward distance if that backward distance exceeds θ'. His experiments show that this does clip off working set peaks, but it may increase or decrease mean resident set size for fixed fault rate, depending on the program, within a range of $\pm 10\%$. One can devise other schemes for detecting transitions—e.g., a run or LRU stack distances (or lifetime intervals) longer (or shorter) than the recent average, a sudden increase in working set size—which can be used to remove pages still inside the normal θ window. It is not known whether such modified working set schemes can operate with low enough overhead to make them practical.

The PFF memory policy may misbehave on programs with phase/transition behavior. For these programs, clusters of short lifetime intervals occur as a result of transitions; PFF responds, as does WS, by adding the new locality set's pages to the resident set without replacing any pages. Whereas WS will remove from residence the pages of the former locality within θ time units after the transition ends. PFF will not do so until the first page fault ending a lifetime interval greater than θ. (In the case of an ideal phase/transition program, as in Figure 8.5, PFF would not remove the a-c unneeded pages until the next transition after time t.) PFF's premise—that short lifetime intervals usually imply too small a resident set—is faulty for phase/transition programs.

8.3.2.   The Information in the WS Lifetime Function

The previous discussion suggests that the WS lifetime curve $g(s)$ of an ideal phase/transition program will tend to flatten out for $\theta > \Delta$ and will tend to drop rapidly for $\theta < \Delta$, as shown in Figure 8.6. The flattening for $\theta > \Delta$ results from increasing the mean WS resident set size without much reducing the paging from transitions. The drop for $\theta < \Delta$ results from the working set being unable to contain the locality set in every phase; hence, significant additional paging is generated during phases themselves. The point at which flattening begins is called the *knee* of the lifetime curve.

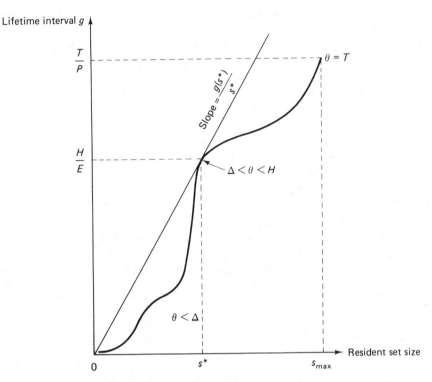

Figure 8.6. Important points on WS lifetime curve of an ideal phase/transition program. (The reference string contains T references over p distinct pages.)

Consistent with Eq. (8.10), the knee lifetime is approximately $g(s^*) = H/E$ in an ideal phase/transition program. A precise definition of the knee is the highest point of tangency between a ray from the origin and the curve—in other words, the point at which the ratio

$$g(s)/s$$

is maximized. (We shall show shortly that this ratio plays an important role in optimal multiprogramming.) The intuition that the knee corresponds to the holding time vs. entering pages ratio H/E has been verified in simulation experiments with ideal phase/transition programs, where H and E could be controlled [Denning and Kahn (1975)]. When there are several levels of identifiable phase behavior—as is observed in the Madison and Batson (1976) experiments—there may be several knees in the WS lifetime curve. The program shown in Figure 8.2 has WS primary knee near 30 pages with lifetime of 3600 time units and a secondary knee near 60 pages with lifetime of 6300 time units. Graham (1976) observed a secondary knee in seven of eight reference strings and a tertiary knee in three. He also observed that the knee slope $g(s)/s$ for the WS lifetime curve was at least as large as the knee slope of other nonlookahead memory policies.

The foregoing discussion leads to the following characterization of a WS lifetime curve. The WS policy differs from the optimal, VMIN, a lookahead policy, primarily because it reacts at transitions by increasing the resident set, while VMIN anticipates by decreasing it. The resulting space difference is measured by $(\theta - 1)f(\theta)$. The knee(s) of the WS lifetime correspond to choice(s) of θ sufficient for WS to observe some level of phase behavior. The portion of the curve below the knee of smallest resident set size tends to be convex. The portion of the curve below a given knee is dominated by the behavior of the program within the phases observed at the θ-value of the knee. The portion of the curve near a knee is dominated by the behavior of single phases and transitions observed at the θ-value of that knee; the knee lifetime is approximated by $H/(D + E)$, where H is the mean phase holding time, E the mean number of pages entering at a transition, and D the mean number of phase page faults. The portion of the curve beyond the knee of largest resident set size tends to flatten for one of two ressons: (a) There is less gain in making the working set larger than the locality sets than there is penalty in making it smaller. (b) There are various external factors—such as the loss of resident set pages during I/O waiting periods or the limitation on maximal lifetime imposed by the ratio T/p, from a T-unit reference string over p pages [Denning and Kahn (1975), Easton and Fagin (1975), and Parent and Potier (1976)].

8.3.3. Dominant Memory Policies and Optimality

The concept of phase/transition behavior suggests that, at the phase level observable by a given value of θ in a given reference string, there is a *locality factor* A that bounds the reward (penalty) for a resident set overestimating (underestimating) locality sets. The interpretation of *locality factor* is that each unit of resident set excess (over the locality set) saves no more than A faults per reference and that each unit of resident deficiency produces at least A faults per reference. The locality factor A may depend on θ, but it otherwise is a program constant independent of the memory policy.

A given memory policy MP is *dominant* among memory policies if, first, each unit of another policy's resident set excess (over MP) reduces the fault rate relative to MP by no more than A and, second, each unit of another policy's resident set deficiency increases the fault rate relative to MP by at least A. Any nonlookahead memory policy that tracks a program's phases will tend to dominate other nonlookahead policies. In particular, the WS policy, possibly modified to clip off space transients near transitions, is dominant among nonlookahead policies when θ is minimally sufficient to track some level of phase behavior. This means that the WS lifetime curve will be larger than another policy's lifetime curve in the vicinity of its primary knee; Figure 8.7 shows the principle, and Figure 8.2 illustrates it for a real program.

In the following discussion, let MP1 denote a given, dominant, memory policy for a given θ. Let MP2 also denote memory policy with a given θ. Possibly MP1 and MP2 are instances of the same MP with different θ values. Neither MP1 nor MP2 has lookahead.

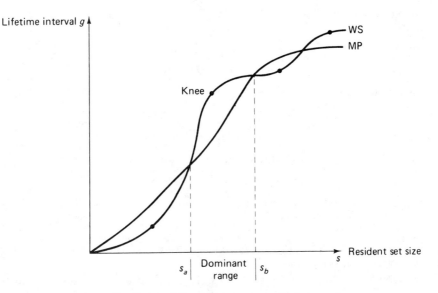

Figure 8.7. Effect of dominance on lifetime.

For $ij = 12$ or 21, define the hit rate attributable to the excess of MPi resident sets over those of MPj,

$$h_{ij} = \frac{1}{T} \sum_{t=1}^{T} H(M_i(t-1) - M_j(t-1), r(t)) \qquad (8.13)$$

where H is the indicator function defined in Eq. (8.4) and $M_i - M_j$ denotes the pages in the resident set M_i but not in the resident set M_j. Similarly, define the mean space excess to be

$$s_{ij} = \frac{1}{T} \sum_{t=1}^{T} |M_i(t) - M_j(t)| \qquad (8.14)$$

Note that $s_{ij} = 0$ implies $h_{ij} = 0$. Define constants B_{ij} so that

$$h_{ij} = B_{ij} s_{ij} \qquad (8.15)$$

If either s_{12} or s_{21} is zero, we can choose $B_{12} = B_{21}$. (Both s_{12} and s_{21} are not zero unless MP1 $=$ MP2.) If MP1 dominates, then each unit of MP2 excess has a reward not larger than the program's locality factor, and each unit of MP2 deficiency has a penalty not smaller than the program's locality factor; therefore,

$$B_{21} \leq A \leq B_{12} \qquad (8.16)$$

We shall show now that the quantity $f + As$ is less at the MP1 demand point (s, f) than at a demand point for any MP2.

Observe that the union of resident sets at each time t can be written in two ways:

$$M_1 \cup (M_2 - M_1) = M_2 \cup (M_1 - M_2) \qquad (8.17)$$

Counting pages and hits on both sides of Eq. (8.17) for all t we obtain, on averaging,

$$s_1 + s_{21} = s_2 + s_{12} \tag{8.18}$$

$$h_1 + h_{21} = h_2 + h_{12} \tag{8.19}$$

We then obtain the relations

$$
\begin{aligned}
h_2 - h_1 &= h_{21} - h_{12} && \text{[from Eq. (8.19)]} \\
&= B_{21}s_{21} - B_{12}s_{12} && \text{[from Eq. (8.15)]} \\
&\leq A(s_{21} - s_{12}) && \text{[from Rel. (8.16)]} \\
&= A(s_2 - s_1) && \text{[from Eq. (8.18)]}
\end{aligned} \tag{8.20}
$$

Applying the definition of fault rate, $f = 1 - h$, this reduces to

$$f_1 + As_1 \leq f_2 + As_2 \tag{8.21}$$

This shows, as claimed, that a dominant policy minimizes the quantity $f + As$ for those θ at which it dominates.

A geometric interpretation of Rel. (8.21) is shown in Figure 8.8: Through the point (s_1, f_1) is a straight line of slope $-A$, below which is an *infeasible region* in which no dominated memory policy can generate a demand point. No dominated policy can simultaneously reduce space and fault rate below the values defined by the dominant policy. If there is a range, say $\theta_a \leq \theta \leq \theta_b$, over which the given MP dominates, then in that range its fault rate curve is at the boundary of the (convex) infeasible region. Figure 8.9 illustrates this. This means that no policy can produce a smaller fault rate in this range and gives rise to the lifetime function pattern as in Figure 8.7.

We argued earlier that the WS policy tracks phase behavior closely when θ is near

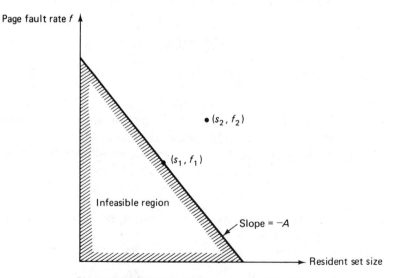

Figure 8.8. Infeasible region associated with demand point (s_1, f_1) of dominant memory policy.

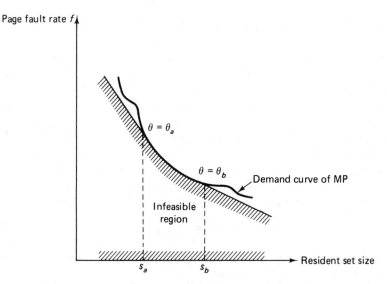

Figure 8.9. Union of infeasible regions for a range
$\theta_a \le \theta \le \theta_b$ in which MP dominates.

the primary knee of the WS lifetime curve. This means that the WS policy should dominate other nonlookahead policies—that is, no nonlookahead policy can generate higher lifetimes in a resident set size range such as (s_a, s_b) in Figure 8.7. A variety of reference strings, generated from an ideal phase/transition model, all fit the pattern of Figure 8.7 when MP = LRU [Denning and Kahn (1975)]. Graham's (1976) eight real reference strings also fit this pattern when MP was LRU or PFF; see also Figure 8.2.

It is important to note that the arguments leading to Rel. (8.21) assume implicitly that the dominated policy (MP2) has no lookahead. With lookahead, MP2 could systematically generate deficiencies $M_1(t) - M_2(t)$ containing no hits, violating the assumption that deficiencies have a penalty. In fact, VMIN's optimality arises from this fact [Denning and Tran-Quoc-Te (1976)]. Moreover, if the locality sets vary widely in size between phases, it is possible for fixed-space lookahead policies (such as the optimal one) to generate paging during phases whose locality sets exceed the space allocated; these policies can be dominated by the WS policy. [Examples are given in Denning and Graham (1975), and empirical observations are given in Prieve and Fabry (1976) and Graham (1976).]

There are theoretical program behaviors for which the WS policy cannot dominate. In the LRU stack model with decreasing distance frequencies, for example, the LRU policy can be proved dominant at all memory sizes (i.e., uniformly optimal) [Denning and Tran-Quoc-Te (1976) and Spirn (1976, 1977)]. In fact, the WS policy is not dominant in any program model in which a page's effective reference probability decreases with time since last reference [Denning and Tran-Quoc-Te (1976)]. That such theoretical assumptions do not appear to be satisfied in practice is further evidence of the need for phase/transition models of program behavior.

8.4. OPTIMAL LOAD CONTROL

The working set principle of memory management holds that each active program must have its working set resident in main memory. This implies a bound on the allowable (multiprogrammed) load n. Our objective in this section is showing that working set memory management achieves a degree of multiprogramming whose throughput closely approximates the optimum, a result already observed in practice [Rodriguez-Rosell and Dupuy (1973)]. [See also Denning et al. (1976).]

Denote by Y_i the memory space time (measured in page seconds) of the ith job. Suppose that a sequence of K jobs requires L seconds to complete and that the memory policy allocates all N available page frames among the n jobs active at all times. Under these assumptions, the jobs consume all the available memory space time:

$$\sum_{i=1}^{K} Y_i = LN \tag{8.22}$$

Dividing by K and noting that the throughput is $T(n) = K/L$, we find that the mean memory space time per job, $\bar{Y}$, satisfies

$$\bar{Y} = \frac{N}{T(n)} \tag{8.23}$$

In other words, maximizing the throughput is equivalent to minimizing the memory space time per job. As will be shown, choosing resident set size at a job's lifetime knee tends to minimize $\bar{Y}$ by minimizing Y_i for all i.

The memory space time of a job is the integral of its resident set size over the period during which it is active in the system. For the ith job, with average resident set size s_i, the space time can be estimated from

$$\hat{Y}_i = s_i(C_i + Df_iT_i) \tag{8.24}$$

where C_i is the total time the job waits for, or receives, service from the central processor and all (nonpaging) I/O devices, D is the mean delay (including queueing) for a page fault, T_i is the length of the job's reference string, and f_i is the job's paging rate. [Graham (1976) found that $\hat{Y}_i$ is actually a crude estimate of the true memory space time.]

The claim is that $\hat{Y}_i$ tends to be near a minimum when s_i is selected at the primary knee of the program's lifetime curve. From the definition, the primary knee maximizes the lifetime/space ratio $g(s)/s$; since $f(s) = 1/g(s)$, this knee minimizes the product $sf(s)$. If the term s_iC_i is a small component of $\hat{Y}_i$, choosing s_i at the knee will clearly tend to minimize $\hat{Y}_i$. If s_i is increased relative to the knee value, the terms s_iC_i and $s_if_iT_i$ will increase; while the corresponding reduction in paging may reduce D slightly, the overall tendency is for $\hat{Y}_i$ to increase. If s_i is decreased relative to the knee value, the term $Ds_if_iT_i$ will increase and the term s_iC_i will decrease; while a decrease in $\hat{Y}_i$ is possible, the sharp increases in f_i when s_i gets small suggest that the overall tendency is for $\hat{Y}_i$ to increase as s_i is decreased from the knee value.

This argument is *not* to be interpreted as a proof that setting the memory policy parameter to cause a job to operate at its WS lifetime knee will minimize the job's memory space time. It is merely a plausibility argument suggesting that an experimental investigation of this heuristic for choosing a policy parameter value is worthwhile.

Preliminary investigations verify this hypothesis. The study by Denning and Kahn (1975) considered a few lifetime functions under a wide range of system conditions, showing that the knee criterion consistently produces throughputs within 5% of optimum in queueing networks [also see Denning et al. (1976) and Kahn (1976)]. Graham (1976) studied the lifetime functions of eight production programs; he found near perfect matches between working set lifetime knees and minima in the estimated memory space time ($\hat{Y}_i$). He also found strong correlation between these knees and optimal multiprogramming loads in queueing network models. The form of the results is sketched in Figure 8.10.

Graham (1976) also studied the overhead inherent in optimal load control. He found that a controller need not vary the memory policy parameter once an initial setting has been determined. He studied the question, "What is the smallest set of distinct parameter values needed, so that one of them suffices to cause (estimated) memory space time to be within p percent of minimum?" For his set of eight reference strings, he found these were the smallest numbers of parameter values:

	p	
	10%	5%
WS	1	2
PFF	3	4

These results suggest that PFF has inherently higher overhead than WS in selecting a near optimal choice of the parameter. Indeed, one global value of WS window suffices to come within 10% of minimum in the space time of all these programs; the controller has nothing to do. [Graham (1976) also found that, with one best parameter, PFF was still 50% from optimal on some programs.]

If the information represented by a program's WS lifetime function is not available, simpler—but less robust—controls can be built. One is based on controlling the system's memory policy parameter so that the observed lifetime interval, averaged over active programs, remains slightly larger than the paging device swap time. It may fail in I/O bound systems. An even simpler control is based on regulating the load so that the paging device's utilization remains near 50%. It may fail in a system in which the memory policy fails to keep working sets resident or in an I/O bound system. These points are discussed in detail by Denning et al. (1976).

8.5. CONCLUSION

When the load (multiprogramming level) of a computer system is properly regulated, the system will realize its work potential: Throughput and processor utilization will be maximized; response time and main memory space time per job will be

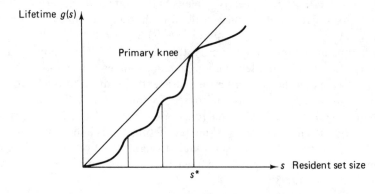

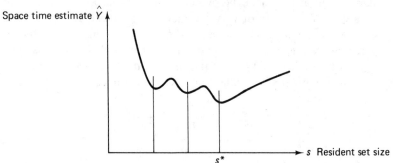

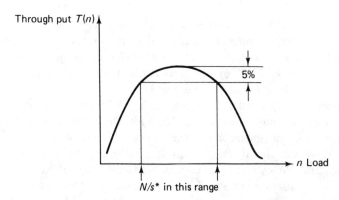

Figure 8.10. Typical optimal loading results.

minimized. The only component of a job's memory space time that depends significantly on load or memory policy is the product of the job's mean resident set size and
fault rate. This product is minimized at the knee of the job's lifetime function for the
given memory policy.

Now considered to be the most reasonable descriptions of program behavior, phase/transition models are supported directly by measurement and indirectly by their abilities to explain phenomena outside the scope of such models as the LRU stack model. Many properties of the working set (WS) policy's lifetime function are easily explained from this model and are supported by experiment: (a) Multiple levels of nested phase behavior in a program will be manifested as multiple knees in the WS lifetime function. (b) The WS lifetime dominates that of other nonlookahead memory policies in the vicinities of its knees, especially its primary knee. (c) The knee slope, defined as the ratio of lifetime to resident set size at the primary knee, tends to be maximized among nonlookahead policies by WS and may exceed that of fixed-space lookahead policies if locality set size variation is significant. These facts explain, in terms of program behavior, why the WS policy's knee minimizes memory space time relative to nonlookahead policies and, hence, maximizes a system's throughput and responsiveness. Efficient one-pass procedures for measuring WS lifetime functions are outlined in the Appendix; these procedures allow for the extraction of information needed to optimize system work capacity.

Critics sometimes suggest that these results are nice in theory but not in practice: "No one implements working set policies due to their overhead." Morris (1972) demonstrated that the hardware required to implement working set memory management was about $20 per main memory page frame at 1972 prices and that with such hardware almost no operating system overhead is generated. Graham (1976) observed from his data that one fixed, global value of the working set parameter is ordinarily sufficient to cause operation near lifetime knees; this value can be determined simply by adjusting the parameter occasionally for best system performance. WS controllers need not, therefore, generate much overhead. In contrast, the PFF (page fault frequency) policy, suggested as an easily implemented approximation to WS [Chu and Opderbeck (1972, 1976b)], tends to be much less controllable—partly because the PFF controller may have a large selection of parameter values among which to choose, partly because the PFF policy may be extremely senstive to minor adjustments in its parameter [Graham (1976)], and partly because of anomalous behavior [Franklin et al. (1978)].

Implementability and overhead of WS policies do not appear to be the primary questions. Theoretical, simulation, and numerical studies repeatedly indicate that properly regulated working set memory management is both useful and ideal for practical systems.

ACKNOWLEDGMENTS

G. Scott Graham and Kevin C. Kahn contributed a significant portion of the data used in the chapter, as well as their keen insights. Alan J. Smith pointed out inconsistencies in the presentation before the chapter was printed. The National Science Foundation's Grant GJ-41289 contributed some of the money to support this work.

APPENDIX: COMPUTATION OF WS
AND VMIN LIFETIME CURVES

The computational procedures of this appendix are condensed versions of those developed by Denning and Slutz (1976); also see Easton and Bennett (1977). Since lifetime g is related to fault rate f by $g = 1/f$, it is sufficient to compute the fault rate. Suppose $\theta_0 = 0$ and $\theta_1, \ldots, \theta_N$ are given integer values of the memory policy parameter such that $\theta_0 < \theta_1 < \ldots < \theta_N$, at which we wish to compute WS and VMIN demand points. Typically $\theta_{k+1} = 2\theta_k$ is sufficient for clear resolution of a lifetime function, whence N approximately $\log_2 T$, for a reference string of length T, gives good results.

In the following, $r(t - u)$ will denote the prior reference to page $i = r(t)$, for $t = 1, 2, \ldots, T$. The quantity u is called an interreference interval. If $r(t)$ is a first reference, u will be set to a value larger than θ_N. The reference string is assumed to contain p distinct pages, conveniently indexed $i = 1, \ldots, p$.

Fault Rate

Let $\{a(k), k = 1, \ldots, N + 1\}$ be counters; $a(k)$ counts the number of times t at which the interreference interval satisfies $\theta_{k-1} < u \leq \theta_k$. These counts can be computed for $t = 1, 2, \ldots, T$ using an array TIME, initialized to $-\theta_N$, in which TIME[i] is the time of prior reference to page i. When reference $i = r(t)$ is observed, we set

$$u := t - \text{TIME}[i]; \quad \text{TIME}[i] := t \qquad (8.A1)$$

Then we find the largest k such that $k \leq N + 1$ and $\theta_{k-1} < u$ and then set

$$a(k) := a(k) + 1 \qquad (8.A2)$$

On a first reference, $u = t + \theta_N > \theta_N$, implying that counter $a(N + 1)$ is updated; thus $a(N + 1)$ contains the p counts from first references. After time T, $a(1) + \ldots + a(N + 1) = T$.

As noted in Section 8.3.1, both VMIN and WS produce a page fault at time t if and only if $u > \theta$ at that time; thus both have the same page fault rate, abbreviated here as $f(k) = f(\theta_k)$:

$$f(k) = \frac{a(k + 1) + \ldots + a(N + 1)}{T} = 1 - \frac{a(1) + \ldots + a(k)}{T} \qquad (8.A3)$$

This gives rise to the simple difference equations

$$f(k) = \begin{cases} 1, & k = 0 \\ f(k - 1) - \dfrac{a(k)}{T}, & k = 1, \ldots, N \end{cases} \qquad (8.A4)$$

VMIN Resident Set Size

The mean VMIN resident set size, abbreviated here as $v(k) = v(\theta_k)$, can be computed by adding up the contributions of $r(t)$ for $t = 1, \ldots, T$. Each $r(t)$ always contributes $1/T$ to $v(k)$, corresponding to the requirement that $r(t)$ be in the resident set during the virtual time unit of reference. The *additional* contribution of $r(t)$ to $v(k)$ is as follows:

1. If $u \leq \theta_k$, $r(t)$ is resident continuously in the interval $[t - u + 1, t]$; its additional contribution is $(u - 1)/T$.

2. If $\theta_k < u$, then either $r(t)$ is a first reference, or else it was removed from residence just before time $t - u + 1$; in either case the additional contribution is 0.

Define counters $\{b(k), k = 1, \ldots, N + 1\}$; $b(k)$ tallies these additional contributions to the virtual space time, $Tv(k)$: Whenever $k \leq N + 1$ is the largest subscript such that $\theta_{k-1} < u$ [according to (8.A1)] we set

$$b(k): = b(k) + u - 1 \tag{8.A5}$$

The VMIN resident set size is

$$v(k) = \frac{T + b(1) + \ldots + b(k)}{T} = 1 + \frac{b(1) + \ldots + b(k)}{T} \tag{8.A6}$$

This gives rise to the difference equation

$$v(k) = \begin{cases} 1, & k = 0 \\ v(k - 1) + \dfrac{b(k)}{T}, & k + 1, \ldots, N \end{cases} \tag{8.A7}$$

WS Resident Set Size

As with VMIN, each reference $r(t)$ contributes $1/T$ to the WS resident set size. An approximation for $s(\theta_k)$, denoted $\hat{s}(k)$, can be computed by tallying these additional contributions:

1. If $u \leq \theta_k$, $r(t)$ is resident continuously in the interval $[t - u + 1, t]$; its additional contribution is $(u - 1)/T$.

2. If $\theta_k < u$, then either $r(t)$ is a first reference, in which case the additional contribution is 0, or it resided until just before $t - u + \theta_k + 1$, in which case its additional contribution is $(\theta_k - 1)/T$.

The initialization we specified earlier for the array TIME forces $u > \theta_N$ on each first reference; corresponding to case 2, therefore, the counter $b(N + 1)$ will be updated [by action (8.A5)] p times when it should not have been. However, this error is unimportant since $b(N + 1)$ is not used. Note that case 1 is the same as for VMIN. Note that case 2 contributes $(\theta_k - 1)/T$ to $\hat{s}(k)$ whenever there is a page fault on a second or subsequent reference; there are $a(k + 1) + \ldots + a(N + 1) - p = Tf(k) - p$ such contributions. Combining the two cases, we have

$$\hat{s}(k) = v(k) + (\theta_k - 1)\left(f(k) - \frac{p}{T}\right) \tag{8.A8}$$

This means that the WS resident set computation is actually more difficult than that of the optimal VMIN.

The foregoing argument for the WS resident set size is not exact: Since the additional contribution of $r(t - u)$ is tallied only when $r(t)$ is recognized, the contributions after final references have been omitted. (This is not a problem for VMIN, which removes pages from residence just after their final references.) The necessary correction for this *end effect* is achieved by pretending that $r(T + 1) = i$ for each page $i = 1, \ldots, p$. In other words, after the counters $a(k)$ and $b(k)$ have been used to compute $f(k)$ and $v(k)$, they are corrected as follows: For $i = 1, \ldots, p$ and $t = T + 1$, add 1 to $a(k)$ and $u - 1$ to $b(k)$, where $k \leq N + 1$ is the largest subscript such that $\theta_{k-1} < u$. Letting $a^*(k)$ and $b^*(k)$ denote the total corrections entered, respectively, into the a- and b-counters, we can apply the previous arguments to the intervals following final references, yielding for the correction

$$s^*(k) = \frac{b^*(1) + \ldots + b^*(k)}{T} + (\theta_k - 1)\frac{a^*(k + 1) + \ldots + a^*(N + 1)}{T} \quad (8.A9)$$

The true WS mean resident set size is $\hat{s}(k) + s^*(k)$. It can be obtained from (8.A8) provided $f(k)$ and $v(k)$ are recomputed using the corrected counters.

Suppose that j of the p corrections are entered into counters of subscripts $1, \ldots, k$. The maximum value of $b^*(1) + \ldots + b^*(k)$ is j time the largest correction that could have been entered, viz., $j(\theta_k - 1)$. Since the remaining $p - j$ corrections are in counters of subscripts $k + 1, \ldots, N + 1$, $a^*(k + 1) + \ldots + a^*(N + 1) = p - j$, so that

$$s^*(k) \leq \frac{j(\theta_k - 1)}{T} + (\theta_k - 1)\frac{p - j}{T} = \frac{(\theta_k - 1)p}{T} \quad (8.A10)$$

This implies that the corrections are insignificant if $\theta_k p$ is small compared to T.

The difference between the true WS resident set size, $\hat{s}(k)$, and the VMIN resident set size, is bounded as follows:

$$s(k) - v(k) = s^*(k) + \hat{s}(k) - v(k)$$

$$= s^*(k) + (\theta_k - 1)f(k) - \frac{(\theta_k - 1)p}{T} \quad \text{[from (8.A8)]}$$

$$< (\theta_k - 1)f(k) \quad \text{[from (8.A10)]} \quad (8.A11)$$

which demonstrates that Eq. (8.11) of the text is an upper bound which is tight when $\theta_k p$ is small compared to T.

CHAPTER 9

AN INTRODUCTION TO MATHEMATICAL PROGRAMMING APPLIED TO COMPUTER SYSTEMS DESIGN

K. MANI CHANDY
University of Texas at Austin
Austin, Texas

9.1. INTRODUCTION

Several system parameters are selected in the process of designing a computing system. Parameters are selected to maximize some *objective function* such as throughput or profit. The design must satisfy several *constraints*, such as the following: The cost of the system should not exceed some given value. In this chapter we shall be concerned with the problem of selecting parameters to maximize an objective function with the requirement that none of the design constraints be violated. This area of constrained optimization or *mathematical programming* is well covered by several excellent texts (see the Appendix), and yet many computer systems analysts do not have any familiarity with the area. Our objective in this chapter is to

1. help the computer systems analyst become aware of the broad categories of mathematical programming problems, so that he can communicate with operations researchers,

2. give the analyst some idea of different solution techniques and to provide him with an intuitive understanding of problems and algorithms,

3. motivate the analyst to study the subject more formally and in depth by illustrating the relevance of mathematical programming techniques, and

4. provide the operations researcher with some examples of applications of mathematical programming to computer systems design.

323

We shall not provide a formal development of optimization theory. However, the reader should gain an intuitive understanding of the area.

This chapter is organized as follows: Section 9.1 is the introduction. In Section 9.2, we present elementary concepts such as convex sets, convex functions, closed and bounded sets, extreme points, and local and global maxima. In Section 9.3, two basic theorems dealing with maximization and minimization are presented. Section 9.4 is an introduction to linear programming. Section 9.5 is a discussion of a branch and bound algorithm for integer programming problems. An application of mathematical programming to memory hierarchy design is presented in Section 9.6. The objective of this section is to make the computer systems analyst aware that an understanding of optimization theory allows the analyst to develop efficient algorithms tailored to specific design problems. The analyst does not have to rely exclusively on canned, general-purpose programs to solve all of his problems. In Section 9.7 we discuss other applications of mathematical programming to computing systems design.

9.2. BASIC CONCEPTS

9.2.1. Line Segment

In this chapter, $x = (x_1, \ldots, x_n)$ will refer to a vector or a point in n-dimensional Euclidean space. The *line segment* joining two points x and y is the set L of all points $px + (1 - p)y$, where p is a scalar and $0 \leq p \leq 1$; i.e.,

$$L = \{px + (1 - p)y \mid 0 \leq p \leq 1\}$$

See Figure 9.1.

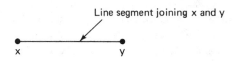

Line segment joining x and y

x   y

Figure 9.1.   The line segment.

9.2.2. Convex Sets

A set of points C is said to be a *convex set* if the line segment joining any two points in C is contained in C.

Note: In most of the following examples, x and y refer to *scalar* variables.

Example 1
$C = \{(x, y) \mid x^2 + y^2 \leq 1\}$. See Figure 9.2.

Example 2
$C = \{(x, y) \mid 0.4 < x^2 + y^2 < 1\}$. See Figure 9.3. C in Figure 9.3 is not a convex set, because points $(0.5, 0.5)$ and $(-0.5, -0.5)$ lie inside the set and the line segment joining these two points does not lie entirely within C.

See Figure 9.4 and 9.5.

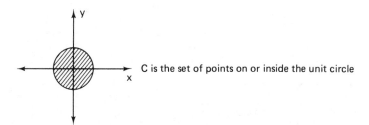

Figure 9.2.   Example of a convex set.

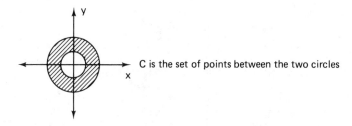

Figure 9.3.   Example of a set that is not convex.

Figure 9.4.   Examples of convex sets.

Figure 9.5.   Examples of sets that are not convex.

9.2.3. Convex Functions

Let C be a convex set and f a function defined over C. f is said to be a *convex function* if for any pair of points x, y in C and any scalar p, $0 \leq p \leq 1$,

$$f(px + (1 - p)y) \leq pf(x) + (1 - p)f(y)$$

f is said to be a *concave function* if $-f$ is a convex function. f is a convex function if the line segment joining the points $(x, f(x))$ and $(y, f(y))$ lies on or above the curve f at points along the line segment joining x and y, as illustrated in Figure 9.6. Examples of convex functions are presented in Figure 9.7, and examples of concave functions are found in Figure 9.8.

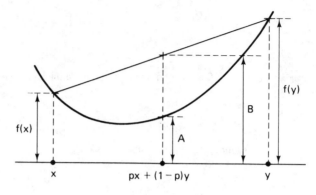

A: $f(px + (1 - p)y)$

b: $pf(x) + (1 - p)f(y)$

Figure 9.6. Convex function only if $B \geq A$.

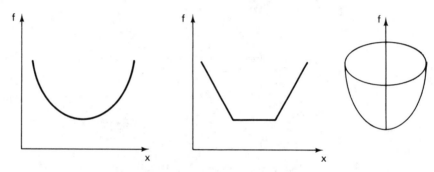

Figure 9.7. Examples of convex functions.

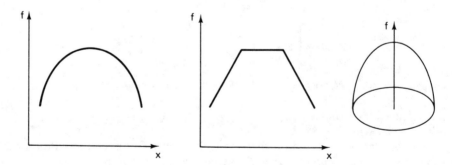

Figure 9.8. Examples of concave functions.

9.2.4. Closed Sets

A point x is said to be a *point of closure* for a set C if for any given positive number ϵ there exists a point in C which is at a distance of less than ϵ from x. In intuitive terms, x is a point of closure of C if x is either in C or is arbitrarily close to C.

Example 3

Let $B = \{x \mid x < 1\}$. The point $x = 1$ is a point of closure of B. In fact all points $x \leq 1$ are points of closure of B.

A set C is said to be a *closed set* if the set of all points of closure of C is equal to C. In Example 3, B is not a closed set since there is a point of closure $(x = 1)$ which is not in B.

Example 4

Examples of closed sets B:

$$B1 = \{x \mid x \leq 1\}, \qquad B2 = \{(x, y) \mid x^2 + y^2 \leq 1\},$$
$$B3 = \{(x, y) \mid x = y\}$$

Example 5

Examples of sets B that are not closed:

$$\{B = x \mid 0 < x \leq 1\}, \qquad B = \{(x, y) \mid 0 \leq x^2 + y^2 < 1\}$$

The difficulty with searching for maxima in sets that are not closed is illustrated by the problem

$$\text{maximize } x \text{ subject to } x < 1$$

In this case, the optimum solution is arbitrarily close to 1 but is not 1 itself. We shall choose to ignore such problems in this chapter since they do not seem to occur in computer or communications systems design.

9.2.5.   Bounded Sets

A set C is said to be *bounded* if there exist numbers a and b such that for any point $x = (x_1, \ldots, x_n)$ in C, $a < x_i < b$ for $i = 1, \ldots, n$. An example of a set that is bounded is $B2$ in Example 4, whereas sets $B1$ and $B3$ in that example are not bounded.

9.2.6.   Extreme Points

A point v in a set C is said to be an *extreme point* of the set C if there does not exist points x and y in C, distinct from v, such that v lies on the line segment between x and y.

Example 6

$C = \{(x, y) \mid x \geq 0, y \geq 0, x + y \leq 1\}$. C is a closed, bounded, convex set with three extreme points: $(0, 0)$, $(1, 0)$, and $(0, 1)$. See Figure 9.9.

Example 7

$C = \{x \mid x \leq 1\}$. C is a closed, convex (but not bounded) set with one extreme point: $x = 1$.

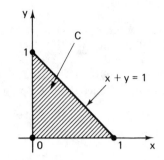

Figure 9.9.   C has three extreme points.

Example 8

$C = \{(x, y) \mid x^2 + y^2 \leq 1\}$. C is a closed, bounded, convex set. Every point on the circumference $x^2 + y^2 = 1$ is an extreme point of the set. See Figure 9.10.

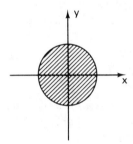

Figure 9.10.   C has an infinite number of extreme points.

9.2.7.   Local and Global Solutions

Let f be function defined over a set C. We now study the problem of searching C to find that point at which f takes on its maximum value. A point x in C is said to be a global solution if $f(x) \geq f(y)$ for all points y in C. A point x in C is said to be a local solution if for some positive ϵ, $f(x) \geq f(y)$ for all points y in C which are at a distance of less than ϵ from x. In intuitive terms, x is a global solution if it is the best solution in C, and it is a local solution if it is the best solution in its immediate vicinity. See Figure 9.11.

9.3.   FUNDAMENTAL THEOREMS

9.3.1.   Functions of One Variable

We now consider the following simple problem: Maximize $f(x)$, where x is a *scalar*, $a \leq x \leq b$, and a and b are arbitrary constants. Analysis of this simple problem will provide insight into more general problems with several variables. Let

$$C = \{x \mid a \leq x \leq b\}$$

C is the set of feasible solutions. C has extreme points at $x = a$ and $x = b$.

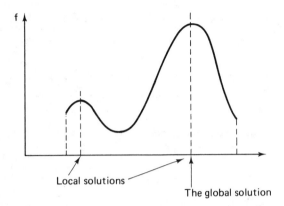

Figure 9.11. Local and global solutions for maxima.

Lemma 1

In the problem, maximize $f(x)$, subject to $a \leq x \leq b$, where $f(x)$ is convex, an extreme point of the set of feasible solutions is a global solution.

Proof: Any point y in C lies on the line segment between the extreme points, $x = a$ and $x = b$. Hence there exists a scalar p, $0 \leq p \leq 1$ such that

$$y = pa + (1 - p)b$$

From the definition of convexity,

$$f(y) \leq pf(a) + (1 - p)f(b)$$

Assume that $f(a) \geq f(b)$. Then

$$pf(a) + (1 - p)f(b) \leq pf(a) + (1 - p)f(a) = f(a)$$

and hence $f(y) \leq f(a)$. By the same argument if $f(b) \geq f(a)$, then $f(y) \leq f(b)$. Hence the value of the function f must be at least as large at one of the extreme points as it is at any point y in C. Therefore, there exists an extreme point which is optimal. See Figure 9.12.

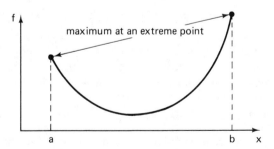

Figure 9.12. Maximizing a convex function.

Lemma 2

In the above problem, if f is a concave function, a local solution is a global solution.

Proof: We shall prove this lemma by contradiction. Let $x = u$ be a local but not global solution, and let $x = v$ be a global solution. The

$$f(v) > f(u)$$

Let y be a point on the line segment between u and v but not the point $x = u$ itself. Then there exists a scalar p, $0 < p \le 1$, such that

$$y = pv + (1 - p)u$$

(Note that p cannot be 0, because if it were 0, then $y = u$.) From the definition of concave functions,

$$f(y) \ge pf(v) + (1 - p)f(u)$$

For $p > 0$,

$$pf(v) + (1 - p)f(u) > pf(u) + (1 - p)f(u) = f(u)$$

Hence, for any point y on the line segment joining u and v, excepting u itself,

$$f(y) > f(u)$$

Hence $x = u$ cannot be a local solution, because an arbitrarily small step from u towards v results in an improvement of the objective function. See Figure 9.13.

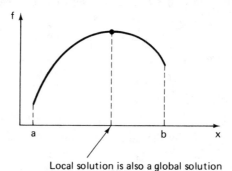

Local solution is also a global solution

Figure 9.13.   Maximizing a concave function.

Lemma 1 tells us which areas of the feasible region to search (or equivalently, which areas of the feasible region may be ignored). Lemma 2 tells us when we may stop our search. If we are maximizing linear functions (which are both concave and convex), we can make use of both lemmas; we need only search extreme points, and we may stop when we have found an extreme point which is a local optima.

9.3.2. Functions of Several Variables

We now present theorems (similar to Lemmas 1 and 2) for more general feasible regions C. The reader should attempt to prove them for himself.

Theorem 1

Let f be a convex function defined over a closed, bounded, convex set C. There exists an extreme point of C at which f assumes its global maximum.

This theorem tells us that to find the maximum value of a convex function over a closed, bounded, convex set, we need only search the extreme points as shown in the examples below.

Example 9

Find x, y to maximize $f(x, y) = x^2 + y^2$ subject to $x \geq 0$, $y \geq 0$, $2x + y \leq 2$. See Figure 9.14. In this example, C is a closed, bounded, convex set, and f is a convex function. We need only search the three extreme points $(0, 0)$, $(1, 0)$, and $(0, 2)$ of C, and of these three, the maximum value is obtained at $(0, 2)$. Hence $(0, 2)$ is the global solution.

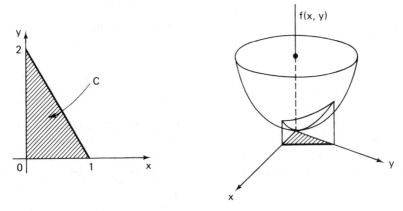

Figure 9.14. An example of maximizing a convex function.

Theorem 2

Let f be a concave function defined over a convex set C. If x is a local solution, then x is a global solution.

This theorem gives us a rule for stopping the search: stop when a local optimum is found. The next example illustrates this theorem.

Example 10

Maximize $f(x, y) = -x^2 - y^2$ (or equivalently, minimize $x^2 + y^2$) subject to

$$x + y \geq 1$$
$$0 \leq x \leq 1$$
$$0 \leq y \leq 1$$

The point $x = y = \frac{1}{2}$ is a local solution and is therefore a global solution. See Figure 9.15.

If the objective function were linear, we could use both Theorems 1 and 2 in devising a search strategy since linear functions are both concave and convex. In this

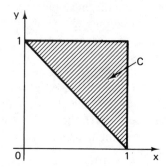

Figure 9.15. The feasible region for Example 10.

case, we need only search extreme points, and we can stop searching as soon as we find an extreme point which is a local solution.

9.3.3. Categories of Mathematical Programming

In linear programming, we wish to find the solution $x = (x_1, \ldots, x_n)$ which maximizes a linear objective function $f(x) = c_1 x_1 + \ldots + c_n x_n$, where the c_i are constants, $i = 1, \ldots, n$. Furthermore, x belongs to the set of feasible solutions C if it satisfies a set of constraints which are linear equalities or inequalities, for instance,

$$a_{11} x_1 + \ldots + a_{1n} x_n \leq b_1$$

or

$$a_{21} x_1 + \ldots + a_{2n} x_n \geq b_2$$

or

$$a_{31} x_1 + \ldots + a_{3n} x_n = b_3$$

where the a_{ij} and b_i are constants. The set C of feasible solutions in linear programs is a convex polyhedron; i.e., they have boundaries which are formed by linear hyperplanes. Figure 9.16 shows examples of sets that are convex polyhedra, and Figure 9.17 has

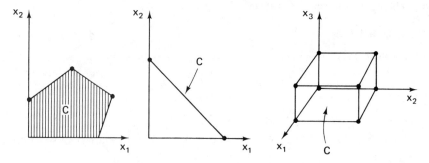

Figure 9.16. Convex polyhedra: extreme points marked by dots.

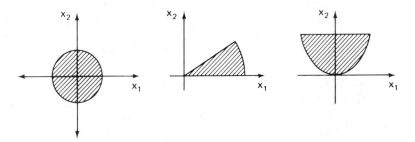

Figure 9.17. Convex sets which are not polyhedra.

examples of sets that are convex but are not convex polyhedra. The examples of Figure 9.16 correspond to the sets of inequalities

(a) $-2 \leq x_2 - x_1 \leq 1, \quad x_1 + x_2 \leq 3, \quad x_1 \geq 0_1, \quad x_2 \geq 0$

(b) $x_1 + x_2 = 2, \quad x_1 \geq 0, \quad x_2 \geq 0$

(c) $0 \leq x_1 \leq 1, \quad 0 \leq x_2 \leq 1, \quad 0 \leq x_3 \leq 1$

The constraints corresponding to the sets in Figure 9.17 are

(a) $x_1^2 + x_2^2 \leq 1$

(b) $x_1^2 + x_2^2 \leq 1, \quad x_1 \geq x_2 \geq 0$

(c) $1 \geq x_2 \geq x_1^2$

An important consequence of C being a convex polyhedron is that C has only a finite number of extreme points. Thus if we were maximizing a convex function over a convex polyhedron, we would have a search strategy that is guaranteed to find an optimal solution in finite time: Inspect all extreme points, and pick the best one. (We are making an implicit assumption that all extreme points can be characterized and listed in finite time.) Furthermore, in a linear program, we rarely need to search all the extreme points because we usually find an extreme point which is a local solution (and hence is also a global solution, since the objective function is linear and, therefore, concave as well) before all extreme points are inspected. If the objective function is convex and *nonlinear*, then even if the very first extreme point picked is the global solution, we would not *know* that it was a global solution (though we may know that it is a local solution) until we had inspected all the other extreme points.

If the set C is not a convex polyhedron or if the objective function is nonlinear, we have a *nonlinear* programming problem. If the objective function is a concave quadratic function and C is a convex polyhedron, relatively simple algorithms to find global solutions exist, and the problem is referred to as a *quadratic programming problem*. If the problem is

$$\max f(x)$$

$$\text{subject to (s.t.) } g_i(x) \leq d_i, \qquad i = 1, \ldots, m$$

$$x \geq 0$$

where $f(x)$ and $g_i(x)$ are posynomials (i.e., they are sums of terms of the form $a_i\pi x_i^{b_i}$), where the a_i are nonnegative, then the problem is a *geometric programming problem*. Special techniques to solve this problem exist. In a *fractional programming* problem, the objective function is the ratio of two polynomials. If the set of feasible solutions C is such that for any $x = (x_1, \ldots, x_n)$ in C all the x_i are restricted to take on integer values, we have an *integer programming problem* (see Figure 9.18); if all the x_i are restricted to take on the values 0 or 1, we have a *0-1 integer programming problem*; if some of the x_i can take on continuous values while others are restricted to take on integer values, we have a *mixed integer programming problem*.

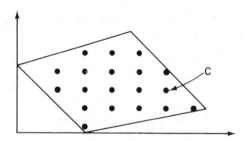

Figure 9.18. The dots correspond to C, the set of feasible solutions in an integer program.

Integer and mixed integer programming problems are generally very difficult. Since the set of feasible solutions C is not a convex set, we cannot use Theorems 1 or 2.

If we are minimizing a convex function (or maximizing a concave function) over a convex set, we have a *convex programming problem*, in which case we may use Theorem 2, which states that a local solution is a global solution. *Hill-climbing* or *ascent* techniques may be used to lead us arbitrarily close to a local solution. The basic idea behind ascent methods is as follows: Let x_0 be any feasible solution; if x_0 is a local solution, stop; otherwise, there is some direction (vector) y such that $f(x_0 + \epsilon y) > f(x_0)$, for some $\epsilon > 0$. Let

$$x_1 = x_0 + ty$$

where t is a scalar; $t > 0$ is the *step size*, which is determined in an appropriate way such that x_1 is also in C. Now check to see if x_1 is a local solution or else ascent up the surface $f(x)$ to a better solution x_2 and so on. There are many aspects of the algorithm which have not been discussed here. For instance, how should the step size t be chosen? These and other questions are discussed in many operations research texts (see the Appendix).

9.4. LINEAR PROGRAMMING

We now turn our attention to linear programs (LPs). Our objective is to get an intuitive grasp of the *simplex algorithm*, which is a method for solving LPs. In what follows, if x is an n-dimensional vector, the statement $x = 0$ implies that $x_i = 0$ for all *i*. In other words, the 0 in $x = 0$ stands for an n-dimensional vector, all of whose elements are zero. The obvious meaning is implied by $x \geq 0$.

LPs can be written in (or transformed, as we show later, by means of artificial variables, into) the form

$$\text{maximize } z = cx$$

$$\text{subject to } Ax \leq b \tag{1}$$

$$x \geq 0$$

where c and x are n-dimensional vectors, cx is the dot or scalar product, A is an $m \times n$ matrix, and b is an m-element vector.

The problem may be cast in the above form with b nonnegative. However, for the purposes of discussion, we shall assume that if any $b_i = 0$, $i = 1, \ldots, m$, then the problem is perturbed slightly, so that $b_i > 0$. If $b_i = 0$ in the original problem, we shall set b_i to an arbitrarily small positive constant ϵ_i. It must be emphasized that the simplex algorithm does not require the problem to be perturbed in this fashion; we choose to do it for ease of exposition. Consider the following simple, contrived example.

Example 11

An electronics company has two kinds of resources (say, integrated circuits). Let us refer to the two types of resources as type A and type B. The company can manufacture three types of instruments: types 1, 2, and 3. Type 1 instruments are fabricated with 2 units of type A resource and 1 unit of type B resource, whereas type 2 instruments require 1 unit of type A and 2 units of type B, and type 3 instruments need only 1 unit of type A and 3 units of type B. The company has 1000 units of resource A and 1000 units of resource B on hand. The company does not wish to buy additional resources or to sell any of its current resources. A profit of \$30 is made on each type 1 and on each type 2 instrument made, and the profit is \$35 on each type 3 instrument. How many instruments of each type should be made to maximize profit?

Let x_i be the number of instruments of type i that are manufactured. Then, we wish to maximize

$$z = 30x_1 + 30x_2 + 35x_3$$

The constraint on resource type A is

$$2x_1 + 1x_2 + 1x_3 \leq 1000$$

and on type B is

$$1x_1 + 2x_2 + 3x_3 \leq 1000$$

We have the added constraint that we cannot manufacture negative amounts of these items, and hence $x_i \geq 0$, $i = 1, 2, 3$. This problem has the standard form (1) with $x = (x_1 \quad x_2 \quad x_3)$, $C = (30 \quad 30 \quad 35)$,

$$A = \begin{pmatrix} 2 & 1 & 1 \\ 1 & 2 & 3 \end{pmatrix}$$

and $b = (1000 \quad 1000)$. If we added the constraint "x_i must be integer" (since fractional instruments cannot be manufactured), we would have an integer programming problem. It is convenient to define a *slack vector* $s = (s_1, \ldots, s_m)$, where s_i is the amount of unused resource of type i. Thus

$$s = b - Ax$$

The linear program (1) can be written as

$$\text{maximize } cx$$

$$\text{subject to } Ax + Is = b \tag{2}$$

$$x \geq 0, s \geq 0$$

where I is the identity matrix.

Let C be the set of all (x, s) which satisfy (2). Let P be the solution $x = 0$, $s = b$. Since this solution is feasible, P is in C.

Theorem 3

P is an extreme point of C.

Proof: We shall use a proof by contradiction. Assume that P is not an extreme point of C. Then there exist two points Q and R distinct from P in C such that P lies on the line segment joining Q and R. Let Q be the point $x_i = q_i$ for all i, $s = b - Aq$, and let R be the point $x_i = r_i$ for all i, $s = b - Ar$, where q and r are n-dimensional vectors. Since Q and R are in C, $q \geq 0$ and $r \geq 0$. Since P lies on the line segment joining Q and R, there is a scalar d, $0 \leq d \leq 1$, such that

$$dq_i + (1 - d)r_i = 0 \qquad \text{for all } i \tag{3}$$

Since P is distinct from Q, $d \neq 1$, and since P is distinct from R, $d \neq 0$, and hence both d and $1 - d$ are strictly positive.

Both terms on the left-hand side of (3) are nonnegative; hence they must both be identically zero. Since d and $1 - d$ are nonzero,

$$q_i = r_i = 0 \qquad \text{for all } i$$

and hence P is identical to Q and R, in contradiction to our initial assumption.

Theorem 4

Recollect that $b_i > 0$, $i = 1, \ldots, m$, in the LP formulation (since the problem was perturbed if $b_i = 0$ for any i). In this case $x = 0$, $s = b$ is a global solution if and only if $c \leq 0$.

Proof: If $c \leq 0$, then since $x \geq 0$ we have $cx \leq 0$ for all x, and hence $cx = 0$ is the maximum value. Hence $x = 0$, $s = b$ is a global solution.

Consider the case where $c_j > 0$. Consider two subcases. Either

(a) $A_{ij} \leq 0$ for all i or

(b)   There exists an i for which $A_{ij} > 0$.

In case (a), the solution $z = c_j x_j$, $x_i = 0$ for $i \neq j$, $s_i = b_i - A_{ij}x_j$ for all i is feasible for any $x_j \geq 0$; hence x_j and z can be made arbitrarily large, which implies that $x = 0$, $z = 0$ is not a global solution. Furthermore, the solution is unbounded.

In case (b), define

$$r = \text{maximum } \{x_j \mid s_i = b_i - A_{ij}x_j \geq 0 \text{ for all } i\}$$

Hence, $r = $ minimum over all positive A_{ij} of

$$\frac{b_i}{A_{ij}}$$

Since $b_i > 0$ for all i, it follows that $r > 0$. The solution $z = c_j x_j$, $x_i = 0$ for $i \neq j$, $x_j = r$, $s_i = b_{ij} - A_{ij}x_j$ is nonnegative and hence feasible. This solution has a strictly positive objective function value $z = c_j r$, and hence $z = 0$, $x = 0$, $s = b$ cannot be optimal.

This theorem suggests an algorithm for linear programs. Consider the problem formulated as follows: F: maximize $z = d + cx$ subject to $Ax \leq b$, $x \geq 0$, where d is an arbitrary scalar constant. (We can ignore d in the optimization process since it is a constant; however, it is convenient to include d in the formulation.) Let the feasible solution $z = d$, $x = 0$, $s = b$ (where s is the slack vector) be called the *basic solution corresponding to formulation F*; this basic solution corresponds to an extreme point P of the set of feasible solutions C. If $c \leq 0$ in the formulation F, the basic solution corresponding to F is optimal, and P is a global solution. If there exists some $c_j > 0$, then P is not a global solution. Now consider two cases.

Case 1

$A_{ij} \leq 0$ for all i in which case the optimum solution is arbitrarily large.

Case 2

There exists some i for which $A_{ij} > 0$. In this case we transform the given problem into an equivalent one:

F': maximize $z = d' + c'x'$, subject to $A'x' \leq b'$, $x' \geq 0$ where $d' > d$. One of the slack variables in F becomes nonslack in F', and one of the nonslack variables in F becomes slack in F'; the set of feasible solutions is unchanged. The basic solution corresponding to F' is $z = d'$, $x' = 0$, $s' = b'$, and it occurs at some extreme point P'; the value of the objective function is greater at P' than at P since $d' > d$. The algorithm now proceeds to the next step: We inspect extreme point P' (i.e., the basic solution corresponding to F'); it is either a global solution or there exists a solution which is arbitrarily large or we obtain a new formulation F'' and a basic solution corresponding to this new formulation at a better extreme point P'', and so on. This algorithm must terminate since there are only a finite number of extreme points, as we show later.

Now we shall focus attention on the transformation of formulation F to F' that is carried out if there exists a $c_j > 0$ and some i such that $A_{ij} > 0$. Pick any j such that $c_j > 0$. Then the larger we make x_j, the larger the value of the objective function $z = d + c_j x_j$; however, we cannot violate the constraints, and hence we must have

$$s_i = b_i - A_{ij} x_j \geq 0$$

Let r be the largest value of x_j which does not violate any constraint, i.e., $r = \max \{x_j \mid s_i = b_i - A_{ij} x_j \geq 0, i = 1, \ldots, m\}$. If $A_{ij} \leq 0$, x_j can be made arbitrarily large without violating the constraint $s_i = b_i - A_{ij} x_j \geq 0$, and if $A_{ij} > 0$, we must have $x_j \leq b_i / A_{ij}$. Hence

$$r = \text{minimum} \left\{ \frac{b_i}{A_{ij}} \, \middle| \, A_{ij} > 0 \right\}$$

Let $r = b_k / A_{kj}$. When we set x_j to r the kth slack s_k is reduced to zero. In the new formulation F' we shall make s_k a nonslack variable and x_j a slack variable. Formulation F is

$$\text{maximize } z = d + c_1 x_1 + \ldots + c_n x_n$$

$$\text{subject to} \qquad A_{11} x_1 + \ldots + A_{1n} x_n + s_1 = b_1$$

$$\vdots \qquad \qquad \vdots$$

$$A_{n1} x_1 + \ldots + A_{mn} x_n + s_m = b_m$$

$$x_1, \ldots, x_n \geq 0$$

Add the kth row multiplied by $-A_{ij}/A_{kj}$ to the ith row, $i \neq k$; add the kth row multiplied by $-c_j/A_{kj}$ to the objective function, and multiply the kth row by $1/A_{kj}$ to get

$$\text{maximize } z = d' + c'x'$$

$$\text{subject to } A'x' + Is' = b'$$

$$x' \geq 0, s' \geq 0$$

where $x' = (x_1, \ldots, x_{j-1}, s_k, x_{j+1}, \ldots, x_n)$ and $s' = (s_1, \ldots, s_{k-1}, x_j, s_{k+1}, \ldots, s_m)$. This process is a *pivot* operation on A_{kj}.

Problem

Determine what d', c', A', and b' are.

Example 12

Consider the electronics manufacturing company problem (Example 11). It is convenient to use variables x_4 and x_5 to represent the slacks s_1 and s_2; it is also convenient to represent the problem in tableau form; see Figure 9.19.

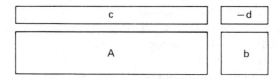

Figure 9.19. The tableau.

The sequence of problem transformations is shown in Figures 9.20 through 9.23. These figures are self-explanatory.

Linear programming codes do not carry out precisely the same steps as in the above example, though the algorithm is essentially the same: Go from extreme point to better extreme point until a global solution is found. Some details have been left out

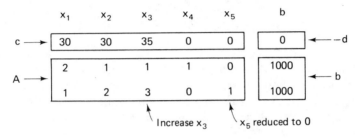

Figure 9.20. Given tableau.

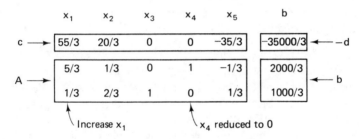

Figure 9.21. Tableau after first step.

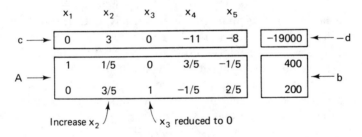

Figure 9.22. Tableau after second step.

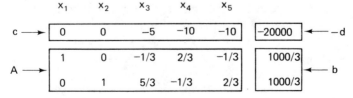

Figure 9.23. The tableau after the third step is optimal.

of this discussion. The interested reader is urged to consult mathematical programming texts.

Converting Problems into the Standard Format

Constraints in linear programs occur in one of three forms:

$$A_{i1}x_1 + \ldots + A_{in}x_n \leq b_i \qquad \text{Case 1}$$
$$A_{i1}x_1 + \ldots + A_{in}x_n = b_i \qquad \text{Case 2}$$
$$A_{i1}x_1 + \ldots + A_{in}x_n \geq b_i \qquad \text{Case 3}$$

where b_i is nonnegative. (If b_i is negative, multiplying the ith constraint by -1 will convert the constraint into one of the above three cases.)

In Case 1, the constraint is already in standard form; however, note that adding a slack variable y_i converts a Case 1 constraint into a Case 2 constraint since the inequality becomes

$$A_{i1}x_1 + \ldots + A_{in}x_n + y_i = b_i, \qquad \text{where } y_i \geq 0$$

Similarly, a Case 3 constraint can be converted into a Case 2 constraint by adding a *surplus* variable y_i to obtain

$$A_{i1}x_1 + \ldots + A_{in}x_n - y_i = b_i, \qquad \text{where } y_i \geq 0$$

We hereafter restrict attention to Case 2 constraints.

Consider the problem P0: max $z = cx$ s.t. $Ax = b$, $x \geq 0$. (We have used the abbreviation "s.t." for "subject to.") This problem is solved in two phases. In the first phase we add a vector of artificial variables $w = w_1, \ldots, w_m$ and change the objective function to get the following: min $z' = \sum_{i=1}^{m} w_i$ s.t. $Ax + w = b$, $x \geq 0$, $w \geq 0$. Substituting for the w_i in the objective function, we get problem P1: min $z' = d + c'x$ s.t. $Ax + w = b$, $x \geq 0$, $w \geq 0$, where $d = \sum_{i=1}^{m} b_i$ and $c'_j = -\sum_{k=1}^{m} A_{jk}$. Problem P1 has the standard form. This minimization problem is equivalent to a maximization problem with the same constraints and the negative of the objective function, i.e., max $z'' = -d' - c'x$. The optimal solution to P1 is found in phase 1. The optimal value of the objective function z' can either be 0 in which case $w_1 = \ldots = w_m = 0$ or be positive. (Note that z' could not be negative since it is a sum of nonnegative variables w_i.) If the original problem, P0, had a feasible solution (i.e., if there exists a nonnegative x, say $x = x'$, such that $Ax' = b$), then $x = x'$, $w = 0$, $z' = 0$ is a solution to P1. Hence if $z' > 0$, there is no solution to P0.

If $z' = 0$, then since $w = 0$ it follows that there is a feasible solution to P0. The tableau at the end of phase 1 will be in the standard format. Phase 2 solves P0 using the standard format obtained at the end of P1 and replacing the objective function used in phase 1 by the original function $z = cx$.

Matrix Operations

The sequence of problem transformations can be described in terms of matrix operations. Generally, the *slack* variables in each tableau are called *basic* variables. Let the vector of basic variables be x_B. The $m \times m$ matrix (where m is the number of constraints) obtained by selecting the columns of the original A matrix (see Figure 9.19) corresponding to the basic variables will be called the *basis*. Let c_B be a vector with m elements, where the elements of c_B are the elements of the original c vector which correspond to the (basic) variables in x_B.

In Figure 9.20 the basic variables are x_4 and x_5. Hence $x_B = (x_4, x_5)$, $c_B = (c_4, c_5) = (0, 0)$, and

$$B = \begin{pmatrix} 1 & 0 \\ 0 & 1 \end{pmatrix}$$

In the next step (Figure 9.21) the basic variables are x_4, x_3. Hence $x_B = (x_4, x_3)$, $c_B = (c_4, c_3) = (0, 35)$, and

$$B = \begin{pmatrix} 1 & 1 \\ 0 & 3 \end{pmatrix}$$

(Note that c_B and B are defined in terms of the given problem, i.e., the original tableau.) In the next step (Figure 9.22), the basic variables are x_1 and x_3. Hence $x_B = (x_1, x_3)$, $c_B = (c_1, c_3) = (30, 35)$, and

$$B = \begin{pmatrix} 2 & 1 \\ 1 & 3 \end{pmatrix}$$

A little algebra shows that we can transform the given problem (the original tableau) into an equivalent problem (any other tableau) with any vector of basic variables by premultiplying the $m + 1$ equations (including the objective function) of Figure 9.19 by the $(m + 1) \times (m + 1)$ matrix

$$H = \begin{pmatrix} 1 & -u \\ 0 & B^{-1} \end{pmatrix}$$

where $u = c_B \cdot B^{-1}$. Thus to transform the problem shown in Figure 9.20 into the equivalent problem shown in Figure 9.21 we premultiply by

$$H = \begin{pmatrix} 1 & 0 & -35/3 \\ 0 & 1 & -1/3 \\ 0 & 0 & 1/3 \end{pmatrix}$$

Similarly, to transform the original problem shown in Figure 9.20 to the equivalent problem shown in Figure 9.22 we premultiply by

$$H = \begin{pmatrix} 1 & -11 & -8 \\ 0 & 3/5 & -1/5 \\ 0 & -1/5 & 2/5 \end{pmatrix}$$

Problem

Determine the linear transformation H for the third step (Figure 9.23).

At each step of the algorithm we need to compute the "new" objective function (i.e., the objective function of the new tableau) to see if there are any positive coefficients; the new objective function vector c' can be obtained from

$$c' = c - u \cdot A$$

This equation is equivalent to premultiplying the original equations (Figure 9.19) by the first row of matrix H. If there are any positive elements in c', we pick x_i to "enter" the basis, to form the basis of the next step where $c'_i = \max_j c'_j$. Let a_i be the ith column of matrix A, and recollect that vector b is the right-hand side in the given problem, i.e., the original tableau (Figure 9.19). Let a'_i and b' be the ith column of the A matrix and the right-hand side, respectively, in the current tableau. To determine which variable in the current basis will be replaced by the incoming, currently nonbasic variable (x_i) we need to compute a'_i and b'. Note that $a'_i = B^{-1}a_i$ and $b' = B^{-1}b$. We see that we do not need to actually transform the problem at each step by premultiplying the entire set of equations by linear transformation H since we do not need the entire tableau; all we need to do is compute $c' = c - u \cdot A$, a'_i, and b'. Thus computational advantage may be gained by storing the original problem (tableau) and the transformation H and computing only c', a'_i, and b' rather than carrying out the pivot operations. Furthermore, the transformation H for any iteration can be relatively quickly computed from the transformation for the previous iteration. Reduction in computation along these lines results in an algorithm called *revised simplex*.

Proof of Convergence of the Simplex Method

Let $x = x'$ be a feasible solution, i.e., $Ax' = b$ and $x' \geq 0$. Let the number of elements of x' which are nonzero be k, where $k = 1, \ldots, n$. Let $x'_{i(1)}, \ldots, x'_{i(k)}$ be the positive elements of x'. Recollect that a_i is the ith column of the (original) matrix A; see Figure 9.19. The k vectors $a_{i(1)} \ldots, a_{i(k)}$ are said to be *linearly independent* if the only solution to the set of equations

$$y_1 a_{i(1)} + \ldots + y_k a_{i(k)} = 0$$

where $y_1, \ldots, y_k$ are scalars, is $y_1 = \ldots = y_k = 0$. The feasible solution $x = x'$ is said to be a *basic* feasible solution if $a_{i(1)}, \ldots, a_{i(k)}$ are linearly independent. At every step of the simplex method a basic feasible solution is checked for optimality. If the solution is not optimal, a variable in the current basis is replaced by a currently nonbasic variable to obtain a new basic feasible solution which is checked for optimality, and so on. We shall now show that every basic feasible solution is an extreme point of the space of feasible solutions; furthermore, every extreme point is a basic feasible solution. Thus we show that the simplex method carries out the search strategy we proposed at the outset of this chapter: Go from extreme point to better extreme point until a locally optimum extreme point is obtained. To show that the algorithm will converge in a finite number of steps all we need to show is that there are a finite number of basic feasible solutions (i.e., extreme points).

Lemma 3

(This lemma is similar to Theorem 3.) Every basic feasible solution is an extreme point of the space of feasible solutions C.

Proof: The proof is very similar to that of Theorem 3 and is left as a problem for the reader. (Hint: Read Lemma 5, which is independent of this lemma, before you attempt the proof.)

Lemma 4

Every extreme point is a basic feasible solution.

Proof: We shall prove this lemma by contradiction. Assume that there exists an extreme point P which is not a basic feasible solution. Let P correspond to feasible solution $x = x'$. Let k be the number of elements of x' which are nonzero. Assume without loss of generality that $x'_1, \ldots, x'_k$ are nonzero and that the remaining $n - k$ elements of x' are zero. Since x' is not a basic solution, it follows that there exists scalars $y_1, \ldots, y_k$, some of which are nonzero, such that

$$y_1 a_1 + \ldots + y_k a_k = 0$$

Assume without loss of generality that $y_1 \neq 0$. Then dividing by y_1, we get

$$a_1 = w_2 a_2 + \ldots + w_k a_k$$

where $w_j = -y_j/y_1, j = 2, \ldots, k$. Now

$$
\begin{aligned}
x'_1 a_1 + x'_2 a_2 + \ldots + x'_k a_k &= (x'_1 - \epsilon)a_1 + \epsilon a_1 + x'_2 a_2 + \ldots + x'_k a_k \\
&= (x'_1 - \epsilon)a_1 + (x'_2 + \epsilon w_2)a_2 + \ldots \\
&\quad + (x'_k + \epsilon w_k)a_k \\
&= b
\end{aligned}
$$

For ϵ positive and sufficiently small, the solution $x = u$ where $u_1 = x'_1 - \epsilon$, $u_2 = x'_2 + \epsilon w_2, \ldots, u_k = x'_k + \epsilon w_k$, and $u_{k+1} = \ldots = u_n = 0$ is a feasible solution. Similarly, the solution $x = v$ where $v_1 = x'_1 + \delta$, $v_2 = x'_2 - \delta w_2$, $\ldots, v_k = x'_k - \delta w_k$ and $v_{k+1} = \ldots = v_n = 0$ is feasible for δ positive and sufficiently small. Hence we have two feasible solutions $x = u$ and $x = v$ distinct from the assumed extreme point $x = x'$ such that

$$pu + (1 - p)v = x'$$

where $p = \delta/(\delta + \epsilon)$. In other words, the assumed extreme point P of C lies on the line segment joining two points in C distinct from P, which is a contradiction.

Lemma 5

For a given problem, any basic feasible solution may be uniquely determined from the identity of its nonzero variables.

Proof: Assume that $x = u$ and $x = v$ are distinct basic feasible solutions in both of which variables $x_{i(1)}, \ldots, x_{i(k)}$ take on nonzero values and all other variables are set to zero; we shall show that this assumption leads to a contradiction.

$$u_{i(1)} a_{i(1)} + \ldots + u_{i(k)} a_{i(k)} = b$$

$$v_{i(1)} a_{i(1)} + \ldots + v_{i(k)} a_{i(k)} = b$$

Subtracting one equation from the other,

$$(u_{i(1)} - v_{i(1)})a_{i(1)} + \ldots + (u_{i(k)} - v_{i(k)})a_{i(k)} = 0$$

Since $u \neq v$, it follows that the vectors $a_{i(1)}, \ldots, a_{i(k)}$ are not linearly independent, which contradicts the assumption that $x = u$ and $x = v$ are basic feasible solutions.

Lemma 6

The set of feasible solutions C has a finite number of extreme points.

Proof: It follows from Lemma 5 that it is possible to enumerate all basic feasible solutions (extreme points) by enumerating corresponding subsets of variables which can take on positive values. The number of subsets of n variables is finite and provides an upper bound on the number of basic feasible solutions.

Lemma 7

The simplex algorithm terminates in a finite number of steps.

Proof: We have assumed that all entries in the right-hand sides in all tableaux are strictly positive; we argued that if any entry were zero the problem would be perturbed to make that entry positive but arbitrarily small (more about perturbation later). Since every element of the right-hand side is strictly positive, it follows that at each iteration step the current basic feasible solution is replaced by a *different* basic feasible solution and that the objective function increases by a *positive* amount. Since the objective increases by a positive amount at each step, it follows that a basic feasible solution obtained at an iteration will never be repeated in subsequent iterations. From earlier theorems there must exist an extreme point (i.e., basic feasible solution) which is optimum. Since there are only a finite number of basic feasible solutions, the algorithm must discover the optimum basic feasible solution in a finite number of iterations.

Problem Perturbation

We have assumed in our proofs that the right-hand sides of the constraint equations (i.e., the b vectors in all tableaux) have no zero elements. In other words, given any basis B, we assumed that $B^{-1}b$, where b is the right-hand side in the original problem, has entirely nonzero entries or that the problem could be perturbed so that all entries were nonzero. We shall perturb the problem in the following way: For ϵ positive but arbitrarily small, replace b by $b + \epsilon^1 a_1 + \ldots + \epsilon^n a_n$, where a_i is the ith column of the original A matrix. Thus given any basis B, the right-hand side in the corresponding tableau may be perturbed to $b' + \epsilon^1 a_1' + \ldots + \epsilon^n a_n'$, where $b' = B^{-1}b$ and $a_i' = B^{-1}a_i$. The jth element of the perturbed right-hand side can be zero only if the jth elements of all vectors a_i', $i = 1, \ldots, n$, are all zero; but this is impossible because one of the a_i' must be the unit vector with a one (1) in the jth place corresponding to the jth vector in the basis. Hence this perturbation ensures that every element in the right-hand side of every tableau is nonzero.

Problem

Show that carrying out this perturbation is equivalent to doing the following: Replace b_j, the jth (scalar) element of b, by the $n + 1$ element vector $(b_j, A_{j1}, \ldots, A_{jn})$, and replace the scalar $d = 0$ in the initial tableau (see Figure

9.19) by the $n + 1$ element vector $d = (0, 0, \ldots, 0)$. Define a k element vector $(u_1, \ldots, u_k)$ to be lexicographically greater than a k element vector $(v_1, \ldots, v_k)$ if and only if there exists some j such that $u_j > v_j$ and $u_i = v_i$ for all $i < j$. Carry out the simplex method as usual except that comparisions between elements of the right-hand side are made lexicographically.

Problem

Show that with the above scheme, at every iteration step of the simplex method the d "vector" increases lexicographically. This will imply that a basic feasible solution will never be repeated in the algorithm.

Sensitivity Analysis

It is interesting to study the behavior of the maximum value of the objective function as a function of the amount of resources available. Let $z(b)$ be a function which maps an m-dimensional vector into reals, where

$$z(b) = \max cx \text{ subject to } Ax = b, x \geq 0$$

We shall now study the function $z(b)$.

Theorem 5

$z(b)$ is a concave function.

Proof: Let b^i, $i = 1, 2$, be two values of the right-hand side b, corresponding to which the global solutions are $x = u^i$, $i = 1, 2$. We need to show that

$$z(pb^1 + (1 - p)b^2) \geq pz(b^1) + (1 - p)z(b^2) \tag{4}$$

for any scalar p, where $0 \leq p \leq 1$. By direct substitution we see that $x = pu^1 + (1 - p)u^2$ is a feasible solution to the problem

$$\max cx \text{ subject to } Ax = pb^1 + (1 - p)b^2, x \geq 0, \text{ where } 0 \leq p \leq 1$$

Hence the maximum value for the objective function to this problem, $z(pb^1 + (1 - p)b^2)$, must be at least as large as $c(pu^1 + (1 - p)u^2)$. Hence Eq. (4) follows.

Suppose we force a variable, say x_i, to take on some definite value y and let the corresponding maximum value of the objective function be $z(y)$. How does $z(y)$ vary with y? In other words, $z(y)$ is defined by $z(y) = \max cx$ subject to $Ax = b$, $x_i = y, x \geq 0$. From Theorem 5, $z(y)$ is concave. Hence the function may have a shape such as that shown in Figure 9.24. Let y^* be the optimal value of x_i in the problem

$$\max cx \text{ s.t. } Ax = b, x \geq 0$$

Then $z(y^*) = \max_y z(y)$. Theorem 6 follows from this argument.

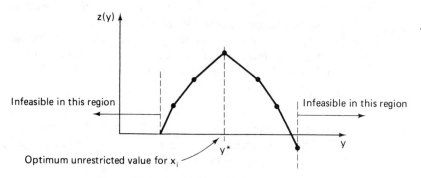

Figure 9.24. Sensitivity with respect to one variable.

Theorem 6

The optimal solution to the problem

P1:   max cx s.t. $Ax = b$, $x_i = y'$, $x \geq 0$

is an optimal solution to the problem

P2:   max cx s.t. $Ax = b$, $x_i \leq y'$, $x \geq 0$ for any $y' \leq y^*$

Similarly, the optimal solution to the problem

P3:   max cx s.t. $Ax = b$, $x_i = y'$, $x \geq 0$

is an optimal solution to the problem

P4:   max cx s.t. $Ax = b$, $x_i \geq y'$, $x \geq 0$ for any $y' \geq y^*$

Proof: Since $z(y)$ is concave, for any $y \leq y' \leq y^*$, $z(y) \leq z(y') \leq z(y^*)$. Thus

$$z(y') = \max_y \{z(y)\,|\,y \leq y'\}$$

Hence, there exists an optimal solution to P2 with $x_i = y'$, and so there is an optimal solution to P1 which is also optimal in P2. The proof of the second part of the theorem is similar.

It is generally easier to solve P1 than P2: Let P2 have n variables and $m + 1$ constraints (including the constraint $x_i \leq y'$). Since x is not a variable in P1 and the constraint $x = y'$ need not be included explicitly (since x can be replaced everywhere by the constant y'), we have $n - 1$ variables and m constraints.

These results lead to a branch and bound algorithm [Doig and Land (1960)] for integer or mixed integer programming; this is discussed next.

9.5. A BRANCH AND BOUND ALGORITHM

The algorithm proceeds by creating increasingly finer partitions of the set of all feasible solutions. Upper bounds on the maximum value of the objective function within each subset of the current partition are computed. We inspect all subsets in the current partition and next search that subset with the largest upper bound; the process of searching this subset will either yield an optimum solution (which is a feasible solution with an objective function value greater than or equal to the upper bounds of all subsets in the partition) or we shall partition this subset into smaller subsets and compute upper bounds for the smaller subsets. Consider the problem

$$\text{P:} \quad \underline{z} = \max z = cx \text{ subject to } Ax = b, x \geq 0, x \text{ integer}$$

$\underline{z}$ is the opimum value of the objective function to this problem. Let C be the set of feasible solutions to this problem; i.e.,

$$C = \{x \mid Ax = b, x \geq 0, x \text{ integer}\}$$

Let $R(C)$ be the set of solutions obtained by relaxing the requirement that x be integer in C; i.e.,

$$R(C) = \{x \mid Ax = b, x \geq 0\}$$

The relation between C and $R(C)$ is shown in Figure 9.25.

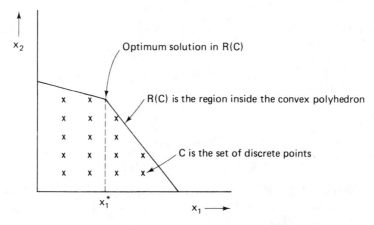

Figure 9.25. Relationship between C and $R(C)$.

Consider the linear programming problem P′:

$$\mathbf{u} = \max u = cx \text{ subject to } x \in R(C)$$

Since $C \subseteq R(C)$, $\underline{z} \leq \mathbf{u}$. Let $\mathbf{x}$ be the optimal solution to P′; then $\mathbf{u} = c\mathbf{x}$. If $\mathbf{x}$ is integer, it lies in C; hence $\underline{z} = \mathbf{u}$, and $\mathbf{x}$ is the optimal solution to P.

Suppose $\mathbf{x}_i$ is not an integer. Let y_i be the largest integer less than or equal to $\mathbf{x}_i$. Let E be the subset of C in which $x_i \leq y_i$, and let F be the subset in which $x_i \geq y_i + 1$. Since x_i must be integer for all elements in C, it follows that it is impossible for x_i to lie in the range $y_i < x_i < y_i + 1$ for any member of C. Hence E and F form a partition of C where

$$E = \{x \mid Ax = b, x_i \leq y_i, x \geq 0, x \text{ integer}\}$$
$$F = \{x \mid Ax = b, x_i \geq y_i + 1, x \geq 0, x \text{ integer}\}$$

Let $R(E)$ be the set of x obtained by removing the requirement that x be integer in the

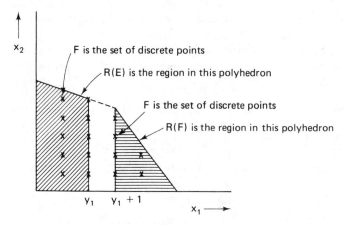

Figure 9.26. Relationship between E, $R(E)$, F and $R(F)$.

definition for E. Let $R(F)$ be defined similarly. Then $R(E) \cup R(F) \neq R(C)$. (see Figure 9.26).

Let

$$v' = \max \{cx \,|\, x \in E\}$$

and

$$\mathbf{v} = \max \{cx \,|\, x \in R(E)\}$$

Similarly, let

$$w' = \max \{cx \,|\, x \in F\}$$

and

$$\mathbf{w} = \max \{cx \,|\, x \in R(F)\}$$

$\mathbf{v}$ and $\mathbf{w}$ are obtained by solving LPs. Theorem 6 is used in simplifying these LPs. To compute $\mathbf{v}$, set $x_i = y_i$, thus yielding a problem with $n - 1$ variables if the original problem had n. Similarly, to compute $\mathbf{w}$, set $x_i = y_i + 1$. Since $E \subseteq R(E)$, $v' \leq \mathbf{v}$, and hence $\mathbf{v}$ is an upper bound on the value of the objective function for any solution in E; similarly, $\mathbf{w}$ is an upper bound for F.

At the end of the initialization phase either the optimum solution is obtained or the set of all solutions C is partitioned into two subsets E and F with associated upper bounds $\mathbf{v}$ and $\mathbf{w}$, respectively, as shown in Figure 9.27. Note that C is partitioned by restricting one variable, say x_i; in E, $x_i \leq y_i$, and in F, $x_i \geq y_i + 1$.

Iteration Step. Let the current partition of C be $C^1, \ldots, C^k$ with associated upper bounds $z^1, \ldots, z^k$, respectively. The upper bounds are computed by solving the LPs Q^j: $z^j = \max \{cx \,|\, x \in R(c^j)\}$, $j = 1, \ldots, k$. Assume without loss of generality that $z^k \geq z^j$, $j = 1, \ldots, k$. We next search C^k, the subset with the largest upper bound, for the optimal solution. At the end of this step, we either would have found an optimal solution or C^k is partitioned into three subsets S, T, and U (some of which may be empty); upper bounds are computed for each of these subsets, and with this finer partition of C (i.e., $C^1, \ldots, C^{k-1}, S, T, U$) we start the next iteration.

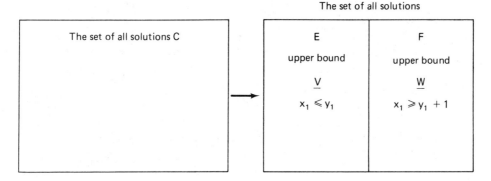

The set of all solutions

The set of all solutions C	E upper bound $\underline{V}$ $x_1 \leqslant y_1$	F upper bound $\underline{W}$ $x_1 \geqslant y_1 + 1$

Figure 9.27. The first partition.

For any solution x in C, there is some subset C^j that contains x and thus $z^j \geq cx$. $z^k \geq z^j$ by assumption, and hence

$$z^k \geq cx \qquad \text{for all } x \text{ in } C \tag{5}$$

Let x^k be an optimal solution to the problem Q^k. Then

$$z^k = cx^k \tag{6}$$

If x^k is integer, then it is in C, and from (5) and (6), x^k is the optimal solution to the given integer programming problem.

Consider the case where x^k is not integer. Any subset C^j of C inherits all the constraints of C and in addition has constraints on certain variables. These additional constraints are of the following form: A certain number (possibly zero) of variables will be set to constant values, while one and only one variable will have either an upper bound or a lower bound placed upon it. To keep the notation simple, assume that in problem Q^k variables $x_1, \ldots, x_{r-1}$ are fixed at constant values and x_r has a bound placed on it; first consider the case of an upper bound. Here Q^k is a linear program of the form

$$Q^k: \quad \max cx \text{ s.t. } Ax = b, \, x_1 = L_1, \ldots,$$
$$x_{r-1} = L_{r-1}, \, x_r \leq L_r, \text{ and } x \geq 0,$$
$$\text{where } L_1, \ldots, L_r \text{ are integers}$$

Let x_r^* be the optimum value of x_r in the problem obtained by removing the bound on x_r in Q^k; in other words, x_r^* is the optimum value of x_r in

$$\max cx \text{ subject to } Ax = b, \, x_1 = L_1, \ldots, x_{r-1} = L_{r-1}, \, x \geq 0$$

L_r is chosen so that $L_r \leq x_r^*$. Hence, by Theorem 6, the optimum value of x_r in Q^k is $x_r = L_r$. Note that Q^k has $n - r$ variables whereas the original problem has n variables and that the number of explicit constraints in Q^i that need to be considered is no more than in the original problem.

If x^k is the optimal value of x in Q^k, we have $x_1^k = L_1, \ldots, x_r^k = L_r$. If x^k is not integer, there must be some x_i^k with a fractional component. Assume without loss of generality that x^k_{r+1} has a fractional component. Let y be the largest integer not exceeding x^k_{r+1}. C^k is partitioned into three subsets S, T, and U (see Figure 9.28). All these subsets inherit all the constraints of C^k. In particular, $x_r \leq L_r$ for all three subsets. In addition, the subsets have the following constraints:

$$\text{in } S, \quad x_r \leq L_r - 1$$
$$\text{in } T, \quad x_r = L_r \text{ and } x_{r+1} \leq y$$
$$\text{in } U, \quad x_r = L_r \text{ and } x_{r+1} \geq y + 1$$

Upper bounds for S, T, and U are computed in the usual way. We now have a finer partition $(C^1, \ldots, C^{k-1}, S, T, U)$ with associated upper bounds to start the next iteration.

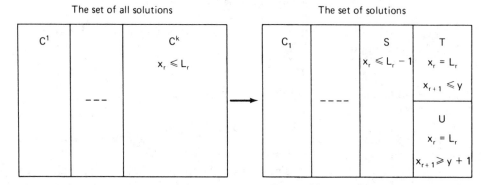

Figure 9.28 Partitioning subset C^k.

Now consider the case where x_r has a lower bound. In this case Q^k is an LP with the form

$$\max cx \text{ s.t. } Ax = b, x_1 = L_1, \ldots, x_{r-1} = L_{r-1}, x_r \geq L_r, \text{ and } x \geq 0$$

Proceeding as in the case where x_r had a lower bound, we either obtain an optimal solution or partition C^k into S, T, and U, where S, T, and U inherit all the constraints of C^k and in addition have the following constraints:

$$\text{in } S, \quad x_r \geq L_r + 1$$
$$\text{in } T, \quad x_r = L_r \text{ and } x_{r+1} \leq y$$
$$\text{in } U, \quad x_r = L_r \text{ and } x_{r+1} \geq y + 1$$

Compute upper bounds for S, T, and U, and proceed to the next iteration with a finer partition.

The process of obtaining increasingly finer partitions terminates, in the worst case, when every subset in the partition contains at most one element; in this case, the branch and bound algorithm is slower than exhaustive enumeration. In practice, there are many problems for which the branch and bound algorithm takes significantly less time than exhaustive enumeration.

Example 13

Consider the electronics manufacturing company problem (Example 11). However, now restrict all variables to be integer. This restriction requires that all
instruments be completely (rather than partially) built. Let C be the set of feasible
solutions. The optimal solution to the LP max $z = cx$ s.t. x in $R(C)$ is

$$z = 20{,}000, \qquad x_1 = 333\tfrac{1}{3}, \qquad x_2 = 333\tfrac{1}{3}, \qquad x_3 = x_4 = x_5 = 0$$

Thus, 20,000 is an upper bound on the objective function of any feasible solution.
We represent this by Figure 9.29. Since x_1 is not integer in the above problem, we
partition C into subsets C_1 and C_2, where $x_1 \leq 333$ in C_1 and $x_1 \geq 334$ in C_2.
We obtain upper bounds for C_1 and C_2 by solving LPs in which x is restricted to
be in $R(C_1)$ and $R(C_2)$, respectively. From Theorem 6, the LP in which x is
restricted to be in $R(C_1)$ has $x_1 = 333$ in the optimal solution. Putting $x_1 = 333$
in the original problem, we have the tableau shown in Figure 9.30. The optimal
solution to this LP is $z = 19{,}995$, $x_2 = 333.5$, $x_3 = 0$, $x_4 = 0.5$, $x_5 = 0$. Thus
19,995 is an upper bound on all solutions in C_1. An upper bound for C_2, computed in a similar way, is 19,990. Since C_1 has a higher bound, we proceed to
partition C_1. This is represented by Figure 9.31. Since x_2 is not an integer in the
optimal solution in $R(C_1)$, we partition C_1 into three subsets D_1, D_2, D_3; these
subsets inherit all the constraints in C_1 and in addition

$$\text{in } D_1, \qquad x_1 \leq 332$$
$$\text{in } D_2, \qquad x_1 = 333, \quad x_2 \leq 333$$
$$\text{in } D_3, \qquad x_1 = 333, \quad x_2 \geq 334$$

The LP in which x is restricted to be in $R(D_2)$ has $x_2 = 333$ in an optimal solution. Making this substitution, the tableau for the LP in which x is restricted to

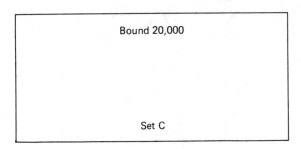

Bound 20,000

Set C

Figure 9.29. Set of feasible solutions.

x_2	x_3	x_4	x_5	
30	35	0	0	-9990
1	1	1	0	334
2	3	0	1	667

Figure 9.30. Tableau for $R(C_1)$.

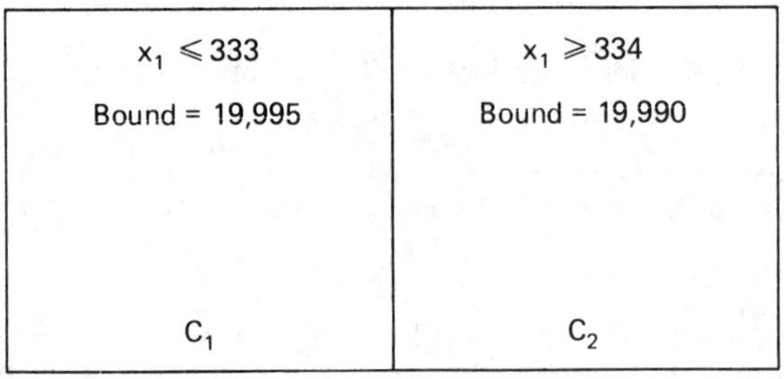

$x_1 \leqslant 333$ Bound = 19,995 C_1	$x_1 \geqslant 334$ Bound = 19,990 C_2

Figure 9.31. First partition.

be in $R(D_2)$ is shown in Figure 9.32. The optimal solution for this problem has $z = 19{,}991\frac{2}{3}$, $x_1 = 333$, $x_2 = 333$, $x_3 = \frac{1}{3}$, $x_4 = \frac{2}{3}$, $x_5 = 0$. Thus $19{,}991\frac{2}{3}$ is a bound on solutions in D_2. Bounds computed similarly for D_1 and D_3 are 19,980 and negative infinity, respectively (since D_3 is the empty set). We now have a partition (D_1, D_2, D_3, C_2) with bounds $(19{,}980; 19{,}991\frac{2}{3}; -\infty; 19{,}990)$, respectively (see Figure 9.33). Since D_2 has the largest bound, we proceed to search D_2 next.

x_3	x_4	x_5	
35	0	0	$-19{,}980$
1	1	0	1
3	0	1	1

Figure 9.32. Tableau for $R(D_2)$.

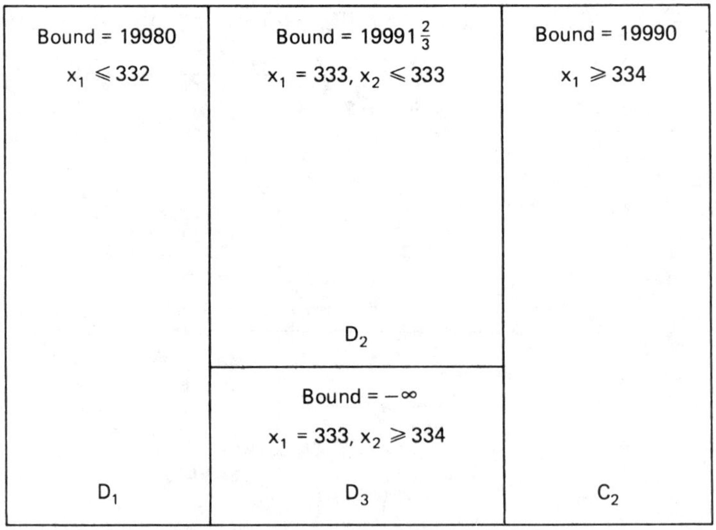

Bound = 19980 $x_1 \leqslant 332$	Bound = 19991$\frac{2}{3}$ $x_1 = 333, x_2 \leqslant 333$	Bound = 19990 $x_1 \geqslant 334$
	D_2	
	Bound = $-\infty$ $x_1 = 333, x_2 \geqslant 334$	
D_1	D_3	C_2

Figure 9.33. Second partition.

x_3 is not integer in the optimal solution to $R(D_2)$; hence we next partition D_2 into subsets E_1, E_2, and E_3; these subsets inherit all the constraints in D_2 and in addition

$$\text{in } E_1, \qquad x_2 \leq 332$$
$$\text{in } E_2, \qquad x_2 = 333, \quad x_3 \leq 0$$
$$\text{in } E_3, \qquad x_2 = 333, \quad x_3 \geq 1$$

Computing bounds in the usual way, we obtain the following partition with associated bounds: $(D_1, E_1, E_2, E_3, D_3, C_2)$ and $(19{,}980; 19{,}985; 19{,}980; -\infty; -\infty; 19{,}990)$, as shown in Figure 9.34. Since C_2 is the subset in the current partition with the largest bound, we next search C_2.

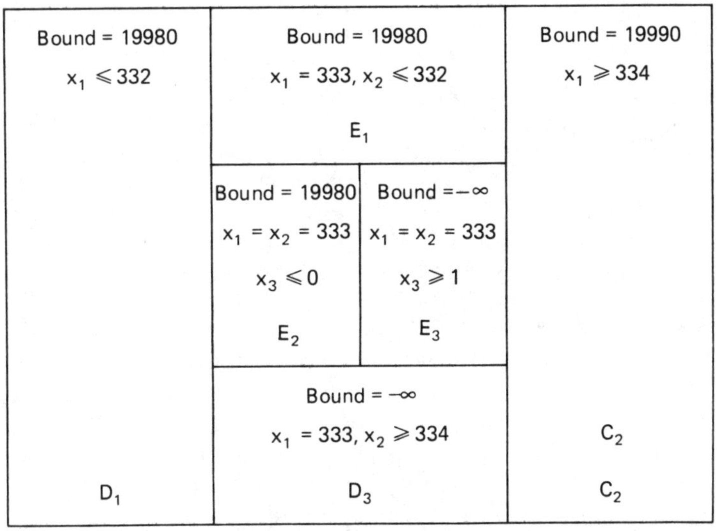

Bound = 19980 $x_1 \leq 332$	Bound = 19980 $x_1 = 333, x_2 \leq 332$ E_1		Bound = 19990 $x_1 \geq 334$
	Bound = 19980 $x_1 = x_2 = 333$ $x_3 \leq 0$ E_2	Bound $= -\infty$ $x_1 = x_2 = 333$ $x_3 \geq 1$ E_3	
	Bound $= -\infty$ $x_1 = 333, x_2 \geq 334$		C_2
D_1	D_3		C_2

Figure 9.34. Third partition.

The optimal solution to the LP with x restricted to be in $R(C_2)$ is $z = 19{,}990$, $x_1 = 334$, $x_2 = 330$, $x_3 = 2$, $x_4 = 0$, $x_5 = 0$. This solution is integer, and hence it is the optimal solution to the given integer programming problem.

It is cumbersome to represent partitions by boxes as in Figure 9.34. It is more convenient to use trees to represent partitions. Each node of the tree represents a subset of solutions (see Figures 9.35 through 9.38), and all the leaves of the tree form a

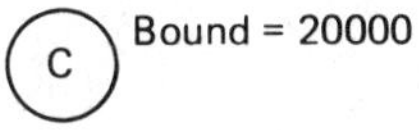

$\bigodot_{C}$ Bound = 20000

Figure 9.35. Set of all feasible solutions.

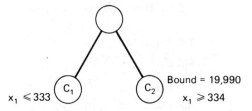

Figure 9.36. First partition.

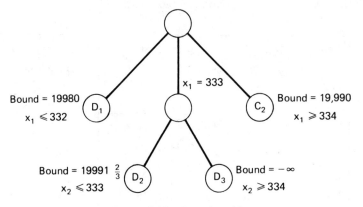

Figure 9.37. Second partition.

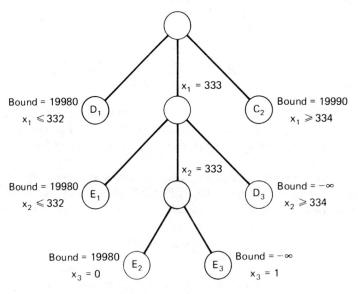

Figure 9.38. Third partition.

partition. Partitioning a subset corresponds to creating descendents of the corresponding nodes, which is often referred to as *branching* (thus yielding the phrase *branch and bound* algorithm).

Next we shall discuss an application of branch and bound algorithms to a problem in computer memory hierarchy design. Our goal is to show that the basic theory of mathematical programming can be used to develop efficient algorithms designed for the specific problem at hand. This is often preferable to using general-purpose "canned" programs.

9.6. APPLICATION TO MEMORY HIERARCHIES

In this section we shall analyze some of the trade-offs that arise in the design of memory hierarchies used as file libraries. Requests are made for specific items of information stored in the library. The item of information is fetched from its storage location, used (and possibly updated), and then replaced in the same location. The information in the library is assumed to be relatively static, i.e., its size does not change rapidly, and the frequency of access for a specific item of information is assumed to be constant over time. The memory hierarchy considered in this chapter is analogous to a library of books. A book is withdrawn from some location in the stacks, used, and then replaced in the same location. The memory hierarchy consists of different types of memories ranging from very fast, expensive types to relatively slow, inexpensive varieties. This is analogous to books being stored in a hierarchy of stacks, some of which are conveniently accessed and others which require a long access time. The questions that we consider are, "What is the optimum mix of memory devices that should constitute the hierarchy given a constraint on the total cost of the hierarchy?" and "Where in the hierarchy should specific items of information be stored?" This problem has been analyzed in [Ramamoorthy and Chandy (1970)].

Each memory device is assumed to be completely described by its cost, capacity, and average access time. Describing a memory device by just three parameters is a gross simplification; however, such simplifications result in tractable models which are useful in providing gross estimates.

We are given a description of the information to be stored in the hierarchy. The information is assumed to be divided into blocks or pages of equal size. Some pages, or collections of pages, are accessed more frequently than others. Associated with a given page is the probability that a random request for information will be a request for that page. There will normally be many pages with approximately the same probability of access, and so it is convenient to describe the *activity profile* of the information stored in the data base by a pair of vectors $P = P_1, \ldots, P_N$ and $W = W_1, \ldots, W_N$, where there are W_i pages, each of which is accessed with probability P_i, $i = 1, \ldots, N$, and there are a total of $\sum_{i=1}^{N} W_i$ pages in the hierarchy. Thus

$$\sum_{i=1}^{N} P_i W_i = 1$$

We shall refer to all the W_i pages which are accessed with frequency P_i as *type i* pages, $i = 1, \ldots, N$. It is convenient to assume that $P_i > P_{i+1}$, for all i.

Simplifying Assumptions

1. The memory hierarchy in our model is essentially a file library. The hierarchy does not include memory within processors or paging devices. The model assumes that the computing system consists of two entities: the central processor and its associated memory (registers, main memory, paging drums, etc.) and the memory hierarchy in which files are stored. Information may move or *percolate* (i.e., change storage locations) within the central processor subsystem, though information is assumed to reside in fixed locations in the memory hierarchy.

2. File sizes are assumed to be small relative to the capacity of memory devices. Our model does not specifically require a file to lie entirely within one memory device. If a file is distributed across more than one device, then two or more access paths will have to be set up, thus increasing the effective average access time. This should be avoided. Files are assumed to be approximately the same size.

3. In a multiprogramming system, two or more tasks may attempt to access the same device, thus resulting in queueing delays. Queueing delays are ignored in our model. The model discussed here is only valid when queueing delays are negligible.

4. Restricting attention to one performance parameter of a memory device, viz., the average access time, and ignoring other parameters such as seek times, rotational delays, and transfer rates is a serious oversimplification when large files are involved.

5. The cost of controllers and channels is ignored in our model. We can handle such costs approximately by amortizing controller costs over several devices.

6. The activity profile of the system is assumed to be static.

It must be emphasized that this model has a very limited objective: to aid in the initial, rough layout of memory hierarchies. The model is too gross to be used for detailed analysis.

Mathematical Model

Let there be M types of memory devices under consideration for the hierarchy. Let the kth device have capacity A_k, cost d_k, and average access time T_k, $k = 1, \ldots, M$. Let G be the maximum allowable expenditure on the hierarchy.

Let y_k be the number of units of type k memory in the hierarchy, $k = 1, \ldots, M$. Let V_{ik} be the number of type i pages stored in type k memories, $i = 1, \ldots, N$ and $k = 1, \ldots, M$.

The probability that a random request to the hierarchy results in an access to a type k device is $\sum_{i=1}^{N} P_i V_{ik}$. Hence the average access time is

$$\bar{T} = \sum_{k=1}^{M} T_k \sum_{i=1}^{N} P_i V_{ik}$$

An integer programming formulation for the problem is

$$\text{minimize } \bar{T} = \sum_i \sum_k P_i T_k V_{ik} \tag{7}$$

$$\text{subject to } \sum_k d_k y_k \leq G \tag{8}$$

$$\sum_i V_{ik} \leq A_k y_k \qquad \text{for all } k \tag{9}$$

$$\sum_k V_{ik} = W_i \qquad \text{for all } i \tag{10}$$

$V_{ik} \geq 0$ for all i, k, $y_k \geq 0$, and y_k must be integer, for all k. Inequality (8) requires that the total cost of the system should not exceed the budget constraint G. Inequality (9) states that the total volume of information stored in type k memories cannot exceed the total capacity of all the type k devices in the hierarchy. Inequality (10) requires that all type i pages be stored somewhere in the hierarchy. V_{ik} and y_k must be nonnegative for obvious reasons. y_k must be integer, since memory units are large and indivisible; for instance, it is not possible to purchase half a drum unit.

There may be up to 10 types of memories under consideration and perhaps 100 page types, resulting in an integer program with a 111 constraints.

The purpose of this model is to aid the designer in a very rough layout of the hierarchy. The designer will make several passes at rough designs before detailed analysis is begun. It is imperative that the rough model be analyzed very rapidly. General-purpose, "canned" integer programs for problems of this size take longer than acceptable. We shall attempt to develop faster algorithms for this specific problem. We shall use a branch and bound algorithm. Bounds are computed by allowing the integer variables to be continuous. Thus bounds are computed by solving linear programs. We next develop special-purpose solutions for the linear program.

The Linear Program

The divisible (as opposed to the indivisible) memory unit problem is one where fractional amounts of memory devices may be purchased; i.e., y_k are not restricted to be integer. In this case we may replace inequality (9) by the equality

$$\sum_i V_{ik} = A_k y_k \qquad \text{for all } k \tag{11}$$

since we may purchase just enough type k memory to accommodate the information to be stored in type k devices. Equation (11) is equivalent to

$$y_k = \sum_i \frac{V_{ik}}{A_k} \qquad \text{for all } k \tag{12}$$

Since the V_{ik} are nonnegative, it follows from (12) that the y_k must also be automatically nonnegative; hence we may remove the explicit constraint that y_k be nonnegative without altering the problem. Substituting for y_k from (12) into (8), we get

$$\sum_k d_k \sum_i \frac{V_{ik}}{A_k} \leq G \tag{13}$$

Let $C_k = d_k/A_k$; i.e., C_k is the cost per page of memory type k. Substituting for C_k, the budget constraint (13) becomes

$$\sum_i \sum_k C_k V_{ik} \leq G$$

The linear program of Eq. (7)–(10) (with y_k continuous) can be solved by solving the simpler problem

$$\text{minimize } \bar{T} = \sum_i \sum_k P_i T_k V_{ik} \tag{14}$$

$$\text{subject to} \quad \sum_i \sum_k C_k V_{ik} \leq G \tag{15}$$

$$\sum_k V_{ik} = W_i \qquad \text{for all } i \tag{16}$$

$$V_{ik} \geq 0$$

Let the optimal solution to this problem be $V_{ik} = V_{ik}^*$. From Eq. (12), set

$$y_k^* = \sum_i \frac{V_{ik}^*}{A_k}$$

Then $y_k = y_k^*$ and $V_{ik} = V_{ik}^*$ are the optimal values in the original linear program.

We now attempt to exploit the structure of the problem consisting of Eq. (14)–(16).

Figure 9.39 shows the cost per page C versus the average access time T for different memory devices under consideration for the hierarchy. If type j devices are slower than type k devices and at least as expensive, then type j devices would never be used in any memory hierarchy in the divisible memory problem, since a better solution is to replace all type j devices by type k devices. In such a case, we shall say that type j

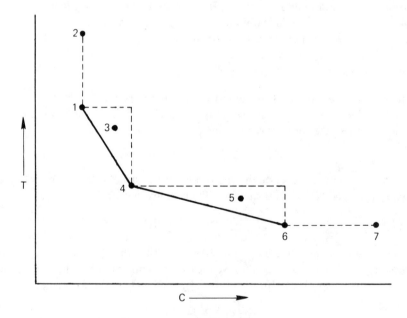

Figure 9.39. Average access time and cost per page for memory devices

is *dominated* by type k. Type k also dominates type j if type j is more expensive than, and as slow as, type k. If types k and j have exactly the same values for both C and T, then we shall arbitrarily state that k dominates j if $k < j$ since the two types are equivalent in the divisible memory problem. For example, in Figure 9.39, type 2 is dominated by type 1 and type 7 is dominated by type 6.

Hereafter, when solving the divisible memory problem, we shall discard all dominated memories from further consideration. In the divisible memory problem we may store a fraction q of a page on a type k device and the remainder of the page $1 - q$ on a type j device. The cost of storing this page is

$$C' = qC_k + (1 - q)C_j$$

The time required to access this page in the divisible memory problem is

$$T' = qT_k + (1 - q)T_j$$

By splitting a page between devices k and j we have effectively simulated a memory device with a cost per page of C' and an access time of T'. By varying the amount of a page stored on devices k and j we can simulate all C, T values lying on the line segment joining (C_k, T_k) and (C_j, T_j).

We shall say that memory type k is dominated by the pair of types i and j if we can simulate a memory type by splitting a page between types i and j such that this simulated type dominates k. For instance, in Figure 9.39, type 3 is dominated by the pair $(1, 4)$. If memory type k is dominated by the pair i and j, then we shall never use type k in any hierarchy, since we could always decrease the average access time by splitting the information stored in k between devices i and j. In the divisible memory problem we may ignore from further consideration any memory type which is dominated by a pair of types. For example, in Figure 9.39 we started out with types 1 to 7, but we shall restrict attention to types 1, 4, and 6, since type 3 is dominated by the pair 1, 4 and type 5 is dominated by the pair 4, 6.

For convenience, renumber the memory types that remain in consideration as $1, 2, \ldots, m$, where $C_k < C_{k+1}, k = 1, \ldots, m - 1$. In the C versus T graph, join the points (C_k, T_k) and (C_{k+1}, T_{k+1}), $k = 1, \ldots, m - 1$, by straight-line segments to obtain a function $C(T)$. Let

$$y_k = \frac{T_{k+1} - T_k}{C_{k+1} - C_k} \qquad k = 1, \ldots, m - 1$$

Then y_k is the slope of the line joining the kth and the $(k + 1)$th memory types in the C-T graph. Note that all the y_k are negative.

Problem

Show that $C(T)$ is convex, or, equivalently, show that $|y_k| > |y_{k+1}|$ for $k = 1, 2, \ldots, m - 1$. Also show that convexity implies that

$$\frac{T_{k+1} - T_k}{C_{k+1} - C_k} < \frac{T_j - T_k}{C_j - C_k} \qquad \text{for } j = k + 2, k + 3, \ldots$$

and

$$\frac{T_{k+1} - T_k}{C_{k+1} - C_k} > \frac{T_{k+1} - T_j}{C_{k+1} - C_j} \qquad \text{for } j = 1, 2, \ldots, k - 1$$

We shall next present a heuristic algorithm and shall postpone until later the question of the algorithm's optimality. This algorithm will be shown to be extremely fast.

A Heuristic Algorithm for the Divisible Memory Problem

For an initial solution, put all the pages on the slowest (and cheapest) memory.

$$V_{ik} = \begin{cases} W_i & \text{for } k = 1 \\ 0 & \text{for } k > 1 \end{cases} \quad \text{all } i$$

Let s be the slack in the budget constraint. Then, in the initial solution

$$s = G - C_1 \sum_i W_i$$

If s is negative, then no feasible solution exists since the budget is not sufficient to buy a sufficient quantity of even the cheapest memory. If $s = 0$, this is the only feasible solution, and hence it is optimal. If $s > 0$, this solution is not optimal since it is possible to purchase faster memory and move a portion of a page into the faster memory, thereby decreasing the average access time.

Consider a feasible solution in which s is positive and not all pages are in the fastest memory. (If all pages are stored in the fastest memory in this solution, then this solution must obviously be optimal.) Let there be a type i page stored in a type j device in this solution. By moving this page onto a type k device, we shall mean

(a)   Purchase an additional page of type k memory (at a cost of C_k),

(b)   Give up a page of type j memory (thus saving C_j), and

(c)   Relocate the type i page on type k memory.

The cost of this move is $C_k - C_j$. The resulting change in the average access time $\bar{T}$ is $P_i(T_k - T_j)$. The change in $\bar{T}$ per dollar is

$$P_i \frac{T_k - T_j}{C_k - C_j}$$

Not all moves are feasible: For instance, it is not possible to change the current solution by moving type i pages out of device j if there are no type i pages in device j in the current solution.

To improve the current solution we shall make that feasible move which results in the largest decrease in $\bar{T}$ per dollar. Suppose this move takes type i pages from device type j and relocates them in type k memory. We shall continue to perform this move until either

(a)   The move is no longer feasible because all the type i pages which were in device j have been moved to device k, or

(b)   The budget is exhausted; i.e., s is reduced to zero.

In case (b) the algorithm stops, and in case (a) we proceed to the next move.

We shall now show that the mechanics of this algorithm can be simplified. From the convexity of $C(T)$ (see Figure 9.39), it follows that

$$\frac{T_{k+1} - T_k}{C_{k+1} - C_k} < \frac{T_j - T_k}{C_j - C_k} \quad \text{for } j = k + 2, k + 3, \ldots$$

Hence, the largest decrease in $\bar{T}$ per dollar always results from moving a page from type k memory to type $k + 1$ memory (and never from moving a page from type k memory directly to memory types $k + 2, k + 3, \ldots$). This substantially reduces the number of feasible moves to be considered. Hereafter, the statement move a page forward from memory type k will imply that the page is moved to memory type $k + 1$. Therefore, the iteration step of the algorithm is as follows: Make that *feasible* forward move resulting in the largest decrease in $\bar{T}$ per dollar.

We shall now show that the move which results in the largest decrease in $\bar{T}$ per dollar is always feasible. Therefore, the iteration step simplifies even further, as shown below:

$$\text{Let } z_{ik} = P_i y_k = P_i \frac{T_{k+1} - T_k}{C_{k+1} - C_k}$$

z_{ik} is the change in $\bar{T}$ per dollar obtained by moving type i pages forward from device k. The z_{ik} are all negative. Arrange all the z_{ik} in increasing order (i.e., decreasing order of magnitude) to obtain the sequence

$$z_{i(1)k(1)}, z_{i(2)k(2)}, z_{i(3)k(3)}, \cdots$$

where

$$z_{i(j)k(j)} \leq z_{i(j+1)k(j+1)}, \quad j = 1, 2, 3, \ldots$$

Consider the following sequence of moves which apparently may not be feasible: First move type $i(1)$ pages forward from memory type $k(1)$, then move type $i(2)$ pages forward from memory type $k(2)$, and so on, moving type $i(j)$ pages forward from memory type $k(j)$ before moving type $i(j + 1)$ pages forward from memory type $k(j+1)$, $j = 1, 2, 3, \ldots$ until either the entire sequence of moves is complete (in which case all the pages are in the fastest memory) or the budget is exhausted.

Theorem 7

Every move in this sequence is feasible.

Proof: From the convexity of $C(T)$,

$$y_1 < y_2 < y_3 < y_4 < \cdots$$

Hence for any i,

$$z_{i1} < z_{i2} < z_{i3} < z_{i4} < \cdots$$

Hence $z_{i1}, z_{i2}, \ldots, z_{i,j-1}$ will always appear earlier than z_{ij}, for any j, in the increasing sequence of all z_{ik}. Thus, if we make a sequence of moves corresponding to the increasing sequence of the z_{ik}, we shall move all type i pages from memory type 1 to memory type 2 before we attempt to move these pages out of memory type 2, and by the same argument we shall move all type i pages from memory type 1 to memory type 2, then from memory type 2 to type 3, . . . , and then from memory type $j - 1$ to memory type j before we attempt to move these pages out of memory type j. Hence every move in the sequence is feasible.

The matrix of z_{ik} is ordered both by row and column, since

$$z_{ik} < z_{i,k+1} \qquad \text{since } y_k < y_{k-1}$$

and

$$z_{ik} < z_{i+1,k} \qquad \text{since } P_i > P_{i+1}$$

Hence we can rapidly arrange all the z_{ik} in increasing order.

The heuristic algorithm is very simple:

1. Discard all dominated memory types.

2. Compute z_{ik} and sort them in increasing order.

3. Perform the sequence of moves corresponding to the increasing sequence of z_{ik} until either the budget is exhausted or all moves have been completed.

We are now faced with the following question: Can we use the theory of mathematical programming either to prove that this algorithm is (always) optimal or to show that it may not be optimal?

Theorem 8

The above algorithm is optimal.

Proof: Since we are dealing with a linear program, it is sufficient to show that the solution (say X) obtained by this algorithm is a *local* optimum; in other words, any small perturbation of X should not result in a better solution. If all pages are stored in the fastest memory in solution X, then X is clearly optimal. Consider the case where not all the pages are stored in the fastest memory in X. A perturbation of solution X in which some pages are moved from their current locations to *slower* memories (and no pages are moved from their current locations to faster memories) cannot be better than X itself. Therefore, restrict attention to perturbations where some information is moved to faster memories. Since the budget is exhausted in solution X, it is not possible to perturb X by merely moving information to faster memory, since doing so would exceed the budget; some pages will have to be moved to slower devices so that the total cost of the system does not increase.

Consider a perturbation of X in which ΔC is saved by moving some pages from their current locations to slower devices, and $\Delta C'$ is the incremental cost of moving some pages from their current locations to faster memories. The budget constraint implies that

$$\Delta C' \leq \Delta C \tag{17}$$

The sequence of moves may have been terminated either

(a)   while the jth move is being carried out, $j = 1, 2, 3, . . .$, or

(b)   Soon after the jth move was completed and just prior to the $(j+1)$th move, $j = 1, 2, 3, \ldots$.

Let u and u' be the rates of change in $\bar{T}$ per dollar due to pages being moved from their current locations to slower and faster devices, respectively, in the perturbation of solution X. The net change in $\bar{T}$ caused by the perturbation is

$$\Delta T = -\Delta C \cdot u + \Delta C' \cdot u' \qquad (18)$$

Consider case (a) in which the algorithm stops during the jth move. At this point, the move which results in the largest decrease in $\bar{T}$ per dollar is the jth move, and hence

$$u' \geq z_{i(j)k(j)} \qquad (19)$$

We now show that the backward move which results in the smallest increase in $\bar{T}$ per dollar saved is also the jth move, i.e., $u \leq z_{i(j)k(j)}$. Suppose page type f is moved backward from its current location in memory type g to a slower memory type h. The rate of change in $\bar{T}$ per dollar due to this move is

$$u = P_f \frac{T_h - T_g}{C_h - C_g} = P_f \frac{T_g - T_h}{C_g - C_h}$$

From the convexity of the $C(T)$ curve (see Figure 9.39) it follows that

$$\frac{T_g - T_h}{C_g - C_h} \leq \frac{T_g - T_{g-1}}{C_g - C_{g-1}} = y_{g-1}$$

Hence

$$u \leq P_f \cdot y_{g-1} = z_{f, g-1} \qquad (20)$$

Since page type f is stored in memory type g in solution X, it follows that in the sequence of moves page type f is moved from memory type $g - 1$ to memory type g before the jth move, i.e., before page type $i(j)$ is moved from memory type $k(j)$ to memory type $k(j) + 1$, and hence

$$z_{f, g-1} \leq z_{i(j)k(j)} \qquad (21)$$

From (19), (20), and (21),

$$u \leq u' \qquad (22)$$

From (17), (18), and (22) and since u and u' are negative, it follows that

$$\Delta T \geq 0$$

Hence any perturbation does not improve solution X. Hence the heuristic algorithm is optimal. A similar argument works for case (b).

Problem

It is instructive to see the correspondence between the sequence of moves and basic feasible solutions. How many nonzero variables are there at the end of a move, in the middle of a move, and at the end of the algorithm? Is the solution at the end of a move a basic solution? Is the solution at the end of the algorithm a basic solution? What is the relationship between the sequence of moves and the extreme points of the set of feasible solutions?

The Indivisible Memory Unit Problem

Consider the case where the y_k are restricted to be integer. We shall use the branch and bound algorithm discussed earlier to solve this problem. The algorithm proceeds by partitioning the set of feasible solutions into subsets, where in a subset some variables are held fixed at constant integer values, while other variables are allowed to take on noninteger values as well. In general, we may partition a subset of solutions by restricting (i.e. fixing) any one of the variables. Consider the following question: For this specific problem, is there any advantage in restricting the y_k in a specific sequence rather than in restricting variables randomly? We shall show that there is a considerable advantage in first fixing the sizes of faster memories.

Consider two pages A and B, where page A is accessed more frequently than page B. Any solution in which page A is stored in a slower device than page B cannot be optimal, since interchanging the locations of pages A and B will result in a lower average access time. Thus, if we know how many units of the fastest memory there are in the hierarchy, we also know which pages should be optimally stored in this memory, viz., the most frequently accessed pages. An algorithm for deciding which pages should be stored in memory type M (the fastest memory), given the number y_M of units of this memory, is as follows: First pack as many of the most frequently accessed pages (type 1 pages) into type M memories as possible; if all these pages fit into this memory, then pack as many of the next most frequently accessed (type 2) pages as possible, and if there is space left, go to type 3, and so on, until either all the pages are packed or the memory is full. Let

$$\sum_{i=1}^{j} W_i \le A_M y_M < \sum_{i=1}^{j+1} W_i$$

The first j types of pages fit into memery type M, but not all of the type $j + 1$ pages do. The optimal contents of type M memory are

$$V_{iM} = \begin{cases} W_i & \text{for } i \le j \\ A_M y_M - \sum_{i=1}^{j} W_i & \text{for } i = j + 1 \\ 0 & \text{for } i > j \end{cases}$$

Thus fixing y_M also fixes V_{iM} for all i, and a total of $N + 1$ variables are fixed. Note that the V_{iM} depend only on y_M and are independent of $y_{M-1}, \ldots, y_1$. By the same argument if we were given $y_M, y_{M-1}, \ldots, y_j$, we could readily compute V_{ik}, $k = M, \ldots, j$, for all i, and these values would be independent of $y_{j-1}, \ldots, y_1$.

Consider a subset of solutions in which $y_M, \ldots, y_j$ are held fixed at integer values and $y_{j-1}, \ldots, y_1$ are free to take on nonnegative values. The V_{ik} for $k = j, \ldots, M$ are fixed for this solution. A bound for this subset of solutions is obtained by solving a linear program with variables y_k, V_{ik}, $k = 1, \ldots, j - 1$. This linear program has the same structure as the one discussed earlier except that there are only $j - 1$ memory devices and the number W'_j of type i pages in this problem consists of all those pages which did not get placed in memory types $j, \ldots, M$. Therefore, the efficient special-purpose algorithm described earlier can be used to obtain bounds for all subsets by solving the appropriate LPs.

It is possible to reduce the amount of computation even further by further utilizing the structure of the problem. However, we shall not do so since we have made the basic point of this exercise: Computer design models often have a special structure, and it is often preferable to utilize the theory of optimization to develop special-purpose algorithms which exploit this structure rather than use general-purpose programs.

APPENDIX

There are several excellent books on mathematical programming. We list an extremely small sample here. These books collectively describe all of the material in this chapter much more thoroughly than we do. We urge the reader to consult these books since this chapter is only a skimpy introduction to an exciting area. The goals of this chapter will have been achieved if the reader feels sufficiently excited about this material to consult any of the following books.

General introductory material is found in [Hillier and Lieberman (1967)], [Wilde and Beightler (1967)] and [Wagner (1969)]. Linear programming is discussed in detail in [Dantzig (1963)] and [Hadley (1962)] and an elementary introduction is found in [Thompson (1971)]. Advanced material pertaining to graph theory and network flows is found in [Berge and Ghouila-Houri (1965)] and [Hu (1969)]. Nonlinear programming is discussed in [Abadie (1967)], [Hadley (1964)], [Himmelblau (1972)] and [Zangwill (1969)]. Geometric programming is discussed in [Duffin et al. (1967)] and integer programming in [Hu (1969)] and [Garfinkel and Nemhauser (1972)].

BIBLIOGRAPHY

1. ABADIE, J. (ed.), *Nonlinear Programming*. New York: John Wiley, 1967.

2. ADAM, T. L., K. M. CHANDY, and J. R. DICKSON, "A Comparison of List Schedules for Parallel Processing Systems," *CACM* 17, no. 12 (1974), 685–90.

3. ADIRI, I., "Queueing Models for Multiprogrammed Computer," *Proc. Symp. on Computer Communication Networks and Teletraffic*, pp. 441–448. New York: Polytechnic Press, 1972.

4. AGERWALA T. and M. FLYNN, "Comments on Capabilities Limitations and 'Correctness' of Petri Nets," *Proc. 1st Symp. on Computer Architecture* (1973), 81–86.

5. AHO, A. V. and J. D. ULLMAN, *The Theory of Parsing, Translation and Compiling, Volume II: Compiling*. Englewood Cliffs, N.J.: Prentice-Hall, 1973.

6. AHO, A. V., J. E. HOPCROFT, and J. D. ULLMAN, *The Design and Analysis of Computer Algorithms*. Reading, Mass.: Addison-Wesley, 1974.

7. ALLEN, F. E. and J. COCKE, "A Program Data Flow Analysis Procedure," *CACM*, 19, no. 3 (1976) 137–47.

8. ANDERSON, H. A., G. L. GALATI, and M. REISER, "The Classification of the Interactive Workload for a Virtual Memory Computer System," *Proceedings of Computer Science and Statistics*, 7th Annual Symposium on the Interface, Ames, Iowa (1973), 30–40.

9. ANDERSON, JR., H. A., M. REISER, and G. L. GALATI, "Tuning a Virtual Storage System," *IBM System J.*, 14, no. 3 (1975), 246–63.

10. ANDERSON, T. W., *An Introduction to Multivariate Statistical Analysis*. New York: John Wiley, 1958.

11. ANDREWS, D. F., "A Robust Method for Multiple Linear Regression," *Technometrics*, 16 (1974), 523–31.

12. ARORA, S. R. and A. GALLO, "The Optimal Organization of Multiprogrammed Multi-level Memory," *Proc. ACM-SIGOPS Workshop on System Performance Evaluation* (1971), 104–41.

13. ARVIND, KAIN, R. Y. and E. SADEH, "On Reference String Generation Processes," *Proc. 4th ACM Symp. on Op. Syst. Princs.* (1973), 80–87.

14. AVI-ITZHAK, B. and D. P. HEYMAN, "Approximate Queueing Models for Multiprogramming Computer Systems," *Oper. Res.*, 21, no. 6 (1973), pp. 1212–230.

15. BADEL, M., E. GELENBE, J. LEROUDIER, and D. POTIER, "Adaptive Optimization of a Time Sharing System's Performance," *Proc. IEEE*, 63, no. 6 (1975), 958–65.

16. BAER, J. L., "A Survey of Some Theoretical Aspects of Multiprocessing," *Comp. Surveys*, 5, no. 1 (1973), 31–80.

17. BAER, J. L., "Optimal Scheduling on Two Processors of Different Speeds," in *Computer Architectures and Networks*, E. Gelenbe and R. Mahl (eds.), pp. 27–45. Amsterdam: North Holland Publishing Co., 1974.

18. BAER, J. L. and R. CAUGHEY, "Segmentation and Optimization of Programs from Cyclic Structure Analysis," *Proc. AFIPS 1972 SJCC*, 40, pp. 23–36. Montvale, N.J.: AFIPS Press, 1972.

19. BAER, J. L., and G. ESTRIN, "Bounds for Maximum Parallelism in a Bilogic Graph Model of Computations," *IEEE-TC*, 18, no. 11 (1969), 1012–1014.

20. BAER, J. L., D. P. BOVET and ESTRIN, G. "Legality and Other Properties of Graph Models of Computations," *J. ACM*, 17, no. 3 (1970), 543–52.

21. BAKER, K., *Introduction to Sequencing and Scheduling*. New York: John Wiley 1974.

22. BARD, Y., "Performance Criteria and Measurement for a Time-Sharing System," *IBM Systems Journal*, 10, no. 3 (1971), 193–216.

23. BARD, Y., "Experimtal Evaluation of System Performance," *IBM Systems Journal*, 12, no. 3 (1973), 302–14.

24. BARD, Y., *Nonlinear Parameter Estimation*. New York: Academic Press, 1974.

25. BARD, Y., "Application of the Page Survival Index (PSI) to Virtual-Memory System Performance," *IBM J. Res. Develop.*, 19 (1975), 212–20.

26. BARD, Y. and K. V. SURYANARAYANA, "On the Structure of CP-67 Overhead," in *Statistical Computer Performance Evaluation*, W. Freiberger (ed.), pp. 329–46. New York: Academic Press, 1972.

27. BASKETT, F., "Mathematical Models of Multiprogrammed Computer Systems," Ph.D. dissertation, Univ. of Texas, Austin, Texas, 1971.

28. BASKETT, F. and R. R. MUNTZ, "Queueing Network Models with Different Classes of Customers," *Proc. Six Annual IEEE Computer Society Int'l. Conf.* (1972), 205–209.

29. BASKETT, F. and R. R. MUNTZ, "Networks of Queues," *Proc. of Seventh Annual Princeton Conf. on Information Sciences and Systems* (1973), 428–34.

30. BASKETT, F., and A. RAFII, "The AO Inversion Model of Program Paging Behavior," Report STAN-CS-76-579 (1976), Stanford Univ., Computer Science Dept.

31. BASKETT, F., K. M. CHANDY R. R. MUNTZ, and F. G. PALACIOS, "Open, Closed and Mixed Networks of Queues with Different Classes of Customers," *J. ACM*, 22, no. 2 (1975), 248–60.

32. BATSON, A. P., "Program Behavior at the Symbolic Level," *Computer*, 9, no. 11 (1976), 21–26.

33. BEALE, E. M. L., "Some Use of Computers in Operational Research," *Industrielle Organisation*, 31 (1962), 27–28.

34. BERGE, C., *Theorie des Graphes et ses Applications*. Paris: Dunod, 1958.

35. BERGE, C. and A. GHOUILA-HOURI, *Programming, Games and Transportation Networks*, translated from French by M. Merrington and C. Ramanijacharyalv. London: Metheun, 1965.

36. BERNSTEIN, A. J., "Analysis of Programs for Parallel Processing," *IEEE-TEC*, 15, no. 5 (1966), 757–62.

37. BHANDARKAR, D. P., "Analysis of Memory Interference in Multiprocessors," *IEEE-TC*, 24, no. 9 (1975), 897–907.

38. BOX, G.E.P. and N. R. DRAPER, *Evolutionary Operation*. New York: John Wiley, 1969.

39. BROWN, D. T., "An Analytic Model of Multiprocessing with Multitasking," unpublished memorandum (1971), IBM, Poughkeepsie, N.Y.

40. BROWNE, J. C., K. M. CHANDY, R. M. BROWN, T. W. KELLER, D. TOWSLEY, and C. W. DISSLEY, "Hierarchical Techniques for Development of Realistic Models of Complex Computer Systems," *IEEE Proceedings*, 63, no. 6 (1975), 966–75.

41. BRUCKER, P., J. K. LENSTRA, and A.H.G. RINNOOY KAN, "Complexity of Machine Scheduling Problems," to appear in *Operations Research.* 1977.

42. BURKE, P. J., "Output Processes and Tandem Queues," *Proc. Symp. on Computer-Communications Networks and Teletraffic*, pp. 419–28. New York: Polytechnic Press, 1972.

43. BUZEN, J. P., "Analysis of System Bottlenecks Using a Queueing Network Model," *Proc. ACM-SIGOPS Workshop on System Performance Evaluation* (1971a), 82–103.

44. BUZEN, J. P., "Queueing Network Models of Multiprogramming," Ph.D. dissertation, Div. Eng. Appl. Phys., Harvard Univ., Cambridge, Mass., 1971b.

45. BUZEN, J. P., "Computational Algorithms for Closed Queueing Networks with Exponential Servers," *CACM*, 16, no. 9 (1973), 527–31.

46. BUZEN, J. P., "Fundamental Operational Laws of Computer System Performance," *Acta Informatica*, 7, no. 2 (1976), 167–82.

47. CHANDY, K. M., "The Analysis and Solutions for General Queueing Networks," *Proc. Six Ann. Princeton Conf. on Information Sciences and Systems*, (1972), 224–28.

48. CHANDY, K. M., and P. F. REYNOLDS, "Scheduling Partially Ordered Tasks with Probabilistic Execution Times," *Proc. 5th Symp. on Operating Systems Principles* (1975), 169–77.

49. CHANDY, K. M., U. HERZOG, and L. WOO, "Parametric Analysis of Queueing Network Models," *IBM J. Res. Develop.*, 19, no. 1 (1975a), 36–42.

50. CHANDY, K. M., U. HERZOG, and L. WOO, "Approximate Analysis of General Queueing Networks," *IBM J. Res. Develop.*, 19, no. 1 (1975b), 43–49.

51. CHANDY, K. M., J. H HOWARD, and D. F TOWSLEY, "Product Form and Local Balance in Queueing Networks," *J. ACM*, 24, no. 2 (1977), 250–63.

52. CHANDY, K. M., T. W. KELLER, and J. C. BROWNE, "Design Automation and Queueing Networks," *Proc. 9th Annual Design Automation Conference* (1972), 357–67.

53. CHANG, H. C., "Analysis of Deadlock Avoidance Schemes and Resource Utilization for Non-Preemptible Resources," Ph.D. thesis, Department of Computer Science, Carnegie-Mellon University, Pittsburgh, Pa., 1975.

54. CHEN, N. F., "An Analysis of Scheduling Algorithms in Multiprocessor Computing Systems," IU-CS: R-75.0724 (1975), University of Illinois.

55. CHEN, N. F. and C. L. LIU, "On a Class of Scheduling Algorithms for Multiprocessors Computing Systems," *Parallel Processing, Lecture Notes in Computer Science*, 24 (1974), 1–16.

56. CHIN, W., D. DUMONT, and R. WOOD, "Performance Analysis of a Multiprogrammed Computer System," *IBM J. Res. Develop.*, 19, no. 3 (1975), 263–71.

57. CHOW, W-M, "A Memory Interference Model for Multiprocessor Systems," IBM Research Report (1974), T. J. Watson Research Center, Yorktown Heights, N.Y.

58. CHOW, W-M., "Central Server Model for Multiprogrammer Computer System with Different Classes of Jobs," *IBM J. Res. Develop.*, 19, no. 3 (1975), 314–20.

59. CHOW, T. S. and H. ROBBINS, "On the Asymptotic Theory of Fixed-Width Sequential Confidence Intervals for the Mean," *Ann. Math. Statist*, 36 (1965), 457–62.

60. CHRISTOFIDES, N., *Graph Theory—An Algorithmic Approach*. New York: Academic, 1975.

61. CHRISTOFIDES, N., "Worst-Case Analysis of a New Heuristic for the Traveling Salesman Problem," 1977.

62. CHU, W. W. and H. OPDERBECK, "The Page Fault Frequency Replacement Algorithm," *Proc. AFIPS 1972 FJCC*, 41 (1972), 597–609.

63. CHU, W. W. and OPDERBECK, H. "Analysis of the PFF Replacement Algorithm Using a Semi-Markov Model," *CACM* 19, no. 5 (1976a), 298–304.

64. CHU, W. W. and H. OPDERBECK, "Program Behavior and the Page Fault Frequency Replacement Algorithm," *Computer*, 9, no. 11 (1976b), 29–38.

65. CINLAR, E., *Introduction to Stochastic Processes*. Englewood Cliffs, N.J.: Prentice-Hall, 1975a.

66. CINLAR, E., "Markov Renewal Theory: A Survey," *Management Sci.*, 21 (1975b), 727–52.

67. COCHI, B. J., "A Stochastic Model of Interleaved Memory Systems," Ph.D. thesis (1973), Dept. of Elec. Eng., Stanford Univ.

68. COCHRAN, W. G. and G. M. COX, *Experimental Designs*. New York: John Wiley, 1957.

69. COFFMAN, JR., E. G. (ed.), *Computer and Job-Shop Scheduling Theory*. New York: John Wiley, 1976.

70. COFFMAN, JR., E. G. and P. J. DENNING, *Operating Systems Theory*. Englewood Cliffs, N.J.: Prentice-Hall, 1973.

71. COFFMAN, JR., E. G. and R. L. GRAHAM, "Optimal Scheduling for Two Processor Systems," *Acta Informatica*, 1, no. 3 (1972), 200–13.

72. COFFMAN, JR., E. G., M. J. ELPHICK, and A. SHOSHANI, "Systems Deadlocks," *Comp. Surveys*, 3, no. 3 (1971), 67–78.

73. COFFMAN, JR., E. G., R. R. MUNTZ, and H. TROTTER, "Waiting Time Distributions for Processor-Sharing Systems," *J. ACM*, 17, no. 1 (1970), 123–30.

74. COMMONER, F., A. HOLT, S. EVEN, and A. PENUELI, "Marked Directed Graphs," *J. Computer and System Sciences*, 5 (1971), 511–23.

75. CONWAY, R. W., W. L. MAXWELL, and L. W. MILLER, *Theory of Scheduling*. Reading, Mass.: Addison-Wesley, 1967.

76. COOK, S. A., "The Complexity of Theorem-Proving Procedures," *Proc. of the 3rd Annaul ACM Symposium on the Theory of Computing* (1971), 151–58.

77. COOPER, R. B, *Introduction to Queueing Theory*. New York: Macmillan, 1972.

78. COURTOIS, P. J., "Decomposability, Instabilities and Saturation in Multiprogramming Systems," *CACM*, 18, no. 7, (1975a) 371–77.

79. COURTOIS, P. J., "Error Analysis in Nearly-Completely Decomposable Stochastic Systems," *Econometrica*, 43 (1975b), 691–709.

80. COURTOIS, P. J. and J. GEORGES, "On a Single-Server Finite Queueing Model with State-Dependent Arrival and Service Process," *Oper. Res.*, 18 (1970), 424–35.

81. COURTOIS, P. J. and H. VANTILBORGH, "A Decomposable Model of Program Paging Behavior," *Acta Informatica*, (1976), 251–76.

82. COX, D. R., "A Use of Complex Probabilities in the Theory of Stochastic Processes," *Proc. Cambridge Phil. Soc.*, 51 (1955), 313–19.

83. COX, D. R. and M. D. MILLER, *The Theory of Stochastic Processes*. New York: John Wiley, 1965.

84. COX, D. R. and W. L. SMITH, *Queues*. London: Methuen, 1968.

85. CRANE, M. A. and D. L. IGLEHART, "A New Approach to Simulating Stable Stochastic Systems," *Proceedings of the 1973 Winter Simulation Conference*, San Francisco (1973), 264–72.

86. CRANE, M. A. and D. L. IGLEHART, "Statistical Analysis of Discrete-Event Simulations," *Proceedings of the 1974 Winter Simulation Conference*, Washington, D.C. (1974a), 513–21.

87. CRANE, M. A. and D. L. IGLEHART, "Simulating Stable Stochastic Systems, I: General Multi-Server Queues," *J. ACM*, 21, no. 1 (1974b), 103–13.

88. CRANE, M. A. and D. L. IGLEHART, "Simulating Stable Stochastic Systems, II: Markov Chains," *J. ACM*, 21, no. 1 (1974c), 114–23.

89. CRANE, M. A. and D. L. IGLEHART, "Simulating Stable Stochastic Systems, III: Regenerative Processes and Discrete-Event Simulations," *Operations Res.*, Vol. 23 (1975a), 33–45.

90. CRANE, M. A. and D. L. IGLEHART, "Simulating Stable Stochastic Systems, IV: Approximation Techniques," *Management Sci.*, 21 (1975b), 1215–224.

91. DANTZIG, G. B., *Linear Programming and Extensions*. Princeton, N. J.: Princeton University Press, 1963.

92. DEMPSTER, A. P., M. SCHATZOFF, and N. WERMUTH, "A Simulation Study of Alternatives to Ordinary Least Squares," *J. Am. Stat. Assoc.*, 72, no. 357 (1977), 77–91.

93. DENNING, P. J., "The Working Set Model for Program Behavior," *CACM*, 11, no. 5 (1968), 323–33.

94. DENNING, P. J., "On Modelling the Behavior of Programs," *Proc. AFIPS 1972 SJCC*, 40 (1972), 937–44.

95. DENNING, P. J. and G. S. GRAHAM, "Multiprogrammed Memory Management," *Proc. IEEE*, 63, no. 6 (1975), 924–39.

96. DENNING, P. J. and K. C. KAHN, "A Study of Program Locality and Lifetime Functions," *Proc. 5th ACM Symp. on Op. Syst. Princs.* (1975), 207–16.

97. DENNING, P. J. and K. C. KAHN, "An L = S Criterion for Optimal Multiprogramming," *Proc. Int'l. Symp. on Comput. Perf. Modlg. Meas. and Eval'n.*, ACM SIGMETRICS and IFIP WG7.3 (1976), 219–29.

98. DENNING, P. J. and S. C. SCHWARTZ, "Properties of the Working Set Model," *CACM* 15, no. 3 (1972), 191–98.

99. DENNING, P. J. and D. R. SLUTZ, "Generalized Working Sets for Segment Reference Strings" Report CSD-TR-178 (1976), Computer Science Dept., Purdue Univ. To appear *CACM*, 1978.

100. DENNING, P. J. and TRAN-QUOC-TE, "On the Optimality of Working Set Policies," Report CSD-TR-176 (1976), Dept. of Computer Science, Purdue Univ.

101. DENNING, P. J., K. C. KAHN, J. LEROUDIER, D. POTIER, and R. SURI, "Optimal Multiprogramming," *Acta Informatica*, 7, no. 2 (1976) 197–216.

102. DEO, N., *Graph Theory with Applications to Engineering and Computer Science*. Englewood Cliffs, N.J.: Prentice-Hall, 1974.

103. DIJKSTRA, E. W., "A Note on Two Problems in Connection with Graphs," *Numerische Math*, 1 (1959), 269–71.

104. DIJKSTRA, E. W., "Cooperating Sequential Processes," in *Programming Languages*, F. Genuys (ed.). New York: Academic Press, 1968, 43–112.

105. DOIG, A. and A. H. LAND, "An Automatic Method of Solving Discrete Programming Problems," *Econometrica*, 28 (1960), 497–520.

106. DRAPER, N. R. and H. SMITH, *Applied Regression Analysis.* New York: John Wiley, 1966.

107. DUDEWICZ, E. J. and S. R. DALAL, "Allocation of Observations in Ranking and Selection with Unequal Variances," to appear in *Sankhya* (1975).

108. DUFFIN, R. J., E. L. PETERSON, and C. ZENER, *Geometric Programming: Theory and Application*. New York: John Wiley, 1967.

109. EASTON, M. C. and B. T. BENNETT, "Transient-Free Working Set Statistics," *CACM*, 20, no. 2 (1977), 93–99.

110. EASTON, M. C. and R. FAGIN, "Cold Start vs. Warm Start Miss Ratios and Multiprogramming Performance," IBM T. J. Watson Research Center Report RC 5715, (1975), Yorktown Height, N.Y.

111. FERNANDEZ, E. B. and B. BUSSELL, "Bounds on the Number of Processors and Time for Multiprocessor Optimal Schedules," *IEEE-TC*, 22, no. 8 (1973), 745–51.

112. FERRARI, D., "Improving Locality By Critical Working Sets," *CACM*, 17, no. 11 (1974), 614–20.

113. FERRARI, D., "Tailoring Programs to Models of Program Behavior," *IBM J. Res. Develop.*, 19, no. 3 (1975), 244–51.

114. FERRARI, D., "The Improvement of Program Behavior," *Computer*, 9, no. 11 (1976), 39–47.

115. FIELLER, E. C., "The Biological Standardization of Insulin," *J. Roy. Statist. Soc. Suppl.*, 7, (1940), 1–64.

116. FISHMAN, G. S., "Statistical Analysis for Queueing Simulations," *Management Sci.*, 20 (1973), 363–69.

117. FISHMAN, G. S., "Simulation Data Analysis Using Continuous Time Markov Processes," Technical Report No. 74–1 (1974a), Operations Research and Systems Analysis, University of North Carolina at Chapel Hill.

118. FISHMAN, G. S., "Achieving Specified Accuracy in Simulation Output Analysis," Technical Report No. 74-4 (1974b), Operations Research and Systems Analysis, University of North Carolina at Chapel Hill.

119. FISHMAN, G. S., "Estimation in Multiserver Queueing Simulations," *Operations Res.*, 20 (1974c), 72–78.

120. FRAILEY, D. J., "A Practical Approach to Managing Resources and Avoiding Deadlocks," *Comm. ACM*, 16, no. 5 (May 1973).

121. FRANKLIN, M. A., G. S. GRAHAM, and R. K. GUPTA, "Anomalies with Variable Partition Paging Algorithms" (1976), Dept. E. E., Washington University, St. Louis. To appear in *CACM*, 1978.

122. FRASER, D. A. S., *Statistics, An Introduction*. New York: John Wiley, 1958.

123. FUJII, M., T. KASAMI, and K. NINOMIYA, "Optimal Sequence of Two Equivalent Processors," *SIAM J. on Applied Math.*, 17, no. 3 (1969), 784–89. Also *Erratum*, 20, no. 1 (1971), 141.

124. GAREY, M. R. and R. L. GRAHAM, "Bounds for Multiprocessor Scheduling with Resource Constraints," *SIAM J. on Computing*, 4 (1975), 187–200.

125. GAREY, M. R. and D. S. JOHNSON, "Complexity Results for Multiprocessor Scheduling Under Resource Constraints," *SIAM J. on Computing*, 4 (1975), 397–411.

126. GAREY, M. R. and D. S. JOHNSON, "Approximation Algorithms for Combinatorial Problems: An Annotated Bibliography," in *Algorithms and Complexity: Recent Results and New Directions*, J. F. Traub (ed.). 1977.

127. GAREY, M. R., D. S. JOHNSON, and L. STOCKMEYER, "Some Simplified NP-Complete Problems," *Proceedings of Sixth Annual ACM Symposium on Theory of Computing* (1974), 47–63.

128. GARFINKEL, R. S. and G. L. NEMHAUSER, *Integer Programming*. New York: John Wiley, 1972.

129. GAVER, D. P., "Probability Models for Multiprogramming Computer Systems," *J.ACM*, 14, no. 3 (1967), 423–38.

130. GAVER, D. P. and G. S. SHEDLER, "Processor Utilization in Multiprogramming Systems via Diffusion Approximations," *Oper. Res.*, 21 (1973), 569–76.

131. GELENBE, E., "On Approximate Computer System Models," *J.ACM*, 22, no. 2 (1975), 261–69.

132. GONZALES, T., O. H. IBARRA, and S. SAHNI, "Bounds for LPT Schedules on Uniform Processors," Computer Science Technical Report (1975), University of Minnesota.

133. GONZALES, T., and S. SAHNI, "P-Complete Approximation Problems," *J.ACM*, 23, no. 3 (1976), 555–65.

134. GORDON, W. J. and G. F. NEWELL, "Closed Queueing Systems with Exponential Servers," *Oper. Res.*, 15, no. 2 (1967), 254–65.

135. GOSTELOW, K., V. CERF, G. ESTRIN, and S. VOLANSKY, "Proper Termination of Flow of Control in Programs Involving Concurrent Processes," *SIGPLAN Notices*, 7, no. 11 (1972), 15–27.

136. GRAHAM, G. S., "A Study of Program and Memory Policy Behavior," Ph.D. thesis (1976), Dept. Computer Sciences, Purdue Univ.

137. GRAHAM, R. L., "Bounds for Certain Multiprocessing Anomalies," *Bell System Tech. J.*, 45 (1966), 1563–581.

138. GRAHAM, R. L., "Bounds on Multiprocessing Timing Anomalies," *SIAM J. on Applied Math.*, 17 (1969), 416–29.

139. GRAHAM, R. L., "Bounds on Multiprocessing Anomalies and Packing Algorithms," *Proc. AFIPS 1972 SJCC.*, 40, pp. 205–17. Montvale, N.J.: AFIPS Press, 1972.

140. GREGORY, M. T., "Discrete Event Simulation of Stable Stochastic Systems," M.S. thesis (1975), Dept. Math. Sciences, Clemson Univ.

141. HABERMANN, A. N., "A New Approach to Avoidance of System Deadlocks," *Lecture Notes on Computer Science*, 16, New York: Springer-Verlag, 1974.

142. HABERMANN, A. N., "Prevention of System Deadlocks," *CACM*, 12, no. 7 (1969), 373–77.

143. HACK, M., "The Recursive Equivalence of the Reachability Problem and the Liveness Problem for Petri Nets and Vector Addition Systems," *Proc. 15th IEEE S.W.A.T.* (1974), 156–64.

144. HACK, M., "Petri Net Languages," MAC-Computer Structures Group Memo. 124 (1975), M.I.T.

145. HANDLEY, G., *Linear Programming*. Reading, Mass.: Addison-Wesley, 1962.

146. HADLEY, G., *Nonlinear and Dynamic Programming*. Reading, Mass.: Addison-Wesley, 1964.

147. HARARY, F., *Graph Theory*. Reading, Mass.: Addison-Wesley, 1969.

148. HATFIELD, D. J. and J. GERALD, "Program Restructuring for Virtual Memory," *IBM Syst. J.*, 10 (1971), 168–72.

149. HEBALKAR, P. G., "Deadlock-Free Sharing of Resources in Asynchronous Systems," Ph.D. thesis, Department of Electrical Engineering, Cambridge, Mass.: Massachusetts Institute of Technology, 1970.

150. HEMMERLE, W. J., An Explicit Solution for Generalized Ridge," *Technometrics*, 17 (1975), 309–14.

151. HERZOG, U., L. WOO, and K. M. CHANDY, "Solution of Queueing Problems by a Recursive Technique," *IBM J. Res. Develop.*, 19, no. 2 (1975), 209–532.

152. HILLER, F. S. and G. J. LIEBERMAN, *Introduction to Operations Research*. Holden-Day, Inc., 1967.

153. HIMMELBLAU, D. M., *Applied Nonlinear Programming*. New York: McGraw-Hill, 1972.

154. HOERL, A. E., "Application of Ridge Analysis to Regression Problems," *Chem. Eng. Progress*, 58 (1962), 54–59.

155. HOERL, A. E. and R. W. KENNARD, "Ridge Regression: Biased Estimation for Nonorthgonal Problems " *Technometrics* Vol. 12 (1970), 55–67.

156. HOLT, R., "Some Deadlock Properties of Computer Systems," *Comp. Surveys*, 4, no. 3 (1972), 179–96.

157. HORDIJK, A., D. L. IGLEHART, and R. SCHASSBERGER, "Discrete Time Methods of Simulating Contunuous Time Markov Chains," *Advances in Applied Probability*, 8, no. 4 (1976), 772–88.

158. HOROWITZ, E. and S. SAHNI, "Exact and Approximate Algorithms for Scheduling Non-Identical Processors," *J.ACM*, Vol. 23, no. 2 (1977), 317–27.

159. HSU, N. C., "Elementary Proof of Hu's Theorem on Isotone Mappings," *Proc. AMS*, 17 (1966), 111–14.

160. HU, T. C., "Parallel Sequencing and Assembly Line Problems," *Operations Research*, 9, no. 6 (1961), 841–48.

161. HU, T. C., *Integer Programming and Network Flows*. New York: Addison-Wesley, 1969.

162. IBARRA, O. H. and KIM, C. E., "Heuristic Algorithms for Scheduling Independent Tasks on Non-Identical Processors," Computer Science Technical Report (1975), University of Minnesota.

163. IBM, *IBM Virtual Machine Facility/370, Introduction*, Form No. GC20–1800 (1972), IBM Corp. Data Processing Div., White Plains, N.Y.

164. IGLEHART, D. L., "Simulating Stable Stochastic Systems, V: Comparison of Ratio Estimators," *Naval Res. Logist. Quart.*, 22 (1975), 553–65.

165. IGLEHART, D. L. "Simulating Stable Stochastic Systems, VI: Quantile Estimation," *J.ACM*, 23, no. 2 (1976), 347–60.

166. IGLEHART, D. L., "Simulating Stable Stochastic Systems, VII: Selecting Best System," *Management Sci.* (1977).

167. JACKSON, J. R., "Jobshop-Like Queueing Systems," *Management Sciences*, 10, no. 1 (1963), 131–42.

168. JOHNSON, D. B., "Finding All the Elementary Circuits of a Directed Graph," *SIAM J. of Computing*, 4, no. 1 (1975), 77–84.

169. JOHNSON, D. S., "Approximation Algorithms for Combinatorial Problems," *J. Computer and Systems Sciences*, 9 (1974), 256–78.

170. KAHN, K. C., "Program Behavior and Load Dependent System Performance," Ph.D. thesis, (1976), Dept. Computer Sciences, Purdue Univ.

171. KARP, R. M., "Reducibility Among Combinatorial Problems," *Complexity of Computer Computations*, R. E. Miller and J. W. Thatcher (ed.), pp. 85–103. New York: Plenum Press, 1972.

172. KARP, R. M. and R. MILLER, "Parallel Program Schemata," *J. Computer and System Sciences*, 3 (1969), 147–95.

173. KAUFMAN, M. T., "An Almost-Optimal Algorithm for the Assembly Line Scheduling Problems," *IEEE-TC*, 23, no. 11 (1974), 1169–174.

174. KELLER, R., "Vector Replacement Systems: A Formalism for Modeling Asynchronous Systems," TR 117 (1972), Dept. of E.E., Princeton Univ.

175. KENDALL, M. G. and A. STUART, *The Advanced Theory of Statistics*, Vol. 1, 2nd ed. New York: Hafner, 1963.

176. KERNIGHAN, B. W., "Optimal Sequential Partitions of Graphs," *J.ACM*, 18, no. 1 (1971), 34–40.

177. KIM, C. E., "A Minimal Spanning Tree and Approximate Tours for a Traveling Salesman Problem" (1977).

178. KLEINROCK, L., "Certain Analytic Results for Time-Shared Processor," *Proc. IFIP Congress 68*, 2, pp. 838–45. Amsterdam: North-Holland Pub. Co., 1969.

179. KLEINROCK, L, *Queueing Systems, Volume I; Theory.* Wiley Interscience, 1975.

180. KLEINROCK, L., *Queueing Systems, Volume II; Computer Applications.* Wiley Interscience, 1976.

181. KLEINROCK, L. and S. LAM, "Packet Switching in a Multiaccess Broadcast Channel: Performance Evaluation," *IEEE-TC*, 23, no. 4 (1975), 410–23.

182. KNUTH, D. E., *The Art of Computer Programming, Vol. 1, Fundamental Algorithms*, 2nd ed. Reading, Mass.: Addison-Wesley, 1973.

183. KNUTH, D. E., *The Art of Computer Programming: Seminumerical Algorithms*, Vol. 2. Reading, Mass.: Addison-Wesley, 1969.

184. KNUTH, D. E., *The Art of Computer Programming, Vol. 3, Searching and Sorting.* Reading, Mass.: Addison-Wesley, 1973.

185. KNUTH, D. E. and F. R. STEVENSON, "Optimal Measurement Points for Program Frequency Counts," *BIT*, 13 (1973), 313–22.

186. KNUTH, D. E. and D. SZWARFICTER, "A Structured Program to Generate All Topological Sorting Arrangements," *Info. Proc. Letters*, 2, no. 6 (1974), 153–57.

187. KOBAYASHI, H., "Some Recent Progress in Analytic Studies of System Performance," *Proc. 1st USA-Japan Comp. Conf.* (1972), 130–38.

188. KOBAYASHI, H., "Application of the Diffusion Approximation to Queueing Networks I: Equilibrium Quene Distributions," *J.ACM*, 21, no. (1974a), 316–28.

189. KOBAYASHI, H., "Applications of the Diffusion Approximation to Queueing Networks II: Nonequilibrium Distributions and Applications to Computer Modeling," *J.ACM*, 21, no. 3 (1974b), 459–69.

190. KOBAYASHI, H., "A Computational Algorithm for Queue Distribution via Palya Theory of Enumeration," IBM Research Report RC-6154 (1976), Yorktown Heights, N.Y.

191. KOBAYASHI, H., *Modeling and Analysis.* Reading, Mass.: Addison-Wesley, 1978.

192. KOBAYASHI, H. and A. G. KONHEIM, "Queueing Models for Computer Communications System Analysis," *IEEE-T. Communications*, 25, no. 1 (1977), 2–29.

193. KOBAYASHI, H. and M. REISER, "On Generalization of Job Routing Behavior in a Queueing Network Model," IBM Research Report RC-5252 (1975), Yorktown Heights, N.Y.

194. KOBAYASHI, H., D. HUYNH, and Y. ONOZATO, "An Approximate Method for Design and Analysis of an ALOHA System," *IEEE Transactions on Communications*, 25, no. 1 (1977), 148–57.

195. KOHLER, W. H., "A Preliminary Evaluation of the Critical Path Method for Scheduling Tasks on Multiprocessor Systems," *IEEE-TC*, 24, no. 12 (1975), 1235–238.

196. KOSARAJU, S., "Limitations of Dijkstra's Semaphore Primitives and Petri Nets," *Proc. 4th Symp. on Operating Systems Principles* (1973), 122–26.

197. LAM, S. S., "On An Extension of Moore's Results for Closed Queueing Networks," IBM Research Report (1975), Yorktown Heights, N.Y.

198. LAM, S. and R. SETHI, "A Bound on Coffman-Graham Schedules for Three or More Processor Systems," TR-156, (1974), Computer Science Dept., Penn. State Univ.

199. LAM, S. and R. SETHI, "Worst Case Analysis of Two Scheduling Algorithms," *SIAM J. on Computing* (1977).

200. LASSETTRE, E. R. and A. L. SCHERR, "Modelling the Performance of the OS/360 Time-Shared Option (TSO)," *Statistical Computer Performance Evaluation*, W. Freiberger (ed.), pp. 57–72. New York: Academic, 1972.

201. LAVENBERG, S. S., "The Steady State Queueing Time Distribution for the M/G/1 Finite Capacity Queue," *Manag. Sci.*, 21, no. 5 (1975a), 501–506.

202. LAVENBERG, S. S., "Stability and Maximum Departure Rate of Certain Open Queueing Networks Having Finite Capacity Constraints," IBM Report RJ1625 (1975b), Yorktown Heights, N.Y.

203. LAVENBERG, S. S., private communication (1976).

204. LAVENBERG, S. S. and G. S. SHEDLER, "A Queueing Model of the DL/I Component of IMS" (1975), IBM Research Laboratory, San Jose Ca.

205. LAVENBERG, S. S. and D. R. SLUTZ, "Regenerative Simulation of a Model of an Automated Tape Library," IBM Research Report RI-1563 (1975a), San Jose, Ca.

206. LAVENBERG, S. S. and D. R. SLUTZ, "Regenerative Simulation: A Tutorial," IBM Research Report RI-1562 (1975b), San Jose, Ca.

207. LAW, A. M., "Efficient Estimators for Simulated Queueing Systems," *Management Sci.*, 22 (1975), 30–41.

208. LAWLER, E., *Combinatorial Optimization*. 1977.

209. LAWSON, C. L. and R. J. HANSON, *Solving Least Squares Problems*. Englewood Cliffs, N.J.: Prentice-Hall, 1974.

210. LEHMAN, E. L., *Testing Statistical Hypotheses*. New York: John Wiley, 1959.

211. LENSTRA, J. K., *Sequencing by Enumerative Methods*. Amsterdam: Mathematisch Centrum, 1976.

212. LEROUDIER, J., "Analyse d'un Systeme a Partage de Resources," *Revue Francaise d'Automatique*, 7B-3 (1973), 3–30, Informatique et Recherche Operationelle.

213. LEWIS, P. A. W. and G. S. SHEDLER, "A Cyclic-Queue Model of System Overhead in Multiprogrammed Computer Systems," *J.ACM*, 18, no. 2 (1971), 199–220.

214. LEWIS, P. M., D. J. ROSENCRANTZ, and R. E. STEARNS, "An Analysis of Several Heuristics for the Traveling Salesmen Problem," *SIAM J. on Computing*, 6, no. 3 (1977), 563–81.

215. LIU, J. W. S. and C. L. LIU, "Bounds on Scheduling Algorithms for Heterogeneous Computing Systems," *Proc. IFIP Congress 74* (1974), 349–53.

216. LOWRY, E. S. and C. W. MEDLOCK, "Object Code Optimization," *CACM*, 12, no. 1 (1969), 13–22.

217. MACNAIR, E. A., private communication (1976).

218. MADISON, A. W. and A. P., BATSON, "Characteristics of Program Localities," *CACM*, 19, no. 5 (1976), 285–94.

219. MADNICK, S. E. and J. J. DONOVAN, *Operating Systems*. New York: McGraw-Hill, 1974.

220. MARGOLIN, B. H., R. P. PARMELEE, and M. SCHATZOFF, "Analysis of Free-Storage Algorithms," *IBM Systems Journal*, 10, no. 4 (1971), 283–304.

221. MARTIN, D. F. and G. ESTRIN, "Models of Computational Systems Cyclic to Acyclic Graph Transformations," *IEEE-TEC*, 16, no. 2 (1967), 70–9.

222. MARTIN, D. F. and G. ESTRIN, "Path Length Computations on Graph Models of Computations," *IEEE-TC*, 18, no. 6 (1969), 530–36.

223. McKINNEY, J. M., "A Survey of Analytic Time-Sharing Models," *Comp. Surveys*, 1, no. (1969), 105–16.

224. MEYER, R. A. and L. H. SEAWRIGHT, "A Virtual Machine Time-Sharing System," *IBM Systems Journal*, 9, no. 3 (1970), 199–218.

225. MILLER, R. G., "The Jackknife—A Review," *Biometrika*, 61, (1974), 1–15.

226. MIRASOL, N. M., "The Output of an $M/G/\infty$ is Poisson," *Oper. Res.*, 11, no. 2 (1963), 282–84.

227. MOELLER, T. L. and C. H. SAUER, "Control Variables in Regenerative Simulation of Queuing Models," IBM Research Report (1977), IBM T. J. Watson Research Center, Yorktown Heights, N.Y.

228. MONTANGERO, C., "An Approach to the Optimal Specification of Read Only Memories in Microprogrammed Digital Computers," *IEEE-TC*, 23, no. 4 (1974), 375–89.

229. MOORE, III, C. G., "Network Models for Large Scale Time-Shring Systems," Tech. Rept. No. 71-1 (1971), Dept. of Ind. Eng., Univ. of Michigan.

230. MOORE, F. R., "Computational Model of a Closed Queueing Network with Exponential Servers," *IBM J. Res. Develop.*, 16, no. 6 (1972), 567–72.

231. MORRIS, J. B., "Demand Paging Through the Use of Working Sets On the Maniac II," *CACM*, 15, no. 10 (1972), 867–72.

232. MUNCH-ANDERSEN, B. and T. U. ZAHLE, "Scheduling According to Job Priority with Prevention of Deadlock and Permanent Blocking," *Acta Information*, 8 (1977), 153–75.

233. MUNRO, I., "Efficient Determination of the Transitive Closure of a Directed Graph," *Info. Proc. Letters*, 1, no. 2 (1971), 56–58.

234. MUNTZ, R. R., "Poisson Departure Processes and Queueing Networks," *Proc. of Seventh Ann. Princeton Conf. on Inf. Sci. and Syst.* (1973), 435–40.

235. MUNTZ, R. R., "Analytic Modeling of Interactive Systems," *Proc. IEEE*, 63, no. 6 (1975), 946–53.

236. MUNTZ, R. R. and E. G. COFFMAN, "Optimal Preemptive Scheduling on Two-Processor Systems," *IEEE-TC*, 18, no. 11 (1969), 1014–1020.

237. MUNTZ, R. R. and WONG, J., "Efficient Computational Procedures for Closed Queueing Network Models," *Proc. of Seventh Hawaii Int'l Conf. on System Sciences*, (1974), 33–36.

238. NEVIUS, T. W., "On Simulating Stable Stochastic Systems," M.S. thesis (1974), Department of Math. Sciences, Clemson Univ.

239. NEWELL, G. F., *Applications of Queueing Theory*. London: Chapman and Hall, Ltd., 1971.

240. O'DONOVAN, T. M., "Direct Solution of $M/G/1$ Processor-Sharing Models," *Oper. Res.*, 22, no. 6 (1974), 1232–235.

241. PAPADIMITRIOU, C. H., "The Euclidean Traveling Salesman Problem is NP-Complete," *Theoretical Computer Science*, 4, no. 3 (1977), 237–44.

242. PAPADIMITRIOU, C. H. and K. STEIGLITZ, "On the Complexity of Local Search for the Traveling Salesman Problem," *SIAM J. on Computing*, 6, no. 1 (1977), 76–83.

243. PARENT, M. and D. POTIER, "A Note on the Influence of Program Loading on the Page Fault Rate," Technical Report (1976), IRIA Laboria, Rocquencourt, 78150 Le Chesnay, France.

244. PATIL, S. S. and J. B. DENNIS, "The Description and Realization of Digital Systems," *COMPCON 72 Digest* (1972), 223–27.

245. PEARSON, E. S. and H. O. HARTLEY, *Biometrika Tables for Statisticians*, Vol. 1, 2nd ed. Cambridge: Cambridge University Press, 1962.

246. PFALTZ, J. L., "Representing Graphs by Knuth Trees," *J.ACM*, 22, no. 3 (1975), 361–66.

247. PRESSER, L., "Multiprogramming Coordination," *Comp. Surveys*, 7, no. 1 (1975), 21–44.

248. PRIEVE, B. G. and FABRY, R. S., "VMIN—An Optimal Variable Space Page Replacement Algorithm," *CACM*, 19, no. 5 (1976), 295–97.

249. QUENOUILLE, M. H., "Approximate Tests of Correlation in Time-Series," *J. Roy. Statist. Soc. Ser B*, 11 (1949), 68–84.

250. QUENOUILLE, M. H., "Notes on Bias in Estimation," *Biometrika*, 43 (1956), 353–60.

251. RAIFFA, H. and R. SCHLAIFER, *Applied Statistical Decision Theory* (1961), Grad. School of Bus. Admin., Harvard Univ.

252. RAMAMOORTHY, C. V., "Analysis of Graph by Connectivity Considerations," *JACM*, 13, no. 2 (1966a), 211–22.

253. RAMAMOORTHY, C. V., "The Analytic Design of a Dynamic Look-ahead and Program Segmenting System for Multiprogramming Computers," *Proc. 21st Nat. ACM Conf.*, pp. 229–240. Thompson Book Co., 1966b.

254. RAMAMOORTHY, C. V. and K. M. CHANDY, "Optimization of Memory Hierarchies in Multiprogrammed Systems," *J.ACM*, 17, no. 3 (1970), 426–45.

255. RAMAMOORTHY, C. V., K. M. CHANDY, and M. J. GONZALEZ, "Optimal Scheduling Strategies in a Multiprocessor System," *IEEE-TC*, 21, no. 2 (1972), 137–46.

256. REISER, M., "QNET4 User's Guide," IBM Research Report RA71 (1975), Yorktown Heights, N.Y.

257. REISER, M., "Modeling of Computer Systems with QNET4," *IBM Systems Journal*, 15, no. 4 (1976a), 309–27.

258. REISER, M., "Numerical Methods in Separable Queueing Networks," IBM Research Report RC5842 (1976b), Yorktown Heights, N.Y. (to appear in *Operations Research*).

259. REISER, M. and H. KOBAYASHI, "Recursive Algorithm for General Queueing Networks with Exponential Servers," IBM Research Rept. RC 4254 (1973), Yorktown Heights, N.Y.

260. REISER, M. and H. KOBAYASHI, "Accuracy of the Diffusion Approximation for Some Queueing Systems," *IBM J. Res. Develop.*, 18, no. 2 (1974a), 110–24.

261. REISER, M. and H. KOBAYASHI, "The Effects of Service Time Distributions on System Performance," *Proc. IFIP Congress 74*, pp. 230–234. Amsterdam: North-Holland Pub. Co., 1974b.

262. REISER, M. and H. KOBAYASHI, "Horner's Rule for the Evaluation of General Closed Queueing Networks," *CACM*, 18, no. 10 (1975a), 592–93.

263. REISER, M. and H. KOBAYASHI, "Numerical Methods in Queueing Networks," *Proc. Comp. Sci. and Statistics, 8th Annual Symp. on the Interface* (1975b), UCLA.

264. REISER, M. and H. KOBAYASHI, "Queueing Networks with Multiple Closed Chains: Theory and Computational Algorithms," *IBM J. Res. Develop.*, 19, no. 3 (1975c), 283–94.

265. REISER, M. and A. G. KONHEIM, "Finite Capacity Queueing Systems with Applications in Computer Modeling," IBM Research Report RC5827 (1976), Yorktown Heights, N.Y.

266. RINNOOY KAN, A. H. G., *Machine Scheduling Problems*. Leiden, Netherlands: H. E. Stenfert Kroese B. V., 1974.

267. RIVERA-GARZA, M., "Labor and Machine Constrained Job Shops: A Simulation Investigation of Dispatching Rules," Engineer thesis (1974), Dept. of Ind. Eng., Stanford Univ.

268. ROBINSON, D. W., "Determination of Run Lengths in Simulations of Stable Stochastic Systems," Technical Report No. 86–21 (1976), Control Analysis Corp., Palo Alto, Ca.

269. RODRIGUEZ-ROSELL, J. and J. P. DUPUY, "The Design, Implementation, and Evaluation of a Working Set Dispatcher," *CACM*, 17, no. 4 (1973), 247–53.

270. ROY, S. N. and R. F. POTTHOFF, "Confidence Bounds on Vector Analogues of the 'Ratio of Mean' and the 'Ratio of Variance' for Two Correlated Normal Variates and Some Associated Tests," *Ann. Math. Statist.*, 29 (1958), 829–41.

271. RUSSELL, E. C. and G. ESTRIN, "Measurement Based Automatic Analysis of FORTRAN Programs," *Proc. AFIPS 1969 SJCC*, 34, pp. 723–32. Montrale, N. J.: AFIPS Press, 1969.

272. SAHNI, S., "Algorithms for Scheduling Independent Tasks," *J.ACM*, 23 (1976), 116–27.

273. SATTERTHWAITE, F. E., "Random Balance Experimentation," *Technometrics*, 1 (1959), 111–37.

274. SAUER, C. H., "Simulation Analysis of Generalized Queueing Networks," *Proc. 1975 Summer Computer Simulation Conference* (1975), 75–81.

275. SAUER, C. H., "Characterization and Simulation of Generalized Queueing Networks," IBM Research Report (1977), IBM T. J. Watson Research Center, Yorktown Heights, N.Y.

276. SAUER, C. H. and K. M. CHANDY, "Approximate Analysis of Central Server Models," *IBM J. Res. Develop.*, 19, no. 3 (1975), 301–13.

277. SAUER, C. H. and L. WOO, "Hybrid Simulation of a Distributed Network," IBM Research Report RC 6341 (1977).

278. SCHATZOFF, M. and C. C. TILLMAN, "Design of Experiments in Simulator Validation," *IBM J. Res. Develop.*, 19, no. 3 (1975), 252–62.

279. SCHEFFE, H., *The Analysis of Variance*. New York: John Wiley, 1959.

280. SCHERR, A. L., *An Analysis of Time-Shared Computer Systems*. Cambridge, Mass.: MIT Press, 1967.

281. SEKINO, A., "Performance Evaluation of a Multiprogrammed Time-Shared Computer System," MIT Project MAC, Report MAC-TR-103, Ph.D. thesis, (1972).

282. SHEDLER, G. S. and C. TUNG, "Locality in Page Reference Strings," *SIAM J. Comput.*, 1, no. 3 (1972), 218–41.

283. SKINNER, C. and J. ASHER, "Effect of storage contention on system performance," *IBM Syst. J.*, 8.4 (1969), 319–33.

284. SLUTZ, D. R. and I. L. TRAIGER, "A Note on the Calculation of Average Working Set Size," *CACM*, 17, no. 10 (1974), 563–65.

285. SMITH, A. J., "Performance Analysis of Computer Systems Components," Ph.D. thesis (1974), Dep. of Computer Science, Stanford Univ.

286. SMITH, A. J., "A Modified Working Set Paging Algorithm," *IEEE-TC*, 25, no. 9 (1976a), 907–14.

287. SMITH, A. J., "Analysis of the Optimal, Lookahead, Demand Paging Algorithms," *SIAM J. Comp.*, 5, no. 4 (1976b), 743–57.

288. SPIRN, J., "Distance String Models for Program Behavior," *Computer*, 9, no. 11 (1976), 14–20.

289. SPIRN, J., *Program Behavior: Models and Measurement*. Series on Operating and Programming Systems. New York: Elsevier/North Holland, 1977.

290. SPIRN, J. and P. J. DENNING, "Experiments with Program Locality," *Proc. AFIPS 1972 FJCC*, 41 (1972), 611–21.

291. STOCKMEYER, L., "Planar 3-Colorability is Polynomial Complete," *SIGACT News*, 5, no. 3 (1973), 19–25.

292. STRASSEN, V., "Gaussian Elimination is Not Optimal," *Numerische Math*, 13 (1969), 354–56.

293. SYSKI, R., *Introduction to Congestion Theory in Telephone Systems*. Edinburgh, Scotland: Oliver and Boyd, 1960.

294. TARJAN, R., "Enumeration of the Elementary Circuits of a Directed Graph," *SIAM J. of Computing*, 2, no. 3 (1973), 211–16.

295. THOMPSON, G. E., *Linear Programming: An Elementary Introduction*. New York: MacMillan, 1971.

296. TIERNAN, J. C., "An Efficient Search Algorithm to Find the Elementary Circuits of a Graph," *CACM*, 13, no. 12 (1970), 722–26.

297. TIN, M., "Comparison of Some Ratio Estimators," *J. Amer. Statist. Assoc.*, 60 (1965), 294–307.

298. TSAO, R. F., L. W. COMEAU, and B. H. MARGOLIN, "A Multi-factor Paging Experiment," in *Statistical Computer Performance Evaluation*, W. Freiberger (ed.), pp. 103–158. New York: Academic Press, 1972.

299. TURNER, C. A., "A Comparison of Ratio Estimators for Simulating Stable Stochastic Systems," M.S. thesis (1975), Dep. of Math. Sciences, Clemson Univ.

300. ULLMAN, J. D., "Polynomial Complete Scheduling Problems," *Proc. 4th Symp. on Operating Systems Principles* (1973), 96–101.

301. WAGNER, H. M., *Principle of Operations Research*. Englewood Cliffs, N.J.: Prentice-Hall, 1969.

302. WALLACE, V. L., "Toward an Algebraic Theory of Markovian Networks," *Proc. Symp. Computer Communications Networks and Teletraffic*, pp. 397–407. New York: Polytechnic Press of the Polytechnic Inst. of Brooklyn, 1972.

303. WALLACE, V. L. and R. S. ROSENBERG, "RQA-1, the Recursive Queue Analyzer," Tech. Rep. 2 (1966), Systems Eng. Lab., Univ. Michigan.

304. WARREN, H. S., "A Modification of Warshall's Algorithm for the Transitive Closure of Binary Relations," *CACM*, 18, no. 4 (1975), 210–20.

305. WARSHALL, S., "A Theorem on Boolean Matrices," *J.ACM*, 9, no. 1 (1962), 11–12.

306. WEBSTER, J. T., R. F. GUNST, and R. L. MASON, "Latent Root Regression Analysis," *Technometrics*, 16 (1974), 513–22.

307. WEIZER, N. and G. OPPENHEIMER, "Virtual Memory Management in a Paging Environment," *Proc. AFIPS 1969 SJCC*, 34 (1969), 249–56.

308. WHITTLE, P., "Equilibrium distributions for an open migration process," *J. Appl. Prob.*, 5 (1968), 567–71.

309. WILDE, D. J. and C. S. BEIGHTHER, *Foundations of Optimization*. Englewood Cliffs, N.J.: Prentice-Hall, 1967.

310. WILHEIM, N. C., "Exact Models for Two Spindle Disk Drives," Ph.D. thesis (1973), Dept. of E. E., Stanford Univ.

311. WOLFF, R. W., "Work-conserving priorities," *J. Appl. Prob.*, 7 (1970), 327–37.

312. YAO, A. C., "On Scheduling Unit-Time Tasks with Limited Resources," *Proc. of the Sagamore Conference on Parallel Processing*. (1974), 17–36.

313. ZANGWILL, W. I., *Non-Linear Programming-A Unified Approach*. Englewood Cliffs, N.J.: Prentice-Hall, 1969.